HAROLD OBER ASSOCIATES, INC.

PENGUIN USA

RANDOM HOUSE, INC.

RONALD PRESS COMPANY

THE SOCIETY OF AUTHORS

Excerpt from *Saint Joan* by Bernard Shaw. The Society of Authors, on behalf of the Bernard Shaw Estate.

PHOTOS *(Each photo is identified separately in the text.)*

Allenari – Art Reference Bureau

Cleveland Museum of Art

College of Southern Idaho

Shakespearean Festival Theatre, Ontario, Canada

Strand Lighting

Topeka Civic Theatre

Topeka West High School

Utah Shakespearean Festival, Fred C. Adams, Founder and Executive Director; Douglas T. Kirchner, Director of Marketing and Public Relations; and Costume Designers.

Wallace Photography

Wichita Collegiate School

Wichita South High School

SKETCHES & DRAWINGS

The Costume Collection, project of Theater Development Fund, for the costume measuring charts found in the Teacher's Manual for *Basic Drama Projects*.

C.W. Hodges, for permission to use his Globe theater sketch and the reconstruction of the Inn-Yard theater.

Forrest A. Newlin, Theater Chairman of Texas Christian University, for the chapter drawings.

Oxford University Press, for permission to use the theater of Epidaurus sketch.

Thanks to Jane Beach Hipp for her hard work and creativity in formatting this Sixth Edition of *Basic Drama Projects*.

Front Cover Photo: *The Good Doctor*
          College of Southern Idaho, Director: Fran Tanner

Back Cover Photos: *Ain't Misbehavin'* & Pirates of Penzance
          Topeka Civic Theatre, Wallace Photography

TABLE OF CONTENTS

UNIT VI THEATRE APPRECIATION

UNIT VII MONOLOGUES & SCENES

PREFACE TO THE SIXTH EDITION

An old proverb states, "If thou has two pennies, with one buy bread. With the other buy a hyacinth for thy soul." In today's world so full of materialistic demands, it is especially important to feed our inner self. The theatre can do this. Not only will theatre study and participation provide an understanding of other people and cultures, it will also encourage introspection and self-knowledge, which can be strong sustenance for our soul.

Theatre classes, therefore, are wise choices for young people. Through drama experience, students creatively explore life's challenges and relationships. Since successful drama classes are action packed, students and teachers enjoy sharing the excitement and satisfaction of performing within the discipline of the theatre's demands.

This sixth edition contains the same philosophy as the previous editions. The changes include updated material and additional information. Specifically, new material includes:

1. Learner outcomes or chapter objectives which focus students on specific knowledge, performances, and critical thinking skills.

2. A new chapter on theatre attendance and appropriate audience behavior.

3. A chapter on theatre history that includes basic material as well as current information on modern theatre.

4. Discussion and comparison of theatre, film, television, and other art forms.

5. Featured sections on the elements of theatre, the value of theatre as a reflection of human experiences, stage fright, theatre safety for actors and technicians, scene construction and painting, and theatre etiquette.

6. Additional acting scenes from various cultures and diverse historical eras.

7. Monologues for both males and females.

8. Additional scenes for males, females, and mixed groups.

9. New photos and drawings.

10. An instructor's edition to assist the teacher with purposeful assignments, pertinent information, assessment tools, and valuable source material.

So, if you are a drama instructor who believes that your students learn best by getting on their feet and performing, you will enjoy teaching from this text. Each chapter consists of a complete activity project worked out in detail and aimed at giving your students practical experiences in drama.

You no longer need to consume hours deciding what to assign and then spend precious class time explaining your wishes. Ample assignments are in this book — one major project for each chapter, plus many additional suggestions that may inspire your students to do further work. Each assignment explains and gives in detail all pertinent information. The teacher need not be harassed by repetitious questions from the class. The students need not be confused by lack of necessary data; when they read each chapter, they know what is expected of them.

All projects involve class members in group or individual participation: pantomimes, improvisations, scenes, extemporaneous talks, discussions, play performances. All projects require careful student preparation in planning, organizing, and rehearsing for class presentation. The requirements are not easy. At first, many students may grumble because they must think out their project in advance of presentation, organize it in outline form on the activity sheet provided for each chapter, repeatedly rehearse and conscientiously time their scenes. They will learn, however, that only through such preparation can they be successful, and they will succeed if they meet the demands of the assignments, all of which have been used in schools around the nation.

Success in drama, of course, does not imply that these students will become professional actors and actresses. That is not the purpose of a basic drama class. It has too many other values to offer, as any dedicated drama teacher realizes. Work in drama stimulates creative abilities, developing inner resources that lead to an enriched life which is so necessary in our world of cold science and hard fact. Drama classes nurture cultural appreciation, exposing students to plays that have been written by some of the world's greatest thinkers — plays that satisfy the aesthetic, intellectual, and emotional needs of participant and spectator.

Study in theatre provides both social and individual development. In belonging to a group that works toward a creative goal, students develop qualities that promote maturity: teamwork, cooperation, and dependability. They also gain deeper insight into people by studying characterization in numerous plays. Personal growth is assured as students gain confidence and poise from frequent participation and as they achieve emotional release and control through the numerous vicarious experiences on stage. Improved body coordination and vocal flexibility that young people need for everyday communication also result from active participation in the drama class.

Furthermore, as students obtain a wide theatre background, they not only gain appreciation of the great arts, they also develop standards of judgment whereby they can recognize, respect, and demand good theatre, while rejecting that which is inferior or shoddy.

The benefits of theatre study are extensive indeed. It is no wonder that drama has a respected position in the field of performing arts!

It would be difficult to write a drama text without drawing from the numerous authors who have contributed outstanding work in the field. I wish to give thanks to the many scholars whose books I have read, "chewed and digested" as a theatre student and teacher. Most of the works that have been helpful in my writing are named in the bibliography. Especially, I want to acknowledge the influence of Rosenstein's *Modern Acting* in Chapters 1 through 6; of McGraw's *Acting is Believing* in Chapters 7 and 15; of Boyle's *Central and Flexible Staging* for suggestions on arena floor arrangements in Chapter 28; and of Wright's *Primer for Playgoers* in Chapter 29.

I am particularly grateful to those people who gave me assistance in preparing the original text. They are Clark Carlile, professor emeritus of speech at Idaho State University, whose constant encouragement and helpful suggestions made this book possible; the late Dr. Vio Mae Powell of Idaho State University, who was an inspiration to me ever since I was her student, and whose kindness and wise advice concerning each chapter I still appreciate; Dr. Forrest Newlin, whose ideas and drawings were most valuable in the production chapters; and the late Byron L. Averett, my father, who always encouraged me, and whose criticism helped me to strengthen my writing. Special thanks also go to those high school and college teachers throughout the nation who unselfishly previewed the projects in class and gave me many worthwhile ideas.

I also wish to express heartfelt appreciation to my mother, Lois, and to my husband, Marion, who assisted me immeasurably; and to Jackie, Lynn, and Dennis for their helping hands.

Fran Averett Tanner
Twin Falls, Idaho

ABOUT THE AUTHOR

Fran Tanner is professor of Speech and Drama at the College of Southern Idaho and department chair. She has a Ph.D. in Theatre and an M.A. in Speech. She teaches both disciplines, directs readers theatre as well as conventional theatre, and coaches forensics. Dr. Tanner was a Fulbright scholar to England, a recipient of the national Woman of Achievement award, was named an Idaho Distinguished Citizen, is listed in the Outstanding Educators of America Index, and has served as a U.S. delegate to the International Amateur Theatre Congress in Austria. She has served as a board member of the Rocky Mountain Theatre Conference, has presented at Western Speech Communication Association, and has conducted theatre workshops in the U.S. and abroad. Recently she received a Professional Achievement Award from Idaho State University and the Academic Teaching Excellence Award from the College of Southern Idaho. At the College of Southern Idaho, Dr. Tanner has directed more than 60 productions and her forensics students have been winners at national Phi Rho Pi tournaments.

Fran Averett Tanner

PROLOGUE

BODY RELAXATION AND WARM-UPS

Basic Routine for Relaxation

Rag doll —

With feet apart in a comfortable balance, stretch up tall. Then bend over by collapsing quickly and loosely from the waist with your relaxed arms and hands dangling to the floor. Keep your arms, hands, and head completely relaxed like a rag doll. Slowly rise up, keeping relaxed. Repeat.

Head roll —

Immediately after the rag doll exercise while your neck is still relaxed with chin close to the chest, slowly move your head to the left, front, right, and up. Reverse the rotation. Be sure to keep your neck relaxed, letting your head roll like a dead weight in a socket.

Arm swing —

Immediately after the head roll, swing relaxed arms in large circles one at a time.

Yawn —

If you have done exercises one and two correctly, your face and neck muscles and vocal chords are completely relaxed. Slowly yawn, sounding an "ahhhhhhh" on exhalation from the yawn. The sound you make is a relaxed sound. You should strive for this relaxation and open quality of the throat whenever you speak.

Basic Routine for Stimulation, to follow Basic Routine for Relaxation

Rhythm hop —

With weight on left foot, hop once on it and at the same time point your right foot in front, extending your arms in front with hands clapping. Now simultaneously hop once on your left foot while placing the right foot way out to the right side and extending arms, shoulder height out to the sides. Again hop once on left foot and simultaneously bring right foot back to touch left foot, putting arms down at your sides. Change weight to right foot and repeat routine with left foot. Do rapidly and smoothly ten to twenty times. Eventually chant short nursery rhymes or selections from Gilbert and Sullivan in rhythm while doing the exercise.

Additional Body Warm-ups

Tug-of-War —

With a team of six to twelve, form a line by standing in front of each other and facing a similarly placed and numbered team. With an imaginary rope, play tug-of-war, trying to get the rope away from the other side. See and feel the rope. Make it so real in your mind that at the end of the game you will be tired from the great physical exertion.

Jump rope —

Singly or in teams of three (two to swing the rope and one to jump, taking turns) jump with an imaginary rope.

Play sport —

With a partner, toss an imaginary ball to each other, or play ping-pong, or fence with imaginary foils.

Numbers —

Using your whole body, write huge numbers from one to ten in the air. Use as much space as you can, traveling around the room, stretching, and bending as you write. If possible, do this to slow, relaxing music.

Balloon blow —

Assume a limp balloon position. Now with your teacher "blowing" you up in three blows, fill with air after each blow, regulating your expansion to be completely filled after blow three. Hold your enlarged position until your teacher "stabs" you with an imaginary pin or "slashes" you with an imaginary knife. Release your air accordingly as a balloon.

Balloon catch —

Try to grab a balloon above you in the air, but it moves just beyond your reach each time. Travel about the room during your reaching.

VOICE WARM-UPS

Basic Routine for the Articulators

Smile-pucker —

Smile with exaggeration letting your teeth show and drawing the lips as tightly as possible, making your cheek muscles hurt. Say "eeeeeeee." Then with exaggeration, pucker or protrude your lips, saying "ooooooooooo." Repeat ten times each in quick succession (eeeeeeee-ooooooo). Repeat with "me-moo," "tee-too," "bee-boo," "gee-goo" "lee-loo."

Open wide —

Open your mouth as wide as possible. Say "ahhhh." Now close your mouth, saying "ooooooo" Repeat "ahhhhh-ooooo" several times, being sure to open your mouth extremely wide.

Tongue tip —

Stretch your tongue, trying to touch the tip of your nose. With your tongue, now try to touch your chin as far as possible. Only one in 1000 can actually do either, so don't worry if you can't succeed. The stretch is the important thing Repeat several times.

Tongue stretch —

Curl up your tongue and touch the soft palate at the back of your throat. Now push out your right cheek and then your left cheek as far as you can with your tongue. Repeat.

Additional Voice Warm-ups

Tongue twisters —

Say quickly with exaggerated tongue, lip, and jaw movements several of the following tongue twisters. (See Chapter 12 for others.)

    a.   Two teamsters tried to steal twenty-two keys.

    b.   Would Wheeler woo Wanda if Woody snoozed woozily.

    c.   Much whirling water makes the mill wheel work well.

    d.   Odd birds always gobble green almonds in the autumn.

    e.   She makes a proper cup of coffee in a copper coffee pot.

Saying "ahhhhhhh" —

Sustain a comfortably pitched tone. Follow your teacher's directions as he or she tells you to intone louder, softer, higher, lower, etc.

Yelling "hi" —

As your teacher counts, in unison with other class members yell out "hi" on the odd numbers, then on the even numbers.

Gibberish —

You and a partner carry on an animated conversation simultaneously with the rest of the class by using gibberish, which consists of nonsense or make believe words. If you find it difficult at first to think up non-words, simply use only the term "da-da-shoon." Sincerely try to communicate.

Singing —

Energetically carry on an argument with your partner by "singing" your sentences as is done in opera. You needn't carry a tune. Just go up and down the scale according to what you think fits your ideas and words — the more exaggerated, the better.

Say a sentence such as —

"Now is the time;" or "Everything is different;" or "There goes the last one;" in each of the following ways: sternly, frightened, eagerly, defiantly, soothingly, shyly, dubiously, drowsily, wistfully, joyfully, airily, ominously, irritably, stunned, sadly, happily, nostalgically, remorsefully.

Say "What are you doing?" as though you were —

    a.   A wild person

    b.   Just learning to read
    c.   Talking to a cute puppy
    d.   A preacher
    e.   Talking to a deaf person
    f.   A burly policeman
    g.   Dictating to a secretary
    h.   A fond young husband to his wife
    i.   A frightened child

Count from one to ten in the following ways —

    a.   Counting pennies on a table
    b.   Counting out a man in a boxing ring
    c.   Counting people in a crowded room
    d.   Counting off in an exercise routine

WHERE ARE YOU GOING IN THIS CLASS?

Drama is doing. The Greek word for drama means "to do" or "to act," so the assignments in this class will ask for your participation. You will be doing projects in each unit:

1. Developing inner resources
2. Moving
3. Speaking
4. Characterizing
5. Producing
6. Appreciating theatre

Every chapter in the above units has its own basic project (hence, the name of the book) with many additional suggestions. Your instructor will lead you through this active process.

Each chapter also has a section called "Promptings," which focuses on basic chapter ideas that ask you to do some critical thinking and problem solving.

There are also terms listed, called "Theatre Language," that you will need to know for each activity.

Ready to start?   "Places," everyone !

UNIT 1

INNER RESOURCES

LOOSENING UP

Time Limits: 3 minutes for each contestant

Activity Sheet: Using the form for this chapter found in the teacher's manual, write in your charade title. Hand the sheet to the leader of your team.

PROMPTINGS

1. Discuss your personal benefits in studying theatre.
2. Relate the cultural values from theatre study.
3. Discuss the actor's basic purpose.
4. List the subject units to be covered in this book and show their relationships to each other.
5. Discuss stage fright and how to control it.

THEATRE LANGUAGE

Amateur
Charades
Communicate
Control
Conventional
Dialogue
Dilettante (Dil-e-tänt)

Illusion of reality
Legitimate theatre (thé-å-ter)
Medium of expression
Pantomime
Professional
Spontaneity
Technique

BACKGROUND NOTES

"Curtain Going Up" is a call that has enticed both theatre patrons and participants for centuries. As the house lights dim, the audience eagerly awaits the plot and the people to be revealed. On the opposite side of the curtain, actors are excited to breathe life into their characters, and stage technicians are challenged to help sustain the theatrical illusion.

As you participate in this drama class you, too, will experience the satisfaction and thrill of theatre. Some of you may be taking this course because you are seriously considering acting as a career; thus, you will approach the course as though entering upon a profession. Or, you may be taking drama because you think it would be fun to participate in school and community plays. Also, you may want to study drama in order to become a more discriminating and well informed audience member.

Whether you are intent upon earning your living as an actor or as a technician in legitimate theatre (live acting in front of a live audience), television, or the movies, or whether you wish to spend your free time as a dilettante in local amateur theatre groups, drama can be a worthwhile and satisfying activity for you throughout your life.

Our emphasis in this class will be primarily on live theatre. Such theatre experiences will help you better to understand life's situations and the people involved. Theatre is truly a mirror of life that when studied provides an appreciation of past and present times. As you create characters, you will learn about people who are different from you. You will also notice that certain human characteristics are universal. Your world will be expanded into a greater understanding of the human race.

Participation in drama will stimulate your creative abilities, allowing you to develop inner resources that lead to an enriched life, which is so necessary in our world of cold science and hard facts.

Because the theatre demands responsible commitment as you work toward a creative goal, you should develop qualities that promote maturity: teamwork, cooperation, and dependability. Your personal growth is also assured as you gain confidence and poise from frequent participation, and as you achieve emotional release and control through numerous vicarious experiences on stage.

Furthermore, you will see improved body coordination and vocal flexibility when you study those units in this class.

As you obtain a wide theatre background, you will not only learn to appreciate the dramatic arts, but you will hopefully develop standards of judgment for recognizing, respecting, and demanding quality theatre, while rejecting that which is inferior or shoddy. The benefits of drama are extensive indeed!

At the beginning, however, beware of the pitfalls. There is more glitter, accolade, and fascination attached to the theatre than perhaps any other area. To the onlooker, actors seem to move in a world of prominence, applause, and huge salary. They appear to possess great charm, personality, and beauty not found in other people. Whether the actors are professional or amateur, they seem to have a glamorous, easy life.

In truth, the actor's job is far from being easy and glamorous. Mistaken is the person who thinks that acting requires only, "I learn my lines, get on the stage, and be myself." Rather, the actor's job is not to be himself or herself, but to create a character on stage that is believable to an audience and appropriate to the play. The actor, then, is creating an illusion of reality. What the audience sees on the stage is not real — it only appears to be real. The actor's task requires hard work, entailing hours of study, concentration, imagination, and determination. A good actor is an artist who has learned discipline and technique.

Every artist has a medium of expression. While the painter has oils and the musician has instruments, the actor's medium is the self. To do well in drama, each actor must have an active mind that is alert and sensitive, and a sound body that is coordinated and pliable. This is where your drama training begins.

Acting class warmups create energy and a feeling of ensemble.

Through definite projects you will learn how to attune your mind, body, and voice to the demands of acting. When this is achieved, you will learn how to create believable characters. Later, you will study production methods of the director and technician. There are few hard and fast rules in drama. Mainly there are principles for you to study and apply. As you learn these principles and do the various assignments, you will be cultivating a technique that will provide a rich resource for achieving the requirements of your role.

ASSIGNMENT AND ITS PURPOSE

Since an actor's body is vital to theatre, you must immediately begin developing your body into an expressive, controlled entity. Body control requires mobile muscles and relaxed, coordinated movements achieved through daily physical exercise and participation in sports. Acting is strenuous work, often involving vigorous fighting, fencing, wrestling, or dancing. You as a student/actor are wise to practice such skills in your everyday routine so that your body will become supple and disciplined.

One way to begin body control and communication is to participate in pantomimed games such as charades. Many of you may be familiar with charades. The game is sometimes featured as a television program, and it is frequently played at both teenage and adult parties. If you haven't been introduced to charades, you have missed much fun!

Charades is a game in which two or more sides team up against each other in guessing pantomimed titles of either a book, movie, play, or song. (Pantomime means movement and gesture without words.) The group who guesses the titles in the least amount of time wins. In playing charades, each member of the team gets a chance to act out a title in hopes of revealing that title to teammates. The more communicative you can make your body, the more chance your side has of guessing correctly.

Suppose you must pantomime the title of Fitzgerald's novel *The Great Gatsby*. Tell your team that you will act out a book title having three words. Perhaps you will begin by acting out the second word, "great." Let your team know that you are working on the second word by holding up two fingers. You may pantomime "grating" carrots, or building a fire in a "grate," or perhaps you may indicate "great" as a size. Any of these clues your side should easily guess.

When the group has guessed the word "great," pantomime the third word "Gatsby" by extending three fingers to let them know which word you are doing. It will be easier to divide this word into syllables. The conventional way to let your team know that you are working on syllables is to pretend, with your right hand, to chop your left arm into as many pieces as there are syllables in the word. Thus, for "Gatsby" you would chop your left arm twice. For the first syllable you may enact a cat or a bat, cueing the group that the word you want, "gat," sounds like (put your hand to your ear) the word you are acting.

The second syllable will be easily guessed if you act out a bee buzzing around flowers or stinging someone. By this time your team will have guessed the complete title, supplying for themselves the initial word.

If you fail, after two or three attempts, to communicate the right word to your team, either approach it with a new idea or give it up temporarily and go on to another word.

The game will go faster and will be more exciting if you use conventional gestures to indicate little words such as "the, an, if, to, a, and." Do this by holding your right hand up with a closed fist, but having your index finger held up in a higher closed position. Avoid spending too much time on these unimportant or connective words. When the rest of the charade has been guessed, these tiny words will become obvious.

Let us examine a second title. Suppose that you are to pantomime the song *Rhapsody in Blue*. Announce that the song has three words and indicate that the initial word will be enacted by syllables. You may enact "wrapping" a package, or "rapping" on a door, or putting on a "wrap." When this is guessed you must advance quickly to the second syllable and perhaps "sew" with a needle. For the third syllable, you may have to enact an approximation instead of the exact sound, as "die" for "dy." Being shot, falling, and lying dead may convey this third syllable.

When the first word is guessed, advance to the third word. You may act like you are sad and "blue," or perhaps "blow" as the wind, or point to someone wearing the color blue. The group should have no difficulty in supplying the complete title.

HOW TO PREPARE

1. Depending on your class size, divide into two, four, or six teams of about six people each. (If you need four or more teams, play simultaneously in different corners of the room.) Appoint an umpire for each two teams to: (a) see that the rules are enforced; and, (b) record the time consumed by each team in the performance of its charades. Next, choose a leader for each team.

2. Each player should write the name of a book, song, play, or movie on the form provided and hand it to your team leader. In selecting a title, be sure that it is short (no more than four words) and that it can be pantomimed. Choose a title that will be known by the group.

3. Each leader should gather the team's titles and hand them to the opposing leader. Place these where each player can draw a turn.

HOW TO PRESENT

The leader of Team A draws the first slip from those submitted by Team B and silently reads it, keeping it a secret from teammates, but showing it to the opposing side so that they will know which of their titles is being enacted.

The leader as contestant immediately begins to pantomime in complete silence, using only bodily action to convey the words. From the performance, teammates try to guess the charade as quickly as possible. They may ask questions, but the performer replies only by movement and gestures. The umpire records the exact time it takes for the team to guess the charade. Remember, three minutes is the maximum time limit for each contestant. If the team doesn't guess in three minutes, they forfeit and the play goes over to the opposing team.

The opposing team, Team B, then takes its turn. Continue alternating teams until every member of each team has enacted a charade. The umpire tallies the time sheets and announces the winning team who took the least amount of time to guess its charades.

Remember, as a contestant your purpose is to communicate the title to your team by using only your body. Since you cannot use your voice, your actions must tell the whole story. Broad gestures and facial expression will help. Make all movements clear and definite.

You may find that as your turn approaches to perform, you feel nervous or scared. Good for you! Nervousness is a perfectly normal reaction which often precedes performance. You are not the only one with "stage fright." Great actors and speakers often experience this feeling. In fact, they want it. Brought under proper control, this nervous energy gives their performance vitality and spontaneity. Without this energy their reaction is dull and lifeless.

Learn to control your nervousness so that it will work for you — with energy —and not against you — with immobile fright. Forget about yourself by becoming completely engrossed in communicating the charade to your team. In this way you will gain control of your nervousness.

Since the purpose of this assignment is to loosen up your body and become communicative, your instructor will not grade you. Relax, put your whole self into the game, and have fun!

"Nothing great was ever achieved without enthusiasm" — *Emerson*

ADDITIONAL PROJECTS ON LOOSENING UP

1. Divide into groups of three or four people, and act out well-known folktales such as *Little Red Riding Hood*, *The Three Bears*, *Rumpelstiltskin*, or *The Three Little Pigs*. Make up your own dialogue and action as you follow the story outline.

2. Working together in groups of five to seven people, act out a machine. Your group may choose a machine used for work (such as a tractor, lawn mower, sewing machine, electric mixer); or a machine used for transportation (such as a train, helicopter, truck, scooter); or a machine used for fun (such as a tilt-a-whirl or a merry-go-round). For example, if you choose a tractor, four of you may be the wheels, one the steering wheel, others the body, etc. Plan to have the tractor move. After you have finished pantomiming your group machine, let the class guess what machine you are enacting.

3. Create a fantasy machine with each student contributing a moving part and a corresponding sound. Use all types of movement such as standing, kneeling, swinging, hopping, bending, etc. For a variation, have each machine part touch in synchronization another moving part.

4. To soft, slow music, use your whole body to print your name in giant numbers. Stretch, kneel, run, and move from one part of the room to another as you print. Don't worry if other class members finish before you. Just pay attention to your task.

5. Divide into groups of four or five. Imagine that you are acting in a television show with a title such as "Work," "Vacation Time," "Sports," "Relaxation," etc. Each group member should think of one thing to communicate the title idea. For example, if the title is "Work," one person may pantomime mowing a lawn, another scrubbing windows, another digging a ditch. Each group member will simultaneously act out the work idea. The class will observe and guess the various actions.

ELEMENTS OF DRAMA

While theatre often incorporates many embellishments with ornate technical devices and elaborate stages, the basic elements of drama are simple. They are:

1. Actors who create believable characters.

2. An audience who observes and responds.

3. A space in which the actor performs.

4. A story with conflict, meaning a struggle of opposing forces. It is this struggle — between characters, or within self, or between people and outside forces — that creates a dramatic clash and rivets audience attention on either serious or comic matters.

5. A belief that bridges player and audience and allows each to enter a theatrical reality in which the "happening" seems real.

— *Stage Fright* —

All of us have experienced the fear of facing an audience. Our throats become dry, our knees shake, our palms feel moist, our voice breaks, and our stomach has butterflies. Stage fright is a debilitating sensation! According to a nationwide survey, stage fright in the form of speaking in front of others is the number one fear of Americans.

In actuality, stage fright is not as much fear as it is an anxiety. We are anxious to do well — to succeed. The feeling of both mental and physical nervousness is produced by an automatic flow of adrenalin, which is our body's way of giving us spurts of energy so that we can cope with unfamiliar situations.

It is true that every person occasionally experiences stage fright. Your favorite movie or TV star, politician, teacher, or singer, all have stage fright at times. It is also true that you should be glad that you have it, for stage fright provides the energy to make you a dynamic person in any performance endeavor. The adrenalin flow gives you the enthusiasm, zest, or animation that is necessary in an actor.

Learn to control stage fright, to be its master, and not its slave. How do you gain control? You gain it through thorough preparation. Know what you have to do and how you are going to do it. Then rehearse the action and lines repeatedly until you feel confident with your performance — over prepare and over learn.

You will never get rid of stage fright, nor should you wish to, because you need the energy it gives. Just learn to control through preparation. As one person stated, "I still have butterflies in my stomach, but now they fly in formation."

Chapter 2 EMPHASIZING BELIEVABLE ACTION

Time Limits: 1-3 minutes

Activity Sheet: Prepare a 50-100 word complete sentence outline of the pantomime you intend to present. Use the form for this chapter, found in the teacher's manual. Hand it to your instructor when you rise to perform.

PROMPTINGS

1. Compare a child's make-believe play to that of an actor in a play.
2. Defend the statement: An actor must communicate with the audience.
3. Discuss belief as it relates to acting.

THEATRE LANGUAGE

Absorbed
Believable action
Technique

BACKGROUND NOTES

In the first assignment we pointed out that with conscious effort and application, you can learn the essential elements of acting technique. The basis of acting is literally a matter of "make-believe." It requires the ability to pretend — an ability that nearly everyone possesses to some degree. Probably you can recall from your earliest childhood the fun you had playing "House" or "Cowboys and Indians." The vacant lot with its uprooted tree became the lonely prairie with the enemy lying in ambush. Crossing the plains were the bison, which you heroically shot with your rifle. It did not matter that your dog Rover was the bison and that your precious rifle happened to be any old stick that was handy. You knew that the bison and rifle were not real, but that didn't stop the excitement or the fun. Your pleasure was great because you had given yourself over completely to the game. You were believing.

The belief that a child brings to play time is similar to the belief that an actor must bring to the part. Actors know that they are not really the characters that they are playing, but like children in make-believe, they act as if they were the characters. This is a difficult task for actors because, unlike children who enjoy unrestrained freedom of play for its own sake, actors must communicate to an audience. Therefore, they must develop a technique or a means that will enable them: (1) to constantly keep action believable to the situation; (2) to repeat that belief each time they perform; and (3) to communicate to an audience that belief. Is it any wonder that actors, to appear real and alive, must really think on the stage? In order to make an audience believe, the actor must believe!

The Lady's Not for Burning
by Christopher Fry
College of Southern Idaho:
Director, Tony Mannen

Body positions suggest
relationships.

ASSIGNMENT AND ITS PURPOSE

In this assignment you are to pantomime an action and make it believable to yourself. Put all of your attention on what you are doing. This means that you must see the situation and objects in your mind's eye, and work within that imaginary setting until it becomes believable to you.

Suppose that you choose bowling for your pantomime. You must "see" the alley, see where the shoes are rented, where the balls are stored, where you obtain your score sheet. You must visualize the action of bowling: wiping your hands on the towel; picking up the ball; feeling its weight; inserting your fingers into the correct holes; and holding the ball as you walk up to the starting line. Begin your approach on the proper foot. Feel the weight of the imaginary ball as you swing it back and then forward. Feel the release and see the ball as it travels down the alley or gutter. Follow through with your reaction. Make everything you do believable. Remember, in this assignment you are not assuming a character; instead you are doing the action in your own person. You will be graded on how true your actions are to the situation.

HOW TO PREPARE

1. Think of an action you want to pantomime. Choose a familiar activity that interests you. The following are suggestions:

    a. Playing a computer game
    b. Building a campfire
    c. Shining shoes
    d. Rowing a canoe
    e. Fishing
    f. Milking a cow
    g. Changing a flat tire
    h. Setting up an exercise machine
    i. Baking something
    j. Building something
    k. Golfing
    l. Your choice

    Study the above list and make your selection quickly. Spend your time in preparing the action rather than in choosing it. Remember that your purpose is well-planned action that is believable. Imaginatively visualize your surroundings. Then think about the action and see it. If you cannot recall the exact action, do the activity or observe someone participating in that activity. Accurately record the details and movement.

2. Outline each step in the action. Divide each main step into smaller actions until you have a complete series of movements. Use the activity form for this chapter, found in the teacher's manual, to write your outline.

3. Now that you have analyzed the action and have seen it in your mind, you are ready to do the action. Be clear and deliberate. Go slowly. Give attention to details. For example, if you are brushing your teeth, you must first remove the cap from the tube before squeezing out the paste.

    Do one thing at a time. Follow through on your movements. Rehearse until you have complete believability in your scene, going over your pantomime at least eight times. Clock yourself to be sure that you are staying within your 1-3 minute time limit.

HOW TO PRESENT

When your name is called, hand your activity sheet to your instructor and walk quietly to the playing area with an attitude of alertness and politeness.

Quickly set up necessary chairs. Give a short, well-worded introduction to awaken audience curiosity. Do your scene. Be sure you take your time and perfect each detail. Remember, if you are immersed in the task at hand, intent on doing your action in a believable way, you will not be worried about what the audience thinks of you. If you are absorbed in belief, the audience will believe with you.

At the conclusion of your scene, pause and then quietly leave the playing area.

ADDITIONAL PROJECTS ON BELIEVABLE ACTION

1. Using an imaginary rope, play Tug-of-War. Teams of equal number should stand in front of each other in a line, facing a similarly positioned team. In your mind see and feel the rope. Pull together as hard as you can to take the rope from the other team. Be careful that the rope does not stretch. If one side gets the advantage, the other side must give. Make the tug so believable to you, that at the end of the game you'll feel tired from the strong physical exertion. Think only of what you are doing. Don't talk. Put all your energy on the tugging.

2. In a 1–2 minute scene, make believable your efforts to escape from a place where you are trapped — perhaps a pit, a cave, a car trunk, an elevator. Visualize the size, shape, and position of where you are trapped. Then use your whole body in trying to escape. Strain, grunt, claw, climb, dig. Make yourself and your audience believe your endeavors. Continue your efforts until your instructor calls "Cut."

MIRROR NATURE TO CREATE BELIEF

In every day life, people follow a sequential order of response to stimuli. The actor must mirror that order on stage. The normal pattern is:

1. Sense the stimulus (idea, words, situation).

2. Register the idea in the brain — let it sink in. This may be a split second or several seconds, depending on the situation.

3. Physically respond to the stimulus.

4. Then, orally respond.

Following this step-by-step pattern will make the audience feel that what you are doing on stage is truthful and believable.

3

DEVELOPING OBSERVATION

Time Limits: 1– 3 minutes

Activity Sheet: Prepare a 50–100 word complete sentence outline of the pantomime you intend to present. Use the form for this chapter, which can be found in the teacher's manual, and hand it to your instructor when you rise to perform.

PROMPTINGS

1. Discuss the importance of creative imagination.
2. Give examples of how imagination is related to the other inner resources.
3. Discuss the importance of observation to an actor.
4. Connect observation to empathy.
5. Compare the value of actual experiences to vicarious ones.
6. Tell why selectivity and accuracy are the goals in observation.

THEATRE LANGUAGE

Accuracy   Inner resources
Analyze   Reenact
Creative imagination   Selectivity
Empathy   Setting
Inanimate object   Vicarious experience

BACKGROUND NOTES

One of the purposes of this course is to help you become a more creative, imaginative person, both on stage and in your everyday life. You and your associates are endowed with a creative ability that functions in numerous areas. Think of the person who creates an individualized computer program for an exam review, or who organizes a different aerobic routine from basic steps, or who plans a unique marathon race, or who designs a new community logo. All of these situations show use of creative imagination, the power to evolve something that is truly yours because you thought it up and did it by yourself.

Not everyone uses their creative imagination. Some people live their life in a dull, prosaic vacuum where they do only what they are told and sense only that which is obvious. Such people have never bothered to develop their creative powers; consequently, they lack the joy of life that comes from being resourceful.

On the other hand, if you are a creative person, you are vividly aware of your environment. Thus, you are able to store within yourself a vast number of ideas and impressions that you can reassemble and create into something freshly new when the situation demands. Being able to draw confidently from inner resources and to accomplish something that is uniquely yours gives you a great sense of satisfaction and adds value to your life.

Not only will a creative imagination help you to be a more interesting person in daily living, it will enable you to become a more responsive person in your artistic endeavors. It should be evident that the soul of all art — music, dance, sculpture, painting, writing, acting — is creative imagination. Perhaps less evident, but equally true, is that you as a student-actor can develop your imagination.

How is this done? One way is by strengthening your faculties of observation, concentration, and sense recall. These three qualities are all closely interrelated with creative imagination, However, for purposes of study, in the next three chapters we will analyze and work separately with each. As you become more aware of these elements and gain proficiency in using them, you will find that you have strengthened your imagination and that you (the actor) have rich inner resources from which you can create the numerous characters that you will play.

At the moment, let us consider observation. As an actor it is your business to portray human beings on the stage. Undoubtedly you do not have within your own personal experience sufficient knowledge to play well all types of people. Therefore, frequent observation of numerous individuals will add to your acting background. You must observe how various people think, how they feel, how they behave. You must notice, for example, how the movements of the old differ from the young, how the emotions of the teenager vary from the adult, how the thoughts of the worker differ from those of the boss. If your observations are vivid and accurate, you will have many experiences to draw upon in your acting.

Easy, you say! It is, if you put your mind to it; but most of us get into a rut and actually seldom observe the people and things around us. Too frequently we have eyes which "see not"; ears which "hear not. There are many reasons, of course, why our senses shut the outside world from us. Life is too complex for us to observe everything and remember it. We become selective, keeping one detail and throwing away others. Still, some people are able to observe and retain a great deal more than their friends. They encompass and are interested in many facets of the life around them. Instead of being overburdened with such acute observations, they appear vitalized and enthusiastic.

Just how observant are you? Can you immediately recall the color of your best friend's eyes? What were the people at breakfast wearing this morning? Without looking right now to see, can you visualize correctly what is on the bulletin board in your drama

Bye Bye Birdie by Michael Stewart, Charles Strouse, and Lee Adams.   College of Southern Idaho: Director, Tony Mannen

Rock and Roll costumes and body stance create the "Fifties."

classroom? Can you list quickly the various sounds within your hearing distance at this moment?

If you cannot accurately answer all of these questions, you need to become a more observant individual. To do this, you will first need determination to get out of your rut and rigorous self-discipline to keep your eyes open and your mind functioning.

Second, you need to widen your interests. Have you ever noticed that the details you observe and remember are those which are of great interest to you? Coming home from a party, a female can often describe in minute detail the clothes her friends were wearing, while a male might be completely oblivious to knowing even what his date was wearing. The reason is that women are generally more interested in clothes, than are men. But ask about the cars you passed while going to that party, and the females may not have noticed, while the men can usually list the cars and model to the last detail.

So, if you want to increase your powers of observation, increase your interests. Decide that you are not going to be such a narrow individual and conscientiously put forth an effort to learn about numerous things.

The third step in becoming a more observant person is to participate widely in many activities. Today, educators realize that students learn by doing. You will understand and retain knowledge longer if you are actively concerned with the subject. Therefore, participate as much as possible in your new interests. Practice using the synthesizer until it is easy; work on your tennis serve until you can put spin on the ball; attend a class meeting and add some worthwhile ideas to the discussion. If you find an area in which it is actually impossible to participate, you can do the next best thing and empathize (feel into the subject) strongly. For example, you probably cannot join an African photo safari right now, even though you may be interested in this activity. Nevertheless you can read extensively about African safaris, see films and documentaries on them, and become emotionally involved to the extent that you empathize or feel identity with the author and cameraman. In this way you gain a vicarious experience, which is often as stimulating as an actual experience.

As you work on developing your power of observation, keep in mind the actor's goals: accuracy and selectivity. Carefully scrutinize what you see so that your memory of the person, scene, or action will be vivid and true. On stage, if your part calls for you to play a ukulele, you must appear to do so convincingly. If you don't know how to handle the instrument, your actions will not be believable and you will lose your audience. So when you see someone play a "uke," watch carefully and remember the details. Better yet, practice playing the instrument yourself. Then you will be ready to transfer the action to the stage.

In addition to being accurate, the actor must be selective. When you observe, decide what actions can be used on stage and dismiss the others. The actor communicates best who can produce an uncluttered effect. At first you may find it difficult to be accurate and selective; but as you practice, you will be surprised at how discriminating you can become.

Try to begin all your studied observations with quiet contemplation. Attempt to discover new things in the life around you. Look at your immediate world with fresh eyes. On your way to school each day, determine to see at least one thing that is unusual or beautiful or funny or dramatic or sad. Look at your neighborhood as though you were a foreign visitor seeing it for the first time. What do you notice that before had fallen on blind eyes? Attune your ears to the sounds around you. Become aware of the various fragrances or odors that you encounter. View individuals. Study the way they look and move. Store in your memory the actions and impressions that you may be able to use in future character-izations.

Often it is necessary to observe in segments. For instance, if you look at an inani-mate object, such as a gnarled piece of wood, you might first contemplate the line of the object, then the color, the texture, the weight, how it feels when you touch it, and the asso-ciations that are called forth. Let your observations disclose not only what the eyes tell you but what the other senses reveal. The taste, smell, touch, sound, and emotion evoked should all be a part of observation.

Take advantage of the places you go. At the airport, in the art gallery, at the restau-rant, in the store, at the dances, in a church, in the dentist's office — train yourself to be aware and to remember what you observe.

ASSIGNMENT AND ITS PURPOSE

This assignment will help you begin developing your powers of observation. You are to choose an action involving an object. Practice and analyze the action at home and then in class reenact the movement by using pantomime.

In order for you to be successful in reenacting your scene, you must observe and analyze your actions carefully while rehearsing. Then, to test your classmates' power of observation, your teacher will call on one of them to redo the action you have just com-pleted. The accuracy of the reproduction will depend on how carefully your classmate scru-tinized your pantomime.

HOW TO PREPARE

1. Choose a simple action that you can readily practice at home. Be sure that an object or property is involved. The following are suggestions:
   a. Crack an egg into a bowl and beat the egg
   b. Scrub a bathtub
   c. Video tape an activity
   d. Wash your hands
   e. Play a musical instrument
   f. Cut and serve several pieces of cake

g. Put on a pair of tight leather gloves

h. Put on sunscreen lotion

i. Saw a board

j. Prepare vegetables for a food processor

k. Practice rollerblading

l. Make a bed

m. Sew on a button

n. Fill the gas tank of your car

o. Gather an arm load of wood for the fireplace

p. Your choice of a simple action

2. Actually perform the activity. While doing so, pay close attention to your movements and to their sequence. If you choose to pantomime putting on a coat, first get your coat from the closet and actually put it on. Do you throw the coat over your head and slip the arms into the sleeves haphazardly, or do you first put in one arm and then the other? Note with what hand you hold the coat, what your initial action is, what arm is first thrust into the sleeve. Feel the weight of the coat. Notice the muscular effort involved in putting it on. Do you button the coat, or do you leave it open and push your hands into the pockets? Observe and see what you do.

3. When you have completed the action, analyze your movements. Divide the activity into its component parts: the preparation, the initial movement, the following action, the completion. Decide what movements are absolutely necessary to accurately convey the pantomime. Be selective. Exclude all unnecessary, random behavior. Outline the action in steps on the activity sheet for this chapter, found in the teacher's manual.

4. Reenact the movements again, but this time without using the object involved. Be concerned not only with the pantomime but with recapturing the whole activity, including a feeling within you of the muscle effort involved, the sense of the weight and feel of the imaginary object, etc. Concentrate on accurately communicating both movement and sense feeling.

5. When you have rehearsed at least ten times, making sure that you have captured the actual and necessary movements, you are ready to perform this assignment.

HOW TO PRESENT

When your name is called, hand your outline to your instructor and walk quietly to the playing area. Announce the activity you are going to reenact. Then do your pantomime as rehearsed.

The class will be carefully observing you because when you are through, one of them will be called upon to reproduce accurately your scene.

When you complete your pantomime, pause, and then return quietly to your seat. Now, as a classmate repeats your scene, it is your turn to scrutinize carefully the reproduction.

ADDITIONAL PROJECTS ON DEVELOPING OBSERVATION

1. Choose a gathering of people that seems interesting to you — a rock concert, a dedication ceremony, an open air band concert, a farm auction, a political rally, a bargain sale, a child's playground, a county fair, a city bus, a hotel lobby, opening night at the theatre, a bus station, an airport, a crowded seashore, a travel agency. Mingle with the people. Observe them. Select one person who appears to be unique. Concentrate on that person's movement, facial expression, behavior. In class reproduce that person's movement, posture, gestures, etc. Try to be exact in showing what you observed and in indicating why the person was acting that particular way.

2. Choose an age group — childhood, teenage, middle age, old age — and note basic movements indicative of that group. Your observations should include movement of the body, head, legs, arms. Discover a rhythmic beat that you would associate with that age. In class, enact the age group you studied, first silently, and then again with a musical background on disc that suggests the rhythm you noted. (Select the music carefully and rehearse with it before class.)

3. Choose an animal that impresses you and study its movements and rhythm. How does the animal handle its body, its front paws, back paws, head? Notice its eyes, claws, tail, and any other identifying factors. In class don't tell what animal you are playing. First, with a drum or on a desk, beat out the rhythm of the animal as you observed it. Then act out the animal. If your portrayal is exact, the class should be able to guess correctly the animal you observed.

4. Do the mirror exercise. Divide into pairs of A and B. Face each other, looking directly into your partner's eyes. Partner A initiates slow movement of arms, hands, and body, as though under water. B is the mirror and must reflect exactly all of A's activities and facial expressions. At a command from your teacher, reverse your roles, with A being the mirror. Communicate with the eyes. Strive to work together, trying not to trick your partner with quick movements. Later, add vocal sounds.

Chapter **4**

DEVELOPING CONCENTRATION

Time Limits: 3 minutes

Activity Sheet: Prepare a 50–100 word complete sentence outline on your group improvisation. Use the activity sheet for this chapter, found in the teacher's manual, and hand it to your instructor when you perform.

PROMPTINGS

1. Give reasons why concentration is important to an actor.
2. Relate concentration to the illusion of the first time.
3. Connect concentration to the actor's dual role.

THEATRE LANGUAGE

Concentration	Illusion of the first time	Self-discipline
Dialogue	Improvise	Sincerity
Double-role	Interplay	Trappings

BACKGROUND NOTES

How surprised we would be while watching our favorite mystery program on television if the main character forgot his lines, nervously laughed about it, and asked blankly, "Where was I?" Not only would we be surprised, we would probably feel irate and disgusted because the whole illusion of a competent attorney in an exciting mystery had been destroyed by an actor who broke character.

It is rare that such things occur in professional show business, for actors who are rigorously trained in their profession have learned how to concentrate and sustain character no matter what happens during production. Therefore, we generally find professional playing believable, and the stage illusion constant.

Unfortunately, such absorption is not readily seen in amateur productions. Too often amateur actors seem more interested in themselves and their own private thoughts or fears than in what their character should be doing or saying. Consequently, we observe a production that is shallow and unconvincing.

In Chapter 2, we stated that student-actors must develop a technique whereby they can believe in their characters and thus allow the audience to believe also. We further pointed out that the actor engenders belief through constant thought or attention to the action at hand. Such attentiveness we call concentration, a second inner resource that is vital to actors.

As you were working on your power of observation in the previous lesson, did you notice that in order to remember everything you saw, you had to concentrate? These two elements — observation and concentration — are working partners for actors who are enlarging their background for later use in building a part.

Not only in preparation work but in actual stage work it is imperative to concentrate. The only way actors can focus audience attention on the right things in the play is to give their attention to those things. When an actor concentrates on an object or person, the audience will give attention to those same items. If you don't believe this, stand on a street corner and gaze up at the sky in continued studied concern. Just see what happens to those who pass by!

You can strengthen your power of concentration if you have a desire to improve and enough self-discipline to get in and do it. Improvement will take time, but you'll find the results are rewarding both on stage and in your daily life, for concentration exercises will benefit you both as actor and person.

Work on some aspect of concentration everyday. Begin with your studies. At the same time each night and in the same place, do your homework. Be sure that you select a quiet corner, free from distraction. Don't make yourself too comfortable. A hard chair and a desk that you must sit up to will keep your body in an alert position, which makes concentration easier. Set yourself a time limit for each subject and make yourself concentrate on the business at hand. Do not allow your thoughts or attention to wander. Keep at your studying. Engender an interest in your subject, which will make it easier to sustain concentration. If you do this each night for a month, you will find that you have increased your concentration and probably have improved your grades as well.

When you have a few spare moments alone, try this. While music is playing loudly, read silently a few paragraphs of difficult expository material. Then, turn off the music and make yourself account for the ideas and details you read in those paragraphs. Or try this. Take a newspaper to the basketball game and during the excitement, make yourself read and understand an editorial. Repeat these exercises until you are master of your attention.

You and your friends can also have fun in checking each other's concentration. At a party have the hostess place fifteen or twenty articles on a table, After one minute, she will cover up the articles, and you and your friends must write down all the objects that were there. Increase the number of objects until you are capable of quick and accurate observation because of high powered concentration. Other games involving concentration are "Simon Says" and "Up Jenkins" (consult a game book for directions).

As you transfer your concentration to the stage you will note that as an actor, your job is unique. You have a double-role to perform, for you must be both character and actor at the same time. For example, in order to make your part believable, you must become absorbed in the character you are portraying, as well as in the interaction of the other characters on stage. At the same time you must as an actor be cognizant of the technical demands of the theatre, of the trappings backstage, and of the audience out front. While accomplishing this task you must ever communicate the illusion of the first time. This means that your action must seem spontaneous and fresh to the audience, even though you have rehearsed it scores of times.

We will further emphasize the actor's double-role and the illusion of the first time in following chapters. At the moment we will be concerned primarily with the basic concentration you should give your character.

No matter how small your part or how short the scene, your attention must constantly be on what your character should be doing or saying or thinking. Whenever your attention wanders to something else, your character portrayal suffers — and so does your audience!

As you work on your portrayal, develop an interest in your character. Concentrate on his or her desires, purpose, and influence on the other characters. Every moment you are on stage (including a few minutes before your actual entrance) you should be thinking as that character would think. Instead of saying to yourself, "I must be excited and act curious because my brother is coming home," you should think as if you were the character: "How wonderful. Bill is coming home, after all these years. He's coming! Will he have changed? Will he know me?" A thought pattern such as this will help you stay in character and will focus attention where it should be placed.

Acting, of course, demands interplay among people. When not talking, your character should be listening as though for the first time to what the others are saying. In this way your character can believably submit or reject ideas.

If you give complete concentration to your character's actions and thoughts, plus to the interplay among the other people on stage, you, the actor, will find that you haven't time or desire to lapse into your own private speculations. You will be thinking into the play, and your audience will be right there, caught in the illusion of reality.

ASSIGNMENT AND ITS PURPOSE

Concentration has two aspects. First you focus your attention on the necessary object, and then you sustain or keep your attention there. In this assignment you will have practice in both focusing and sustaining concentration.

With a classmate you are to improvise a scene. To improvise means that you are given a situation in which you must make up dialogue and action as you play out the scene. You do not learn definite lines, nor do you plan specific movement. You create your own dialogue and movement as you act. This technique alone demands concentration if you are to think creatively on your feet while keeping within the boundaries of the situation and character.

The Good Doctor by Neil Simon
College of Southern Idaho: Director, Fran Tanner

Character concentration and intense facial expression contribute to the illusion of reality.

For this assignment choose a situation where you play yourself but where you and your partner have contrasting or opposing purposes. As the scene progresses, each of you will attempt to carry out your particular purpose. This means that you must focus on your desire or want and keep trying to achieve it, despite what your partner says or does to divert you.

Suppose you choose a scene in which you are studying for an exam tomorrow. Your friend arrives and tries to get you to go to the school play. You are intent on studying. Your friend is equally intent on getting you to go to the play. You may give your reasons for having to study: you must pass the exam tomorrow or you will flunk the course; you made a promise to your father that you would pass the exam; your parents won't allow you to go out on a school night, etc. You may do certain things to carry out your purpose: continue studying; try to get your friend to leave; stuff your ears with cotton, etc. Your friend may give you a rebuttal to persuade you to go. The result will depend on which argument is the stronger.

Both of you should determine to achieve your purpose and should enter into the spirit of the improvisation with determination and vigor. You will not be graded on your dialogue or action, but on the extent to which you achieve your purpose. Concentration and sincerity of desire are most important.

HOW TO PREPARE

1. Your teacher will assign you a partner and allow class time for the next two steps.

2. Together, you and your partner will choose a situation where there are opposing lines of interest and where the two of you can play yourselves. Quickly choose a scene that will involve action, conflict, and dialogue. Keep the basic scene simple. The following are suggestions:

   a. Two of you are in the family room at home. One of you wants to clean up the clutter; the other is lazy and tries to prolong the cleaning job.

   b. Two of you are hanging a picture. One wants the picture put above the fireplace. The other wants it put on the wall.

   c. A girl is at a party and a boy attempts to make friends with her. She doesn't think she should accept a date with him because she has just met him. He is determined to get a date with her.

   d. Two cheerleaders are working out a yell routine. One wants to jump in the air after each yell. The other insists they should bow at the end of each routine.

   e. Two boys are packing their small car for a ski trip. One thinks that the skis should be carried on top of the car. The other insists they should be mounted on the back.

   f. Two of you are camping in the forest. One insists that the roast should be cooked over the open fire on a spit. The other thinks the roast should be wrapped in leaves and placed in a cooking pit.

   g. Co-chairpersons are decorating the gym for a Thanksgiving dance. One wants to hang the theme-decoration, a huge cornucopia, from the center of the ceiling. The other wants to place it on the floor by the entrance.

   h. Two girls are helping each other with a home permanent. One girl wants to cut off her long hair. The other doesn't want her to and attempts to keep her from it.

   i. Two boys are trying to decide what to do after they graduate. One thinks they should both go to college. He shows his friend the college catalogue and tries to get him to fill out an application form. The other boy thinks they should join the Army. He wants to telephone the enlistment officer and complete an enlistment form.

    j. Two girls are staying all night with each other. One is on a diet and is determined not to snack between meals. The other is snacking and tries to get her friend to do likewise.

    k. One of you is packing a suitcase, determined to take a trip. A friend thinks you are foolish to leave and attempts to keep you from packing.

    l. Your choice.

3. Decide what part you will take, the purpose each of you will try to achieve, and the skeleton action you will do. Also decide which of you will announce the scene before presentation. Now your work together ends until you play your scene in class.

4. Before class, each of you should include on the activity sheet for this chapter:

    a. The skeleton situation you and your partner have chosen.

    b. Four good reasons that you may use in trying to convince your partner to do what you want done.

    c. Four things you may do (action) to try and achieve your purpose.

You may practice, but do not try to memorize lines or action. These two lists on your outline are merely to get you thinking within the situation. You may or may not use what is on the list. As you play the scene, better ideas and action may come to mind.

HOW TO PRESENT

When you and your partner are called to perform, hand the activity sheet to your instructor and quietly go to the playing area. Set up chairs and tables if needed, by placing them in such a way that both of you will be able to play toward the audience.

Announce the scene before beginning the action and dialogue. Immediately dig into the conflict and move quickly toward achieving your purpose. Say and do all you can to arrive at your goal. Do not give in to your partner's wishes. Be forceful and maintain concentration. Do not break character, giggle, or feel embarrassed. You have a job to do, so do it!

At the end of three minutes, your instructor will call "cut"; you will then quit playing and return with poise to your seat. Your instructor may want to offer constructive criticism. Accept it cheerfully, for your purpose here is to learn.

ADDITIONAL PROJECTS ON DEVELOPING CONCENTRATION

1. Have the class divide into circles of about 15 people each. One person says one word; the second person repeats that word and then adds a different word to associate with the first. Example: butter followed by bread. Proceed adding words around the circle. Actors forgetting a word must drop out.

2. Have each class member read in turn for 3-4 minutes some expository material from an unfamiliar essay or article. While he or she is reading, the class will heckle (talk and make noise) in hopes of diverting the reader's attention from the article. At the end of three minutes, the heckling ceases and the reader must relate in detail what has been read.

3. Choose a situation in which you can play yourself and in which you are about to do something. Briefly describe the situation to the class, then improvise out loud what your thoughts would be before you begin the action. For example, you have been called into the dean's office at school and are in the outer room waiting for the door to open. Vocalize your thoughts, fears, and hopes.

4. With a partner, start an argument involving both of you. Talk simultaneously and without pause, concentrating on your own line of reasoning. Example lines to initiate argument: "You were driving too fast," "You are late," "Turn off that TV."

HINTS FOR IMPROVISATION

1. Get into the scene immediately — trying to achieve your specific goal.

2. Keep the scene going. Play from moment to moment. If something doesn't work, try another action.

3. Listen and react to your scene partner. Don't negate your partner's lines. Accept the statement and be creative in responding to it.

4. Believe in what you are doing and saying.

5. Be spontaneous. Limit pre-planning.

6. Keep the scene from being a question/answer routine. Talk about the situation and your feelings. Better yet, show how you feel both facially and physically.

Chapter 5
STRENGTHENING SENSE RECALL

Time Limits: 4 minutes for observation; 5 minutes for writing description

Activity Sheet: Write three or four short descriptive paragraphs recalling an object. Use the form for this chapter, found in the teacher's manual.

PROMPTINGS

1. Discuss the importance of sense recall to an actor.
2. List the various senses.
3. Describe how to activate sense recall.

THEATRE LANGUAGE

Auditory	Scrutinize
Gustatory	Sense recall
Kinesthetic	Stimuli
Olfactory	Tactile

BACKGROUND NOTES

When browsing through a magazine, have you ever gazed at a colored photograph of a favorite food of yours, such as a velvety-looking chocolate cake with thick, creamy frosting, and found that as you looked at the picture and thought of the sweetness and richness of chocolate cake, your mouth actually began to water? Probably this has happened to you, whether the picture was of a cake, a juicy steak, or a bowl of salty, buttered popcorn.

Looking back you may wonder why a mere colored photograph made your salivary glands so active. You realize that the smell and sight of actual food, and the knowledge that you will soon be eating it, can produce such an effect in your mouth, but by what power did the picture of that food produce those results?

In the theatre we term this power sense memory or sense recall. With sense recall you are able to experience past sensations when you wish, or when you come in contact with certain artificial stimuli such as a picture. To show you how sense recall may work, let us return to the picture of the cake. If you like this type of dessert, the picture of it may very well call forth a memory in your mind of how delicious such a cake has tasted. Since taste is the major factor in this situation, the salivary glands are quickly activated.

As you think about the cake you may call to mind additional sensations. You may remember the faint chocolate odor of the cake as it was cut and placed on your plate. You may visualize the creamy, thick frosting on the top, the sides, and between the two layers. You may recall the few crumbs scattered around the plate. Possibly you remember the touch of the cool, silver dessert fork as you picked it up and balanced its weight in your hand before cutting into the spongy-textured food. Thinking of the first bite, you may sense again the feeling of the slightly porous cake on your tongue and palate, the sweet smoothness of the frosting on your lips. You may recall the muscular movement of your tongue, jaws, and throat as you chewed and then swallowed.

Thus, having started with a dominant sensation of remembering how good chocolate cake tastes, you have found it possible to recall a whole range of sensations in eating that cake: the taste, sight, smell, touch, and kinesthetic (muscular) reaction.

This ability of sense recall is of primary importance to an actor, for it is an established fact that the stage provides imaginary stimuli to which the actor must respond with authority. The valuable diamond necklace is really cheap glass, the beautiful velvet gown is inexpensive flannel, the fragrant spring air is only in the word description of a character. Obviously, the set is not actually a wooded New England park. Nevertheless, competent actors are able to make these artificial items appear real. They do this by training themselves to recall the sensations that are associated with the real objects and to apply those remembered sensations to the artificial properties at hand.

For instance, suppose an actor's part calls for holding a bouquet of carnations. These flowers will probably be artificial. If the actor can recall real carnations — the spicy fragrance when freshly cut, the softness of their petals, the brittle rigidity of their slim-leafed stems — he or she will be able to handle the artificial carnations so that they will seem vivid and real to the audience.

If you have faithfully worked on the previous exercises and projects in observation and concentration, you should now realize the necessity of being alert to the world around you. Habitual acceptance of your surroundings is enervating. Constantly you need to be aware of all your sense impressions, not just the visual, but the tactile, auditory, olfactory, and gustatory as well. When you put all of your senses to work, your impressions will be more vivid than if you receive them from a single sense organ. Of course one of the sense impressions will be stronger than all of the others. In the example of the cake, the taste impression was greatest, but remembering this dominant sensory factor allowed you to recall all of the other sense impressions until you had reconstructed the complete image. In like manner, you can successfully recall any sense impression as long as you strengthen your original impression by using every sensory aspect.

Unfortunately, many of us rely solely on the visual sense to gain an impression. We often accept or reject people and articles by how they look to us. Consequently, our other senses become lazy or dormant. You may need to test yourself to discover how acute your various senses are and how well you can recall the impressions they give you. For purposes of exercise, concentrate on each sense separately. When you have activated each basic sense, use them together to gain impressions of the world around you.

The Dining Room by A.R. Gurney
College of Southern Idaho: Director, Fran Tanner

Eye focus on the male character at the table's end creates necessary focus as a toast is given.

5 Basic Senses

1. *Taste* —

   We have been talking about chocolate cake and in so doing you may have re-called its taste. Now can you recall the taste of a spice cake, a fruit cake, a pound cake, an angel food? Each of these cakes has a distinctive flavor. Can you differ-entiate among them? What associations does each taste call forth?

   Think of the taste of other items: mustard, dill pickles, fried chicken, raisins. You should be able to recall each. If you cannot, you should actually sample these foods and concentrate on their flavors. Later, attempt to recall the taste without having the foods in sight.

2. *Hear* —

Now concentrate on hearing. What noises can you detect in the room? Listen carefully. What you thought was a quiet room is actually a room filled with many sounds. Apply this same test outside. As you listen intently, what noises do you hear? Can you detect sounds that generally go unnoticed?

Think about various sounds. Can you recall that of a helicopter flying overhead, a mousetrap being sprung, a piggy bank being shaken, a bugler blowing taps? If you can actually recall these sounds you will not have to pretend on stage that you hear them; you will be hearing them in your mind, and your subsequent responses will be valid.

3. *Touch* —

Recall touching a cold ice cube tray. How did it feel to you? What associations does the ice cube tray bring forth? Attempt to recall the feel of a cocker spaniel's ears, a velvet handbag, a worm as you bait your fish hook, a hot water bottle on your back.

4. *Smell* —

Try to recall from your memory various smells, such as fresh paint, moth balls, your favorite perfume, cooked fish, wet fur, burning rubber, gasoline, or bees wax candles. If you can't remember these odors, smell the actual articles and as you do so, note their distinguishing quality. Later, attempt to recall them accurately. Think of the associations these odors project. What would you choose as being a "friendly fragrance"? What for you is the most "unfriendly odor"?

5. *See* —

Bring to your mind's eye the following: a brilliant red and orange sunset, varied neon lights downtown, a snake slithering through underbrush, a single candle burning in the dark, a dilapidated easy chair.

As you work on these individual exercises, make your own additions to each list. When you have activated each of these sense organs, you are ready to use them all in gaining a many sided memory-impression of the objects you scrutinize.

Keep in mind that your ability to recall sense impressions depends on the strength of the impression, its recency of occurrence, and how frequently you recall it. Only concerted practice will enable you to become skilled in this technique of sense memory.

ASSIGNMENT AND ITS PURPOSE

In this assignment you will gain practice in creating a strong sense impression and in recalling it. You are to select a small object out of class and after scrutinizing it carefully, you are to write a description of it from memory. Bring your description and object to class.

Your instructor will arrange a trade of objects, giving you one that a classmate has brought and giving your article to another student.

The whole class will be given four minutes to examine their individually assigned articles. Then the articles will be covered or put into a box, and the class will be given five minutes to recall the objects and to write a description from memory. The two descriptions of the same article (one done in class and one at home) will be read aloud by each author and compared and graded for sensitivity of awareness and accuracy of recall.

HOW TO PREPARE

1. Choose an object that is readily accessible and that you can bring to class. The object may be something as unusual as a brass samovar, or it may be as ordinary as a white pottery cup. The following are suggestions:

   a. An unusual paperweight

   b. A silk umbrella

   c. A shaving brush

   d. A teapot

   e. A bottle of cologne

   f. An earthenware jug

   g. A dried prune

   h. A wicker basket

   i. A pen knife

   j. Salt and pepper shakers

   k. A house plant

   l. A cloisonné vase

   m. A half lemon

   n. A dinner bell

   o. A carved ivory chessman

   p. Fur earmuffs

   q. Your choice

2. Using as many of your senses as possible, inspect the object. Let your ears, nose, tongue, hands, and eyes tell you as much as possible. If you pick a familiar object, do not be satisfied with what you already know. Observe the object as if looking at it for the first time. Delve in deeply. Make your impressions of the article so strong you can later recall them quickly and easily.

For example, suppose your choice of objects is a red cut glass candy bowl that is sitting on the coffee table in your front room. You have seen it many times, but you have never really bothered to take a good look. Now is your chance. Scrutinize this candy bowl from every aspect you can imagine. Notice the size and conformation, the symmetry of the lines, the balance of the bowl to its base and to its lid. What is the basic shape of the dish? View the workmanship on the hand cut glass, its pattern, its sharpness of design, its repeat motif. Give attention to its finish. Is it smooth, shiny, dull, rough? Look at the inside of the bowl as well as the outside. Even observe the bottom of its stand or base. Feel the weight of the bowl and feel the glass. How does the bowl sound when the lid is carefully hit against the top of the bowl?

Notice the color. Is the color consistent, variegated, bright, subdued? Of what does the color remind you? In the case of this deep red dish, perhaps it reminds you of the dark juice of the pomegranate. In one word, how would you describe the candy dish? Besides its basic function of holding sweets, what other associations does the bowl suggest? If it is an exquisite work of art it may intimate an elegant manor in Austria with crystal chandeliers and women in long gowns. Or it may suggest a red-pieced kaleidoscope where the glass fragments move and fit together in myriads of patterns. Of course the associations that this bowl, or any other article, gives to you will depend on your background and personality.

3. After five or six minutes, when you are satisfied that you have captured the article in your sense memory, cover the article and write three to four short paragraphs describing it. Don't peek! To gain practice in recall, your description must be from memory! Write your description on the front of the activity sheet for this chapter, found in the teacher's manual.

4. Bring the article and your description to class. Your instructor will assign your article to someone else and give you one brought by a fellow classmate. The class will now work simultaneously, but on their individual objects.

5. You will have four minutes to gain a sense impression. Survey the object as thoroughly as you did the one at home. Notice the following:

    a. Line
    b. Balance and proportion
    c. Composition
    d. Weight
    e. Color
    f. Function
    g. Associations it calls forth.

6. After four minutes your instructor will call time and will put the objects in a box. You will be given five minutes to write a description on the back of the outline

sheet for this chapter. Try to recall everything you observed. If necessary, for speed, jot down your thoughts in phrases rather than in complete sentences. Work quickly to complete your description within the allotted five minutes.

HOW TO PRESENT

When your instructor displays the article you brought from home, turn in the bottom part of your activity sheet for this chapter. Be sure your name is on it and take the top part with you to the front of the room. The student who scrutinized your article in class will accompany you.

With the object in full view on a table, read carefully and clearly the description you wrote before class. Then your partner will read the one written in class. Listen carefully to your partner's description. When you are both through, your instructor will ask you and the class to join in a short informal discussion on such aspects as:

1. What are the significant differences between the two analyses?

2. What are the similarities?

3. Which description shows the more sensitive awareness (taking into account the time discrepancy between class and homework)?

4. How do personality and background contribute to the varied or similar sense observations?

In like manner you will later read the description of the article you observed and described in class and make a comparison with the description your classmate wrote about it at home.

ADDITIONAL PROJECTS ON STRENGTHENING SENSE RECALL

1. Choose a category such as flowers, beverages, cups, chairs, fruit. Outside of class, observe four different types of objects within the genre you have chosen. Note similarities and differences. For example, how do you handle a china tea cup, a coffee mug, a tin cup, a small demitasse cup? Or how do the tastes of milk, tea, orange juice, and hot chocolate differ?

In class, recall the sense impression of each article and pantomime your contact with each. Attempt honestly to recall the actual sensation as you pantomime. Feel the china cup in your hand or taste the tart, pulpy orange juice as it trickles down your throat.

2. Choose an activity that can occur in various situations. For example, walking in sand, mud, rain, snow; or carrying a suitcase that is heavy, empty, bulky. Observe how you would walk in the various elements, or how you would carry the different suitcases. Let all your senses give you a strong impression. Then recall that impression in class as you pantomime the activities.

3. Divide into groups of four or five, with each group choosing a simple item to "eat." In turn, each group goes to the stage and proceeds to "taste," "smell," and "eat" the imaginary food. Work on recalling the real food as you eat it.

4. Divide into groups, each deciding a sport event to watch as a group. Go on stage and observe the sport, "seeing" it with your whole body.

Chapter 6 STRENGTHENING IMAGINATION

Time Limits: 40 minutes class preparation; 4-5 minutes presentation

Activity Sheet: Prepare a full sentence outline of 50-75 words on the situation for improvisation. Use the special form for this chapter, found in the teacher's manual.

PROMPTINGS

1. Discuss the role of imagination in creating an illusion of reality.
2. Understand the difference between artistic reality and life.
3. Describe an activity that will stimulate imagination.

THEATRE LANGUAGE

Aesthetic (es-thet´-ik)   Impromptu
Control   Second awareness
Imagination   Stage conventions

BACKGROUND NOTES

There is one most important aspect in all theatre. Without it an actor is nothing. Without it a production is void. It is the vital spirit that gives drama its life. It is imagination.

In Chapter 3, we briefly discussed imagination and the way we use it in our daily lives. We pointed out that imagination, observation, concentration, and sense recall are all integrally related and that they function together in the imaginative process.

In previous lessons we have also noted that the actor's purpose, as well as the purpose of the theatre, is to create an illusion of reality. Plays are not real life; they only appear real. They give us a heightened interpretation, rather than an actual reproduction of life.

In fact, the only reality that exists in the theatre is an aesthetic or an artistic reality, created by the imagination of actor and audience. Actors know that they are not really the characters in the play, but through imagination they act as if they were the characters.

The audience knows that the hero is not really dying on stage, that tomorrow night and as long as the play runs he will "die" each performance, yet through its imagination the audience is able to believe in the characters and situations. Let us repeat: to participate in the illusion of reality, both actor and audience must "suspend disbelief" and let their imaginations flow freely.

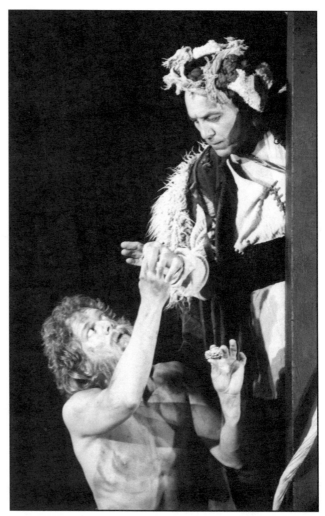

Timon of Athens
by William Shakespeare
Utah Shakespearean Festival
Photo by John Running

Timon shares his new-found fortune with Apemantus.

However, an active imagination does not imply a lack of control. If the theatre is to give pleasure, both actor and audience must realize that they are engulfed in art and not in life. Control, in the form of a second awareness, prevents the actor from getting carried away with the part and actually strangling the villain. Control, in the form of stage conventions, such as a front curtain, act intermission, and applause, assists the audience in maintaining a proper aesthetic balance.

Accepting the importance of imagination, let us focus on how it can vitalize your acting. Its greatest service is to bring to your mind detailed pictures from which you can create a unique and yet appropriate character in the play. The pictures you visualize spring from your insight and your past life experiences. If your imagination is vivid, the pictures will stimulate you into acting, believing and feeling your part.

As a child you probably exercised your imagination often, but as you matured you might have grown lazy in using it. If so, you must learn to revitalize your imagination and to call it forth when you need.

An old saying purports that "variety is the spice of life," and most of us will agree that reprieve from everyday routine is what stimulates us and makes life interesting. Unfortunately, many people inertly wait, hoping for something different to happen, without realizing that they have within themselves the power to add a new, fresh quality to life. Through their imagination they can perk up their old routine and energize events and people around them.

Keeping in mind that imagination implies a new synthesis or combination of ideas, think about yourself and how active your imagination is. What can you do that will put sparkle into your associations and add a pleasant worthwhile uniqueness to the life around you? Put your imagination to work. If you have a date and then find to your chagrin that you have no money, think of something wholesome you can do that doesn't require money. A brisk bicycle ride to the country, a leisurely walk through the city to take colored slides, an evening of reading a musical and playing the songs that accompany it may not be the usual date fare, but just may be a refreshingly enjoyable time for both of you.

Put your imagination to work. How can you make your home surroundings more pleasant? What individual note can you add to the conversation, or to the dessert, or table centerpiece that will make your family dinner a more enjoyable occasion? What different gift can you create — one that doesn't cost money — to present to a friend? From your practice in observation, concentration, and sense recall you should have a background of material from which to draw.

Since imagination, like the other inner resources, takes time to develop, you should work on it as much as possible. If you have some spare time while babysitting, or some free moments during the weekend hunting trip, write an original description of a mermaid's living room, a giant's kitchen, Jeanne d'Arc's prison cell, Napoleon's ballroom, the cloister of a Tibetan monastery, Montezuma's treasury room, or Beethovan's study. Visualize the places as you write. Be exact in your imaginative description. See the details so that when you are finished you can quickly recall the whole room.

Another enjoyable exercise is to observe objects around your house and imagine what you can use them for, in addition to their normal function. You can use a small string of beads as a light switch pull; or when fastened together, as a key chain or as a band for holding a roll of paper. A clothespin, with a name written on it, may be used in place of a napkin ring.

Something else that can be done individually or in a group, is to imagine in detail the reasons for an unusual situation you have observed in life. For example, why would a person walk through the mall wearing scuba gear? Why would a person order a banana split and then eat the ice cream and toppings but leave the banana? Why would a person carry an umbrella under his arm in a heavy rainstorm? Observe such real situations in life and then supply the imagined reasons that lead up to them.

At a party or in class, a game that helps stimulate the imagination is "spin-a-yarn." The leader begins telling a fantastic tale. At the end of one minute (the host or teacher can time you) the leader stops, and the story is continued by the next person in the group. It is the job of each participant to immediately pick up the story where the previous teller stopped and to keep the story moving with exciting episodes.

If you have extra time in class, you may ask your teacher to try this. Take a book and pass it from one student to another, handling the article as though it were a baby, a hot potato, a wet mop, a parakeet, or a puppy. You must be observant to see which end of the book is established as the baby's head, etc. You must use sense memory, concentration, and imagination in order to handle the book as though it were the real article you are establishing.

ASSIGNMENT AND ITS PURPOSE

Here is a chance to let your imagination flow freely. You and two other classmates, working as a group, are to improvise a five minute scene around three unrelated words. As soon as you select the group of words, set your imagination to work and incorporate the words as an integral part of a fantastic scene that your group can play. Your combined imaginations should enable you to visualize the scene structure and the details. As you improvise, your imagination will help supply the dialogue and action.

You will be graded on how uniquely you work the words into a scene and how far-fetched the situation is. You will be graded also on your concentration in maintaining character and developing the scene.

HOW TO PREPARE

1. Your instructor will group you with two other classmates. Together you are to pick a series of three unrelated words. The following are suggestions:
   a. toothbrush — horse — earring
   b. paper clip — telephone — baked potato
   c. pizza — Duke — typewriter
   d. lamp — rifle — zipper
   e. rug — zebra — rosebush
   f. paint brush — parsnips — dishwasher
   g. trumpet — sea shell — tractor
   h. aspirin — diamonds — cactus
   i. cookie jar — snow shovel — swimming suit
   j. door knob — newspaper — monkey
   k. spoon — dice — bath towel
   l. patio — haystack — elevator

A Midsummer Night's Dream
by William Shakespeare
Utah Shakespearean Festival
Photo by John Running

Oberon and Puck discuss the strange turn of events.

     m. angle worm — boxing gloves — postage stamp

     n. mink coat — shovel — toaster

     o. compass — rabbit — dictionary

     p. your choice

2. You will be allowed 40 minutes in class for planning and rehearsing the scene. Using your combined imaginations, create a strange situation in which the three words play an integral part as important objects. Be sure that the association of the articles is fantastic and that your story contains much action (movement you can do). Plan the basic sequence of action, arranging the scene for completion within 4-5 minutes. You may play yourself in the situation or you may assume a different person. Either way, be sure you "stay in character" by concentrating on what that person would say and do in that particular situation.

Suppose your group selects the following words: eraser, ladder, cabbage. You may concoct a story like this:

a. You are a nanny to a ten year old girl, who receives a letter saying that she will receive within the week a large sum of candy left her by a wealthy old uncle. The only stipulation is that the child must have long, pointed ears before she can receive the goodies.

b. Hoping to make the child's ears longer, you attach a string to them, tie the string to a door knob, and pull the child away from the door. This doesn't work. Her ears remain the same.

c. Frantically you take the child to a noted German psychologist. After referring to his large book, he finds the formula for growing pointed ears: eat a special rabbit's diet which consists of art-gum eraser bits and three drops of cabbage juice.

d. The child eagerly writes a letter and then erases it to obtain the art-gum eraser scraps. To secure the cabbage juice, the child is instructed to climb a tall ladder and to drop a cabbage head into a bucket. This she does three times, to obtain the three drops of juice. Each time she drops it, you and the doctor say loudly, "Gesundheit."

e. The child descends the ladder, eats the food, and her ears begin to grow. Soon they are long and pointed like those of a rabbit. She is elated. But suddenly she begins to feel strange, and in a few seconds she quickly turns into a rabbit, hopping out of the office with you and the doctor pursuing her.

3. Outline the improvisation, using the form at the end of this chapter. Be sure that each of you knows the sequence of the planned story. Also decide which of you will announce the scene in class.

4. Quietly rehearse your scene, using your imaginations to add sparkle to the action and dialogue Do not memorize specific movement and words. The rehearsal is only to attune you to playing together.

HOW TO PRESENT

When your group is called upon, hand your activity sheet to the instructor and go quietly to the playing area. Two of you may arrange needed chairs and tables, while the third may write the three words on the board and then announce the scene to the class.

With vivid imagination improvise the scene following the basic planned situation as rehearsed, but making up words and action as you play. Be sure you stay within the 4-5 minute time limit. The timekeeper will signal you at four minutes by standing up. You should be able to notice the timekeeper without breaking character or continuity. You will then have to supply the necessary dialogue and action so that the scene can be completed soon. When you have finished the improvisation, return quietly to your desk

 "An actor is as great as his or her imagination"

ADDITIONAL PROJECTS ON STRENGTHENING IMAGINATION

1. Your instructor will assign you an article such as a carrot, a French poodle, a wet dish-cloth, a watermelon, a thick billfold, a fried egg, or an ostrich feather. Observing or recalling these articles, you are to abstract the predominant features of the article and improvise, in a situation, a character having those qualities. For example, a water-melon may suggest a short fat man with a smooth head, chubby cheeks, and a waddle to his walk. Place such a character in a situation and improvise dialogue and action.

2. Select an abstract word such as freedom, vacation, recreation, dishonesty, etc., and pantomime what the word means to you.

3. Write out a line of dialogue that can be used as a "tag line," or the last line in a scene or play. Put your contribution with those of the class in a box. Divide into groups of three or four and choose at random a tag line from the box. Improvise a group situation, with dialogue that builds toward and ends the scene with the specific tag line your group selected. Examples of tag lines: "There's never time for rain"; "Oh, no, not you too"; "She's out planting pickles"; "And that, Mr. Smith, is that"; "Finally, the mouse is in the trap"; "The taxi's waiting."

4. Divide into groups of four or five. Your teacher will give each group member a specific physical position (bowing, arms above head, hand on toe, etc.) that you must naturally assume once during an improvisation the group creates. Be sure you motivate the as-signed movement.

5. A player goes on stage and moves as a part of a machine. Each class member, as soon as he thinks he knows what the machine is, quietly joins the first player and becomes another part of the machine. For example, the first player may be a windshield wiper on a car; the second may be a wheel; the third, a piston, etc.

Chapter 7

DEVELOPING EMOTIONAL RESPONSE

Time Limits: 3-5 minutes for emotional recall; 2-4 minutes for improvisation

Activity Sheet: Prepare a short full-sentence outline on your emotional recall and improvised scene. Use the special form for this chapter, found in the teacher's
manual.

PROMPTINGS

1. Define emotional recall.
2. Compare emotional response to Stanislavski's and James-Lange's acting theories.
3. List in order three steps in emotional recall.
4. Connect emotional response to aesthetic distance.
5. Discuss the relationship of emotional response to empathy.
6. Explain the meaning of Joseph Jefferson's statement, "The actor should have
a warm heart and a cool head."

THEATRE LANGUAGE

Aesthetic distance
Cliché movement
Emotional recall
James-Lange
Project (pro -jekt´)

Restraint
Stanislavski
Suggestion
Thespis

BACKGROUND NOTES

Does this sound familiar to you? One morning you wake up and find that you have
overslept. If you don't hurry, you'll be late for school. You feel angry. Quickly you dress,
putting on anything that is handy. The faster you move, the angrier you become. Why didn't
you set your alarm? Why didn't Dad call you? You dash into the hallway to grab your coat
and to leave, but Mom intervenes and insists you eat breakfast. Putting up a fight will only

prolong matters, so you hurry into the kitchen, your anger mounting. You scowl at your parents. You're late, and they think of breakfast! You gulp your food quickly, snatch an extra piece of toast, and leave, slamming the front door.

Whether or not this exact scene has happened to you, it is certain that every day you have numerous emotional experiences that motivate you into action. In the above situation, you felt angry, but notice that although you felt anger you did not think about that emotion. Instead, you were concerned with what caused the feeling (sleeping in and perhaps being late for class) and in doing something about it (dressing quickly, gulping breakfast, and hurrying to school).

This normal attention to the cause of an emotion and to dealing with that cause provides a basic key to portraying emotions on stage. If you learn how to use this key, it will open the favored door to communicating believable feeling to an audience, which is an ability that defines an actor's greatness.

Since portraying emotion is considered the most crucial aspect in the actor's craft, countless theories and techniques have been developed, with many noted theatre authorities advocating diverse ideas on achieving emotional response. Stanislavski, of the Moscow Art Theatre, believed that the actor should concentrate on the thoughts and the inner psychological workings of the character. While Stanislavski also stressed the need of a disciplined voice and body, his early followers only emphasized the internal aspect. Consequently, "The Method" is frequently identified with the idea that if you know your character's thoughts, the proper vocal and bodily expression will naturally follow. Opposing this internal approach is the James-Lange theory which teaches that certain body positions, when assumed, will automatically result in a corresponding emotion. For example, if you put your shoulders back, your head up, and smile, the emotion of happiness will follow.

Today most teachers of acting and most professional directors choose a middle course between the extremities of these two theories. We shall accept what they have found: that effective emotional response depends upon both internal and external development. You accomplish this development by following three basic steps:

1. Recalling a past emotional experience.

2. Transferring the recall to your character's part.

3. Heightening your response and action for communication to an audience.

Step 1 — Recalling a past emotional experience

When you begin working on an emotional scene, you should first vividly recall a similar emotion that you have experienced in the past. It may be a situation that happened recently, or it may have occurred during your childhood. The situation need not be similar to the scene you must play, but the emotion should approximate that which your character is to project. For example, there is no need to have a murder in your past in order to feel murderous intent. Simply recalling your strong desire to kill a bothersome and evasive fly can be a source from which your imagination can draw. Just be sure that you choose a past situation that vividly impressed you. If you think about it, there are numerous incidents that stand out in your memory; for whatever you observe and experience, you store away in your mind. What you must do is bring that stored memory to the surface.

Speaking aloud, recall your past experience as though it is happening to you again. Forget about the emotion. Focus, instead, on definite details of that past situation. Use your newly acquired skill of sensory recall to help recreate your experience by stating how objects looked, felt, sounded, tasted, etc. (Sometimes, just the remembering of these simple sensations will evoke the feeling for which you are searching.) Recall particularly what you did, for emotion is always accompanied by action.

As an example, suppose that the character you are playing must show a mounting fear, because of slowing realizing that he or she has been trapped in a hideout by a pursuer. As you begin study of your role, search your past for a situation in which you acutely felt a mounting fear. Perhaps it happened when you were a child. Recall that experience. For instance, you may remember that . . . you awoke from an afternoon nap; you recall lying on your back and gazing sleepily at the cotton quilt that covered you. It was a light-blue quilt, appliqued with girls in flowered pioneer dresses and yellow sunbonnets. Your mother had made it. Where was Mother now? You jumped out of bed and called. No answer. You listened but heard nothing except the even tick-tock of the cuckoo clock in the hallway. You ran to the window and pulled open the soft dark-green drapes; and as they parted, the late October sun slanted in and felt warm on your cheeks. No sign of Mother outside. All you saw was your battered red tricycle tipped over on its side, next to a small pile of dry, fallen leaves. Then you noticed the garage door was open and Mother's car was gone. Mother, who never left without you, was gone! You remember running across the slick, highly waxed hardwood floor, your bare feet making a smack-smack sound. You reached for the doorknob and yanked back hard, but the door would not open. You felt your arm and back muscles pull from the strain of the unexpected obstacle. The door was locked! Frantically you called out, "Mommy," and banged against the door as tears began to smart your eyes and roll down your face....

Repeat the recall of your own past experiences until you can actually visualize the scene (as in the above example, see the quilt, the drapes, the empty garage; hear your feet patter on the floor). Become so engrossed that you sense the emotion and automatically respond to the action you describe (for example, looking out the window, yanking at the locked door, calling to Mother). At first you may need to recall your past experience eight or ten times before you capture the feeling and movement, but as you gain proficiency in emotional recall, less repetition will be necessary to achieve the desired result.

Step 2 — Transferring the recall to your character's part

Now proceed to the second step in producing an emotional response. Immediately transfer the sensations of your recall to the particular part in the play that requires a parallel emotion. Using your imagination as a spring board, incorporate the recalled feelings into the scene as you rehearse it. Now here is the crux of the skill. Do not think about the emotion itself. The actor who thinks, "I must be afraid, I must be angry," is doomed to failure. After recall you should feel the emotion, but as happens in real life, you should think about what caused the emotion and what you are going to do about it. You feel fear, but you don't dwell on that state of fear. You find the cause (being trapped in your hideout by a man who has followed you), and then you deal with it (lock doors, barricade windows,

The Lion in Winter by James Goldman
College of Southern Idaho: Director, Ed Collins

The upstage character and the person three-quarters right throw emphasis to the middle character. Notice costumes and setting to suggest the England of Henry II.

load gun, etc.). If you know the play well, you will be able to find out why your character feels a specific emotion, and then you will be able to create logical action that the character would do because of situation and personality. Remember, your character will be believable to yourself and to the audience mainly by what he or she does in response to the emotions.

So base your character's feelings and their intensity on the recall of your past experiences, and base your character's actions on what you think you would do if you were the character in that situation.

A note of warning: avoid cliché movement and gestures, such as putting your hand to your ear to denote deafness or hitting your arms against your sides to denote coldness. Such stereotype action is rarely seen in real life. In your portrayal use only movement that is believable and artistically true to the character.

Step 3 — *Heightening your response and action for communication to an audience*

Follow the above two basic steps in early rehearsals as you begin to develop your characterization. A little later in rehearsals you will want to incorporate the third step, which is to heighten or exaggerate certain facets of the emotion and action while subordinating less important aspects. This is a necessary procedure as you artistically fuse your part with the whole play and as you concentrate on projecting emotion to the audience. It is at this level that the "external" qualities are emphasized, and you concentrate particularly on your voice and body. You will notice that your emotions are influenced by the use of certain basic movements. For example, exuberance doesn't lend itself to stooped shoulders and bent head. You will also notice that your voice can either compliment or destroy an emotional scene.

As you rehearse, you will gradually develop a planned sequence for dealing with the portrayed emotion, and later that sequence will become habitual. We do not mean that it should become mechanical or lifeless. Thespis forbid! Once the emotion and action are "set," you must constantly use your imagination to provide spontaneity and that "first-time" quality.

You may wonder, "Should I really feel the part? Cry real tears? Let myself go?" In early rehearsals when you are working with recall, you will find it necessary to completely feel the emotion; but as you later work on projection to an audience, you need not feel the emotion intensely. If you strongly felt the emotion (hysteria, depression, fear, etc.) as you played night after night, you would undoubtedly break down. The strain would be too great. You would lose control of your acting skill, being concerned mainly with your own tears and handkerchief and forgetting about communicating an aesthetic impression to the audience.

It may seem strange to you, but to be enjoyed, all work of art needs detachment from the actual world. This detachment we call aesthetic distance. It is maintained when the painter puts a frame around the picture, the sculptor places a pedestal under the statue, and the skilled actor controls emotion with a fine balance between empathy (see Chapter 3) and aesthetic distance. The actor's purpose is to make the audience empathize with the character's feeling but only to a certain degree. When the emotion on stage becomes too great, too much, audience members find themselves so involved that they begin to actively participate. Such overt physical response immediately destroys the illusion of make-believe, and the audience is jarred into embarrassment, displeasure, and disbelief.

As you perform, remember that to be successful, you must establish a definite feeling and mood within the audience, while yet maintaining enough aesthetic distance or detachment to prevent you and the audience from losing control. You accomplish this fine emotional balance by using restraint. Even in the most passionate scenes, never get completely carried away. As the great actor Joseph Jefferson observed, you must keep your heart warm and your head cool. Be selective in both movement and feeling. Suggestion, rather than complete portrayal, is always more effective. Audience imagination is powerful if only you set it free.

As you work with emotional response, constantly keep in mind that your success depends on audience reaction. If the audience believes throughout the play, if it is attentive and responsive, you are projecting the right amount and type of emotion and are neither underacting nor overacting. If your audience laughs in the wrong places, is noisy and inattentive, you have failed in your purpose and will have to change your portrayal.

ASSIGNMENT AND ITS PURPOSE

This assignment will give you practice in two of the three steps we have discussed: recalling an emotion and applying the feeling of that recall to an improvised scene. Be sure that your recall is from an actual experience that greatly impressed you, and that you succeed in recreating the emotion and action of the original situation. As you transfer the recall to the improvisation, strive to maintain the same emotion while applying it to the action and dialogue of the assigned scene.

You will be graded on the sincerity and vividness of your recall and on the believability of your improvised scene.

HOW TO PREPARE

1. Choose one of the following emotions and scenes for improvisation:

    a. *Happiness.* You are waiting for your date to arrive and take you to the ballet. You are happy and excited because this will be the first ballet you have attended, and you are wearing a new dress.

    b. *Sorrow.* You receive a phone call that two friends of yours have been killed in a car accident.

    c. *Relaxation.* You are at the beach where you have a whole carefree day ahead of you. You have brought along a hamper of items to help you relax and enjoy yourself.

    d. *Fright.* You are walking in the woods, collecting specimens for your botany class, when you hear a noise at the side of you and see a rattlesnake coiled to strike. Snakes terrify you.

e. *Surprise*. You are sitting at an awards assembly when the chairman announces that you are to be given a five thousand dollar scholarship for advanced study.

f. *Revenge*. Because it was checked out in your name, you have had to pay a ten dollar replacement fee for a book which your classmate lost. He denies ever having borrowed the book from you. You decide you'll get even by taking his term paper and destroying it.

g. *Curiosity*. Your friend has given you a Christmas present with orders not to open it until Christmas. You know you shouldn't peek, but you are alone in the house and can hardly stand not knowing what the package contains.

h. *Indecision*. You are buying a CD player with your own money. You can't decide whether to buy the cheaper set which is at regular price, or to buy a more expensive model which is on sale but is still forty dollars more than the cheaper set.

i. *Pain*. You are doing an experiment in the chemistry lab when you accidently break the test tube and cut a deep gash in your finger. Blood gushes out and your finger throbs with pain.

j. *Coldness*. It is subzero weather, and you have had no heat in your house all evening because the furnace is broken. Even though your fingers can hardly move, you attempt to type a research paper which is due in the morning.

k. *Boredom*. You are attending a lecture, and the speaker is so uninteresting that you are completely bored. You would like to leave, but you aren't sure how you can legitimately do it.

l. *Tiredness*. You have been skiing all day, and although you are happy, you are extremely tired. Upon arriving home late at night, you hardly have enough energy to unpack the car and put away your gear.

m. *Anger*. You are inside when you hear noises in the front yard. You go outside and see your new neighbor viciously hitting your old faithful dog with a broom. You furiously take action.

n. *Your own choice*. Use yourself as the character.

2. Using your powers of sense memory and concentration, recall a vivid past experience in which you felt an emotion similar to the one you have chosen above. The remembered situation need not be the same as the one for your improvisation, but the emotion should be similar. Recall your past experience out loud, focusing on the exact details of sensory impression (what you saw, smelled, tasted, heard, etc.) as well as on what you did. Relate the experience as though it is happening to you again. You may need to recall the scene many times before you

actually feel the emotion and involuntarily respond to the action you describe. Since this recall is the most important aspect of this assignment, don't be satisfied until you have actually recreated the past experience.

3. On the activity sheet for this chapter, found in the teacher's manual, outline the past experience that you have recalled. Note specifically on your outline the emotion felt, the cause of that emotion, and what you did about it.

4. Read over your scene for improvisation and quickly plan what you will do. Think of three or four specific actions that would be believable within the situation and that would relate to the cause of the emotion. Outline the improvisation on the back of the activity sheet, stating the emotion, its cause, and the ensuing action.

5. Rehearse your improvisation, saying aloud the character's thoughts as dialogue. Practice the scene until it is believable.

HOW TO PRESENT

When you are called upon, hand your outline to your instructor and proceed quietly to the playing area. Set up chairs and tables if you need them for the improvisation. Announce: (1) the experience you are going to recall; (2) the situation you will improvise.

Recall aloud the same experience you recreated at home. Concentrate so that you can succeed in creating the emotion and action. Don't feel embarrassed or silly because the class is listening. Be concerned solely with your recall.

When you have finished, pause a moment for transition and then begin the improvisation, attempting to maintain the same emotion and mood you established in recall and saying aloud the character's thoughts. You will be given 3-5 minutes for recall; 2-4 minutes for improvisation.

Upon completion of your scene, pause briefly and then return quietly to your desk.

"The drama's laws the drama's patrons give,
And we that live to please must please to live."
— Dr. Samuel Johnson

ADDITIONAL PROJECTS ON DEVELOPING EMOTIONAL RESPONSE

1. While seated at your desk scream silently. As you do, scream with your whole body — your stomach, back, arms, legs, wrists, etc. If you scream correctly, you will experience a feeling of inner action which all emotion must have. Check to be sure that something dynamic is happening inside of you. Now repeat the inner scream, and at the ripe moment, when your whole body is primed, your teacher will ask you to release by screaming out loud.

2. Play a 1–3 minute scene in which you do some simple activities with a specific emotion. Then reverse the emotion while doing the same activities in reverse order. For example, in pantomime a girl might excitedly get ready for a dance by putting on her new formal, her dance shoes, and pinning a corsage on. Then the phone rings and her date cancels. Now she sadly takes off the corsage, her shoes, her dress. In each action she shows her intense disappointment.

3. Recall from your own life a situation where you felt a mingling of emotion: joy and sorrow, anger and fear, love and hate, admiration and disgust, etc. Create a situation containing the mixed emotion that you recalled and improvise a scene around it.

    Example: Recall an experience combining the mixed emotion of happiness and sorrow. Then improvise a scene in which you are happy at the prospects of graduating from school, but sorrowful at the idea of leaving friends and home behind as you venture into a new life.

4. Recall from your past an experience where you quickly changed from one emotion to its opposite: joy to sorrow, fear to happiness, sympathy to anger. Improvise a scene around that change of emotion.

    Example: Joy to Sorrow. Improvise a scene in which you are playing happily with your dog by throwing a stick for him to retrieve. As he darts into the street after the stick, a car turns the corner and hits your dog. Your joy immediately changes to sorrow.

5. As a class, attend a play given either by a community group, a professional touring company, or a nearby university drama department. In class, discuss the acting: Did the acting seem spontaneous or have the illusion of the first time? Did the characters' feelings seem genuine? Could you tell what the characters were thinking? Could you tell the characters' purposes for moving and talking as they did? Could you easily hear the dialogue? Did you understand the character relationships? Did you believe in the characters throughout the play? Why or why not?

6. Bring to class a current movie or television review you have read in a national magazine such as *Time, The New Yorker, Saturday Review;* or in a newspaper such as *The New York Times* or *The National Observer*. Discuss the critic's response to the acting.

UNIT II

MOVEMENT

Time Limits: 1-3 minutes

Activity Sheet: Fill in your stage directions on the activity sheet for this chapter, found in the teacher's manual. Hand it to your instructor at the beginning of class.

PROMPTINGS

1. Relate technique to spontaneity.
2. Define stage direction terms.
3. Discuss stage areas and their placement.
4. Demonstrate crosses and counter-crosses.

THEATRE LANGUAGE

Above	"Give" a scene	"Share" a scene
Backstage	Offstage	Stage left
Below	One quarter	Stage right
Counter-cross	On-stage	"Take" a scene
Downstage	Out-front	Three quarter
Full back	Planes	Upstage
Full front	Profile	Wings

BACKGROUND NOTES

If you are to handle your body effectively on stage, you must learn the skills or techniques inherent in the theatre. Every art form embodies a technique, gradually developed by artists throughout the ages as a guide for achieving their purpose effectively and efficiently. The ballerina must learn how to dance on point; the clarinetist must learn the technique of properly fingering the instrument; the swimmer must learn correct breathing in water; the basketball player must become skilled in dribbling and shooting the ball; and the actor must learn the established form of moving on stage.

As a student actor you must practice movement techniques until you can use them so effectively that they appear natural to the audience. *Note: Technique should never be obvious!* Of course movement principles and rules are not absolute. At times they must be modified to achieve a particular purpose. But in general the techniques we discuss in this and the following chapters are practical and should be employed. Always conform to basic rules unless you can add something much more feasible!

In this chapter we will discuss stage directions, stage areas, body positions, and crosses. Learn these well so that you will be able to take directions with poise and assurance.

Stage Directions

Stage Directions always apply to the actor as he or she faces the audience:

Stage right or R:	the actor's right, facing the audience.
Stage left or L:	the actor's left, facing the audience.
Downstage or D:	nearest the audience.
Upstage or U:	away from the audience (this originated from the old theatres where the stage floor sloped toward the audience).
Below:	same as downstage; toward the audience.
Above:	same as upstage; away from the audience.

Stage Areas

The acting area on stage is generally divided into nine locations. The abbreviations are the same as those for stage directions; "C" means stage center. The diagram, at the top of page 74, indicates these stage areas. Notice that the sides of the set are always slanted toward upstage center so that the audience may easily see the whole acting area.

Generally, the downstage area, or plane, is stronger than the upstage area because it is nearer the audience. The reason that the notorious "upstaging" trick is sometimes used by unscrupulous stars is that when they move upstage to the weaker plane, the other characters must turn their back to the audience in order to see the upstage figure. This focuses audience attention on the upstage actor (even when that should not happen) because of the weak three quarter body position of the other actors.

Stage right is stronger than stage left because the audience is conditioned to look from left to right in reading and carries this habit into all observations. (Audience left, or course, is stage right.) Because of the strength of downstage and stage right, important scenes will often be played there.

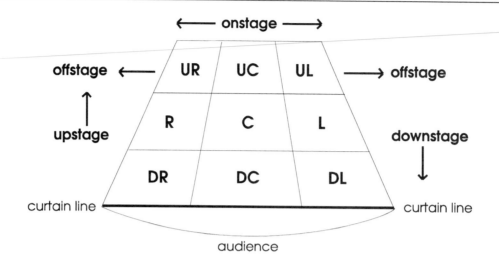

Other terms you should know regarding stage areas are:

On-stage: the acting area within the set, visible to the audience.

Offstage: the parts of the stage not enclosed by the setting.

Backstage: the area behind the setting.

Wings: the offstage area to the right and left of the acting area.

Out-front: the auditorium where the audience sits. Sometimes referred to as the "house."

Body Positions

Body positions apply to the actor as he or she faces the audience. There are five basic positions:

1. *One quarter:* The body is a quarter turn away from the audience. This position is the most frequently used when two actors "share" a scene, for it places each of their bodies so that the audience can easily see them. In this position the upstage foot is almost parallel to the front edge of the stage, and the downstage foot is turned toward the audience, making a 45-degree angle. The upstage shoulder is turned slightly toward the stage center. Notice that in this, as in all positions, the body and the head should follow the angle of the feet.

2. *Full front:* The actor faces directly front. This position is used for important lines.

3. *Profile:* Two actors face each other with the upstage foot advanced slightly toward center. This position is used for intense scenes such as quarreling, accusing, etc. It is sometimes used to obtain comic effects.

4. *Three quarter:* The actor turns away from the audience so that they see three quarters of the actor's back and only one quarter of the face. This position is used when it is necessary for an actor to "give" a scene, or turn all attention to another actor upstage who "takes" the scene.

5. *Full back:* The actor stands with back to the audience. This position is used only in special cases.

Notice that the one quarter, three quarter, and profile positions can be turned toward the right or left. For example, one quarter right would be when the actor assumes the one quarter position with his body slightly facing the right.

Stage Crosses

Stage Crosses, indicated by "X," are movements from one stage area to another. Generally the actor takes the shortest, most direct route, which is a straight cross. Straight crosses indicate strength and determination. At times a curved cross is necessary to indicate indecision, casualness, grace, or ease.

Always begin a cross with the foot nearest your destination. This keeps the body turned toward the audience. For example, if you are on stage right, crossing to the left, you should take your first step with the left foot, which is nearest your destination.

If you are speaking and must cross the stage, walk in front of the other characters. If you need to cross when others are speaking, cross quietly behind them. However, it is generally best to avoid moving when another character is talking, as your movement will steal attention away from the speaker. *Note: The moving figure dominates! If two actors cross stage together, the one with more lines should be upstage, a short step ahead of the other actor.*

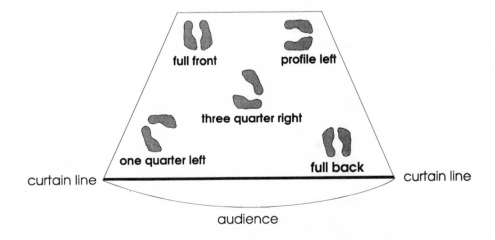

It is usually necessary for actors to adjust to each other's cross by using a counter-cross. If you find yourself in the direct path of another's cross you may "counter" by giving way a little and then by adjusting your position after the cross. For example, in the following diagram, B, the speaker, crosses right and moves in front of A. When B is directly in front of A, A "counters" by moving casually in the opposite direction a step or two and by turning toward B. A and B finish their movement at the same time. On his next speech, A drops down to B's level so that they may share the scene.

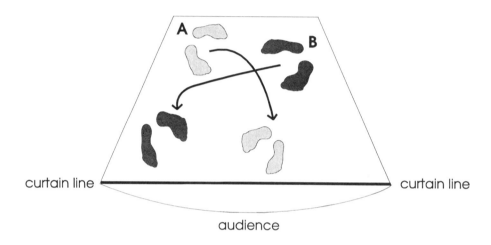

ASSIGNMENT AND ITS PURPOSE

You will want to become so familiar with stage areas and body positions that your responses will be quick and correct. This assignment will give you practice in following stage directions and assuming body positions given you by a classmate.

You will be graded on how confidently you make your crosses and assume your positions, and on how accurately you follow the directions.

HOW TO PREPARE

1. On the activity sheet for this chapter, found in the teacher's manual, list six stage crosses and body positions and plot them on a stage diagram. You may list any combination of crosses and positions you wish. The following (continued on the next page) should serve only as an example.

Sample Directions:

   a. X   DR;   stand quarter position left;
   b. X   UC;   stand in a full front position;

c. X   UR;   stand in a one quarter position left;

d. X   C;   stand in a profile, facing left;

e. X   DL;   stand in a three quarter position, facing right;

f. X   UL;   stand in a full front position.

Example: Sample Plotting of Directions

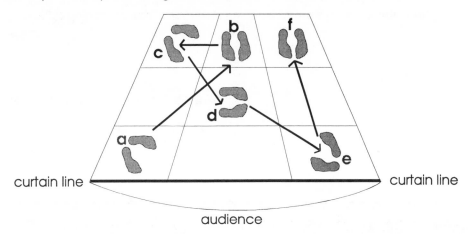

2. Fill in the remainder of the activity sheet. Be sure your name appears on both the top and bottom sections of the sheet. Divide the page by cutting it along the dashed lines.

3. Practice following your own stage directions until you know the nine stage areas and the five body positions. Overlearn so that you can take directions effortlessly.

HOW TO PRESENT

At the beginning of class, hand your instructor the critique form, which is on the bottom half of the activity sheet. Fold the top half and place it in a class box that the teacher will provide for you.

When the instructor selects your critique sheet, rise and draw at random a set of directions from the class box. Be sure you do not get your own. Hand the directions to their originator. Then go to the playing area, and as your classmate calls out directions, follow them as though you were on stage. Be sure you begin each cross on the foot nearest your destination and cross to the correct stage area as directed. Finish your cross by assuming the proper body position required.

Execute the directions quickly and with poise. If you have adequately practiced outside of class you will have no difficulty.

When a classmate selects your set of directions from the class box and hands them to you, read each slowly in a clear voice. Proceed to the next direction only after your partner has correctly followed your previous order.

When you are not actively involved in giving or taking stage directions, quietly watch those who are performing. You can learn much from observing others.

"I hear what you say, but I see what you do." — Chinese proverb

ADDITIONAL PROJECTS ON FOLLOWING STAGE DIRECTIONS

1. Go to the stage area and make several crosses, ending with varied body positions. The class will identify each stage area you are in and the body position you are assuming.

2. Take a partner and demonstrate a counter-cross. Start from a shared position as though you were talking to each other. Then make a downstage cross to the opposite side while your partner counters and adjusts to another shared position.

Chapter **9**   # PRACTICING BASIC MOVEMENT

Time Limits: 3 – 5 minutes

Activity Sheet: Outline your pantomime, incorporating three basic stage movements. Use the form for this chapter, found in the teacher's manual.

PROMPTINGS

1. Explain the six basic principles of stage movement.
2. Discuss the differences between stage movement and business.
3. Demonstrate correct body posture.
4. Understand how to correctly use basic movement.

THEATRE LANGUAGE

Body control
Body flexibility
Business
Inhibitions

Covering
Dressing the stage
Gestures

Motivated
Open
Point Up

BACKGROUND NOTES

An actor and an athlete have much in common. Whether you are playing a strenuous game on a field or acting a demanding role on stage, you must have a body that is both flexible and controlled in order to be successful. The crafts of actor and athlete demand strong, coordinated, and efficient movements. In both areas participants must be physically fit. In both you must observe physical training. Adequate rest, proper exercises, regular hours, and wholesome food are needed to keep actor as well as athlete in prime condition.

These pantomimes and improvisations that you have previously been doing in class should have helped to release your inhibitions about movement. You can gain further flexibility by participating in sports that require coordination and action of the whole body. Tennis, swimming, fencing, and dancing will afford muscular tonus and body responsiveness. Basic principles of stage movement and a few specific rules will provide you with further tools for developing flexibility tempered by control. Only when you have learned expressive body control will your mind be free to concentrate on dialogue and characterization.

Basic Principles of Stage Movement

1. All movement must be *motivated* or justified. Shuffling your feet, fidgeting, or nervously moving at random is unforgivable. An actor should never move without a purpose! (We will discuss more about motivation in Chapter 10.)

2. Movement must be *simplified*. While action in real life is often complex and detailed, art must be more selective if it is to communicate. An actor must use only carefully chosen movement that quickly and lucidly conveys the idea.

3. Movement must be *heightened*. To compensate for the distance between actor and audience, some exaggeration or heightening is necessary. This is particularly true when you must "point up" or draw special attention to an idea or object that has an important bearing on the rest of the play. For example, the hiding of a letter in Act I that must later be found in Act III needs special heightening. Allow your sense of good taste to restrain you from over exaggerating. Too much is worse than too little.

4. Movement must *delineate character*. As you have learned from your lessons in observation, a character's personality, attitude, health, and age are all revealed in movement. A fat person moves differently from a thin person. An easygoing individual moves differently from a nervous person. Youth's actions vary from those of older people. Always move in character if you are to give a convincing portrayal.

5. Movement must *"open" to the audience* without appearing obvious. In theatre the audience is all important. Unless you have a legitimate reason for not doing so, always play toward the "house." Use a one-quarter body position, make turns toward the audience, and use your upstage foot and hand so that your body won't be covered from view. For example, when you are telephoning, hold the receiver with your upstage hand so you can "open" your face to the audience.

6. Movement must *adjust to the characters on stage*. Always keep in mind your relationship to the other characters. People who dislike each other generally keep at a distance; those fond of each other will feel the need of closeness.

7. Movement must *maintain pleasing stage pictures*. To give aesthetic pleasure, the stage must appear balanced. The actor achieves balance by "dressing the stage" or taking a position to ensure an artistic composition. Since the stage picture is constantly changing, the actor must constantly be aware of maintaining balance. The groups the director has planned during rehearsals should always be maintained. Avoid monotonous stage placement such as standing in

straight lines, standing in a semicircle, or keeping an equal distance from others in a group.

Usually, the most pleasing stage pictures are formed by using varied distances among characters, using different levels — sitting, kneeling, standing — and using the triangular form of character placement where emphasis is focused on the character at the apex of the triangle. (See Chapter 24, "Assuming the Directors Duties.")

The actor should learn to "give" the stage to those who need it. Avoid "covering" or standing in front of another actor. If covering takes place, it is the responsibility of the upstage actor to casually move until no longer covered. Occasionally, the actor must purposely cover so as to mask certain actions. For example, an actor may need to cover the lighting of a lamp that is actually controlled off stage. Or an actor may cover the body of an opponent during a fight scene that calls for knifing or shooting.

Training Your Body

Posture —

The above seven basic principles indicate that stage movement demands a well-trained body. It is of great importance that you acquire perfect posture if you are to move efficiently and gracefully, both on stage and in everyday life. It is true that for some characterizations you may need to assume a poor posture as an eccentricity of the role. But like any type of mannerism, bad posture for a characterization should be assumed and not a natural thing with the actor. Let us repeat. Perfect posture is basic to all stage movement!

Check your posture in a full-length mirror. If your head projects forward, your chest caves in, and your abdomen sticks out, your posture is wrong, and you have unnecessary fatigue because the weight of your body is falling on muscles instead of on bones.

Perfect posture means that body weight is correctly balanced and evenly distributed. It requires that you stand tall, with a chest that is high but relaxed, with a back that is straight, and with the hip bones rotated under and forward so that the stomach and buttocks are drawn in.

With determination you can correct faulty posture. It will take several weeks of faithful practice and constant effort, but you will be rewarded by a more attractive, alert appearance. Males and females alike will profit by following this exercise:

Stand against a wall that has no baseboard. Place your heels against it with your weight on the balls of your feet and with the back of your head touching the wall. Imagine that you are a marionette and that strings are attached to the crown of your head, pulling your body erect but without tilting your head back. Hold your chest high, though relaxed. Allow your shoulders to hang free, relaxed. Now flatten the curve in your back by tilting the pelvic or hip bones under and forward. This action pulls in the abdomen and tucks under the buttocks. Holding this posture, slide your right foot forward and transfer your weight to it by moving from the wall. Bring your left foot parallel to it until your weight is on the balls of both feet. If you have followed these directions carefully, your weight is evenly distributed and you are standing with perfect posture!

Now that you have read this exercise, do it! Practice it every day. Be constantly aware of posture. Look at your reflection in mirrors and windows to see how you appear to others. Walk with a book on your head. At first you may find a good posture tiring because you are holding your body in an unaccustomed position. But gradually the fatigue will leave, and you will find yourself feeling better as well as looking better when you maintain perfect posture.

The Crucible by Arthur Miller
Topeka West High School: Director, Doug Goheen

Tituba discusses her incantation.

Standing —

When you stand on stage, keep your body weight on the balls of your feet. For a "straight" role, males should stand with their feet a few inches apart — about the same width as their shoulders. Females should keep their knees and feet closer together. For "character" roles, vary your foot placement. A wide base with feet far apart suggests uncouthness, ignorance, or sporty vitality. The smaller the base, the more proper and prim your character. Unless you have purposeful movement to make, always stand still. Shuffling feet show the actor's nervousness and lack of experience.

Walking —

Walking should be rhythmical and smooth, with even steps that are not too long for your body. In walking, your thigh should lift up and forward. The calf of your leg and your foot should swing from the knee. Learn to push forward with your back foot and transfer your weight effortlessly to the front foot, as in ballroom dancing. Put enough impetus forward so that you feel you must keep on walking or you will fall. Keep your feet pointed straight ahead with the weight on the balls of the feet. Eyes up! Look ahead, not down at the floor.

Turning —

When making a turn on stage, keep the audience in mind and turn toward them. The only exception to this rule is when such a turn would be obviously awkward because the actor is already in a three-quarter position. In this case turn upstage directly.

Climbing Up and Down Stairs —

Keep your posture erect and your head up. Point your feet straight ahead. Reach for each step with your toes and come down on your heel. Smoothly transfer your weight to the balls of each foot.

Sitting —

Usually your aim on stage is to sit casually and unobtrusively. Approach the chair with poise. Feel its front edge with the back of your leg. If you can feel it, you know the chair is there and it is safe to sit. Avoid turning around to find the chair (this looks awkward and gives too much emphasis to your movement). Put your body weight on the leg that felt the chair and lower yourself into the chair by bending your legs, not your whole body. Sit up straight with your hands in your lap unless your character requires a slouched position. If you are sitting on an overstuffed chair or couch, don't sit too far back, as this makes it difficult to rise gracefully.

When sitting, females should keep their knees together. Extend one foot slightly in front of the other, or cross your ankles. Never cross your knees on stage unless your role calls for it. Generally, males should keep both feet on the floor when sitting.

Rising —

Without making it obvious, anticipate your rise by easing to the edge of the chair. Place your upstage foot back and your other foot forward. Keeping your spine straight, rise with your weight on the upstage foot and then transfer it to the other foot, if it is necessary to free the upstage foot for your cross.

Entering —

Good timing is necessary for an effective entrance. Prepare for your entrance several lines before you actually go on stage. Start walking in character back in the wings. Concentrate on where your character has been and is now going. Enter with your upstage foot. Keep your eyes and head up, and come well onto the stage so that you can be seen. Avoid lingering at the entrance. If several characters enter at the same time, the one who speaks first usually enters first.

Exits —

Begin your exit on your upstage foot. Often it is effective to divide your exit line. Say the first part of it, walk to the door, and then as if suddenly adding a thought, finish your line and exit. This emphasizes your speech and your departure. It also ensures that the other characters can immediately begin talking without having an awkward pause between your last line and your walk to the door. Be sure you stay in character until you are well into the wings.

Opening and Closing Doors —

Keep your body toward the audience as much as possible when you are opening and closing doors. If the doors are on the side of the set, they will be hinged upstage. Therefore, open the door with your upstage hand, enter, and without turning around, change hands behind your back and close the door with your downstage hand. Doors in the rear wall may be hinged on either side. If they are hinged on the right, open and close them with your right hand. If hinged on the left, use your left hand. *Note: Always close the door on stage unless otherwise specified by your director. An open door worries the audience and destroys the aesthetic illusion if a crew member scurries past it.*

Gestures —

Gestures are expressive bodily actions such as lifting an eyebrow, shrugging the shoulders, pointing, kicking, etc. Gestures should be definite and clear. If you feel strongly about your part and are able to release your inhibitions or "let yourself go," you will usually gesture with expression. Practice freeing your body for gestures with the following exercises:

1. *Face.* The face helps to project emotions and attitudes. In a mirror, work on registering various emotions such as happiness, surprise, disgust. When your face can communicate these individual emotions, work on transitions from one emotion to its opposite.

2. *Eyes.* Eyes are subtle tools for the actor, for they can reveal intense feeling by flashing hatred, conveying tenderness, showing acceptance, etc. What you are thinking about will determine where you look, but generally you should look at the character to whom you are speaking. In long, reflective speeches you may wish to establish eye contact with the other person and then slowly turn toward the audience and focus your eyes above them, not on them. This places you in full front position

which aids in full projection. At the end of your reflective speech, turn back to the other character.

Exercise your eyes by rotating them from the left to the right, then vice versa. Squint with half closed eyes as though you had an evil intent. Open your eyes widely as though in surprise.

3. *Arms.* Arm gestures should begin with the shoulders and end with the fingers. This allows free, unrestrained movement that looks natural. Unfortunately, many amateurs move their arms as though their elbows were stuck to their sides. Such movement looks awkward and ridiculous. Arm gestures should seldom cross the body; instead use your upstage arm when gesturing. Avoid constant use of arm or hand movement. Punctuate your lines with movement only when necessary. Remember, gestures slightly precede the lines, unless a comic effect is desired.

Exercise your arms by swinging them freely with exaggerated movement as you give a speech at home. Exaggerated practice movements will replace stiffness with grace. Also, use wide free arm movements as you pantomime writing in the air the numbers one through ten. Do this to the background of soft, easy-to-listen-to music. Use your right arm first; then your left. Make your air drawings big and graceful.

4. *Hands.* If you are in character you will seldom question what to do with your hands. Generally, for straight parts they should hang quietly at your sides when not in use. Hands help establish character and emotion. A closed hand shows fear, hardness, selfishness, or determination. An open hand signifies welcome, acceptance, pleading, giving. Busy hands convey nervousness.

Exercise your hands by quickly opening and closing them several times while stretching your fingers far apart. Relax your hands by vigorously shaking them. Work on communicating emotion with your hands. Stand behind a curtain with only your hands showing through. See if your classmates can correctly guess the emotion your hands are trying to project.

"Stage" Business

Stage business refers to small actions that the character performs without moving from one place to another. Sometimes business is written into the script as directions, such as "he combs his hair"; but generally it is added by an imaginative director and actor. Business can aid characterization. Your character may knit, or may forever be whittling a piece of wood. Business may communicate the time of day or the season. If you toast bread at the table, it suggests morning. Fanning yourself with a newspaper may indicate that it is summertime. Business can also create atmosphere or add interest to the play. Whatever specific business is used, it should be planned early in the rehearsals and practiced at each one. As you execute the business, eliminate all needless movement but take time for the necessary "touches."

ASSIGNMENT AND ITS PURPOSE

Only by resolute practice will you be able to move correctly on stage without having to think about it constantly. This assignment will help you develop your "muscular memory." With a partner you are to do a 3 – 5 minute pantomime that incorporates basic movement principles and action. You will be graded on how well you carry out your movement, gestures, and business.

HOW TO PREPARE

1. Your instructor will assign you a partner. Together, choose a simple situation for pantomime that involves two people and that utilizes three of the following stage actions: (1) sitting or rising, (2) opening or closing doors, (3) climbing or descending stairs, (4) entering or exiting, or (5) counter-crossing.

    Make your story clear without the use of words. If possible, build toward a climax. The following are suggestions:

    a. Awaiting a friend to come and play chess, you prepare the chessboard. When your friend arrives, you both begin to play. The game is close and your friend loses. He accuses you of cheating, and there is a heated argument. He walks out angrily.

    b. You are polishing your shoes when there is a knock at the door, left, and a gushy neighbor enters who wants to sell you five tickets to a school carnival. She sits on the sofa DR with you and gives her sales talk. Although you don't want any, in desperation you finally buy one ticket and succeed in getting her out the door.

    c. You are a new waiter (or waitress) in a small cafe, setting a table for service. A domineering customer enters and sits at your table. He places his order: one baked potato with sour cream and one cup of coffee. When you question his strange order, he repeats it irately. As you leave for the kitchen, he reads his newspaper and drinks the coffee you have brought him. When he finishes his coffee, he puts a quarter on the table and walks out, just as you return with the baked potato.

    d. You enter a shoe store and sit to be waited on. You describe to the clerk the type of shoe you want. He brings three pairs. You try on two pairs and decide to take the first pair. The clerk thinks the second pair looks better and attempts to change your mind. The scene ends with your buying both pairs.

e. You stealthily enter the kitchen from a door UC. Quietly you close it. Then you place a step stool near the cupboard and climb to where you can reach the cake box on the top shelf. You get it down and cut yourself a slice of the freshly baked cake. Just then your sister enters from UR. When she sees what you have done, she is furious because the cake was for a cooked food sale. You make a flippant remark, and she grabs the nearest implement and chases you out the door. She then reenters, discouraged. Feeling defeated she begins to eat the piece of cake you cut.

f. You are carefully painting the top of a table. When you are almost finished, the telephone rings and you answer it. You are carrying on such an animated conversation that you don't see your aunt (or uncle) enter with an arm load of packages. She immediately puts them on the newly painted table. Then she relaxes on the couch. You hang up the phone and discover the packages. When your aunt hears what she has done, she is very apologetic. You both remove the sticky bundles.

g. You enter an exclusive hotel lobby where you have arranged to meet a person whom you have never seen. You walk around, undecided as to what to do. Finally you sit where you can survey the whole lobby. You notice another person waiting but decide that he (or she) must not be the right one. When no one else shows up, you both gradually realize that you have been waiting for each other.

h. You are DR sitting in the public library and reading a very humorous book. You are so amused you laugh aloud. The librarian walks over and reminds you that you must maintain silence. You are embarrassed and apologize but return to your reading. Again you laugh aloud and again the librarian rebukes you. You move to another seat and resume reading. This time when you laugh, the librarian asks you to leave. Instead, you persuade her (or him) to read a paragraph from your book. She does and breaks into loud laughter.

i. You are nervously waiting to be interviewed for a job. The employer shows you into his office and asks you to be seated. He questions you about your qualifications. Then he asks you to go to the typewriter and type a sentence or two. Nervously you type and make so many errors that the employer has difficulty reading the words. You explain that you are nervous, and he agrees to give you a two-week trial period on the job. You are happily relieved as you exit.

j. Your own choice.

2. In planning your pantomime, be sure you adhere to the basic movement principles. Keep all movement motivated, simplified, and heightened. Plan your action so that you "open" to the audience. Remember, always move in character and "dress the stage." Execute correctly such actions as sitting, opening doors,

climbing stairs, etc. Reread the instructions in this chapter and practice them until you are sure of the technique.

3. Outline your pantomime step by step on the activity sheet for this chapter, found in the teacher's manual.

4. Rehearse your pantomime with your partner, concentrating on proper execution of movement. Rehearse at least ten times before you perform this assignment.

HOW TO PERFORM

When you are called upon, hand your instructor your activity sheet and with your partner go quietly to the playing area. Set up necessary chairs and tables. Announce the title of your pantomime and then perform it with good stage movement.

The class will carefully observe so that they may offer a critique. When you are through, pause, and then quietly return to your desk. Your instructor will call on class members for constructive suggestions on movement. Be a good sport about the criticism. You can learn from others' suggestions.

ADDITIONAL PROJECTS ON BASIC MOVEMENT

1. During class have your instructor analyze your posture and that of your classmates. Then practice proper exercises for posture and gestures as listed in this chapter.

2. Your instructor will establish a situation such as waiting at a depot for an approaching train or standing at a corner waiting for your ride in a car pool. Individually select an age and write it on a paper. Hand it to your instructor. Then go to the playing area and show that aged person in the established situation. You will have two minutes. Communicate body rhythm, basic movement, and attitude of that age group. Be selective in what you do.

3. Scrutinize an animal or bird at the zoo, on a farm, in the woods, or around your neighborhood. Observe basic body action and rhythm. Study the individual movements of its head, paws, nose, tail, wings, etc. Observe any particular mannerisms. In class portray the animal with action and sound in a suitable situation. Then in a brief scene transfer those characteristics into human action and sounds. Your human portrayal should maintain the basic movement, rhythm, and sound pattern of the animal.

tain the basic movement, rhythm, and sound pattern of the animal.

4. Determine basic movement that you can use to communicate the following characters: an ignorant person; a nervous, "high-strung" individual; a vigorous, healthy athlete; an exceptionally fat person; a weak, sickly person; a timid, self-conscious individual; etc. Pay particular attention to your weight placement and foot base, to the degree of tension in your movements, and to the selected mannerisms of that type person. Reproduce the behavior of these people so that the class won't have any doubt as to whom you are portraying.

5. Attend a dance performance, preferably a modern dance group or a ballet. Notice how the trained dancers convey character solely through rhythm, movement, and posture. Discuss the movement in class.

Oklahoma! by Rodgers and Hammerstein
Wichita Collegiate School: Director, James Ockerman

Chapter
10 UTILIZING MOTIVATION

Time Limits: 2-3 minutes

Activity Sheet: Fill out your motivated action on the activity sheet for this chapter, found in the teacher's manual.

PROMPTINGS

1. Relate motivation to justification.
2. Defend the statement: "The why influences the how."
3. Explain how motivation leads to relaxed control.

THEATRE LANGUAGE

Circumstances   Motivation
Desires   Relaxed control
Justification   Sub-text

BACKGROUND NOTES

Suppose your instructor asks you to go on stage and "just move around, looking at the floor." You will probably feel quite silly. Other than staring at it, you won't know what to do. Your movements will be random and meaningless because you have no definite purpose for looking.

But when you know why you are to gaze at the floor, you will also know how to do it. If you have lost the stone out of your ring and you want to find it, your looking around at the floor takes on meaning. If you have been hired to refinish the floor and you want to determine the size job it will be, you will scrutinize it in another way. If you have heard that there is a trapdoor in the floor and you want to hide some money, you will observe and move quite differently from the other two situations.

In each of these examples your action becomes clear and believable because you have a definite reason for doing it; you have motivated or justified your movement. Motivation or justification means that you communicate your character's desires in believable action.

On stage, as in everyday life, movement (and line delivery) will change as the purpose or motivation changes. Your reason for doing something will determine the way you do it. The why influences the how. Therefore, all stage movement must be motivated, if it is to be believable to actor and audience.

The Royal Family
by Kaufman and Ferber
Utah Shakespearean Festival,
Photo by John Running

A dramatic entrance with flowing gestures.

Before playing a scene, you must determine two things: the circumstances leading up to the scene; and the character's desires or wishes because of those circumstances. Sometimes the circumstances are shown on stage in the previous action. Other times they are only suggested in the script, and you must ferret out for yourself the exact situation that precedes the immediate scene. You do this by using your imagination and your power of sense recall to visualize precisely what happened before your entrance. Becoming imaginatively familiar with the situation will enable you to discover the character's desire, which in turn will assist you in playing the scene with belief.

For example, suppose the script, or your director, tells you to cross to the fireplace. Why you move to the fireplace will determine the way you move. If you have been caught in a snow storm while hunting antelope and have had to walk miles to find shelter (circumstances), you will want to warm yourself (desire), and so you cross to the fire. If you possess a letter that incriminates you and the police are arriving to search the house (circumstances), you will want to burn the letter (desire), and so you hurry to the fireplace with that idea in mind. If you haven't eaten for hours and your electric stove won't heat because the electricity has gone off (circumstances) you will want to eat something warm (desire), and so you go to the fireplace to roast a hot dog. In all of these examples the basic action is the same. But the way you do it is determined by your motivation.

Besides providing for believable action, motivation leads to relaxed control. In previous chapters we have established that stage movement must be efficient and effective, using as little action as possible to communicate your purpose. Unfortunately, amateur actors often fail to achieve this desired movement because of nervous tension. As soon as amateurs appear before a group, they nervously think of themselves and wonder what the audience thinks of them. "Stage fright" is disabling. When you think of yourself, it is impossible to think of the character. The only way that you will relieve your nervousness is by forgetting yourself. Concentrate, instead, on justifying or motivating your action. When you do this, excess tension will disappear, and in its place you will possess the relaxed control necessary for efficient, effective movement.

To further stress the relationship between motivation and relaxed control, let us consider the male athlete playing a basketball game. There are hundreds of spectators to make him nervous, to incapacitate him with fright, yet he plays the game with skill and ease. Why isn't he embarrassed with his strange movements (they are, if you think about them) of guarding his man, dribbling and shooting the ball? The reason is that he is so absorbed in his desire to play well and win the game that he forgets himself. His actions are justified because he knows why he is doing them. Furthermore, he has learned a technique that gives him control when he is relaxed or free from excess tension.

Like the athlete, you must learn to forget yourself by concentrating on your character's wishes instead of on the audience's. The audience will think well of you if you accomplish your purpose: a believable character through motivated action.

ASSIGNMENT AND ITS PURPOSE

You are to play an action and become so absorbed in why you are doing it that you forget yourself and create believable movement. Remember, your motivation or desire for doing the action will determine the way you do it. You will present your scene twice: first, by saying aloud your character's thoughts as a sub text; and second, by saying the thoughts to yourself as you redo the scene.

You will be graded on how well you motivate your action by forgetting yourself and concentrating on why you are moving. You will also be graded on the appropriateness of your sub text in defining your character's wishes.

HOW TO PREPARE

1. Choose an activity that you can do easily and choose a character who may do that action. The following are suggestions:

   Character suggestions:

old person	athlete	child
soldier	hobo	teacher
farmer	gardener	chauffeur
butler	scientist	dancer
police officer	politician	your own choice
salesperson	miser	

   Activity suggestions:

doing exercises	chopping wood	scrubbing floors
flying a kite	shoveling snow	ironing clothes
washing a car	doing dishes	raking a lawn
bridling a horse	washing windows	building a fence
picking a bouquet	shaking rugs	your own choice
typing a letter		

   Scene example:

   You are an old person who needs money to buy food. You have been hired to dig out dandelions in a woman's yard. You want to do a good job so you will be rehired to do more yard work. As you dig carefully, feel the implement in your hand (Is it a regular dandelion digger or a small trowel?). See the dandelions. Visualize the yard and house. Feel the sunshine beat down on your head. As you work, you grow thirsty and tired. How you would like a drink of water! But you keep on working, your action justified by your wish to do a good job so that you will be rehired.

2. Determine:

   a. The type of person your character is — personality and temperament, background, age, appearance, etc.

   b. The circumstances leading up to your scene.

   c. Your character's motivating desire or wishes in that scene. (The reason for doing the action.)

3. Fill out the activity sheet for this chapter, found in the teacher's manual, outlining your scene step by step.

4. Rehearse your 2-3 minute scene by concentrating on the reason you are doing the action. Forget yourself and the way you do the action. In real life you are seldom as concerned with how you do something as you are with why you are doing it. For example, you are cleaning your room because you want to impress

your grandmother who is visiting you; you are hoeing the garden because you can't have the car until you are through; you are painting a fence because you need to earn money for your Saturday date.

As you rehearse, use sensory recall to vitalize the situation. "See" the fence you are painting, "smell" the paint, "feel" the brush in your hand, etc. Make the situation come alive for you.

Rehearse by saying your character's thoughts aloud. This will help you concentrate on the purpose of your action. Rehearse eight to ten times before you perform.

HOW TO PERFORM

Hand your activity sheet to your instructor before going to the playing area. Announce your scene by briefly describing the situation and the setting.

With motivated action, play your scene, saying aloud the character's thoughts. When you are through, pause, and then redo the scene by saying the thoughts to yourself as you play. Return to your seat with poise.

Your instructor may wish to lead the class in a short discussion comparing the effectiveness of the motivated action in the two scenes.

ADDITIONAL PROJECTS ON UTILIZING MOTIVATION

1. Modify the childhood game of "Statues." Assume a pose — any position — as basic or as farfetched as you wish. Let your classmates justify that pose by finding a logical reason for maintaining it. For example, if you stand on tiptoe with your arms in the air, you may justify your action by believing you are picking apples. Notice that when you find a reason, your pose becomes believable.

2. Create two unrelated lines of dialogue for Character A and Character B. Have the class justify these lines by supplying the thought pattern of Character B, so that the lines will relate to what Character A has said:

    Example:

    A: There are roses growing in our back yard.

    B: Oh, to be in Paris right now.

    (Justify B's speech so that it relates to A's line.)

3. Justify specific actions that the class suggests by supplying the factors which lead up to the action. For example, justify the following:

    a.   Giving the dog a T-bone steak that you have cooked for your dinner.

    b.   Secretly putting twenty dollars in your friend's purse.

    c.   Making a hasty trip to the florist.

4. With a partner, memorize the following short scene. Play it with as many different interpretations as you can, perhaps rotating around the class with different actors doing the same scene.

    Scene:

    A.   You're late.

    B.   I know. I couldn't help it.

    A.   I understand.

    B.   I thought you would.

    A.   I have something to give you.

    B.   Really?

    A.   Yes, this.

Play the above as a quarrel scene; a love scene (teasing lovers or parting lovers); murder scene (nervous criminals); parting scene (a son from his mother, son is happy or sad, mother is happy or sad); a death scene (between combat soldiers, old man and nurse, sweethearts). Notice that your interpretation will depend on the situation as well as on your character's attitude and motivating desire.

"Suit the action to the word, the word to the action; with this special observance, that you o'erstep not the modesty of nature." — Shakespeare , Hamlet, Act III, Scene ii

Hamlet's Advice to the Players, (III, ii)
by William Shakespeare

Hamlet. Speak the speech, I pray you, as I pronounced it to you, trippingly on the tongue; but if you mouth it as many of our players do, I had as lief the town-crier spoke my lines. Nor do not saw the air too much with your hand thus, but use all gently, for in the very torrent, tempest, and as I may say, whirlwind of your passion, you must acquire and beget a temperance that may give it smoothness.... Be not too tame neither, but let your own discretion be your tutor. Suit the action to the word, the word to the action, with this special observance, that you o'erstep not the modesty of nature; for anything so o'erdone is from the purpose of playing, whose end both at the first, and now, was and is, to hold as 'twere the mirror up to nature, to show virtue her own feature, scorn her own image, and the very age and body of the time his form and pressure.

Chapter 11   HANDLING SPECIAL MOVEMENT PROBLEMS

Time Limits: 5-8 minutes

Activity Sheet: Outline your group scene on the activity sheet for this chapter, found in the teacher's manual.

PROMPTINGS

1. Discuss reasons for careful training in stage combat.

2. Describe techniques involved with special movement problems, such as fighting scenes, romantic scenes, or falling.

THEATRE LANGUAGE

Curtsy
Fabricate
Mask

BACKGROUND NOTES

As you act in plays, you will discover there are often special movement problems needing your careful attention. Scenes that carry fighting, dying, bowing, and embracing demand special acting skills.

Stage Combat

Violence technique is called stage combat. Such action is very complex, and if done improperly can be dangerous to the actors. Careful training by combat specialists is necessary, so the following information gives only guidelines. Consult a combat text for details.

Fighting —

When you are struggling against another character, breathe in and tense your body muscles as you would in a regular fight but avoid using your strength against the other actor. If the script calls for a fist fight, double your fists tightly and aim at your opponent's chin. Your blow should pass slightly in front of the chin. At that same instant, your victim should fabricate the sound of the blow by clapping his or her hands together, or the person giving the blow can hit their own chest. The person receiving the blow should react both physically and vocally. If this is well-timed and quickly done, the action will look like a real blow, and the audience will not see the hand clapping.

You and your opponent should practice the fight scene in slow motion, with each of you responsible for specific movement. Practice developing a planned sequence of action. Use good judgment in what you do. If the scene is too tame, the audience won't believe in it; if it is too violent, the audience may laugh to release excess tension.

When your movements are smooth, speed them up and include them in regular rehearsals. Be sure you do exactly the same movements each time so that you, as well as the others on stage, will always know what to expect.

Shooting —

Scenes that involve shooting should be believable to the audience and yet safe for the actors. The killer should be downstage of the victim, so that he can fire

Actors in Renaissance costumes practice stage combat with fencing foils. Scenes must be choreographed and practiced precisely to avoid injury while creating believability. College of Southern Idaho: Director, Tony Mannen

upstage, away from the audience. Never fire toward the audience or directly toward any actor! The killer and the victim should have as much space between them as is feasible — at least four feet apart to lessen the danger of injury or burns from the blanks. Other actors on stage should stand well away. The killer should shoot slightly downstage of the victim, who turns his back and head away when the shot is fired. The shot should be timed accurately with the movement in order to be convincing.

To prevent stage shots from being excessively loud, the blanks should be lightly loaded with a fast-burning powder. As a safety measure, avoid loading the gun until right before the killer's entrance. Load it in the presence of the director or stage manager. After the gun has been used on stage, it should be returned immediately to the director.

Stabbing —

Stabbing is always covered or masked. Sometimes it is done behind furniture. If not, the killer must cover the stabbing with his body. The great force needed for stabbing should lessen as the knife approaches the body. As soon as the killer's body covers the dagger, he directs the thrust away from the victim, who acts as though he had been stabbed. If the killer is using a sword, he slides it between the victim's upstage arm and body. The dagger or sword is withdrawn with more force than it took to plunge it in. Immediately dispose of the weapon so that the audience won't notice the lack of blood. Either throw the knife on the floor upstage, return it to the scabbard, or quickly wipe it off.

Dying —

A person who is shot, tenses immediately, inhales, and doubles toward the wound. If he is shot in the back he twists backwards and falls stiffly to the side or the front. If he is shot in the stomach, his hand goes to that spot before he crumples and falls.

A person who is stabbed, grasps the part of the body that is wounded and staggers or sways before falling. If a death scene follows, it should generally be played slowly. The dying person should be short of breath. He speaks broken lines in a voice that suggests weakness but can yet be heard by the audience.

Falling —

The secret of falling on stage (for fainting, a shooting, or a stabbing, etc.) is to keep relaxed. Falls are dangerous only when the muscles are tensed. To lessen the shock, break your fall a little at a time. When you do this quickly, it looks natural.

To fall forward, relax, and crumple down, breaking the fall first with your knees. As your torso leans forward, slide out your arm and let your head fall on it. To fall sidewards, bend your knees and lean toward the side you want to fall on. Hit first with the ankles, then break with the knee, hip, and shoulder. Extend your arm to protect your head. If possible, break your fall by dropping against the furniture before sliding to the floor. Always fall with your head, rather than your feet, downstage. Feet that stick up toward the audience may provoke laughter.

Practice relaxed stage falls by using a pillow or an acrobatic pad on the floor. Rehearse until you can do the falls convincingly without hurting yourself.

Carrying Bodies —

Sometimes a male must carry a female because she has fainted or has been hurt. To make balancing easier, the person being carried should relax and bring her body weight close to the carrier. She should put her head on his shoulder and her arms around his neck, unless she is supposed to be unconscious. This position will help her support some of her own weight. In other situations, such as carrying a person against her will, the carrier picks up the female and slings her halfway over his shoulder, like a sack of flour.

In some plays, such as Shakespeare's, it is often necessary to carry bodies off the stage. This should be done by several men who serve to cover as well as carry the body. The body should be carried off head first, with the head higher than the feet.

Slapping —

While stage slaps must be convincing, they must not hurt the victim. Stage slaps are difficult to fake and must be carefully practiced. The basic slap has partners standing and facing each other, slightly more than arms length apart. The downstage partner (who will receive the slap) has the back to the audience. As the slapper pulls back the slapping hand, the partner drops both arms to the front of the body. As the slapper swings an open palm within an inch of the partner's face, the partner simultaneously slaps hands together and quickly moves the head to simulate the reaction to the slap. The slapper follows through with the arm.

Other versions that involve the slapper hitting the partner's upraised hand can produce louder and more dramatic results after careful practice.

Other Special Movements

Eating and Drinking —

When scenes call for eating, you must actually eat on stage, unless you are seated with your back to the audience. Of course, your eating must be carefully timed so that your chewing and swallowing won't interfere with your lines. Put only

tiny pieces in your mouth and exaggerate your jaw movement to look like regular eating. Never take a bite just before you speak. Actually, you need eat very little. Much of your time at the table may be spent cutting up your food; thus, you may leave on your plate almost everything you were served.

If possible, stage food should be something that the actors like and that can be eaten and swallowed easily. Stay away from food that crackles, such as celery and crackers. Scrambled eggs, bananas, cooked apples, and macaroni are easy to cut and eat. Always serve small portions of food to be eaten on stage.

When drinking, it is best to use opaque glasses. The audience won't be able to see the liquid, so you can either use water, or leave the glasses empty. Just be sure that you swallow, even if there is nothing in the glass. If you use liquid, never fill the glass more than two-thirds full. Drink only a little, unless the script makes it necessary that you empty the glass. Keeping your hands around a transparent glass will mask from the audience how little you have drunk. In place of coffee, you may use grape juice which looks like coffee to the audience. Lemonade may be used for various drinks and is good for clearing the throat.

Bowing —

The type bow you use will depend on the character and the situation. A humble bow is relaxed with the head and back bent forward. In a genteel bow, bend at

Ketchum Justice by Mel Schubert
College of Southern Idaho: Director, Fran Tanner

Fishing gear and attire help create humor for this play set in the Idaho mountains.

the hips, keeping your back straight and your head dropped slightly. If you must kiss a lady's hand, bow low and lift her hand to your lips.

Curtsying —

A bob curtsy is used by women servants to show respect and obedience. Keep your feet close together, swing one foot slightly behind the other, bend your knees quickly, and bob your head.

A court curtsy is used by ladies and gentlewomen. Hold your skirt out at each side. Cross your right leg in back of your left, with the toe pointed toward the left heel. Keeping your back, neck, and head straight, bow from the hips and lower yourself by bending your knees. The more formal the affair, the lower you curtsy.

Kneeling —

Keep your back straight. With your weight on your upstage foot, drop to the floor on your downstage knee. Change your weight to the downstage knee. Slide your other leg slightly forward until it is at a right angle with the floor. Keep your foot flat on the floor.

Embracing and Kissing —

Love scenes should be carefully rehearsed with attention to details. An audience will readily empathize with a love scene if it is built for beauty with gentle and graceful actions. Nothing should be done to make such scenes embarrassing or funny, unless, of course, it is a comic effect you want.

Embraces are usually easier if entered from a sitting position. The male should be downstage of the female. As he leans toward the female, his shoulders and head mask the kiss.

If you are standing, you assume something like a dance position, except that you should look directly into your partner's eyes. The male stands with his feet apart. The female puts her upstage foot between the boy's feet, while using her downstage foot for balance. Usually her heels are lifted slightly from the floor to create a graceful line. Be sure this footwork is followed. Only when you are standing very close to your partner is the embrace attractive.

The male's downstage arm goes under the female's and his hand rests slightly above her waist. His upstage arm goes over hers and is placed on her back, between her shoulder blades. The female's downstage arm goes over the male's and rests on his shoulder or around his neck. Her upstage arm rests on his chest.

The male usually turns the female slightly so that her face is upstage. The audience will see her hair and it will look like the two are kissing, even if they are not. The kiss breaks with the her face open toward the audience. Some directors prefer having the male turn upstage, thus masking the female and the kiss with the male's shoulders.

While the director will want to include love scenes within later rehearsals, the director should begin working separately with just the two actors involved until the mechanical details of the embrace are technically smooth.

Telephoning —

Hold the receiver with your upstage hand and keep the phone below your chin to prevent covering your mouth. As you talk, think of the conversation you are hearing. Work on timing so that your listening pauses are neither too short to be ridiculous nor too long to be boring.

ASSIGNMENT AND ITS PURPOSE

Only through practice will you be able to convincingly handle these special movement problems. This assignment will give you such experience. You will work in groups of three or four and create a short scene built around a set of four special stage movements. You will be graded on how well you execute the movement problems.

HOW TO PREPARE

1. Divide into groups of three or four.

2. Select a set of four special stage problems. The following are sample sets:
   a. Telephoning, eating and drinking, kneeling, sitting
   b. Bowing, stabbing, falling, dying
   c. Carrying a body, falling sidewards, kissing a lady's hand, opening and closing a door
   d. Drinking, fighting, answering a phone call, making a curtsy
   e. Embracing, bowing, rising from a chair, serving tea
   f. Eating, shooting, falling forward, struggling
   g. Kneeling, slapping a face, stabbing with a sword, embracing
   h. Your choice

3. In your group, plan a short scene involving the four movement problems. Each member of the group should execute at least one special movement problem. Plan to use dialogue.

4. On the activity sheet for this chapter, found in the teacher's manual, outline the sequence of events in your scene.

5. Decide who in your group will announce the scene.

6. Rehearse your scene in class. Practice the special movement problems until you can do them correctly and convincingly. You may need to reread the technical instructions in this chapter. Create dialogue as you rehearse. You will need several well-conducted rehearsals before you are ready to present your scene.

HOW TO PRESENT

When your group is called upon, hand your outline to your instructor and go to the playing area. Set up necessary tables and chairs. Give a brief, well-worded introduction telling the situation and the movement problems involved. Then do your scene with belief and finesse. Be sure that you concentrate and stay in character.

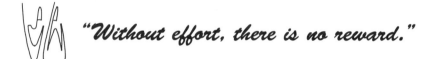

"Without effort, there is no reward."

ADDITIONAL PROJECTS ON HANDLING SPECIAL MOVEMENT PROBLEMS

1. Your instructor will assign you and a partner a special movement problem as listed previously in this chapter. Practice the problem outside of class until you can execute it well. Then demonstrate your technique in class.

2. Rent and see the film, *Period Style in Acting Technique.* 20 minutes. Color. University of Arizona, Audio Visual, Tucson, Arizona 85706.

3. Study the three video tapes, entitled *Combat for the Stage and Screen,* by David Boushey; Combat Video, 4720 38th N.E., Seattle, Washington 98105.

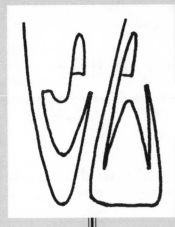

UNIT III

VOICE

Chapter 12 IMPROVING VOICE

Time Limits: 3 – 5 minutes

Activity Sheet: Fill out the special form for this chapter, found in the teacher's manual. Hand it to your instructor when you do your vocal exercise.

PROMPTINGS

1. Describe the process of voice production.
2. Explain why abdominal breathing is important to acting.
3. Discuss the four vocal variables.
4. Describe how to correct basic articulation problems.
5. Explain criteria for determining correct pronunciation.

THEATRE LANGUAGE

Articulation
Articulators
Audible
Diacritical markings
Dialect
Diaphragm

Flexible
Inflection
International Phonetic
   Alphabet
Larynx
Pitch

Pronunciation
Rate
Resonance
Stage wings
Vocal quality
Volume

BACKGROUND NOTES

An actor's voice is basic to his or her craft. Foremost, voice should be audible. Audience members should have no difficulty hearing it, regardless of where they sit. Nothing irritates an audience more than inability to hear the dialogue of a play. Nevertheless, actors frequently swallow their lines, or use their voices so ineffectively that the audience is oblivious to what has been said. Second, an actor's voice should be flexible in order to communicate a variety of characters, meanings, and emotions. Furthermore, voice must be able to withstand arduous rehearsals and performances.

Unless you have serious vocal problems that need a specialist's attention, you can do much to train your voice in audibility and flexibility by practicing vocal exercises every day. This lesson will help you begin. From here it will take you two or three years of daily exercise (preferably with the aid of a good speech teacher) to develop a pliable voice, plus the rest of your life to keep that voice in condition. An actor's training is continuous! Even if you are not intent on becoming a professional actor, your voice will benefit from proper exercise. The best of voices can be improved if only their owners will put forth the effort.

Vocal training begins by taking care of the voice you have. Avoid colds, for they are one of the greatest threats to voice. Smoking and drinking are also detrimental. Never strain your voice by shouting when you have a cold or singing in an improper range. Never, never shout yourself hoarse at a ball game! Such strain makes throat membranes sore and invites infection that can do permanent damage. When in doubt, don't shout. Keep your voice free from strain and irritation!

In exercising your voice, strive for controlled breathing; a trained ear; a rich, resonant quality; variety in pitch, volume, and rate; clear articulation; and proper pronunciation. Let us note each of these areas.

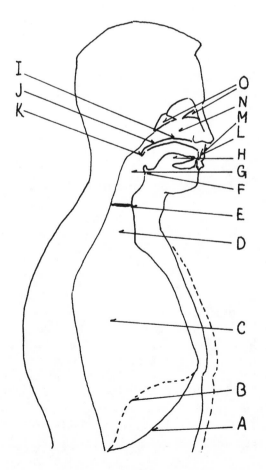

A. Diaphragm in inhalation
B. Diaphragm in exhalation
C. Lungs
D. Trachea or windpipe
E. Vocal folds
F. Epiglottis
G. Pharynx or throat cavity
H. Tongue
I. Hard palate
J. Soft palate
K. Uvula
L. Teeth
M. Lips
N. Nasal cavity
O. Sinus cavity

Controlled Breathing

Speech sounds are produced by air that has been forced through the lungs by the action of certain rib muscles and the diaphragm, a flat muscle separating the chest from the abdominal cavity. The exhaled air vibrates the vocal folds in the larynx. The sound produced is modified by the resonators (throat, nose, mouth, sinuses) and formed into vowels and consonants by the articulators (tongue, jaw, teeth, cheeks, lips, hard and soft palates). For placement of these organs, study the following diagram.

To have the necessary air control for efficient speaking, it is advisable to breathe from your diaphragm. This means that your chest cavity is relatively still, while your waistline expands and contracts, and your lower ribs slightly rise and fall. Diaphragmatic breathing requires less effort than chest breathing, allows you to breathe deeply, and provides the necessary waist control that enables you to project long passages without running out of breath. For controlled breathing, practice these exercises:

1. Lie flat on your back with one hand on your abdomen and the other on your chest. Keep the chest still. The abdomen should move out when you inhale and in when you exhale. Now stand up and (with this same diaphragmatic action) pant like a dog, with only the abdomen pushing in and out. Keep the chest area motionless.

2. Using diaphragmatic breathing, take a deep breath and see how far you can count as you exhale on one breath. Do not force the count. When you grow tense, breathe, start again, and exhale the air slowly for control. Work until you can effortlessly count up to sixty.

Trained Ear

Unless you can discriminate between quality, pitch, pronunciation, etc., you cannot improve your voice. So learn to listen to the varied ways that voice is projected. Listen to others as they speak. Listen to recordings by famous actors and readers. Listen to yourself on the tape recorder. If possible, ask your instructor to criticize your voice so that you will be aware of the particular aspects you need to improve.

Rich Tone Quality

Quality is that characteristic which distinguishes your voice from any other voice. While basic quality depends to a large extent on the shape and size of your vocal mechanism, you can still learn to produce clear, resonant tones. Unless your part calls for it, avoid harshness and breathlessness. A harsh voice is strained and raspy from lack of an open throat. A breathy voice indicates that more air is being used than is needed for vocal production. Test yourself for breathlessness. Light a candle and speak directly in front of it. If it flickers or goes out, you are using too much air. Clear tones require little breath and allows the candle to burn without a flicker. These clear tones result from a relaxed, open throat that allows the air to flow easily through, as though nothing were stopping it. To relax your throat, do the following exercises:

1. Drop your head forward as though you had fallen asleep. Let the jaw drop open and become completely relaxed. Keeping the jaw, neck, and face relaxed, move your head around slowly to the right, up, left, and down. Repeat, rolling it in the opposite direction. Keep your neck relaxed.

2. Yawn lazily. Take a deep breath, stretch, and yawn again. With your throat open and relaxed, quietly, slowly say the following while prolonging the vowel sounds: a-a-ah, ma; o-o-o-oh, blow; aw; ah; ay; ee; oo. Yawn again to relax. Read a passage from your literature book, prolonging the vowels. Vachel Lindsay's *The Congo,* and Tennyson's *Break, Break, Break*, provide good passages with vowel sounds.

Vocal quality or tone is a valuable tool for expressing personality. As an actor, you should find the tone that best conveys your character and should practice using that tone throughout rehearsals, so that by performance you can reproduce it without strain. Tone also conveys emotion, even when words are not distinguishable. Try this experiment. In a tone that conveys kindness and love, tell your dog that he is a naughty, ugly, and worthless mongrel. Your dog will wag his tail, happily satisfied. Now reverse the procedure; use a reprimanding tone with endearing words and watch your dog cower and hide.

Vary your tone as follows:

1. Say each of these words, "oh," "yes," "well," "really," "possibly," conveying each of these emotions: happiness, pride, fatigue, fright, anger, suspicion, innocence, pleading, sorrow.

2. Reproduce the tone color of these words by making your voice sound like the meaning of the words: bang, crackle, swish, grunt, tinkle, roar, coo, thin, wheeze, bubble, buzz, splash, clang, and gurgle.

Variety in Pitch

Pitch is the highness or lowness of your voice. A medium pitch produced by a relaxed throat is the most pleasant to hear and projects the farthest. Although your speaking voice is capable of a two-octave range, you probably are utilizing only a limited area. Learn to use your complete range. In acting, a high pitch expresses excitement, anger, timidity, etc. A low pitch conveys despair, disgust, pathos.

Pitch inflection allows you to glide from one pitch level to another on a single word or syllable. Rising inflection ⟋ connotes questioning. Falling inflection ⟍ signifies finality. Circumflex ⌒ or ⌄ is a combination of the two, expressing sarcasm, doubt, and innuendos.

Practice the following pitch exercises:

1. Read the following phrases aloud at the pitch level designated by the meaning of each phrase:

> Begin high — a little higher still — now very low — now very high — speak at a medium pitch — again very low — can you make it lower? — and back to medium again.

2. Say the word "oh" with the inflection that conveys the meaning indicated:

> oh — (that hurts!)   oh — (how lovely!)
>
> oh — (so what)   oh — (well, perhaps...)
>
> oh — (look out!)   oh — (don't be so rude)
>
> oh — (do you expect me to believe that?)

Variety in Volume

In controlling the general volume of your voice, strive for audibility without shouting, but without speaking too low. If you purposely project your words out to the audience, a whisper will carry to the last row!

Varying volume on individual words within the dialogue helps to communicate meaning. Notice how the change of emphasis or volume shifts the meaning:

> **Was** Dave going home?   (You said so, but did he really?)
>
> Was **Dave** going home?   (Or was it Bill?)
>
> Was Dave **going** home?   (Or was he returning from there?)
>
> Was Dave going **home**?   (Or someplace else?)

Variety in Rate

The speed at which you talk suggests both age and emotion. A slow rate usually indicates old age, important ideas, and/or the emotions of sorrow, reverence, deliberation, and doubt. A fast rate indicates youth, a subordination of unimportant ideas, and/or the emotions of excitement, happiness, and anger.

As an actor you should aim at a general rate that is slow enough to be understood and yet rapid enough to keep the audience's attention. Rate is influenced by: (1) *pause*, which gives emphasis to the word it follows or draws attention to the word it precedes; and (2) *duration* of sound, which means that vowels and consonants can be prolonged or clipped short. Do the following exercise:

Vary the rate as the meaning suggests —

> a.   They climbed slowly, wearily up the summit.
>
> b.   What an exquisite formal you are wearing.
>
> c.   This shrimp pizza is delicious!

    d.   Hurray! We won!

    e.   I am proud to accept this honor.

    f.   Hurry up; we're late.

    g.   I'm so tired, I can hardly move.

    h.   Don't tell me we've got to listen to that again.

Clear Articulation

Most inaudibility results not from lack of volume but from lack of clarity in utterance. Too many people have careless and sluggish speech because of lazy tongue, lips, and jaw. "Jeet jet" instead of "Did you eat yet" "Hoozyer fren" for "Who is your friend" "Whatjado" for "What did you do," show inexcusable sloppiness.

Work on enunciating clearly whenever you speak. Don't be afraid to open your mouth widely. It is impossible to articulate well with a half-closed mouth. When you are on stage, the words need to be even clearer and more exact than in everyday talk. Pay particular attention to enunciating the final consonants, such as in the words "dead,' "friend," "talking," "walking," "want." While your aim is clarity, avoid such preciseness that calls attention to itself and distracts from the dramatic action. Affected articulation is as offensive as slovenly articulation.

1.   Practice the following tongue twisters to help restore precision in your lips, tongue, jaw, and palates. Open your mouth widely and say the twisters clearly, picking up speed as you gain control.

    a.   Six slim sleek saplings.

    b.   Round and round the rugged rock the ragged rascal ran.

    c.   A big black bug bit a big black bear.

    d.   Fill the sieve with thistles; then sift the thistles through the sieve.

    e.   Better buy the bigger rubber baby buggy bumpers.

2.   Say these lines from *Hamlet* with clear articulation:

> "Speak the speech, I pray you, as I pronounced it to you, trippingly on the tongue; but if you mouth it, as many of your players do, I had as lief the town-crier spoke my lines."

Proper Pronunciation

Correct pronunciation means accurately producing the speech sounds with proper division into syllables and correct accent or stress. Learn the diacritical markings used in dictionaries or learn the International Phonetic Alphabet used in pronunciation dictionaries, so that you can read the accurate pronunciation of words.

In a play, your pronunciation will depend somewhat on the character you are portraying and the locale of the action. If there are no identifying character and area factors, then your pronunciation should meet these requirements:

1. Used by the educated people in your locale

2. Free from regional limitations

3. Similar to the other actors

4. Acceptable to the audience

Professional actors use a stage diction that is a compromise between a "too" British and a "too" American pronunciation. High school, college, and little theatre productions seldom use stage diction. They adhere to the educated speech within their community and meet the four requirements just described.

Practice the following pronunciation exercises:

1. Make the proper distinction between words that are similar:

   access / excess   lightning / lighting

   celery / salary   personal / personnel

   breath / breathe   weather / whether

   conscious / conscience   formally / formerly

   statue / statute

2. The following is a list of words frequently mispronounced. Learn to say them correctly, concentrating primarily on the vowels shown in the correct and incorrect rhyme word.

Word	Correct Rhyme	Incorrect Rhyme
a. get	bet	bit
b. for	ore	fur
c. again	pen	pin
d. just	must	mist
e. because	pause	buzz
f. any	penny	skinny
g. our	hour	are
h. duty	beauty	booty
i. assume	fume	doom
j. new	mew	moo
k. poor	sewer	sore
l. route	boot	bout

Word	Correct Rhyme	Incorrect Rhyme
m. your	sewer	per
n. roof	proof	foot
o. suite	sweet	boot
p. I'll	aisle	all
q. them	hem	hum
r. sure	sewer	per

A word here about dialect. It is difficult to assume a dialect and it takes time. You are wise to delay a dialect part until you have had some experience. Then your aim should be to suggest the dialect. You are after effect and audibility, not an imitation of the actual. When learning dialect, listen to one who naturally speaks it or listen to dialect recordings, so that you can hear the melody of the dialect (pitch changes, inflection, rhythm, etc.) as well as the sound substitutions.

As you put into practice all of the ideas in this chapter, keep in mind that as an actor your goal is projection. All your life you have been trained to project only a few feet for normal conversation. When you take the stage, you have a larger area in which you must use your voice. *Note: projection does not mean shouting.* Instead, it aims at "throwing" your voice so that the "deaf person in the last row" can hear you clearly. Proper breathing, resonant tones, medium pitch, and medium rate will help you project. In addition, keep your body in such a position on stage that you neither talk to the floor or the stage wings. Position yourself to throw your important lines directly to the audience, without its being evident.

ASSIGNMENT AND ITS PURPOSE

You are to do three vocal exercises that will aid your voice and start you on a program of exercises that you should enlarge and practice daily.

You will be graded on breath control, clear articulation, and a fusing of all the vocal requirements discussed in this chapter.

HOW TO PREPARE

1. Choose a four-line nursery rhyme such as *Mary Had a Little Lamb*, or *Twinkle, Twinkle, Little Star*. Using controlled diaphragmatic breathing, practice saying the complete four lines from memory until you can say them slowly, two times on one exhalation. Control the output of air so it is depleted as the second jingle ends.

2. Select a tongue twister and practice saying it from memory until you can repeat it clearly three times with moderate speed.

3. Write a 50-100 word paragraph incorporating at least five words from the pronunciation list previously listed. Practice reading your paragraph with concentration on the following: controlled breathing; rich, clear, tone quality; variety of pitch, volume, and rate to convey meaning and feeling; clear articulation; and proper pronunciation.

4. Write on the activity sheet for this chapter, found in the teacher's manual, the nursery rhyme you chose previously, the tongue twister selected, and your original paragraph. Make a duplicate copy of the paragraph to use when performing.

HOW TO PRESENT

When you are called upon, hand your activity sheet to your instructor and take your paragraph to the front of the room. Put it aside for the moment. With audibility and flexibility, perform the three exercises in the order prepared: (1) nursery rhyme and (2) tongue twister, said from memory, and (3) original paragraph, read aloud from script. Take your time. Make every sound you utter your best!

NOTE: If possible, your instructor may tape your presentation, and later let you listen and criticize your own voice.

 "Speech is the index of the mind." — Seneca

ADDITIONAL PROJECTS ON IMPROVING VOICE

1. Select short (2 – 4 minutes) scenes where two characters speak to each other. In reading the scenes, employ the various vocal techniques you have learned.

2. Read aloud two poems that express contrasting or varied emotions. Imagine that you are in a large auditorium. Work on audibility and flexibility of voice.

Chapter

13   READING ORALLY

Time Limits: 3-5 minutes

Activity Sheet: Fill out the analysis form on the activity sheet for this chapter, found in the teacher's manual. Hand it and the accompanying critique sheet to your instructor before you read your poem.

PROMPTINGS

1. Compare the oral reader's purpose to that of the actor.
2. Discuss the values of a theatre student learning oral interpretation techniques.
3. Explain the components of material having literary value.
4. Describe how to analyze literature for reading aloud.

THEATRE LANGUAGE

Climax   Expression   Intermediary
Connotative   Extemporaneous   Readers Theatre
Criteria   Imagery   Suggestion
Denotative   Impression   Transition

BACKGROUND NOTES

       If you were to count the number of times you have read aloud or have heard someone else read aloud this past week, you would find the occasions numerous. Periodically you are asked to read aloud in your classes. Your instructor undoubtedly reads aloud daily school announcements. If you attend club meetings, the minutes and various reports are read aloud. If you turn on your car radio driving home from school, you hear the announcer reading the news report. At home you may find your mother reading stories to your young brothers and sisters. Your father may find an interesting article in the newspaper which he reads aloud for the family to hear. If you listen to a poetry cassette, you may hear any number of famous people reading selections. If you attend civic auditorium events, you may see a renowned actor or actress in a reading program or enjoy a group presenting Readers Theatre.

The Scythe by Ray Bradbury
College of Southern Idaho:
Director, Fran Tanner

Two oral readers create a scene in the audience's imagination through the use of suggestion and off stage focus.

It is evident that oral reading is an important aspect in everyday life. It is equally important in the field of drama, where actors must be able to interpret and communicate the written page, whether they are reading for tryouts, delivering memorized dialogue, doing radio, presenting Readers Theatre, or reporting over television.

Because of the importance of oral reading in all phases of life, you should learn the art of oral interpretation, of reading aloud. Don't make the mistake of believing that to read well simply involves opening your book and your mouth. With such a lackadaisical attitude you will succeed only in stumbling over words and breaking up thought groups until your listeners are completely bored. Effective and interesting oral reading requires training and practice. In return you will be rewarded with a skill that brings great enjoyment!

As an oral reader, it is your purpose to serve as an intermediary in communicating to an audience the author's thoughts and feelings. It is this idea of intermediary that distinguishes reading from acting. We know that the actor represents a character and asks the audience to believe for a time that he or she is that character. The reader, on the other hand, is constantly before the audience as self, and asks to be considered only as an agent, bringing author and audience together. Through vocal and physical suggestion, the reader enables the listeners to recreate imaginatively in their minds the characters and situations.

As a reader your particular responsibility is to be as faithful as possible to the author's intentions. This means that you must thoroughly understand what you are reading. Of course there is no absolute meaning in literature. As in all art, you interpret the material according to your own background. If your background is limited, you may find it difficult to share the author's experience. However, through adequate research, you as a reader should be able to arrive at an interpretation that is basically consistent with the interpretation of other students of that particular work.

Notice that we are stressing your understanding of the material rather than your flexibility of voice. Both aspects are important, and you should reread the chapter on voice. But remember that expression is built upon impression. If you do not understand the material, vocal inflection and technique will be meaningless.

ASSIGNMENT AND ITS PURPOSE

In this assignment you will be given a chance to read aloud in your class. This one assignment, of course, will not make you a master of the art of oral reading, but it will give you a better understanding of what is involved.

Oral reading embraces all types of material — prose, poetry, drama — but for this assignment, you are to read poetry. You are to choose one or two poems that can be read within the 3 – 5 minute time limit. If you read two poems, you may wish to have them embrace one theme such as war, spring, love. This will make your introduction and transitions easier.

Whereas the preparation and reading of poetry and prose is similar, you are assigned poetry because its qualities of imagery, thought, feeling, and rhythm provide you with a worthwhile challenge. You will be graded according to the evaluation chart for this chapter, found in the teacher's manual. Become familiar with the criteria for judging your oral reading on the evaluation chart .

HOW TO PREPARE

1. Choose your poetry selection. Choose quickly, but carefully, making sure that the selection is —

    a. *Of literary value*. This means that the selection should have universality: experiences and motives common to all people; individuality: a unique way of expressing the material; and suggestivity: images that call forth numerous associations.

    b. *Suitable for the audience*. Do not insult or offend your classmates by reading literature unworthy of their attention, thought, and feeling.

    c. *One that you like*. To read a selection well, you must sincerely enjoy and appreciate it.

The following poems are suggested for oral reading. All should be readily accessible in anthologies and in your own literature books.

W. H. Auden, "The Unknown Citizen," "Musée des Beaux Arts"

Rupert Brooke, "The Great Lover," " The Soldier"

E. E. Cummings, "Chanson Innocente," "Sweet Spring"

Walter de la Mare, "The Listeners"

Emily Dickinson, "Success Is Counted Sweetest," "Because I Could Not Stop for Death"

Robert Frost, "The Mending Wall," "Birches"

A. E. Houseman, "When I Was One and Twenty," "Reveille"

Langston Hughes, "The Negro Speaks of Rivers," "Mother to Son"

Vachel Lindsay, "The Congo," "Abraham Lincoln Walks At Midnight"

Edgar Lee Masters, "Silence," "Lucinda Matlock"

Edna St. Vincent Millay, "Dirge Without Music," "To Jesus on His Birthday"

Ogden Nash, "Kindly Unhitch that Star," "Buddy, Bankers Are Like Everybody Else, Except Richer"

Edward Arlington Robinson, "Richard Cory," "Mr. Flood's Party"

Christina Rosetti, "When I Am Dead," "Remember"

Carl Sandburg, "Jazz Fantasia," "Cool Tombs"

Lew Sarett, "Four Little Foxes," "The World Has a Way With Eyes"

Karl Shapiro, "Auto Wreck," "Buick"

Dylan Thomas, "Poem in October," "Do Not Go Gentle Into That Goodnight"

William Butler Yeats, "Lake Isle of Innisfree," "The Second Coming"

2. Analyze the selection —

a. Read the poem completely and quickly to gain the general meaning, the author's purpose, and the mood instilled.

b. Acquaint yourself with the author and times. Look for information that is pertinent to your understanding of the selection.

c. Carefully study the poem for meanings. Be sure you understand the meaning of all the words. Be aware of connotative (implied or suggested) meanings as well as denotative meanings (strict dictionary definition).

Concentrate on word groupings, for they have a great influence on meaning. For example, notice how the meaning changes in the following sentences according to the way the words are grouped:

(1) "The senator says the president is a fool." "The senator," says the president, "is a fool."

(2) "What do you think! I'll invite you to my party!" "What! Do you think I'll invite you to my party?"

You must pay particular attention to word groupings in poetry. Your aim is to project the idea, emotion, and rhythmical feeling without adapting the grade school "sing-song" effect that destroys all meaning. Remember, the end of a poetic line does not necessarily indicate the end of an idea, so beware of stopping at the end of each line. Often the idea is continued into the following line of poetry. For example, see if you can meaningfully group the words in the following verse:

> I saw a peacock with a fiery tail
> I saw a blazing comet pour down hail
> I saw a cloud all wrapt with ivy round
> I saw a lofty oak creep on the ground
> I saw a beetle swallow up a whale
> I saw a foaming sea brimful of ale
> I saw a pewter cup sixteen feet deep
> I saw a well full of men's tears that weep
> I saw wet eyes in flames of living fire
> I saw a house as high as the moon and higher
> I saw the glorious sun at deep midnight
> I saw the man who saw this wondrous sight...[1]

d. Note words that carry emphasis in the selection. Generally nouns and verbs carry the main ideas and should be stressed by saying them either loudly, more slowly, or more forcefully. You will also need to emphasize new ideas in each line, as well as contrasting ideas.

e. Subordinate words that are less important or that have been repeated, by saying them in a lower tone or by saying them faster so that you almost "throw them away." Generally you should subordinate ideas that have already been mentioned, ideas that are implied, and words such as "and," "a" "the," etc.

f. Study the images: words or phrases that affect the senses. You will find your ability of sense recall an asset in visualizing these word pictures. If you are reading about a hotdog stand, "see" the picture that the words form. Read with tone color in your voice so that your audience can imaginatively see that stand, can smell the franks, and can taste them and the mustard. Be sure your voice projects the implied emotional quality of each word picture. If you are reading about something being happy, your voice and body must suggest happiness.

---

[1] *Ambiguous Lines*, appearing in *Reading Aloud*, 3rd ed. by Wayland Maxfield Parrish, 1953. New York: The Ronald Press Company. (Now with John Wiley and Sons, Publishing)

g. Coordinate your reading rate with the poem's content. Certain ideas and moods require a slow rate; but as you build progressively toward the climax, your tempo should increase with the excitement. Also learn to "point up" ideas with a meaningful pause. Used before a word, a pause adds suspense; used after a word, it provides emphasis.

h. Note the organization of ideas, the transitions, and the climax. As you read, provide for the transitions and build toward the highest point of emotional intensity.

3. Fill out the analysis chart on your activity sheet for this chapter, found in the teacher's manual.

4. Prepare a one-minute introduction of your selection. Your introduction should give the title and author, should catch and hold audience attention, and should give any information that will prepare the audience for understanding and enjoying the selection.

5. Rehearse aloud your introduction and poem. Stand up tall and give the introduction extemporaneously in a conversational style. Then, read your poem aloud with the intent of communicating the ideas as well as the emotions. Rehearse orally at least ten times. You should become so familiar with the selection that you can lift your eyes from the page and establish eye contact with the audience about ninety percent of the time.

Hold your manuscript high enough for easy reading without having to bob your head up and down as you look from audience to book. If the book is difficult to handle, type your selection and insert it in a dark-colored theme binder.

Remember, you are to suggest — not portray — character and movement. If you have several characters with dialogue, keep your head placement consistent for each character. For instance, turn a little to the left when Character A speaks, center for Character B, and a little to the right for Character C, etc.

HOW TO PRESENT

When you are called upon, hand both the activity and critique sheets to your instructor and walk quietly and confidently to the front of the room. Take time to get ready; pause before starting your introduction. Project the attitude that you are interested in what you are reading, and your audience will be interested too.

After your introduction, pause, and then begin your reading as rehearsed. Be sure you establish eye contact. When you are through, pause, and then quietly close your manuscript. Don't destroy the effect you have created by startling the audience with a big bang of the book.

ADDITIONAL PROJECTS ON READING ORALLY

1. Select each of the following types of literature for separate oral readings: narrative prose, expository prose, narrative poetry, lyrics, sonnets, humorous verse. Prepare an analysis, as described previously in this chapter, and present the selection orally to your class.

2. Write your own poetry or prose and present it orally to the class.

3. Choose a theme such as nature, childhood, death, animals, city life, war, spring, Christmas, etc., and prepare a ten-minute oral reading program around that theme. Include at least one prose selection and two poems. Prepare an introduction to the program and appropriate transitions between each selection.

4. In groups of three or four select a poem that can be divided into parts for each voice in the group. Use solo as well as unison and choral parts. Create meaning and mood with your voices. Thoroughly rehearse before presenting your selection.

14 RETELLING STORIES

Time Limits: 5-7 minutes

Activity Sheet: Prepare a brief outline of the story's plot on the activity sheet for this chapter, found in the teacher's manual. Hand it to your instructor when you tell your story.

PROMPTINGS

1. Discuss the importance of the storyteller's skill as it relates to the theatre student.
2. Explain basic structure for dividing a story's action.
3. Describe how to handle language in storytelling.
4. Indicate how tempo is an important aspect for telling stories.

THEATRE LANGUAGE

Climax   Tempo
Conflict   Visualization
Plot

BACKGROUND NOTES

> " . . . let us sit upon the ground,
> And tell sad stories of the death of kings."

With these words, Shakespeare vocalized the pastime and pleasure of people throughout the ages. Perhaps you have never told stories about kings dying, but if you have ever gone camping, you may have sat around a campfire retelling adventure stories that you have read or listening to an older member of the circle recall exploits of "the good old days."

Of course you needn't sit on the ground around a fire to tell or hear stories. You find a form of storytelling everywhere: at the dinner table, where the guest relates a strange incident; on a street corner, where you tell a friend about a "funny thing that happened the other day;" at a party, when low lights set the mood for retelling ghost stories; or in a family circle, where grandmother relates folktales to her grandchildren.

Everyone is a storyteller, vocally repeating adventures as soon as speech is learned. The difference among storytellers is in quality. Some people so lack the rudiments of telling a tale that their listeners are painfully bored. Others recreate stories so vividly that the experience is exciting and stimulating.

An oral interpretor shares a story with her audience.

College of Southern Idaho

It is this invigorating quality for both audience and performer that makes storytelling such a rewarding activity. If you become an effective storyteller, your audience, whether adults or children, will give you such wholehearted response that you will have a heady sensation of delight and accomplishment.

In addition, storytelling is a fine discipline for your acting skills, providing you with ample material for acquiring vocal flexibility as you imaginatively suggest character and mood. Then, too, there is something about the informal retelling that relaxes you, gets rid of your stage fright, and allows you to enjoy the tale with your listeners.

As you retell stories, your purpose is similar to that of the oral reader. You must imaginatively suggest the situations so that the audience can live them vicariously. You differ from the oral reader, however, in that you commit the outline of the story to memory and retell it in your own words to the listener.

Storytelling requires that your voice be pleasant and medium-pitched. If it is too high it produces shrillness; if too low it produces a dull mumbling. Your voice must be flexible to suggest the various people, animals, witches, giants, etc., which frequently appear in stories. Because words are your tools for building the story, you need a rich vocabulary of strong words that arouses the imagination. Furthermore, you must have clear articulation if these words are to be understood.

Every community has some outstanding storytellers, and since much can be learned from hearing these people, you may find it helpful to invite them to class. Listen to their stories and see if you can identify the factors that make their telling effective.

ASSIGNMENT AND ITS PURPOSE

Here is your opportunity to learn the storyteller's skill, while improving your vocal flexibility, exercising your imagination, and losing some of your excess stage fright. You are to retell in your own words a folktale in such a colorful, delightful way that it stirs your listeners' imagination and makes them "live" every word you utter.

If possible, your teacher will arrange to have a small group of children from the first, second, or third grades visit your class and become your audience, while your classmates sit on the sidelines, listening and observing. You will be rated according to the evaluation chart on the back of the activity sheet for this chapter, found in the teacher's manual. Read the criteria before preparing for the performance.

HOW TO PREPARE

1. Choose a folktale that merits telling. It should have a closely constructed plot with a short, interesting beginning; logical development of episodes; spirited conflict; and a definite climax that is followed quickly by a brief, satisfying conclusion.

   The story you choose should increase your listeners' understanding of life. It should contain universal emotions, show respect for character, and have a genuine sense of earnestness about it that makes it memorable.

   Be sure you choose a story that you sincerely like and one that will be appropriate for your audience, occasion, and the 5-7 minute time limit. The following are suggestions of good stories to tell. Consult the children's section of the local library for copies:

   Available in collections:
   Bremen Town Musicians
   Clever Manka
   The Elves and the Shoemaker
   The Emperor's Clothes
   Epaminondas
   The Lad Who Went to the North Wind
   Master of All Masters
   Rumpelstiltskin
   Ugly Duckling
   What the Good Man Does is Always Right
   The Wonderful Pear tree

Available in separate books:

Ask Mr. Bear, by Marjory Flack

The Five Chinese Brothers, by Claire Bishop

Journey Cake, Ho! by Ruth Sawyer

Millions of Cats, by Wanda Gag

Paddy's Christmas, by Helen Monsell

Stone Soup, by Marcia Brown

Story of Ferdinand, by Munro Leaf

Tale of Peter Rabbit, by Beattrix Potter

2. Read the story silently for enjoyment. Why do you like the story? Be specific. Keep your answers in mind so that you can incorporate those qualities into your telling.

3. Read the story slowly once or twice in order to visualize each scene. This is the secret of good storytelling. You must "see" in your imagination each event and character in the story until you feel as though you have actually lived that experience. Visualize what each character looks like. Are they brown bears or black bears? Do they wear clothes or are they content in their fur? Visualize the setting, until you know exactly the rooms Goldilocks visited. Sense the emotions of the situation: Goldilocks' tiredness, the Bears' surprise, etc. Accomplish this visualization by using your powers of imagination, concentration, and sense recall.

4. Close your book and think silently through the story. Usually the action divides itself into: (a) the problem; (b) the complication; and (c) the solution. Attempt to see each picture as the plot unfolds.

5. Now read the story aloud and listen to the particular phrases of narration and dialogue that add color. You are to tell the story in your own simple, direct language, avoiding any attempts to memorize the story word for word, but retaining those particular words or phrases that are used for special effect. "Once upon a time" adds a mystic touch, so use it. Avoid changing such words "ogre" to a "mean little man:' because such changes destroy the intended flavor. Also resist adding such modernisms as "o.k." or "wow," for they destroy the magical illusion.

Keep your language simple, powerful, and consistent with the story's setting. You will find that after having told the story three or four times, the words will fit the pictures if your imagination and memory are working together.

Note: There are a few stories written by stylists, such as Kipling or Dr. Seuss, that must be memorized for retelling because the exact words are necessary for enjoyment. Most stories, however, do not fit in this category.

6. Outline the sequence of events on the activity sheet for this chapter, found in the teacher's manual.

7. Rehearse the story aloud seven or eight times. Make it come alive! Give it oomph and spontaneity! Be sure your voice is flexible so that your listeners can easily distinguish the various characters. For example, Papa Bear will be gruffer than Mama Bear, who in turn will sound different from Baby Bear. Keep both vocal and bodily response simple and informal, yet full of vitality.

Polish the beginning of the tale, setting the mood and starting the plot immediately. Polish the end until it rings with enthusiasm and conviction. Lift out difficult sections of dialogue or emotional scenes and work on them until they come easily.

Pay particular attention to tempo. It is boring to hear anything — music, speeches, lines of a play, stories — at the same dreary pace. Variety is necessary to communicate thought and feeling Some moments will be leisurely, but as the action progresses and things begin to happen, your tempo should increase and build toward the exciting climax. Remember, too, that pause is a necessary tool to gain suspense or to allow an important fact to sink in before continuing to the next event. As you learn to coordinate story and tempo you will find the tales become alive and smack of fun!

8. Overlearn your story. Think it through whenever you have a moment doing dishes or riding on the bus to school. If you live with it for a while, it will be yours forever.

HOW TO PRESENT

Hand your activity sheet to your instructor when it is your turn to give your story. Gather the children around you in a circle where you can see each other. You may wish to sit on the floor with them, or you may pull a chair into the circle. Or stand up and seat the children on chairs. Your classmates will sit quietly and attentively around the room.

Before you begin your story, introduce it to the children by relating it to something within their experience. Explain any unfamiliar words, so that the children will not break into the story's continuity with questions. Maintain a relaxed, happy, informal atmosphere.

As you tell the story, be aware of your audience. If they don't seem to understand what you are saying, you may need to rephrase. Also, you may wish to let the children participate in the story by making certain necessary sounds that contribute to the tale, such as the blowing of the North Wind, or the sound the Bremen Town musicians make.

ADDITIONAL PROJECTS ON RETELLING STORIES

1. Plan a series of storytelling hours for small children on Saturday at the local library. Each member of the class should be responsible for telling a story during the series.

2. See and study the video: *Word Weaving: The Art of Storytelling*. 25 minutes. Color. Lifelong Learning, University of California, Berkeley, California 94720.

15 INTERPRETING THE CHARACTER'S LINES

Time Limits: 3 – 5 minutes

Activity Sheet: Fill out the activity sheet for this chapter, found in the teacher's manual. Hand it to your instructor when you read your scene.

PROMPTINGS

1. Discuss the importance of proper line interpretation.
2. Describe the methods of correctly analyzing dialogue.
3. Compare factual and sub-meanings.
4. Discuss motivating desire as it relates to dialogue.
5. Relate spontaneity to line reading.
6. Explain the techniques for picking up cues.
7. Describe the techniques for laughing and crying on stage and for other special line demands.

THEATRE LANGUAGE

Ad-lib	Form	Sub-meaning
Content	Motivating desire	Theme
Cues	Plot	Topping
Focus	"Pointing"	

BACKGROUND NOTES

Line interpretation is vitally important to you as an actor, for it is mainly through dialogue that the actor communicates the dramatist's purpose to the audience. Effective line interpretation demands that you have an active mind to understand the relationships of ideas and emotions in the play, and a well-trained voice to express those thoughts and feelings. As a prerequisite for this chapter you will be wise to reread Chapter 12 "Improving Voice," and put its principles into practice.

Regardless of whether your part is a meaty lead or a thin bit, you are obligated to achieve three aims:

1. Lines must arouse audience belief;

2. Lines must have spontaneity;

3. Lines must be heightened for desired effects.

Let us see how you can meet these demands.

In order to make dialogue sound believable, you must incorporate the same mental process on stage that you use in everyday conversation. Your talk with friends is genuine because you formulate the ideas and words as you speak. You are convincing when you communicate your own thoughts, for your mind is at work. But memorize another person's words, and they often sound stilted and artificial. Why? Because you have failed to provide the mental activity necessary to convey belief. Since dialogue is the dramatist's creation, the actor must learn to recreate the thoughts in his memorized lines so that they sound as his own. Believable dialogue comes from an active mind!

As you approach the content of your lines, you will be concerned with communicating the factual meaning. You will want to study your script in a method similar to that used by the oral reader (see Chapter 13). You should understand the denotative and connotative values of all words. You should divide your speeches into thought groups or words that are fused together into a single idea. For example, when you say, "The big white house," you should convey the single idea rather than the separate words, "the," "big," "white," "house."

You will also need to "point" certain ideas or provide emphasis within your thought groups. Generally you should focus on the most important ideas in the group, on new ideas, and on contrasting ideas. In the following dialogue from *The Importance of Being Earnest* by Oscar Wilde, the words in bold print could be effectively emphasized. See if you can determine why:

Lady Bracknell: Are your ***parents*** living?

Jack: I have ***lost*** both my parents.

Lady Bracknell: Both? That seems like ***carelessness***. Who was your ***father***?

Jack: I am afraid I really don't know. The ***fact*** is, Lady Bracknell, I said I had lost my parents. It would be nearer the ***truth*** to say that my parents seem to have lost ***me***. I ***don't*** actually know who I ***am*** by birth. I was — well, I was ***found***.

As you emphasize main ideas, you must subordinate those of less importance. Words such as "to," "in," "of," "a," etc. need subordination. So do words that have been previously mentioned and those that carry obvious meanings such as "wet" rain (rain always is). Also, provide oral punctuation between thought groups by using pause for emphasis and suspense.

In addition to communicating thought as you deliver dialogue, you must also project your character's attitudes and emotions. Generally, a character's attitude reveals relationships within the play more than the words do. Lines are not separate entities. They relate to the play as a whole, furthering the dramatist's theme. They relate to the particular scene they are in, as well as to the character's purpose. With these associations in mind, determine why your character says each line. What is the motivation? What are the feelings behind the line?

Every line has at least two meanings. There is the factual surface meaning that is usually evident at a glance. But like an iceberg that carries much of its weight beneath the water, lines carry emotional sub-meanings hidden below the surface. For example, the surface meaning of the following lines is evident:

> Bill: It's raining.
> Mary: I know.

But the lines lack real meaning until we understand their relationship to the play's action and to the character's desire or feelings. In one play the speakers may have needed rain desperately, and the lines indicate:

> Bill: Our prayers have been answered!
> Mary: Our crops will grow!

In another play Bill and Mary may be in a flooded area, and the lines suggest:

> Bill: Our lives are in danger.
> Mary: We'll be trapped.

Again, the play may be a light whimsy where Bill is asking Mary out, and the rain lines mean:

> Bill: Do you really want to go with me?
> Mary: Sure do!

As you look for the sub-meaning, determine your character's motivating desire or what he or she wants from having said the line. In the first example, Bill's motivating desire when he says, "It's raining," and means, "Our prayers have been answered," is to give divine thanks. When he means, "Our lives are in danger," his desire is to get away from the flood; and when he means, "Do you really want to go?" his desire is to take Mary for a walk.

Whenever you say a line, be sure you communicate the sub-meaning, realizing your character's desire in having spoken. Understand the relationship of your lines not only to the immediate situation but to the circumstances that happened before the scene.

Up to now we have been concerned with the content of lines — what they say intellectually and emotionally. Of equal importance to interpretation is the form of the dialogue or how the character expresses ideas. Form takes into consideration the grammar, vocabulary, pronunciation, articulation, and length of sentences. Form reveals much about the character. For example, a person who states, "He sez I ain't gonna buy no hat now," and the one who says, "It has been brought to my attention that I shall be unable to procure a chapeau at the moment," may mean the same thing (content), but the form provides the difference and sets the character.

As an actor you must discover your character's background, influences, likes, dislikes, etc., in order to understand why your character speaks as he or she does. Only when you have justified the manner of speech, will you be able to convincingly project personality.

Remember, to arouse audience belief in the dialogue, you must project your lines with spontaneity. Avoid the rut of sounding mechanical. Strive always to have your speeches appear fresh and new, as though you are saying them for the first time. Your success here will greatly depend upon your feeling and thinking within the part.

While we have indicated that lines need a natural, conversational quality, we do not mean that they should be exactly like normal conversation. Stage lines must be clearer and more interesting than in real life, and they must project to the audience. The following techniques will assist you in heightening lines and in handling special problems.

Preparing for Cues —

Cues are the last few words of the actor's speech that precede your lines. Sometimes a certain sound or movement will be your cue, such as a knock on the door, but generally your cue is the speech that precedes yours. In order to "pick up your cues" in time, you should learn to take a breath before the other person has stopped talking, so you are ready to immediately begin your lines.

Picking up Cues —

Most plays demand a fast pickup of cues. This means that there should be no pause between the end of one character's speech and the beginning of another character's speech. Quick pickup of cues provides a tempo which holds interest. Within the speech, of course, rate should be varied according to idea and emotion.

Anticipating cues —

Never anticipate cues. Picking up the phone before it rings, or crying two seconds before you learn of grandma's death makes your acting ludicrous.

Interrupted sentences —

When the script indicates an interrupted sentence, practice cutting in on the other person's speech until your timing is accurate. If someone is to cut in on your speech, prepare to finish the sentence, in case the cue is late and your speech is not interrupted.

Topping —

Topping lines provides a build to the climactic part in the scene. To top means to say each line faster, stronger, and with a higher pitch than the preceding line. The secret of topping is to start at a level low enough to permit building to the climax. The following scene from Molière's *The Imaginary Invalid* calls for topping of lines:

Toinette:	What does your doctor prescribe for your diet?
Argan:	He lets me eat soup.
Toinette:	Stupidity!
Argan:	Chicken.
Toinette:	Chicanery!
Argan:	Beef.
Toinette:	Baloney!
Argan:	Fresh eggs and Italian cheese.
Toinette:	Ignorantus, ignoranta, ignorantum!

Ad-lib —

Ad-lib means to make up your own words and business. Ad-lib is used to cover up mistakes on stage, such as when an actor forgets a speech or makes a late entrance. Of course, ad-libbing should be used only in emergencies and then should be given in full voice and with confidence, so that it does not sound like ad-libbing.

Calling off stage —

Be sure you mentally picture the distance and increase your volume and force to account for that distance.

Stage Whisper —

Use strong diaphragmatic breathing, a low pitch, and little voice to project the whispered effect.

Laughing —

Laughing requires expelling the air stream in explosive spurts from the region of the diaphragm. To keep your lines from being blurred, laugh only between lines or words. For technique on holding for laughs, see Chapter 19, "Playing Humorous Scenes."

Crying —

Inhale in little gasping sobs. Sob between words, rather then on them. Be sure that the "tears" are revealed in your voice. Don't get carried away, though. Deep grief will communicate more effectively if it is restrained.

ASSIGNMENT AND ITS PURPOSE

This assignment will give you practice in analyzing and presenting dialogue. You and a classmate are to prepare a 3 – 5 minute scene from a play and read it aloud to the class. You will be graded on how well you arouse belief, provide spontaneity, and handle special dialogue problems.

HOW TO PREPARE

1. You and your partner are to choose a two-character scene from a noted full-length or one-act play. Decide which character you will be. Read the complete play, relating your scene to the whole.

2. After you have read the complete play, condense the plot (the play's story) into one sentence. Decide on the theme of the play, or the main idea that the dramatist is trying to project. Study your character. What kind of person is he or she mentally? emotionally? physically? How have family, education, and environment influenced ideas, feelings, and manner of speaking? What is this character's main purpose in the play? What are the basic wants or desires? (See Chapters 17 and 18.)

3. Work on the scene you will read aloud. Identify the general mood of the scene. Concentrate on understanding the factual meaning. Then concentrate on the sub-meaning and on your character's attitudes and desires. Fill out the activity sheet for this chapter, found in the teacher's manual.

4. Plan a one-minute introduction in which you briefly relate the background events leading up to the scene you are giving. Decide which of you will give the introduction.

5. Practice reading the scene aloud, working for vocal audibility and flexibility. Now rehearse the scene seven or eight times with your partner. Work on picking up cues, building to the climax, etc. (Your instructor may give you class time for rehearsal.)

HOW TO PRESENT

When you are called upon, hand your activity sheet to your instructor and go to the playing area with your partner. Clearly and concisely introduce the scene.

Read the scene with your partner. Be sure that you establish eye contact with your partner and the audience. Hold your script high enough to prevent head bobbing. When you are through with the scene, pause, and then return quietly to your desk.

"Language springs out of the inmost parts of us. No glass renders a man's likeness so true as his speech."

— Ben Jonson

ADDITIONAL PROJECTS ON INTERPRETING THE CHARACTER'S LINES

1. Plan a Shakespearean program. Select short scenes from Shakespeare's plays for analysis and reading presentation. A list of Shakespearean scenes appears in Chapter 28, or consult Samuel Selden's *Shakespeare: A Player's Handbook of Short Scenes.* Holiday House, 1960.

2. Find a soliloquy or long speech either in modern or classical drama. Analyze and interpret it for oral presentation. Title suggestions of plays with long speeches: *Elizabeth the Queen, Mary of Scotland, Electra, Macbeth, Hamlet, Death of a Salesman, Our Town, Medea, J.B., The Lark, Noah, Glass Menagerie, The Miracle Worker.* In preparation, see the video cassette *Set Speeches and Soliloquies,* Films for the Humanities.

Our Town by Thornton Wilder
Utah Shakespearean Festival, Photo by John Running

The Soda fountain scene.

Chapter 16   MEMORIZING

Time Limits: 3 – 5 minutes

Activity Sheet: Fill out the activity sheet for this chapter, found in the teacher's manual. Hand it to your instructor before you present your memorized scene.

PROMPTINGS

1. Discuss reasons for unit memorization being preferred over rote.
2. Explain how movement and memorization are related.
3. Relate an effective routine for memorization.

THEATRE LANGUAGE

Rote memorization
Unit memorization
Verbatim

BACKGROUND NOTES

The story goes that on opening night of a new play, a famous acting team was in the middle of a romantic scene when suddenly the dialogue stopped. Feeling his call to duty, the prompter whispered the line, "Darling, I love you," and waited for the two actors to pick it up. Nothing happened. The prompter, thinking they didn't hear him, said in a louder tone, "Darling, I love you." Still nothing happened on stage. By this time the prompter was frantic and loudly shouted, "Darling, I love you." With an air of cool concern, the male lead turned to the prompter and queried, "We know the line, now which one of us says it?"

Let's hope that such a situation never happens to you either as an actor or a prompter. Exaggerated as the story is, it does serve to focus on the actor's dilemma of line memorization.

There are many ways to learn lines, and your director may tell you his or her preference. You are probably already familiar with rote memory in which you learn lines one by one through labored drills. Although this method allows you quick mastery of material, it is generally not recommended for acting because you more easily forget the material and your delivery tends to be stilted.

Most drama authorities prefer unit memorization in which you learn the material scene by scene and coordinate the lines with the assigned movement. Unit memorization, while slower than rote, will provide better line retention and a more fluid, convincing delivery. Let us discuss how you can effectively use this method.

The Belle of Amherst
by William Luce
College of Southern Idaho: Directors,
Fran Tanner and Tony Mannen

This one-woman play, based on the life of the poet Emily Dickinson, demands intensive memorization.

Highlight or underline your character's name and your cues. Then before you begin to memorize your part, check with your director. Usually he or she will want to "set" movement within the scenes before asking actors to learn lines. When the director tells you to start memorizing, read the whole play to become familiar again with its purpose, mood, rhythm, character relationships, and structure.

Repeatedly read your individual scenes aloud. Read the complete scene from your entrance to your exit, including all the other characters' lines. As you read, concentrate on the continuity of the scene and the progression of ideas and emotions. Familiarity with the scene's purpose will allow you to carry through even if someone accidentally "blows" lines in performance.

Now read your own speeches with their cues. Repeatedly go over them, focusing on what your lines convey to the audience, and how they further the play's progression. After repeated readings you will find that lines start to fall into place, and you begin to remember the unit as a whole.

It would be comfortable to sit in a cozy chair and relax while you study your part. But don't just sit there! Get up and go through your movement as you say your lines. Roughly set the stage in your room, and as you move, visualize the other players and their positions. Be sure you say your lines with interpretation. Glibly running through them will establish bad habits that may be difficult to break. If something prevents you from moving during line study, at least visualize movement in your mind as you repeat your lines.

In addition to cast rehearsal time, set aside an hour or so each day for memorization of your lines. A quiet place free from interruptions is best. Concentrate as you work. If necessary, review Chapter 4, "Concentration."

As you progress, you will want to have someone "cue" you. That person will read your cues and then check as you say your lines. If you cannot get someone to help you, write your cues in succession on cards. Flash the cards and then say the corresponding lines.

You may find that later you will have to "polish" by drilling yourself on difficult lines or scenes. Try to learn lines verbatim. You are obligated to the dramatist to be as faithful as possible to his script. It is also your responsibility to give correct cues to your fellow players. Nothing is worse than to have a presumptuous actor rewrite the lines until no one knows what the cues are.

Free yourself from all doubts of forgetting dialogue by overlearning your lines. Say them to yourself before going to sleep at night, and let your subconscious work on them. Never wait until the last minute to learn lines! You should have them letter-perfect half way through the rehearsal schedule. This will give you and the director time to work without the hindrance of a script, enabling scenes to be polished.

ASSIGNMENT AND ITS PURPOSE

Working with the same scene and partner you had in the assignment for Chapter 15, memorize your part for presentation. This will give you practice in learning unit memorization. You will be graded on how well you learn your lines and on how convincing they sound.

HOW TO PREPARE

1. Choose the same scene and partner as for the assignment in Chapter 15. If this is not feasible, choose a new partner and a different two-character scene for presentation. Read the whole play from which the scene is taken. Summarize the plot and identify the theme and mood. Analyze the character's personality. Note the motivating desire in the scene. (This step may be deleted if already done in the assignment for Chapter 15.)

2. Fill out the activity sheet for this chapter, found in the teacher's manual.

3. Familiarize yourself with the complete scene, focusing on the purpose of your lines. Read aloud your lines and cues consecutively, over and over again. Repeat

at intervals until you assimilate them as your own. Do not memorize line by line. Study the scene as a unit! While you will not have definite movement to follow, you and your partner may wish to plan necessary action, or you may want to follow the dramatist's stage directions. Either way, practice your lines with the movement.

4. You and your partner may "cue" each other by running through the scene together, or you may get someone at home to feed you your lines.

5. Before presentation, rehearse your memorized scene at least six times with your partner. Your instructor may allow class time for rehearsal.

HOW TO PRESENT

Hand your activity sheet to your instructor when you are called upon. Go quietly to the playing area with your partner. Set up chairs and tables needed.

Announce the scene; then play it convincingly with expression and purpose. If you have memorized well, your lines will come easily, even though you may be nervous. If something happens that you should forget your lines, you are familiar enough with the ideas in the scene so that you can ad-lib and get back to your set dialogue.

Pause after you complete your scene, then quietly return to your desk.

"A man's real possession is his memory. In nothing else is he rich, in nothing else is he poor." — Alexander Smith

ADDITIONAL PROJECT ON MEMORIZING

Prepare for memorized presentation a 2-3 minute monologue or soliloquy (a long speech delivered by one character) from a familiar play or from the sources listed below. Read the complete play from which the monologue is taken. Analyze the play, the character, and the motivating desire in the monologue. Then unit memorize your lines while adding necessary characterized movement. Present your memorized characterization to the class. For a selection of monologues, see Unit VII.

UNIT IV

CHARACTERIZATION

Chapter 17   ANALYZING A CHARACTER

Time Limits: 6-8 minutes

Activity Sheet: On the form for this chapter, found in the teacher's manual, fill out the character analysis for the group improvisation.

PROMPTINGS

1. List ways to obtain information about a character.
2. Discuss internal qualities of character.
3. Discuss external qualities of character.
4. Explain artistic selectivity in characterization.
5. Relate characterization to the actor's dual role.

THEATRE LANGUAGE

Actor's dual role
Artistic selectivity
Character

External qualities
Internal qualities

BACKGROUND NOTES

Your ultimate aim as an actor is to create a stage role or character that satisfies the playwright's intention and that engenders audience belief throughout your performance. The projects that you have previously been assigned have been focused on helping you prepare for characterization. If you have adequately equipped yourself, you will discover that the experience of moving, talking, and thinking in character is highly stimulating and enjoyable.

Your knowledge of people is a valuable ingredient for creating a role. Past experiences with family, friends, and acquaintances; remembered observations of the study of individuals; and vicarious experiences from reading will provide creative inspiration. Vivid sensory and emotional recall plus an active imagination further contribute to characterization material.

Regardless of your background and imagination, the development of a believable character takes time. Characterization demands intensive study of both the play and the part. If you are a devoted artist, you will find your role gradually developing throughout rehearsals. If your play has a long run, your portrayal will grow during performances.

Initial study of the part will give you general ideas about the character you are to play. As you progress, you will modify those ideas, selecting specific qualities from your background and imagination that lend themselves to your voice and body. This process prevents any two actors from developing the same character, even though they study the same part. Experience and imagination provide each actor with a distinctive touch!

To obtain a well-rounded concept of your character's personality, analyze both internal and external qualities. The internal aspect includes the following:

1. *Background* —
   What can you discover about the character's family, environment, occupation, education, interests, and hobbies?

2. *Mental characteristics* —
   Intelligent, clever, dull, slow, average?

3. *Spiritual qualities* —
   Ideals, ethical code, religion? Attitude toward other people and toward life?

4. *Emotional characteristics* —
   Confident, outgoing, happy, poised? Sullen, confused, nervous, cynical, timid? Likes and dislikes? Response to other people? How is the character's temperament similar to yours? How is it different?

Answering the questions listed concerning internal and external qualities should give you a basic idea about your character's personality. Now become more specific by determining his or her motivating desire within the play or scene. What does your character want? To determine this desire, you may need to supply imaginatively the circumstances that precede the play or scene, in addition to studying the script. (See Chapter 10, "Utilizing Motivation.") If possible, state the desire in terms of action: what your character will do to satisfy his or her wishes. It may help you to use the resourceful "if." Ask yourself, "What would I do in the situation if I were the character?" Concentrate on the desire and the action. These, in turn, should release the proper emotion. (See Chapter 7, "Developing Emotional Response.")

The external qualities of your character apply to those aspects that the audience sees. These outward forms are important because they can communicate inward traits. Externals include your character's physical appearance, costume, facial makeup, movement, and voice. You must develop these facets carefully, so they will be consistent as well as believable to the character and to the play.

The following is a checklist of external qualities:

1. *Posture* —

   Is it slumped, stiff, relaxed, attractive? Does it suggest timidity, assuredness, awkwardness, grace?

2. *Movement and gesture* —

   Does it convey poise, nervousness, weakness, strength? Does your character walk with a stride, plod, shuffle, bounce? How does the movement indicate age, health, attitude?

3. *Mannerisms* —

   Does he or she bite nails, clear throat, keep hands in pockets, chew gum, scratch head when thinking, doodle on paper?

4. *Voice* —

   Is it pleasant, high-pitched, resonant? Does your character have a twang, a drawl?

5. *Dress* —

   Is appearance neat, casual, sloppy, prim, clean, dirty? Are clothes in good taste, flashy, fashionable?

Our Town by Thornton Wilder
College of Southern Idaho:
Director, Fran Tanner

Profile body positions create an intimate scene.

As you develop your character's external qualities, avoid cliché or commonplace movements. Choose action that is consistent with your role and yet that is imaginative and refreshing. Be sure your movement conveys the same general idea throughout. Also, avoid trite hand properties. Dark glasses for the Hollywood actor, a pencil behind a reporter's ear, are examples of overworked hand properties.

The external and internal checklists listed previously indicate that character analysis produces a wealth of material — much more than you can effectively use. The actor's problem becomes one of artistic selectivity. Instead of asking yourself how much you can do with your part, decide how little you can do and still communicate the necessary ideas and emotions. As a creative artist you must select, combine, and discard. The secret of artistic success is in knowing what to leave out! Your aim should be to produce an uncluttered effect that communicates with precision and clarity. You should simplify rather than elaborate. Economy is the keynote of all great art!

In previous chapters we have mentioned the actor's dual or double role. You are both actor-as-character and actor-as-actor. If you are to play with conviction, you must maintain an imaginative belief in what the character is doing, feeling, and saying. When not speaking in character, you should think as he or she would think and listen to others as he or she would listen in that situation. Concentrate within your character and try to satisfy the desires. On the other hand, as an actor you must maintain technical control. Your voice must be heard; your movement, clear; your tempo, right; your position, in proper relation to the others on stage. It should be evident that this double role must be balanced if you are to do your best. Character and actor must work together with precision.

Characterization is a demanding job, but don't allow it to become a strain. Tension inhibits. Relax and enjoy yourself as you create a believable individual on stage.

ASSIGNMENT AND ITS PURPOSE

Your resourcefulness in analyzing and creating a role will be challenged with this assignment. You are to create a believable character within a group improvisation. Draw from your background and your imagination to supply the details of character within a given situation. You will be graded on the completeness of your characterization (internal and external traits); the projection of your character's motivating desire; your artistic selectivity of movement, mannerisms, hand properties, etc.; and the belief your character instills in the audience.

HOW TO PREPARE

1. Divide into mixed groups of five. (Your instructor may wish to assign groups, scenes, and roles.)

2. Select a situation for improvisation and the character you will play in it. The following are suggestions:

    a. *Situation:* A spring garage sale in an empty building downtown.

    Characters:

        Antique dealer — has hopes of finding something valuable

        Old woman — wants woolens for a braided rug

        Costume chairperson — needs costumes for a university play

        Poor woman — needs to outfit three boys

        Salesperson — wants to have a profitable sale

    b. *Situation*: Waiting at an airport for takeoff which will be delayed until the plane can be repaired.

    Characters:

        Ticket agent

        Business executive — keeping an important appointment

        Model — flying to the Caribbean on her job

        Orphan — being sent to a foster family

        College student — going back to school

    c. *Situation:* Young man picking up date for the first time.

    Characters:

        Young man

        His date

        Her mother

        Her father

        Her aunt — who is visiting

    d. *Situation:* A family reunion after a wedding reception. All are happy until an old argument is renewed.

    Characters:

        Grandfather — retired railroad engineer

        His brother — owner of an orange grove

        His oldest daughter — mother of the bride

        Nephew — a minister

        Distant cousin — a librarian

    e. *Situation:* A group of vacationers being welcomed by the manager of a lakeside resort.

    Characters:

        Wealthy society matron

        Her young secretary

        Newspaper reporter

Olympic swimmer — in training

Manager of the resort

f. *Situation:* A detective is questioning a group of people in connection with a recent murder in a boarding house.

    Characters:

Chinese cook

College professor of mathematics

Middle-aged landlady

Crippled girl — who is a seamstress

Detective

g. *Situation:* A group of citizens are meeting with the city manager to discuss a proposed dog leash law for the town.

    Characters:

City manager

Young attorney

President of the local kennel club

Housewife who is tired of dogs in her yard

Local veterinarian

h. Your choice

3. As a group, decide the basic step-by-step action of the scene, including how it will begin, what will happen, the climax, and how it will end. Plan so that you can stay within the 6-8 minute time limit. Be sure you know the action sequence. Keep it simple; emphasis should be on characterization.

4. Decide who will introduce your scene. Your work as a group now ends until you perform your improvisation in class.

5. Outside of class, analyze your character in the situation. Drawing from your background and imagination, supply the necessary internal and external traits. Determine your character's motivating desire in this scene.

Get to know your character as much as you can in the time allowed for preparation. Decide what your character will do and say. Avoid memorizing specific movement and words, but have a general idea in your mind that you can modify as you improvise the scene.

6. Fill out the activity form for this chapter, found in the teacher's manual.

7. Rehearse your characterization, working on movement, speech, thoughts, and mannerisms that will help to satisfy the motivating desire.

HOW TO PRESENT

When your group is called upon to perform, go quietly to the playing area. Set up necessary properties. Introduce your scene by describing the setting and by briefly giving any information pertinent to understanding the scene.

Play with conviction and belief. Move, think, and talk as your character. Keep alert, readily adjusting to the action and dialogue. Stay in character no matter what happens!

At the completion of your scene, return with poise to your seat. Your instructor may wish to lead a class discussion on character effectiveness and then have you redo your scene.

ADDITIONAL PROJECTS ON ANALYZING A CHARACTER

1. Select newspaper human interest stories. In groups, supply the necessary characters for the action. Analyze the characters. Then improvise a scene built around the printed story.

2. In groups, build a scene around an historical event, such as Lewis and Clark's first meeting with Sacajawea, Madam Curie's discovery of radium, Alexander Graham Bell's first successful use of the telephone. Be sure your story has dramatic value, a clearly defined plot, and a climax.

3. Select a picture from a magazine or from a reproduction of a famous painting that shows an interesting looking person. Analyze that person in the light of what you see in the picture. In class, show the picture and report what feelings, thoughts, and behavior make this character distinctive.

4. Choose an external hand property or costume accessory, such as a pair of white gloves, a colorful silk umbrella, a pocket watch, dangle bracelets, a battered hat, a nosegay of violets, a rusty pocket knife. Create a brief scene in which you portray a character suggested by the object.

5. Select partners. B goes on stage and waits for A to enter. A decides upon a definite character relationship with B, but does not tell B. B must discover who he or she is by the way A relates and talks. B must play the scene throughout, responding as best as possible until discovering who he or she is. Then continue playing the scene until the teacher calls cut.

Suggestions:

    a. A is a teenager coming home late. B is the mother.

    b. A is an antique shop clerk who has broken an expensive bowl. B is the manager.

6. Show character and situation through door knocking only. If possible, students participating should stand outside the class room door and knock without being seen by the class.

    Examples: Knock as —

    a. A policeman at night, demanding the door to be opened.

    b. A very young child unable to reach the door knob.

    c. A gangster entering a hideaway.

    d. A delivery person with a pizza.

7. Indicate character and situation through use of your legs and feet only. Have two classmates hold a covering in front of your torso and head, showing only your legs and feet. Create a character and situation.

8. Indicate character and situation through your hands only by having them show from a partition in a curtain.

Chapter

18

CREATING A CHARACTER IN A PLAY

Time Limits: 7–10 minutes

Activity Sheet: Fill out the analysis of play and character on the form for this chapter, found in the teacher's manual.

PROMPTINGS

1. Relate how play analysis is vital to character analysis.
2. Note differences in the two basic styles of plays.
3. Compare representational theatre to presentational.
4. Explain characteristics of tragedy.
5. Explain characteristics of comedy.
6. Discuss differences between melodrama and serious drama.
7. Diagram basic play structure.
8. Determine the difference between plot and theme.

THEATRE LANGUAGE

Antagonist	Initial incident	Representational
Asides	Melodrama	Rising action
Catharsis	Mood	Serious drama
Climax	Nonrealistic	Soliloquy
Comedy	Plot	Structure
Conflict	Presentational	Style
Falling action	Protagonist	Theme
Form	Realistic	Tragedy
Fourth wall		

BACKGROUND NOTES

In the previous chapter you learned an important characterization process: analyzing the internal and external facets of your role. But since a character moves in a play, he or she must also be understood in relationship to that play. Through study of the script, you will learn pertinent facts about your part that will allow you to portray the character close to the playwright's intention.

Since depth of characterization depends on depth of study, you must be able to understand the author's treatment of the play and to relate your character's behavior to the action, atmosphere, and theme.

Plays are categorized in many ways. In fact, terms are so numerous their meaning sometimes overlaps. For our purpose, we will discuss only the basic divisions as an aid to understanding the play and to portraying your character. These divisions are style, form, type, theme, plot, structure, and mood. Keep in mind that these terms apply to the methods the playwright uses in selecting and arranging the material to express his or her ideas. It is the playwright's attitude toward the subject that determines how we label the play. Also realize that not all plays fit neatly into a specific division. Some are combinations of the basic groups.

Steel Magnolias by Richard Harling.   Topeka West High School: Director, Doug Goheen

A realistic beauty shop is part of the Southern setting.

Realistic and Nonrealistic Styles

The style of plays can be divided into realistic and nonrealistic. Realistic plays center on characters and action that create an illusion of real life. The scenery looks like a real room and the actors respond in a way that the audience recognizes as lifelike. Examples of realistic plays are: O'Neill's *Ah Wilderness!*; Ibsen's *The Doll House*; Miller's *All My Sons*; and Lawrence and Lee's *Inherit the Wind*.

Nonrealistic plays contain characters, events, and scenery that are exaggerated to the extent that they obviously depart from real life. Nonrealistic plays include fantasies where animals may speak like people, spirits walk about, etc.; symbolic plays where the characters and setting suggest or represent ideas; and romantic plays where life is pictured ideally and imaginatively, dreams come true, and language is often lyrical. Many nonrealistic plays combine several of these elements. Examples of nonrealistic plays include: Maeterlinck's *The Blue Bird* (fantasy and symbolic); Rice's *The Adding Machine* (fantasy and symbolic); Millay's *Aria da Capo* (fantasy and symbolic); Shakespeare's *Midsummer Night's Dream* (fantasy); Rostand's *Cyrano de Bergerac* (romantic); and Shakespeare's *Twelfth Night* (romantic).

Representational and Presentational Forms

After you identify the basic style of the play, determine its form. Today most plays have a representational approach. They are written with the "fourth wall" in mind — the invisible wall that extends between stage and audience and that establishes the fourth side of the set. In these plays the author and actors seemingly ignore the audience who merely "look in" on the action. This representational treatment maintains a constant stage illusion, whether it is a realistic or nonrealistic play.

When the playwright recognizes the presence of the audience and directly presents the play to them, a presentational approach is being used. Actors break into the stage illusion by talking directly to the audience or by permitting the audience to see the theatrical devices. Many classic plays, such as those of Shakespeare and Sheridan, are presentational with their use of soliloquies and asides said straight to the audience. Modern presentational plays are: Wilder's *Our Town*; Brecht's *The Caucasian Chalk Circle*; and William's *The Glass Menagerie*.

Types or Categories of Plays

Tragedy —

Tragedy is considered to be the highest form of drama. Through the intensity of profound emotions, tragedy shows humans achieving a sense of nobility in their unswerving sacrifice and suffering. In a tragedy the protagonist, struggling with a problem or with opposing forces, eventually goes down to defeat — usually death — but with an aura of dignity. Because of the depth of emotion, the audience experiences pity and terror, resulting in a catharsis, a purging of these emotions that uplifts the soul and leaves the spectator calm. This emotional exultation results from audience belief in a person's capacity for greatness and in their belief that the human spirit will ultimately triumph over its own weakness, wickedness, or fate. Calmness evolves from audience acceptance of the tragic ending. Examples of tragedies are: Sophocles' *Oedipus Rex* and *Electra*; Shakespeare's *Hamlet, Macbeth,* and *King Lear*; Anderson's *Winterset*; or Miller's *The Crucible*.

Comedy —

In a comedy the audience is invited to be amused or to laugh at playful incongruities, contrasts, and comparisons . There is more emotional detachment in comedy than in tragedy. The audience enjoys the hero's antics and minor catastrophes, knowing that in the end the hero will solve the problem successfully. There are many types of comedies, ranging from the subtle satirical, to the rollicking farce, to the "pie-throwing" slapstick. Examples of comedies are: Molière's *The Imaginary Invalid*, Shakespeare's *Taming of the Shrew*, Hart and Kauffman's *You Can't Take It With You*, and Goldsmith's *She Stoops to Conquer*.

Serious or *social drama* —

Serious drama or social drama are terms applied to those plays that treat their subject seriously and yet do not fall into the tragic division with its tragic hero, self-realization, catharsis, and catastrophic ending. Serious drama focuses on several problems, indicating what is right and wrong with society. Many modern plays are serious dramas, such as: Gibson's *The Miracle Worker*; Wouk's *The Caine Mutiny Court-Martial*; Goodrich and Hackett's *Dairy of Anne Frank;* and Lawrence and Lee's *Inherit the Wind*.

Melodrama —

Another type of play is the melodrama. While it has a happy ending, its purpose is to arouse great suspense, excitement, and thrills in the audience. Emphasis is on action and chance rather than on character and social problems. Examples of modern melodrama include: Hamilton's *Angel Street*; Knott's *Dial M for Murder*; and Anderson's *The Bad Seed*. The old-fashioned Gay Nineties' melodramas have such exaggerated values of right and wrong with the mustached villain and the sweet, innocent heroine that the plays are humorous to modern audiences. Examples of these old-fashioned melodramas are: *Curse You, Jack Dalton*; *A Fate Worse Than Death*; and *Bertha, the Sewing Machine Girl*.

Theme

Upon establishing the play's style, form, and type, concentrate on its theme. The theme encompasses a generally accepted truth of life, and it embodies the author's purpose or point in writing the play. Theme unifies the characters and story. Sometimes the theme is suggested in the play's title, such as Sherwood's *Idiot's Delight*, or Hart and Kauffman's *You Can't Take It With You*. Sometimes the author will provide a pertinent quote at the beginning of the work, as Lillian Hellman did in *The Little Foxes* when she quoted the Biblical passage, "Take us the foxes the little foxes that spoil the vines; for our vines have tender grapes." Often the theme is revealed in a key speech of the main character. Other times it is only subtly present in the impression the author creates with the work. Elusive as it may seem, you must discover the theme, or you may distort the play's meaning with your characterization. Examples of possible themes are: *Macbeth*, vaulting ambition bring destruction; and *Romeo and Juliet*, love triumphs over hate.

Plot and Structure

Next, determine the plot and the play's structure. The plot consists of a series of incidents unified by the theme. It involves conflict or struggle that is resolved in action which ultimately leads to a climax and to a logical conclusion. As you study the play, condense the plot into three or four sentences so that you will know exactly what basic events occur.

A play should begin with a dramatic situation so strained and unstable that it leads to action. This action either progresses, delays, or reverses the events. Either way, it presents a new situation that is often less stable than the first. This process repeats itself until certain events result in a stable situation. The following is an outline of a play's structure.

1. *Opening situation —*

   Events at the rise of the curtain. (Includes the exposition that give the background or reveals what has happened before the curtain rises.)

2. *Initial incident —*

   First event that suggests there will be a change in the situation; an incident to which you can trace all future action.

3. *Rising action —*

   Additional events with their scene or act climaxes.

4. *Climax —*

   Highest point of emotional intensity that occurs near the end of the play and to which all action has been leading.

5. *Falling action —*

   Brief events after the climax in which the outcome is resolved.

Most modern plays are divided into three acts, with the acts frequently divided into scenes. If the playwright does not provide definite scene divisions, your director may do so to aid rehearsal. These scenes will encompass a definite situation with its accompanying action and minor climax. You must build toward these scene climaxes, yet never allow them to overshadow the major play climax.

Mood

The mood of the play is its emotional aura. Contributors to the mood are the characters, dialogue, setting, and lighting. The audience should quickly sense the mood during the exposition.

Character Portrayal

When you have completed the above analysis of the play in which you are cast, turn to your character and his or her relationship to that play. Decide the character's place in the conflict: on the side of the protagonist; the leading character? Or with the antagonist who opposes the central figure? Characters generally identify with one of these forces, though sometimes they are neutral with a purpose of providing background information, local color, or atmosphere.

By now you will be familiar with the size of your role. Remember, while there are short parts, there are never any unimportant parts! Each character is needed in the play's progression. Short parts are often more difficult than long ones. When you have only a few lines with which to work, you need a highly active imagination in order to characterize.

As you build your part, formulate your character's internal and external traits, motivating desire, and general attitudes. (See Chapter 17.) Be able to justify everything your character does. The play will provide you with many clues. Work from the author's description of your character. Analyze what your character does (often written in stage directions) and says. Look particularly for meanings beneath the surface of words. (See Chapter 15.) In addition, notice what the other characters say about your character and how they react. Lastly, be aware of the changes that occur in your character between Act I and the final curtain.

Drawing from this information, as well as from your background and imagination, you should be able to develop your part into a living, breathing individual who is faithful to the playwright's idea.

ASSIGNMENT AND ITS PURPOSE

In this assignment you are to incorporate the analysis described in this chapter while creating a character from a one-act play. You will individually analyze the play and your part in it. Then working in groups of two or three you will prepare for presentation a memorized scene from the play, concentrating on vivid characterization. This assignment will take several class periods for rehearsal before actual class presentation.

You will be graded according to the evaluation chart for this chapter, found in the teacher's manual. Turn there now to familiarize yourself with the criteria.

HOW TO PREPARE

1. In groups of two or three, select a one-act play and a 7-10 minute scene from it. Choose a character for each of you to portray in that scene. Select plays from: Kozelka's *Fifteen American One-Act Plays*, Cerf and Cartmell's *24 Favorite One-Act Plays*; or Zachar's *Plays as Experience* . (Rather than have you choose, your instructor may wish to assign you a group, play, scene, and character.)

2. Before class, quickly read the whole play to understand its general approach. Avoid concentrating on your specific role. Work toward obtaining a unified view of the complete play.

3. Determine the author's dramatic treatment by identifying the style, form, type, theme, plot, structure, and mood. Delve into this analyzation immediately so that you will have ample time to concentrate on your characterization.

4. Reread the play and this time identify with your part. See the action through your character's eyes. Understand your character's behavior and dialogue in view of the motivating desire. Determine your character's internal and external qualities, as well as your character's relationships.

5. Now concentrate on your group scene. Note its atmosphere, basic action, and scene climax.

6. Fill out the activity sheet for this chapter, found in the teacher's manual.

7. Work on your role in the scene. Develop an imaginative belief in the character's actions, feelings, and words.

8. With your group, rehearse the scene in class. Provide basic movement and business. When you are not speaking your lines, listen in character to the others. Memorize the dialogue. Lines and movement must be learned before you can achieve complete character concentration! When your character is well established and the scene runs effectively, you are ready to perform.

HOW TO PRESENT

When your group is called upon, hand both the activity and critique sheets to your instructor and go to the playing area. Set up necessary props. A selected person should announce your play and briefly give pertinent, background information. Play the scene as you rehearsed. Be sure you establish and maintain character.

"The actor who lets the dust accumulate on his Ibsen, his Shakespeare, and his Bible, but pours greedily over every little column of theatrical news, is a lost soul."

— Minnie Maddern Fiske

(one of America's greatest actresses)

ADDITIONAL PROJECTS ON CREATING A CHARACTER IN A PLAY

1. Repeat the assignment described previously, but select a character and scene from a three-act play. See Unit VII for Scenes. Become familiar with the complete play as preparation for building your character.

2. Write a biography of the character you are portraying in a scene. Include as many facets of the character as possible, such as: family background; schooling; leisure time activities; favorite food; most memorable experience; greatest disappointment; happy events at home; unhappy home situations. Base your writing on your character study from the play.

3. Attend a three-act play staged by either a professional or amateur group. Write a critique on the play, answering the following questions. Did the play's theme convey a universal concept true to life? Did the plot consist of related events that rose to an exciting climax and that reached a logical conclusion? Were the characters lifelike? Were they interesting? Did the dialogue reveal the characters and advance the story effectively? Was the author's style distinctive? Did the audience respond to the play the way you think the author intended them to? Did you like the play? Why or why not?

4. Read a full length play and write an analysis of it from today's information and dramatic criticism.

Chapter

19

PLAYING HUMOROUS SCENES

Time Limits: 3 – 5 minutes

Activity Sheet: Fill out the character and scene outline on the form for this chapter, found in the teacher's manual.

PROMPTINGS

1. Compare four types of comedy.
2. Describe what is meant by a comic sense.
3. Discuss six requirements for playing comedy effectively.
4. Explain how to hold for laughs.

THEATRE LANGUAGE

Comic sense   Incongruity   Objectivity
Farce   Light comedy   Turn of phrase
High comedy   Low comedy

BACKGROUND NOTES

"The world is a comedy to those who think; a tragedy to those who feel." These lines of Horace Walpole epitomize the greatest difference between humorous and serious drama. Comedies approach life objectively, with less emotional involvement than do serious plays. They mentally dance through incongruities, contrasts, exaggerations, or under-emphasis. With comedy there is a feeling of thoughtful fun that the actor must catch and transfer to the audience.

There are many types of comedies. Low comedy projects physical humor and aggression that often approaches cruelty with its exaggerated slapstick beatings, pie throwings, etc., or with its burlesqued ridicule of life. Farce, another type of comedy, is built around greatly exaggerated situations that are usually possible but highly improbable. Farcical characters are always in "hot water" with the entanglements becoming complicated. Examples of farce are Thomas's *Charley's Aunt* and Wilder's *The Matchmaker*.

Light comedy has more realistic characters than does farce but with a humor that is still quite broad. Examples of light comedy are: Thurber and Nugent's *The Male Animal;* and Lindsay and Crouse's *Life With Father*. High comedy, sometimes called drawing room comedy, contains subtle lines that are witty and satirical. These comedies provoke "thoughtful laughter." Sheridan's *School for Scandal* and Shaw's *Pygmalion* fall within this category.

In order to play comedy well, you must be skilled. Good comedy is precise. An actor's slightest miscalculation will destroy the humor. For this reason, many authorities believe that light material is more difficult to play than serious. A discussion of the requirements for playing comedy follow.

The Good Doctor by Neil Simon
College of Southern Idaho: Director, Fran Tanner

The use of levels and furniture reinforcement creates focus on the female character.

Playing Comedy Essentials

Comic sense —

> Above all, you need a comic sense. Not only must you possess a spirit of fun, you must realize what is comic, what is to be laughed at, what needs to be emphasized. Sometimes humor is born from an intellectual turn of phrase. You must then project these witty lines and ideas. Often you will need to practice saying the lines in various ways until you discover the most effective manner for communicating their humor. An example of witty lines that requires pointing occurs in Wilde's *The Importance of Being Earnest* when Algernon says:

> > "I really don't see anything romantic in proposing. It is very romantic to be in love. But there is nothing romantic about a definite proposal. Why, one may be accepted. One usually is, I believe. Then the excitement is all over. The very essence of romance is uncertainty."

> Sometimes humor evolves if audience members are allowed to feel superior to the character, because that person is awkward or unnecessarily over exerts. Other humor is awakened when the audience is allowed to see things that the character does not. In *The Imaginary Invalid* the servant Toinette disguises herself as a doctor in order to treat her hypochondriac master. The situation provides audience enjoyment because they are "in the know" while the master is not.

> An audience is also amused at incongruity. When extremes exist, you must emphasize the difference between the expected and the actual. Be aware of contrasts not only in lines and character but in moods and feelings as well. An example of comic incongruity occurs in Shaw's *Androcles and the Lion*. Androcles greatly fears his wife but is unfrightened by a huge roaring lion he encounters in the forest.

> Laughter is also provoked when the audience shares similar experiences with the characters. In these instances you must get the audience to feel that "something like this has happened to me."

Objectivity —

> For playing comedy, you need objectivity. Comedy demands that you have the ability to "stand outside" of your part to a certain degree. Of course you must diligently study your character and determine that person's motivating desire so that you can think, feel, speak, and act as he or she would. Yet at the same time, you must be able to point up the humorous aspects of character and situation to the audience. This does not imply exhibitionism. Never try to show yourself clever and funny. Your duty is to bring out the author's humor.

Projection —

> You need a sense of projection. Through wise selection and emphasis, your voice

and actions should communicate the comic. For example, in high comedy the business will be small and precise, and the lines will be stressed. In broad comedy, movement will be enlarged and emphasized. Sometimes student actors worry that the audience will not be amused. Yet, if you have developed an imaginative belief in your character's actions — no matter how farfetched they are — the audience will also believe and the humor will tickle. One word here about lines. Learn them verbatim. There are no two ways of saying good lines. They require the specific rhythm and words that the playwright has labored to achieve, so keep them in their original form.

Restraint —

For playing comedy you need suitable restraint. Learn the technique of exaggerating without its being too obvious. Use suggestion. Never demand that the audience laugh, and never laugh at your own jokes. If you try too hard, the fun dies. Humor should seem easy, effervescent, and spontaneous.

Variety —

You need to use variety in your part. The same thing done over and over ceases to be funny. That which is humorous in Act I will seldom bring laughs in Act III. Vary your line delivery as well as your movement and business. Remember, employ only those touches that will project the character and add humor to the situation.

Sense of Timing —

You must possess a good sense of timing. Comic plays have a faster pace than serious plays. Of course this does not mean that you should deliver your dialogue at lightning speed. Rather, you must allow time for the audience to savor the humor. Emphasize the comic by pointing with a pause. Subordinate the less humorous lines with a faster rate. The quick pace of comedy comes not from within the lines but from a rapid pickup of cues. Usually there should be no pause between speeches. In scenes of fast-moving dialogue that build to a climax, lines should be topped. (See Chapter 15.)

If you play the comedy well, you will receive laughs. Never obviously wait for laughs, but when they come, know how to handle them. You should not talk when the audience is laughing. They will see you talking and will immediately stop chuckling. On the next funny line they will be afraid to laugh for fear of missing something. Therefore, hold for laughs. While you are waiting for the laughter to ease, maintain your position in character, or if the laugh is long, execute some applicable business. It is important that you sense how long to hold. The laugh will rise to a peak. If you speak then, the audience still won't be able to hear you. So wait until the laughter starts to drop. Then come in with your line. Do not wait until the laughter dies down completely. This has a depressing effect, for it destroys the mood and tempo. *Note: Never break character and laugh with the audience.*

If you can follow the essentials of playing comedy, you should be able to play comedy in such a way that it brings enjoyment to both you and your audience.

ASSIGNMENT AND ITS PURPOSE

This assignment will allow you to try the suggestions given previously in an original humorous scene. Work on a character until you can believe in that person. Your purpose is not to be funny yourself, but to portray a character in a comic situation.

You will be graded on your technique of communicating the comic through proper projection, variety, restraint, and timing. Remember that although you are portraying character, you must objectively emphasize the humorous elements.

HOW TO PREPARE

1. Select a situation that is humorous because of its incongruity or because it makes the audience feel superior. The following are examples:
   a. Situations of incongruity:
      (1) Prim person at an exciting horse race.
      (2) Big, muscular athlete sipping tea with retired women.
      (3) Sedate man buying women's cosmetics in an exclusive store.
      (4) Heavyset person entering a telephone booth.
      (5) Parent with four children, arms full of bundles, tries to find change for their bus ride.
      (6) Society matron tries to bait a worm on a fish hook.
   b. Situations where the audience feels superior because of character awkwardness or overexertion:
      (1) Tourist attempting to learn the hula.
      (2) Person trying to economize by doing own wallpapering.
      (3) A teenager learning how to drive a car.
      (4) A person building a bookcase and being unable to understand the do-it-yourself directions.
      (5) A bachelor attempting to thread a needle so he can sew on a button.
      (6) A grandparent trying to learn how to use a VCR.
2. Prepare a short 3 – 5 minute scene. Determine and analyze your character to achieve imaginative belief. Carefully select movement and business. If you wish, use dialogue. Work on adequately projecting the comic element, while using

sufficient restraint to make the situation believable for the moment. Be sure you communicate a spirit of fun!

3. Fill in the activity sheet for this chapter, found in the teacher's manual.

4. Rehearse your scene until you are skillfully sure of your character, movement, and dialogue. Your audience will enjoy the scene only when they can relax, confident that you are well prepared.

HOW TO PRESENT

When you are called upon, hand the activity sheet to your instructor and go to the playing area and announce your scene. Take time to get into character; then do your scene. When you are through, leave the playing area with poise.

ADDITIONAL PROJECTS ON PLAYING HUMOROUS SCENES

1. Portray to the class your most humorous experience. Be sure to show it, not tell it.

2. In groups of two or three, choose a humorous scene from either a long play or a one-act play. Prepare the scene for class presentation only after you have read the whole play. The following are play suggestions:

  a. Long Plays:

   Charley's Aunt, Thomas

   Blithe Spirit, Coward

   You Can't Take It With You, Kaufman and Hart

   Arsenic and Old Lace, Kesselring

   Life With Father, Lindsay and Crouse

   The Imaginary Invalid, Molière

   Barefoot in the Park, Simon

   No Time for Sergeants, Levin and Hyman

   Taming of the Shrew, Shakespeare

   Twelfth Night, Shakespeare

b. One-Acts:

The Boor, Chekhov

The Trysting Place, Tarkington

Dear Departed, Houghton

The Marriage Proposal, Chekhov

The Still Alarm, Kaufman

I'm a Fool, Sergel

Box and Cox, Morton

Master Pierre Patelin, Stone (trans)

Spreading the News, Gregory

3. Present a humorous, memorized 2-3 minute monologue (a long speech given by one character). Read the complete play from which the monologue is taken before preparing characterization and mood. Plays having usable humorous monologues include: *The Women*, by Boothe; *Mad Woman of Chaillot*, by Giraudoux; *The Matchmaker*, by Wilder; *Little Murders*, by Fieffer; *Everymom*, by Powell; *Send Me No Flowers*, by Barasch and Moore; *Barefoot in the Park*, by Simon; and *Star Spangled Girl*, by Simon.

"Though laughter seems like a trifle, yet it has a power perhaps more despotic than anything else, and one that is well-nigh irresistible; it often changes the tendency of the greatest affairs, as it very often dissipates hatred and anger." — *Quintilian*

Chapter 20 PLAYING SERIOUS SCENES

Time Limits: 3 – 5 minutes

Activity Sheet: Fill out the character and scene outline on the form for this chapter, found in the teacher's manual.

PROMPTINGS

1. Explain how antagonizing forces in tragedy have changed over the centuries.
3. Contrast tragedy and serious drama.
3. Describe the pitfalls to avoid in playing tragedy.
4. Explain the four basic essentials for playing serious scenes.

THEATRE LANGUAGE

Catharsis   Tragic flaw

BACKGROUND NOTES

You will recall from your study of Chapter 18, that plays which treat their subject seriously are categorized either as tragedy or serious drama. In order to enact these two types well, you must understand their essence and approach.

Tragedy evolves around an impressive personality who suffers greatly while unsuccessfully trying to cope with life. The basis of the character's conflict will depend upon the period in which the tragedy was written. The classic Greek tragedies, such as *Oedipus Rex*, *Prometheus Bound*, and *Medea*, present the tragic hero in conflict with the gods. Events happen over which the protagonist has no control; catastrophe occurs because the gods are displeased.

In Shakespearean tragedies, man is at struggle with himself. The protagonist has a "tragic flaw," a weakness of character that ultimately brings about his tragic end. Macbeth's flaw is his insatiable ambition; Hamlet's is his inability to decisively act; and Othello's is his uncontrollable jealousy.

Richard II by William Shakespeare
Utah Shakespearean Festival, Photo by John Running

Notice the costumes and scenery, with emphasis on the kneeling king.

In modern plays the protagonist is usually in conflict with the surroundings. Social conditions, environment, or heredity create defeat. There is some controversy about what constitutes modern tragedy. However, Anderson's *Winterset*, Miller's *Death of a Salesman*, and O'Neill's *Emperor Jones* are examples of what many critics would label tragedy.

Whatever causes the conflict, whether it be the gods, a person's own weakness, or the environment, the consequences are always profound. The severity of the situation is emphasized by the strength of the protagonist's character in trying to overcome the obstacles. The tragic hero, in spite of everything, is always impressive. One admires the hero's spunk, dynamic will, and finally, the ability to suffer intensely. Despite a magnitude of spirit, the tragic hero finds the obstacles insuperable. It is inevitable that there is a defeat. But in the defeat there is also triumph, as the protagonist, recognizing the error, achieves an emotional cleansing. Because of this enlightenment, the tragic ending brings a sense of elevation (catharsis) to the audience who feel reaffirmation in the majesty of the human spirit, applied not only to the play but to life in general. (It is regarding the absence of the hero's enlightenment and the lack of a subsequent catharsis that today's critics disagree about labeling modern tragedies.)

Turning to serious drama, we find that although it too has dignity, its' protagonist does not always meet catastrophic defeat. The ending is often happy or at least hopeful. The emotions are not generally as great or as deep as those found in tragedy. Also, the struggle is not as dynamic, although it must have intensity if the play is to be interesting and dramatic.

Because of the profound nature of tragedy and serious drama, an amateur actor sometimes blunders by assuming foreboding vocal tones, eloquent movement, and studied "theatrical" gestures. Or, the actor is so intent on being sincere that over-zealousness brings ridicule and laughter from the audience. Avoid these dangers by calling upon your sense of discretion and good taste in your portrayal.

Essential Acting Requirements

What basically are the acting requirements for tragedy and serious drama? There are four essentials: strong characterization, controlled emotional intensity, simplicity; and an awareness of the play's universal elements. Let us briefly discuss each of these.

Strong Characterization —

In serious and tragic plays, the characters are usually well-rounded individuals. While they are fully drawn, they often have one dominant trait that you, the actor, must project. Hamlet is indecisive; Iago is cunning; Anne Sullivan (*The Miracle Worker*) has stubborn determination; and Henry (*The Night Thoreau Spent in Jail*) is a sensitive, bold thinker. We have stated previously that the protagonist is always impressive. This is true not only because of an indomitable spirit, but because the hero has the gumption to stand up against a great force. This means that the antagonist must be played with strength, to provide adequate conflict for the hero.

Controlled Emotional Intensity —

The deep emotions that are involved in tragedy and serious drama must be portrayed with conviction and sincerity, while yet maintaining a certain dignity and poise inherent in the play. To create the emotions, you may need to employ emotional recall (Chapter 7). As you develop the character's feelings, work on achieving controlled intensity. Build up to the big emotional scenes gradually, both with your voice and body. Never completely drain yourself by giving your all, for the effect will cease to be aesthetic and will become either ugly or ludicrous. Use suggestion and maintain a reserved power. Although you may look like you're acting with abandon, in reality you should be using wise restraint.

Simplicity —

Simplicity is necessary in serious roles. It provides the strength and directness needed to complement the mood. Be selective in what you do. One well chosen movement can effectively suggest much more than a series of cluttered, inconsequential activity. In a scene in Brecht's *Mother Courage,* a character becomes extremely cold as he waits outside in the severe weather. In the notable London production the character stood for that scene. He did not blow on his hands, he did not beat his sides with his arms, nor did he do any of the cluttered cliché movements one usually associates with being cold. Instead, he seemed to make himself as small as he could by drawing himself in while still standing upright. And then he slowly, almost painfully, lifted one foot up and held it closely to his other leg. This one simple action was all that was needed to impressively suggest to the audience the character's feeling of extreme coldness. There is strength in simplicity!

Universal Elements —

When you act in serious plays, you must be aware not only of the immediate problem but of the larger implication involved. A skilled actor is able to portray the character, as well as to suggest to the audience the play's universal elements. To accomplish this, the double role of actor and character must function with great sensitivity and balance.

ASSIGNMENT AND ITS PURPOSE

What would you consider to be one of the most tragic events that could happen to someone? Dramatize your ideas in this assignment. Play the scene by yourself with dialogue and/or sub-text. If necessary, move and respond as though there are other characters sharing the scene with you.

You will be graded on the depth of your characterization, your emotional intensity, and your use of proper control and simplicity.

HOW TO PREPARE

1. Create a scene that dramatizes one of the most tragic events you feel could ever happen to an individual. Choose quickly so you can spend most of your time in preparing the scene. The following are suggestions:

   a. A brilliant scientist finds that he or she is going blind.

   b. A mother learns that her only child has been killed.

   c. A foreigner who has been granted political asylum is told that the family he left behind has been cruelly tortured because of his escape.

   d. A young woman about to be married is told that she has an incurable disease.

   e. A father is sentenced to life imprisonment for a crime he did not commit.

   f. An old man sees his whole life's work destroyed by a catastrophic earthquake.

   g. A woman with a proud family background discovers that her brother is the key figure in a crime syndicate.

   h. A seriously injured victim of a plane crash appeals for help to get out of the wreckage, but there is no one around to heed the cries.

   i. A young man is starving to death because he cannot find work and is too proud to ask friends to help him.

   j. A crippled woman, confined to a wheelchair, helplessly watches a small child drown.

   k. Your choice.

2. Analyze the character and situation; then plan a sequence of action that leads to a climax.

3. Outline your scene and character analysis on the activity sheet for this chapter, found in the teacher's manual.

4. Rehearse the scene, creating necessary movement and dialogue. When not using dialogue, employ a sub-text where you vocalize the character's thoughts.

   You may need to employ emotional recall and sensory recall to help you realize the situation. Concentrate on what your character does rather than on the emotion. Make your scene and character believable both to yourself and to your audience. Stay in character and keep in control.

HOW TO PRESENT

Hand your outline to your instructor when you are called upon. Go to the playing area and arrange the necessary furniture. Briefly announce your scene and the setting. Before playing your scene, take time to get into character. When you are finished, pause, and then return quietly to your seat.

ADDITIONAL PROJECTS ON PLAYING SERIOUS SCENES

1. Dramatize the most unhappy event in your life.

2. Improvise serious group scenes that build to a climax. Keep the scenes believable. Build slowly to the peak. Make it climactic but still maintain control. The following are scene suggestions:

   a. A group of coal miners working underground sense something is wrong. As they prepare to go up, a huge slide gradually caves in on them.

   b. A group of people on strike are demonstrating outside the management's office building. There is much complaining and unrest until in climax, they break into the building.

   c. A political speaker is heckled at an outdoor rally until all bedlam breaks loose.

   d. A ship's crew is in a raging storm at sea. The captain is trying to maintain order and save the ship.

3. Rehearse and perform group scenes from either a tragedy or a serious drama. Be sure you read the complete play before choosing, analyzing, and preparing the scene. The following are play suggestions:

   a. Long Plays:

   Macbeth, Shakespeare

   Hamlet, Shakespeare

   Julius Caesar, Shakespeare

   Romeo and Juliet, Shakespeare

   Inherit the Wind, Lawrence and Lee

   Glass Menagerie, Williams

   The Crucible, Miller

   Death of a Salesman, Miller

> *J.B.*, MacLeish
>
> *The Lark*, Anouilh

  b. One-Act Plays:

> *Where the Cross is Made*, O'Neill
>
> *The Lottery*, Duffield (Adaptor)
>
> *Trifles*, Glaspell
>
> *Riders to the Sea*, Synge
>
> *The Valiant*, Hall and Middlemas
>
> *Ile*, O'Neill
>
> *Dust of the Road*, Goodman
>
> *The Last of the Loweries*, Green

4. Present a memorized monologue (a long speech given by one character) from either a tragedy or a serious drama. Read the complete play from which the monologue is taken before preparing the characterization and creating the mood. See Unit VII, Monologues.

The Miracle Worker by William Gibson
College of Southern Idaho: Director, Laine Steel

The water pump scene.

A Midsummer Night's Dream by William Shakespeare
Wichita South High School

Various costumes help create the different characters.

UNIT V

PRODUCTION

Chapter

21 DOING STRAIGHT MAKEUP

Time Limits: 25 minutes

Activity Sheet: Fill out the makeup form on the activity sheet for this chapter, found in the teacher's manual.

PROMPTINGS

1. Discuss the five aspects that determine the type of makeup for each role.
2. Compare the four kinds of foundation.
3. Discuss the contents of a makeup kit.
4. Explain "straight" makeup.
5. Describe the procedural steps in applying straight makeup.

THEATRE LANGUAGE

Acetone	Greasepaint	Modeling
Base	Highlight	Shadow
"Character" makeup	Liner	Spirit gum
Complementary colors	Liquid latex	"Straight" makeup
Crepe hair	"Makeup morgue"	

BACKGROUND NOTES

To actors, the smell of "greasepaint" is one of the exciting preludes to performance. Ideally, actors should learn to apply their own makeup. They can then project their personal ideas of the character's facial appearance, obtaining help from the makeup crew only on elaborate or difficult jobs.

This and the following chapter will introduce you to the basic principles of makeup. If you find this area fascinating and want to learn more, study an inclusive makeup text or take a class in makeup.

Certainly you should observe faces of people around you, as well as scrutinize the untouched photographs of individuals in magazines, such as *The National Geographic* and *Time*. Make mental notes of facial characteristics, contours, and coloring. Observe portraits by such famous artists as Rembrandt, Vermeer, and Holbein for use of color, highlight, and shadow. To assist you in learning about faces, keep a "makeup morgue," or a file of picture clippings showing various people and different age groups.

Effective makeup requires good judgment and much experience. When you have learned the guiding principles, you must practice and experiment until you can skillfully and rapidly create plausible makeup of all kinds.

Influences on Makeup

Whether you are working on yourself or other actors, the type of makeup you do for each role depends on five aspects: *actor, character, play, theatre,* and *stage lighting.*

Actor —

Since every actor's face is individual, modify makeup to fit the actor's particular bone structure, eyes, and coloring. If the actor looks almost like the part being played, apply "straight" makeup. If the actor must change appearance to look like the part (older, fatter, thinner, younger), "character" makeup is applied.

Character —

The role itself provides clues to makeup. A character's age, health, occupation, personality, and attitude must be reflected in makeup. For example, a young character who plays tennis everyday should have a ruddy or tanned face to look like an athlete.

Play's Style —

The play's style also determines makeup. If the play is realistic, makeup should look natural to the audience. If the play is a fantasy, or if it is symbolic, you may use limitless imaginative makeup to heighten certain features or to obtain special effects. Unusual colors, strange eyebrows, unique wrinkles and shadings may all be part of unrealistic makeup.

Theatre Size —

The size of the theatre has a great effect on makeup. If the distance between actor and audience is slight, as in arena or thrust theatre, makeup must be subtle. When the theatre is large and the audience is 100 feet or more away from the actors, makeup must be stronger and bolder if the actor's features are to carry. Of course, it is impossible for makeup to appear the same in all parts of the house. The makeup artist compromises by obtaining an acceptable effect in the first few rows, while yet assuring reasonable projection to the back rows.

Stage Lighting, amount and color —

The makeup artist should also consider the amount of stage light. Strong lights fade facial color. If you were to stand on stage under strong light and without any makeup, you would look completely "washed out." In order to project your natural coloring to an audience, males and females alike must have a tinted foundation, some rouge, and darker eyebrows. Besides the amount of stage light, the source of light is important. Since we are used to the overhead light of the sun and to the shadows that it creates, any deviation appears strange to the audience. Therefore, when stage footlights are strong, or when side lights are used, makeup must replace the normal sun shadows.

Colored lights also affect makeup. Even though today's lighting technicians often use light pink and light lavender lamps, there is usually more yellow in stage lights than in the sun's rays. To compensate, makeup adds the necessary red tints to the complexion, cheeks, and lips. Since stage lighting varies in each show, you must check all makeup under the actual lights and experiment until you obtain the desired effect. Remember, colored lights dim similar colors on stage and completely darken complementary colors.

For example —

A red light subdues red makeup and makes green (red's complementary color) look black. Consequently, if you have red lights on stage, you'll need a heavy pink base and a rouge with a blue tint. If you have strong amber stage lights, apply rouge heavily and use a pink base, since amber "eats up" red. With blue lights the reds look purple or black, so for a blue moonlight scene use a light foundation and very little rouge. Since green light makes the face look ghastly, it is rarely used unless that effect is needed.

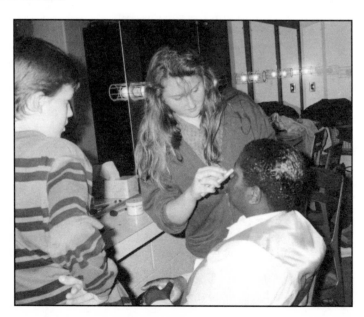

Makeup crew assists actor.
Wichita South High School

General Principles of Makeup Applications

Now that you have seen how makeup varies according to actor, character, play, theatre, and lights, let us state the two general principles of makeup application.

1. Always follow the basic lines, shadows, and highlights of the face you are making up; and then modify according to the character, play, theatre, and lights.

2. Lighten areas that you want emphasized and darken those that you want subordinated.

Makeup Necessities

You will soon learn to apply these principles, but first you must equip yourself with the proper materials.

In the United States and Canada theatrical makeup is available from Stein, Nye, Kelly, Factor, Mehron, and Leichner. All have good products and many makeup artists patronize all. However, since each manufacturer numbers colors differently, it is usually easier to buy makeup from one company so that you become acquainted with their colors and identifying numbers. See what type your local theatre carries, or order directly from a theatrical supply house or from the makeup companies.

If possible, for sanitary reasons you should have your own individual makeup kit. Many actors outfit a metal fishing box or tool chest; or you may purchase a small student makeup kit from most of the makeup companies. If your school has its own group kit, your instructor may allow you to use it for classroom practice. A word of caution. Makeup is expensive, so avoid being wasteful. Use only what is necessary and always replace lids tightly to prevent makeup from drying out.

The following list contains the essential materials and basic colors that you will need in your makeup kit. For a list of all available colors, consult the catalogs of each makeup company.

Foundation or Base —

Gives the basic color to the face, neck, and ears, and when necessary to the arms, hands, and legs. Foundation colors suggest race, physical condition, age, and environment. There are four types of base:

1. Creme makeup, in a stick or a jar, is preferred for its ease in blending and use with liners;

2. Soft greasepaint, which comes in tubes, is economical and blends well, but does require more powder touch-up than creme;

3. Pancake, which is a water base in cakes, is applied with a damp sponge, so it washes off easily; it is harder to blend and mix and to use with liners, and melts under strong lights.

4. Liquid (sometimes called body makeup) comes in bottles, and is used for covering legs and arms.

In creme and greasepaint you will want four basic colors: light, medium, dark red, and yellow brown. You can mix these in the palm of your hand to obtain many other usable shades.

Liners or Shading Colors —

Give the face a three-dimensional effect by providing shadows and highlights. The highlights or light colors advance and make areas seem larger; the dark colors or shadows recede and make areas appear smaller. Basic liners are brown, maroon, white, blue, and grey.

Rouge —

Helps to suggest age and physical condition. You will need moist rouge for applying directly on top of the base, and dry rouge for touching up after powdering. Choose medium-red in both moist and dry rouge, as well as a moist reddish-brown for men's lips.

Powder —

Sets the grease paint so that it won't smudge. Choose a shade lighter than the base, or use a neutral tone you can apply over any base.

Eyebrow pencils —

Darken eyebrows and provide eye lines. Use either medium or dark brown. Avoid black; it looks hard and artificial.

Powder Puff & Brush —

Apply powder with the puff and use the brush (a soft baby brush will work) to remove excess powder.

Lining brushes —

Use sable brushes to apply fine lines and wrinkles. Buy size 3/16 and 3/8 or 1/4 inch brushes for blending.

Cold cream & facial tissue —

Use for removing and wiping off makeup.

Additional Makeup Materials

In addition, the class should have the following materials available:

1. *Nose putty* — to make three dimensional changes in the face, such as a different nose, a scar, etc.

2. *Wool crepe hair* (for men) — to make mustaches, beards, and sideburns. Crepe hair comes in yard length braids. Purchase gray-brown, light gray, and a color to match your own hair.

3. *Liquid latex* — to mold beards so that they can be reused.

4. *Spirit gum* — fastens the beard to the face.

5. *Rubbing alcohol* or *acetone* — removes spirit gum from the face.

6. *Liquid hair whitener* or *white shoe polish* — to gray the hair and eyebrows. Apply with an old toothbrush. Whitener and most shoe polish easily wash out of the hair.

7. *Large mirror*

8. *Scissors* — for cutting crepe hair.

9. *Mascara* — to accent eyelashes.

Guidelines for Applying Straight Makeup

The purpose of "straight" makeup is to make actors more attractive or handsome by accenting their own features while overcoming any facial defects they may have, such as a face that is too long or a nose that is too short. The following is a guide for applying "straight" makeup on yourself, using a grease base:

1. *Clean your face.* Remove all street makeup with soap and water. Contrary to what you may hear, do not coat your face with cold cream if you are using grease base. Modern grease base does not work well over cold cream.

2. *Apply the base.* For "straight" makeup you'll want a color that is a shade darker than your own skin. Dab the base in a few spots on the forehead, nose, cheeks, chin, and jaw. Spread the base over your face with fingers or with a damp, silk sponge. Keep a light touch, applying the base on, not into, the skin. Blend from the center out in a smooth, even effect. Work up to the hair line, being careful not to coat the hair. Then cover your ears and entire neck with base.

    When you are through, rub a clean finger over your face. If the base comes off easily, or your finger leaves a print, you have used too much foundation and will have to wipe some off with a facial tissue. Your aim is a thin coating. A thick base looks bad and makes you perspire.

3. *Shadow and highlight the face.* This is called modeling. For "straight" makeup you will want to shadow the areas that are too prominent and highlight those areas that need emphasis.

    If your face is too wide, use a darker base on the sides. If your nose is too long, shadow the tip and highlight the ridge in a broad, short line. If your nose is too short, shadow the sides and use a narrow highlight on the ridge and over the tip. For a too prominent jaw, dust under the chin with dry rouge, using a down powder puff or a rabbit's foot. Blend so that there is no definite demarcation.

4. *Apply rouge.* Use sparingly, because rouge goes a long way. Dot the rouge in a triangle shape, usually at the highest point of each cheekbone. Blend with the

finger tips toward the eyes, temples, nose, and jaw. The color should be strongest on the cheekbone and should grow weaker as it moves away until it blends unnoticed into the base. There should not be a sharp delineation. For a healthy glow, males should carry rouge farther into the temples than females, and farther down the jaw.

5. *Accent the eyes.* To make eyes look bigger and to compensate for the distance between actor and audience, surround the eyes with shadow. The whites of the eyes will look bigger by contrast, so darken the lids with brown shading that you blend and fade out gradually. If your eyes protrude too much, try shading with violet. If they are deeply sunk, highlight the upper lids with a lighter base. After you properly shade the lids, draw a fine eye line along the roots of the lashes

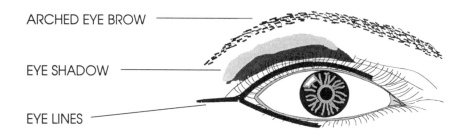

ARCHED EYE BROW

EYE SHADOW

EYE LINES

with a dark brown pencil or with a brush and brown liner. Do not use black. On the upper lid start at the corner by the nose and follow close to the lashes, extending the line about 1/4 inch beyond the outside corner. Powder immediately to prevent smearing. On the lower lids, start the line in the middle and draw it to meet the upper line at the outer corner.

Eye lines are meant to look like heavy eyelashes. They should be attractive without drawing undue attention to themselves.

6. *Accent eyebrows.* Darken eyebrows if necessary. Using a medium or dark brown pencil, apply little feathery lines, drawn in the normal direction eyebrow hairs grow. The heaviest color should be near the center, with the brows tapering at the outer end in a line that parallels the curve of the eye. Keep a soft effect. You can lower eyebrows to make a nose look shorter. Block out the natural brows with base, or rub them with a cake of wet soap. When they are dry, apply base over them and then draw the brows a little lower. To make a nose look longer, raise the eyebrows slightly.

7. *Accent the lips.* Females should use their own lipstick in a shade that matches the rouge. If their lips are an irregular shape — the lower or the upper lip too small or too full — cover them with foundation and then carefully paint and shape them with a lipstick brush. If one lip is larger than the other, use a darker

shade of lipstick on it and a lighter shade on the smaller lip. If males need to accent their lips, they can either softly outline them with a brown pencil or apply a brownish-red moist rouge that they then gently wipe off, leaving only a suggestion of color. Males should avoid accenting a cupid's bow of the upper lip.

8. *Apply powder.* Set the makeup so it won't smudge by applying powder. Be sure you are through with your makeup before you powder, as there is little you can correct once the powder is on. Pat on ample powder. Do not rub. Apply thoroughly and evenly. Then brush off excess powder with a soft baby brush. If necessary, touch up the cheeks with dry rouge. Women may wish to apply mascara to darken their eyelashes and to touch up lipstick. You may need to powder between scenes if you perspire and your makeup becomes shiny.

If you use a pancake base, instead of a creme or grease base, apply moist rouge, shadows, and highlights directly to your clean face. Apply heavily enough to show through the base. Then with a moist sponge, carefully stroke on a thin coating of pancake. Touch up your cheeks with dry rouge if necessary. Do not powder.

Always be careful of using too much makeup. You want your makeup to carry to the house without looking exaggerated. Too much is worse than too little! Apply only that which you need. Many amateurs use far too much. Be sure that the director gives final approval of your makeup before the show begins. Once your makeup is approved, leave it alone, despite what well-meaning friends or relatives say.

It is extremely "amateurish" to appear outside of the theatre while wearing stage makeup. As soon as the play is over and curtain calls are complete, remove your makeup with cold cream and facial tissue. Close your pores by splashing cold water on your face.

Some young actors believe that stage makeup will cause their face to break out. This is highly unlikely, unless they are allergic to all cosmetics. Excitement, tension, or worry about a part, however, may cause skin problems. If you clean your face before putting on makeup, and then remove the makeup immediately after performance, you should have no complexion problems from the makeup.

ASSIGNMENT AND ITS PURPOSE

Here is your opportunity to experiment with basic makeup. You are to do "straight" makeup on yourself, correcting any facial faults you may have. Apply the makeup in relation to the size of your school theatre, assuming that there is ample stage light. Work according to the procedure described in this chapter. You will be graded on the color, amount, and application of the makeup, as well as on its general appearance from the audience.

HOW TO PREPARE

Outside of class:

1. Secure a makeup kit. Your instructor will either have you buy your own student kit or allow you to use the school's group kit. In addition, you will need a large stand-up mirror and a smock or old shirt.

2. Fill out the makeup chart for yourself on the activity sheet for this chapter, found in the teacher's manual. Know what colors you should use and know what corrective makeup you need for your particular face.

3. Learn the step-by-step procedure (as described in this chapter) for applying makeup:

    a. Clean your face

    b. Apply grease base

    c. Shade and highlight

    d. Apply rouge

    e. Accent eyes and eyebrows

    f. Accent lips

    g. Apply powder

In class:

4. Prepare your desk or table for makeup by spreading papers over it and placing it near a light source. Have a large wastepaper basket handy. Lay out your makeup, including cold cream, facial tissues, and a large mirror. Don your smock to protect your clothes. Tie back your hair.

HOW TO PRESENT

Following the procedures and instructions in this chapter, do a "straight" makeup on yourself. Be careful of using too much makeup. Work quickly and quietly. You should be able to finish in twenty-five minutes if you work seriously; avoid "goofing off." (If the class is large, your instructor may wish only half the class to do makeup at a time, while the others quietly observe so that they can work well when their turn comes. Or, if time is limited, your instructor may ask you to makeup only one side of your face.)

After twenty-five minutes, time will be called. When it is your turn, hand your activity sheet to the instructor, who will look closely at your makeup for blending, rouge placement, and corrective modeling. Your teacher will then ask you to go to the lighted playing area on stage to see how your makeup carries to the audience.

As soon as your work is checked, remove all makeup and clean your face. Also, clean up your makeup table, put lids on containers, and straighten up the room.

ADDITIONAL PROJECTS ON DOING STRAIGHT MAKEUP

1. Begin a "makeup morgue" by collecting magazine pictures of various faces. Paste the clippings in a loose-leaf notebook and classify them according to age — youth, maturity, old age; characters — fictional, historical, stylized; special noses, scars; hair styles; beards and mustaches. Refer to this "morgue" when you need to get ideas for makeup.

2. Divide into pairs and apply "straight" makeup on each other.

Time Limits: 35 minutes for makeup

Activity Sheet: Fill out the makeup form on the activity sheet for this chapter, found in the teacher's manual.

PROMPTINGS

1. Explain "character" makeup.
2. Describe the general changes in facial appearance as people grow older.
3. Discuss the goals and procedures for applying old-age makeup on a young person.
4. Discuss the procedure for making a beard.
5. Explain the use of nose putty.

THEATRE LANGUAGE

Collodion   Crow's feet   Nose putty

BACKGROUND NOTES

"Character" makeup involves changing the actor's facial appearance to fit a particular role in the play. Since a person's face discloses personality, emotional experiences, age, health, and attitude, it is necessary to understand these aspects before you begin doing a particular makeup.

Intelligent observation of the faces you see in life will provide you with numerous ideas for makeup. There are many ways to disclose character. You can make the eyes, which are one of the most expressive parts of the face, appear larger. You can make them appear farther apart to suggest unfriendliness or appear sunken for an ominous or threatening attitude. You can change eyebrows to show character by raising or lowering them or by making them look thinner or bushier. The following sketches indicate a few of the eyebrows you can create.

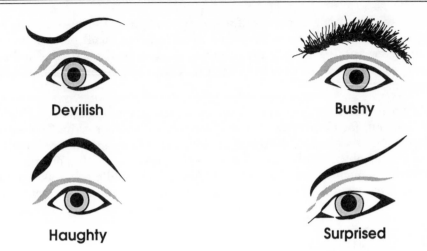

Devilish   Bushy

Haughty   Surprised

You can vary nose proportions with shadow and highlight, or with nose putty that creates a three-dimensional change such as a huge or misshapen nose or one with a big bump on it. You can alter the size of the mouth and change its expression by painting the corners up to suggest happiness or painting them down to indicate sadness, pain, or meanness (notice the comedy and tragedy masks). You can add wrinkles to show the age or the emotional experiences of the character. When using wrinkles, always accent the natural lines on the actor's face. Have the actor frown, smile, etc., and then while holding that position, outline the natural wrinkles with liner.

"Old Age" Makeup

Most "character" makeup involves changing the face to look older. From your observations you will note that as people grow old, specific changes occur. The complexion becomes more sallow or pale, the facial muscles sag, and the skin on the cheeks and neck becomes loose. Wrinkles appear, teeth may fall out, the lips usually become thinner, and the hair gets sparse and gray. In addition to these changes, the face now readily shows the type of life the person had lead. People who have been constantly cross or worried, will have more pronounced frown wrinkles in their foreheads and above their noses than will people who have been generally happy. The happy person's wrinkles will fall at the corner of the eyes and in the laugh lines that extend from the nose to the corners of the mouth.

Of course, age occurs gradually, and in your makeup you must guard against making everyone look either young or ancient. Actors playing people in their forties and fifties need different makeup from those playing people in their sixties or seventies or eighties.

To make actors look in their forties, use a more sallow base than for youth and apply darker rouge lower down on the cheeks to indicate the beginning of sagging facial muscles. Use less lipstick on women and use brown liner for the men's lips. Model subtle pouches under the eyes and wrinkle the outer eye corners (crow's feet). You may slightly gray the hair at the temples.

To make actors appear in their fifties or sixties, lighten the base and use little if any lipstick. Eye pouches should be more pronounced. Indicate facial hollows and sags with brown shading and subtly highlight them with white. Emphasize wrinkles in the forehead, around the eyes, and from the nose to the mouth. Gray the hair at the temples, with a few gray streaks elsewhere.

Old age makeup requires a pale base and a face that is shadowed and highlighted to convey the sagging facial muscles and the loose cheek and eye skin. The wrinkles that appeared in the fifties are now deep and pronounced. The eyebrows are often bushy and both they and the hair are white. Let us discuss the makeup for "thin old age" and "fat old age." You can then modify these suggestions when doing middle-age makeup. Remember, the following hints should serve only as a guide. You must vary treatment according to individual faces and characters. For example, on a thin face adapt thin old age makeup.

"Thin Old Age" Makeup

Apply makeup according to the following steps:

1. Apply a pale creme or grease base.

2. Using a maroon or brown liner, with brush or fingertips shade the:
    a. Eye sockets (these should have the heaviest shadows)
    b. Indention below cheek bones
    c. Temple hollows
    d. Side of nose
    e. Mouth corners
    f. Under jaw and chin
    g. Depressions on both sides of throat cartilage

3. Using maroon or brown liner (do not use pencil) draw wrinkles where they naturally form in the:
    a. Forehead
    b. Between the eyes
    c. Outer eye corners (called crow's feet lines)
    d. Curved smile line from nose to mouth corners
    e. Vertical lines below and above the lips

4. With white liner, highlight above all the wrinkles.

5. Using white liner, above each shadow, highlight the bones:
    a. Over the eyebrows
    b. Cheekbones
    c. Chin point

    d.   Line of lower jar

    e.   Throat cartilage

6. With your fingertips carefully blend together the edges of highlight, shadow, and base. The effect should be subtle. Avoid the stark wrinkle lines that plague many amateur jobs.

7. Thin the lips by applying foundation over them. Allow only a small thin portion of the natural lip coloring to show.

8. Whiten hair and eyebrows. Make the latter bushy by brushing them the wrong way.

9. Powder the makeup.

10. Apply the beard and mustache, if needed.

11. Make up the hands by shading the depressions with gray or brown and highlighting the bones with yellow or white.

12. Properly arrange the character's hair.

"Fat old age" Makeup

Apply makeup according to the following steps:

1. Apply a pale creme or grease base that has a pink tinge.

2. Using maroon or brownish red liner, shade crescents:

    a.   Under the eye

    b.   Under the cheekbones

    c.   Between the cheekbones and nose

    d.   On lower cheek jowls

    e.   Around the chin

    f.   At mouth corners

    g.   On throat

3. Add crow's feet and forehead wrinkles.

4. With white, highlight the wrinkles and shadows, including:

    a.   The center of each cheek

    b.   Each side of the forehead

    c.   Under the eyebrows

    d.   On the eyelids

    e.   Under each eye (for puffiness)

    f.   On top of nose

    g.   On the chin bone

    h.   Lower front of each cheek (to suggest jowls)

5. Blend edges of highlight, shadow, and base so there is no definite demarcation line.

6. Make the mouth appear larger by applying reddish-brown rouge; highlight the lower lip with a lighter color in the middle.

7. Whiten hair and brows.

8. Powder face with a powder having a pink cast.

9. Apply beard and mustache, if needed.

10. Properly arrange the character's hair.

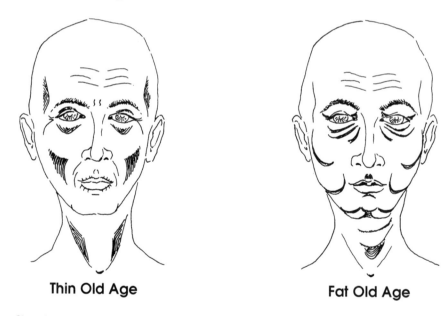

Thin Old Age   **Fat Old Age**

Shadows and wrinkles shown must be highlighted and blended well.

Beards & Mustaches

Many male characters must have beards or mustaches. Before you apply a beard, observe men who have them. You will notice that facial hair has certain boundaries and that it grows forward under the chin and downward at the sides. It is thinner where the growth starts and becomes thicker farther down on the face.

To make beards, prepare the crepe hair the day before. Unbraid the amount and colors you'll need. To straighten the kinks, dampen the hair, put it between two towels, and press it with an iron. Since beards are rarely one solid color, combine the colors needed and then comb the pressed hair.

Below is a step-by-step procedure for applying beards:

1. Be sure the face is shaved and the part to be covered is free of foundation.

2. Define the bearded area by applying the adhesive. If you want to use the beard several times, apply liquid latex. Otherwise, use spirit gum. Put on two coats, allowing each to dry.

3. Hold a small piece of crepe hair in your hand and cut the ends on the bias. Do not use too thick a piece of hair, but have it longer than the desired finished length.

4. Paint the third and last coat of adhesive just above the larynx and apply a layer of hair, sticking it out toward the front. Hold until it is dry. Latex dries quickly. If you use spirit gum, press the layered hair firmly with a towel until the adhesive is dry.

5. In this same manner, cut the hair, apply the adhesive, and work up in layers — like shingles on a roof — until the front of the chin is covered with hair pointing down.

6. In this same manner, work up in layers on each side.

7. When completed, hold the beard firmly and gently comb out any loose hairs.

8. Trim to the desired shape.

9. At the top of each beard, you may need to pencil in hairs to blend the beard's edge so that it looks natural.

10. To remove latex beards, lift up one edge and gently pull off. Powder the back of the beard so it won't stick to itself. Trim off the rough edges of the latex. When you use the beard again, attach it with spirit gum. To remove spirit gum, use rubbing alcohol or acetone.

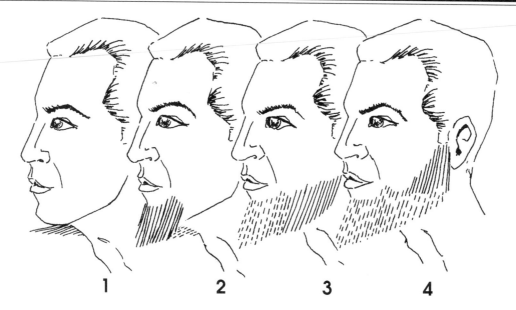

Illustrated above are the four basic steps of beard application. Each step may take several layers.

1. Cover under chin, pointing hair out.
2. Cover chin, pointing hair down.
3. Cover lower sides, pointing hair down.
4. Cover upper sides, pointing hair down.

When making a mustache, prepare the crepe hair and the face as for beards. Then:

1. With brown pencil draw the desired outline of the mustache.
2. Cover the area with liquid latex or spirit gum. Allow two or three coats.
3. Cut crepe hair on a bias.
4. Start applying the hair at the outer corner of the lip and work in several layers toward the center, following the lip line. With the scissors, hold each layer in place until dry.
5. Hold firmly and comb out loose hairs.
6. Trim. If you need to shape the ends, first apply a little spirit gum to the hair.

For an unshaven appearance stipple grey-blue liner on the face with a sponge, or cut crepe hair about 1/8 inch long and apply evenly over the area with spirit gum.

Hair, Nose Putty, & Teeth

The hair is an integral part of makeup, often providing by itself the character's credulity. Hair can be slickly combed, messy, or bouffant, and it can be parted in various ways. If necessary, females can make their hair look longer by using hair switches. If the color cannot be suitably matched, spray the hair and switch with a colored hair spray that can be washed out after the performance. Males should avoid having a haircut close to performance, for it makes them look like "skinned rabbits" from the stage. Actually, males should have a haircut three to four weeks before performance and then they should let their hair grow till after the show. Since wigs are expensive to rent and difficult to fit, avoid their use if possible. For sketches on period hair styles, see Richard Corson's *Stage Makeup*.

Nose putty can be used on any part of the face. Prepare the putty by molding it with greased fingers until it is soft and pliable. Then:

1. Clean the area to be covered.

2. Apply a coating of spirit gum.

3. Place the putty over the gum, forcing it down until it sticks.

4. Smooth out the edges until they blend into the face.

5. Cover the putty with base and any other makeup needed.

6. To remove, pull a thread tightly and run it along the area, under the putty. Save the putty for reuse.

You can use nose putty to make scars, since most scars are welts. Build up the center of the scar in an irregular shape. Smooth down the edges. Color the raised surface with gray-blue liner. If indentations instead of welts are desired, apply three or four coats of collodion directly to the skin, drying between each coat. Collodion will give a drawn, indented look. Remove collodion with acetone.

To make teeth look like they are missing, use black tooth wax. Place the wax between the teeth unless several teeth are to be blackened. Then place the wax directly over the teeth.

Stylized Makeup

In fantasies and in abstract or symbolic plays, stylized makeup is often used. Pictures and your own imagination will provide you with many makeup ideas. The following stylized types are presented only as suggestions:

Clowns —

Usually have a white base and imaginative facial shadings with red, blue, green, etc. Their mouth and nose are often large. The eyebrows are unusual and there are imaginative markings around the eyes.

Pirates —

Need a dark base with eyes heavily shadowed for a sinister look. Emphasize their cheek bones, add a scar, and black out some teeth.

Elves —

Often have turned-up noses and round open eyes. Use your imagination for eyebrows, markings, and ears.

Witches —

Need a yellow or green tint to their base. Create sunken cheeks, thin lips, pointed nose, sharp chin. Witches often have many wrinkles, scraggly hair, and few teeth.

Devils —

The devil sometimes has a red base. His features are sharp and pointed, with narrow eyes, a long thin nose, and prominent cheek bones. Blacken the eyebrows and slant them upward. You may apply a small pointed mustache and goatee.

Pierrot & Pierrette —

Have either a clown-white or pink base. Their lips are small and red with a definite cupid's bow. The eyebrows are arched and often are painted black. Use green, blue, or violet eye shadow. Pierrette has two small dots of rouge on her cheeks.

ASSIGNMENT AND ITS PURPOSE

In this assignment you will practice applying old-age makeup on a classmate. Follow the suggestions given in this chapter. You will be graded on proper use of colors; correct application of shadows, highlights, and wrinkles; and the overall effect in projecting the appearance of old age to the audience.

HOW TO PREPARE

1. Your instructor will pair you with a classmate and will assign you a day for you to apply makeup. Scrutinize your partner's face; you must modify your makeup treatment according to his or her facial structure.

2. Outside of class fill in the makeup chart on the activity sheet for this chapter, found in the teacher's manual. Know the background, age, personality, etc., of the character you are to make up. You should reveal these aspects in makeup.

3. Familiarize yourself with the proper steps for applying makeup:
    a. Apply grease base
    b. Model shadows (eyes, cheek hollows, nose, temples, etc.)
    c. Draw wrinkles (forehead, eyes, mouth, etc.)
    d. Highlight and blend the shadows and wrinkles

    e.   Adjust the lip line

    f.   Apply nose putty (if any)

    g.   Powder

    h.   Whiten brows and hair

    i.   Apply beard and mustache (if any)

    j.   Arrange hair

4. In class, prepare your makeup table, as suggested in Chapter 21.

HOW TO PRESENT

Apply makeup on your partner according to your planned chart. Work quietly and quickly. You will have thirty-five minutes to complete the old-age makeup. (If class time is short, your instructor may have you make up only one side of your partner's face.)

When the instructor calls your name, hand in your activity sheet. Your instructor will check the sheet and will closely scrutinize the makeup you have done. Then, ask your partner to stand in the lighted stage area so that the instructor can check the makeup at a distance.

Afterwards, your partner will clean his or her own face while you straighten up the table and put away the makeup.

"The teeth lie, the hair deceives, but wrinkles tell the truth." — *Spanish proverb*

ADDITIONAL PROJECTS ON DOING CHARACTER MAKEUP

1. Working with a partner, analyze a character, prepare a makeup chart, and create one of the following on each other:

    a. A forty year old person

    b. A fifty year old person

    c. A stylized character, such as: Caliban in *The Tempest*, Titania in *A Midsummer Night's Dream*, Scratch in The *Devil and Daniel Webster*, Pierrot in *Aria da Capo*, or Long John Silver in *Treasure Island*.

2. Demonstrate on a classmate the application of a beard, a mustache, or nose putty. See how many varied beards, noses, etc., the class can create.

3. Observe in life and study a makeup text on various racial characteristics. Then, divide the class into groups and do the following makeup: Oriental, Arab, Spaniard, Greek, Black, and Indian.

4. Report on special makeup techniques used in the movies and in television.

5. Create an "available materials" makeup. Choose any character you wish from storybook to real-life people. For makeup, use only the materials you have available at home other than genuine makeup. Also, avoid anything that will cause stain to the face, such as some food dyes. An example of available materials makeup is to create old age using white liquid glue as a base and potting soil as a beard. Or, an owl might be created with wheat paste and raw oatmeal on your face. The Snow Queen might effectively combine table salt, cotton, and glitter. Use your creative imagination.

Chapter
23 DRESSING IN CHARACTER

Time Limits: 5 – 7 minutes for extemporaneous oral report on costume

Activity Sheet: Fill out the costume chart on the activity sheet for this chapter, found in the teacher's manual.

PROMPTINGS

1. Describe the five basic requirements for stage costuming.

2. Explain the four factors to consider in costume design.

3. Discuss costume silhouette.

4. Tell the demands on actors of period play costumes.

5. Relate what determines whether the producing group borrows, rents, or builds costumes.

THEATRE LANGUAGE

Accessories
Anachronism (å nak´ro nizm)
Chiton (ki´ton)
Draped line
Extemporaneous

Fitted line
Hoops
Period costume
Sari (sä´re)

Silhouette
Stencil
Toga
Trim

BACKGROUND NOTES

One of the satisfying facets of acting is to don your costume while you are in complete makeup and view the externals of your character in a full-length mirror. Careful choice of costume provides the final touch for converting the actor into a stage role!

Dressing in character is no trivial matter, for costumes differ from everyday clothes. Even for a modern show your personal wardrobe may not meet the demands of the play. Fabrics, styles, and colors that are attractive in life may be unsuitable for the theatre.

Costume Design — Requirements

All stage costumes must meet certain requirements:

1. Costumes should readily reveal to the audience your character's personality, taste, age, wealth, and social position.

   In addition, your costume must enable the audience to differentiate between your attire and that of the other characters.

2. Costumes must be appropriate to the physical theatre.

   If the auditorium is small and intimate, as in arena theatre, the audience can easily see the costumes. Therefore, such attire must be carefully made with precise details and authentic material and style. In intimate productions, costumes must stand close inspection.

   Plays that are produced in large theatres make less rigid demands on dress detail. For big auditoriums, costumes are simplified and heightened for projection to the audience. Trim is slightly exaggerated and used sparingly; inexpensive, durable material is substituted for costly or fragile fabric; and while the sewing is strong and stable, the costumes do not need the "finish" required for intimate theatre.

3. Costumes should reflect the mood and style of production.

   In comedies, actors usually dress in bright colors and lightweight fabrics. In tragedies, colors are subdued to denote gloom, and fabrics are often heavy. Costumes for fantasies are generally stylized. In period plays they must conform to the fashion, line, and material used in that particular time.

4. Costumes should be unified with the whole production.

   Just one costume out of harmony with the show may ruin the whole artistic effect. Stage attire should subtly catch audience attention without distracting from the play.

5. Costumes should be acceptable to the actor who wears them.

   However, this does not allow you to be finicky and demanding. You should wear your assigned costume like a trouper. It does mean that your costume should correctly fit you, and that it should allow for the individual movements that your role requires.

   If you must do a high-kicking dance on stage, you will need a full skirt rather than a tight one. If you have a quick change, your costumes should be designed for it. For example, Rosalind in *As You Like It* must quickly change from her disguise as a boy to her usual girlish dress. Therefore, her attire must be planned with this in mind. Of course some costumes, particularly period costumes, will not be comfortable. But if they convey the desired picture and allow for the proper movement, you should wear them without complaint.

Costume Design — Line

In designing costumes, consider the line, fabric, color, and decoration. The line or silhouette projects the period of the play. A short, straight "sack" silhouette is indicative of the 1920s; a tiny waist and a bell-shaped skirt suggest the Civil War period. For stage use, line is simplified, and the basic impression is slightly exaggerated to carry to the audience. Throughout the history of costume, there evolve three main types of silhouette.

1. The *draped* line is achieved by a rectangular piece of material that falls in folds over the body and that is held by pins or gathers at the shoulders and sometimes by belts at the waist.

    In this silhouette the body outline is obscured, with attention being on the drape of the fabric. Examples are the chiton of Greece, the toga of Rome, and the sari of India.

2. In the *fitted* silhouette the material is cut and sewn to emphasize the body. Examples of a fitted line are the men's tights used in Shakespearean times, the matador costumes in Spain, and the sheath dresses of the 1950s and 1960s.

3. Many silhouettes are a *combination* of fit and drape. The fitted bodice and draped skirt of the "Empire" dress, or the bloused top and fitted tights of Elizabethan men are examples of this combination.

Besides indicating the period, line of costume and trim can be used to produce a psychological effect on the observer. Vertical lines give an actor height, and imply stateliness, dignity, and strength; horizontal lines add width and suggest calmness; diagonal or slanting lines convey action and excitement.

Costume Design — Fabric

When choosing costume fabric, you should consider price. Most schools are on a limited budget, so avoid expensive material. In all but intimate theatre you can use substitutes for costly fabric. For example, instead of brocade, use muslin stenciled with a design. To stencil, use either dye or poster paint. First apply an undercoat the same color as the fabric. Then the final painted design won't soak into the cloth and smear. Fabric substitutes for wool are burlap, monk's cloth, and terry cloth. Instead of velvet, use cotton flannel or corduroy. Unbleached muslin looks like linen at a distance. For lace collars and cuffs, use paper or plastic doilies. Observe all fabric under stage lights before purchasing or using it, to be sure that the material communicates the proper effect. Also be sure that any fabric print measures over three inches in order to be seen in the proscenium theatre. Dainty prints are ineffectual.

The weight or texture of the fabric is important because it determines how the costume will hang and move. A stately, regal robe requiring dignified vertical folds needs bulky material such as terry cloth, monk's cloth, or outing flannel. The fairies' costumes in *Midsummer Night's Dream* need lightweight material such as cheesecloth or nylon chiffon that will allow dainty, fluid motion.

Costume Design — Color

Costume colors must harmonize or contrast with each other, with the set, and with the furniture. If the costume is the same color as the background, the audience "loses" the actor. Since prints seldom carry well at a distance, solid colors are generally used. To be distinguished from the other actors, principal characters should wear the more dominant colors — either the brightest or the darkest on stage. White, red, and black should be reserved for main characters. Sometimes groups of characters are dressed in the same color with varying shades. Romeo's family may be in gradations of the same color; Juliet's family may all be dressed in shades of a different hue.

Proper choice of color will help establish the play's mood. For example, blues and greens are restful, red conveys danger or anger, black denotes tragedy, purple suggests royalty, and white is associated with purity and innocence. If you are unable to find the color you want in a certain fabric, dye the cloth. Be sure you allow for the color changes that your stage lights will produce. (See "Color Changes" in Chapter 21,)

Costume Design — Decoration

Besides line, fabric, and color, costume effectiveness is also dependent upon decoration. Decoration includes the trim (such as buttons and lace) that is part of the costume; accessories (such as hats, shoes, fans, canes) that are separate from the costume; and jewelry. All decoration must be used sparingly if it is to emphasize and project; and it must be slightly exaggerated. For instance, if it is necessary for buttons to show, use oversized ones.

Stretch your ingenuity in providing decoration. Lace, feathers, imitation jewels, and fur can often be purchased from a discount store, or can be bought inexpensively from the Salvation Army or from garage sales. Avoid wearing glitter on stage because it distracts audience attention from the other actors. Also avoid white footwear because it is too eye-catching. Men should wear dark, not bright stockings. When wearing your costume, you should remember to take off all personal jewelry such as class rings and watches, for an audience is quick to see such items. An actor who wears a watch in a classic Greek play may destroy the whole illusion because of the anachronism!

Period Costumes

Many schools present at least one play a year that demands period costumes. Such plays as: *School for Scandal, Little Women, She Stoops to Conquer, The Barretts of Wimpole Street*, and Shakespearean plays need period dress. In the theatre, period costume requires modified authenticity. This means that stage attire should be as authentic as is feasible. Some costume factors will be discarded while others will be stressed to project the familiar characteristics of that period. For instance, silhouettes may be simplified for clarity; hats and hoods may be modified so that the actor's face is visible.

When planning the costume, study the period. Understand why the fashions developed as they did, for fashion reveals manners and thoughts of the time. Only with such understanding will you be able to effectively select and modify the clothes for stage use. Remember, the costume must be easily identified with its particular period. Research in costume books, encyclopedias, old magazines, and paintings provides a storehouse of accurate information on historical clothing.

In order to obtain the proper silhouette in period costumes, you will need special undergarments. A "Gay Nineties" dress needs a corseted form for the smooth, snug bodice. Greek robes require long slips to prevent body shadows. The skirts of the middle 1800s need many crinoline petticoats to produce the shape and fullness.

Accessories for period costumes need careful selection to be appropriate for the time and to be in harmony with the outfit. Use only accessories that are necessary. There must be an acceptable reason for using each costume piece. Since shoes are important in adding period atmosphere, provide something that looks authentic. Acquire accessories such as snuff boxes, fans, and muffs early in rehearsal and practice using them.

The most memorable period costumes will be of little value unless you learn how to properly wear them. Since historic garments are so different from modern dress, you will need special training in handling them. Hoop skirts, swords, armor, trains, and headgear present problems that must be carefully worked out in rehearsal for several weeks prior to production! Since it is often impossible to use the actual costume until the week of dress rehearsal, wear a practice garment that presents the same movement problems. For example, if the women are to wear hoop skirts, they must practice in hoops, learning to sit in them by lightly lifting the hoop from behind so that the front will stay down. Women must also learn to take short, smooth steps when wearing a hoop. Males need to rehearse wearing swords, armor, plumed hats, etc., if they are to move with ease.

Costume Sources

Where do you obtain costumes? There are three sources — borrow, rent, or make them. Although family attics sometimes provide authentic period clothes which can be adapted for the proper effect, these garments are often precious and the material is fragile; therefore, it is generally inadvisable to use them. If you do borrow, handle the items with great care to avoid tearing and soiling. Any article borrowed should be returned in good condition.

Some groups rent costumes, but rental can be expensive if many garments are needed, and sometimes rental costumes do not fit properly. Rented garments must be carefully chosen to coordinate with the production's artistic design. When renting, send exact

Costume Designs For Theatre Productions, Utah Shakespearean Festival

Blithe Spirit, designer James Berton Harris '92

The Merry Wives of Windsor, designer Bill Black '92

A Midsummer Night's Dream, designer Bill Black '93

Our Town, designer Rosemary Ingham '93

Costume Designs For Theatre Productions, Utah Shakespearean Festival

King Lear, designer Colleen Muscha '92

Cyrano de Bergerac, designer Linda Melloy '92

The Royal Family, designer James Berton Harris '93

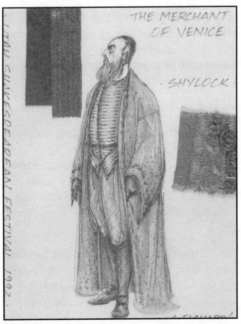

The Merchant of Venice, designer Chris Flaharty '92

measurements (including height and weight) of each actor, as well as the color, fabric, and style needed for each costume. Since you will want to rehearse in them and make necessary sewing alterations, obtain rentals at least one week before performance.

Schools that can make their own costumes and have space for storing them for future use are fortunate indeed. Then costumes can be designed to fit each production and character. Making costumes for the group is inexpensive in the long run because the garments can be easily reused with small changes. For instance, a dress with a plain fitted top and long full skirt can be used for numerous periods with slight changes. A padded roll at the hips will provide a farthingale of the Elizabethan period. A bustle and petticoats will change the dress to an 1880 style.

If your group makes its own costumes, a sewing committee is needed. Often the home economics department will assist. Sketches of each costume (including fabric, color, style) that have been approved by the director and costume chairman are given to the sewing committee. The committee then selects or creates patterns for the garments. Most costume books carry basic patterns and explain how they can be modified, or adequate patterns can sometimes be purchased in department stores. The committee takes the actor's measurements, buys the material, cuts, and sews the costume.

The sewing should be durable enough to withstand rehearsals and performance. Broad effects are desired. Except in intimate theatre, the audience cannot see the stitches, so the sewing need not be as neat and finished as for street clothes. Allow wide seams for future altering. Make skirts longer than what is required for street use, for most of the audience is below the stage floor level and skirts appear about two inches shorter than they actually are. Be sure skirt hems are even. To look attractive, the length of skirts and sleeves should cover the nearest joint or else should allow ample area above. For example, a sleeve that ends right at the elbow is less attractive than if it falls a few inches below or above. The same is true of skirt lengths in relation to knee and ankle.

Costumes should be completed at least one week before performance. Actors then have time to become accustomed to the garments and to wear off the "new" look.

Whether you borrow, rent, or make costumes, each production must have a costume committee with chairperson and crew. As soon as the play is cast, this committee assists the director with the costume design and makes a costume chart for each actor. The committee is then responsible for obtaining or making all costumes, although in the case of a modern play, the actors often assist the crew by finding their own dress. All clothing must be approved by the chairperson and director, for each costume needs to be unified with the production.

During rehearsals and performance the committee presses the costumes, helps the actors dress, makes any emergency repairs, and maintains clean dressing rooms and floors. Actors should assist the costume crew by hanging up their costumes after each use and by protecting their costumes from makeup around the collars, etc. The costume chairperson sits out front during dress rehearsals to be sure that costumes and accessories are suitable and are being worn properly.

ASSIGNMENT AND ITS PURPOSE

Costume design requires much study and experience. This assignment will initiate you into the field of costuming so that you will be better able to dress in your various roles. You are to select a character from a one-act play and design one of that person's costumes for that play. Your design should reveal the character, convey the play's mood, project to the audience, and allow for the role's required movement. Decide upon silhouette, fabric, color, and decoration. You will be graded on all of these factors. Substantiate your costume choice from the script and from library references. Plan to explain your costume choice in a 5-7 minute extemporaneous talk to the class.

HOW TO PREPARE

1. Read a one-act play from Kozelka's *Fifteen American One-Act Plays*, Cerf and Cartmell's *24 Favorite One-Act Plays*, or Zachar's *Plays and Experience*; or choose from other recommended one-acts.

2. In the play select a character you wish to costume. The following are suggestions:

   Scratch . . . . in *The Devil and Daniel Webster*

   Tessie . . . . in *The Lottery*

   Pierrot . . . . in *Aria da Capo*

   Judge Gookin . . . . in *Feathertop*

   Leonard Botal . . . in *The Man Who Married a Dumb Wife*

   Jessie . . . . in *The Trysting Place*

   Natalia . . . . in *The Marriage Proposal*

3. Plan the costume to reveal character, mood, and period. Refer to both script and library references. Determine silhouette, fabric, color, trim, and accessories. Be sure the garment will carry to the audience.

4. Fill in the costume chart on the activity sheet for this chapter, found in the teacher's manual.

5. Prepare a 5 – 7 minute oral report on the costume. This report should begin with a brief, interesting introduction; include a short description of the character's personality, age, and social status, as well as the mood and period of the play. The body of your talk should include detailed remarks about the costume you designed, telling why you chose the fabric, color, line, and decoration. You may wish to show your costume sketch to the class. Conclude with a well-planned, appropriate statement.

6. Rehearse your talk before class until you have it well in mind and can give it in an interesting, fluid way. Stay within the time limits.

HOW TO PRESENT

When your name is called, hand your activity sheet to your instructor and go to the front of the class. Pause and look at the class before you begin to speak. With poise and with a pleasant, audible voice, present your extemporaneous talk. Look directly at your audience. If you must refer to notes, do so briefly. If you show sketches (and this is a good thing to do), be sure that they are large enough for all to see. When you are through, pause, and return to your desk.

ADDITIONAL PROJECTS ON DRESSING IN CHARACTER

1. Divide the class into groups and have each group report on a specific costume period. Include the Greek, Roman, Medieval, and Renaissance periods, and the 17th, 18th, and 19th centuries. From library research explain the reason for the style, its basic characteristics and accessories. Show pictures.

2. Using sheets, demonstrate correct draping of the Greek chiton and Roman toga.

3. Report on the influence that men's fashions have had on ladies' fashions throughout the ages.

4. Prepare a chart showing the silhouettes of basic costume periods in America.

5. Report on men's shoes from Greek to modern times.

6. Dress small dolls in various period costumes.

Chapter 24 ASSUMING THE DIRECTOR'S DUTIES

Time Limits: 4 – 6 minute scene for blocking; class periods for rehearsing

Activity Sheet: Fill out the special form on the activity sheet for this chapter, found in the teacher's manual.

PROMPTINGS

1. Describe the director's purpose.
2. Relate the duties a director must meet prior to holding auditions.
3. Explain the content and purpose of a prompt book.
4. Discuss the three requirements for stage composition.
5. List and explain various ways a director creates emphasis to influence audience focus.
6. Explain how the director plots blocking.

THEATRE LANGUAGE

Aesthetic balance
Artistic
Asymmetrical balance
Blocking
Counter focus

Direct focus
Dressing the stage
Functional
Ground or floor plan

Reinforcement
Symmetrical balance
Unity
Variety

BACKGROUND NOTES

If you are to intelligently follow the director's suggestions during rehearsals, you must understand the basic aspects of directing. While directing is a course in itself that demands intensive study, this chapter, as well as Chapter 27 "Producing a Play," will give you some preliminary experiences as a director.

The director's purpose is to create living theatre out of the written script. He or she must be faithful to the playwright, coordinating all of the theatrical elements — actors, scenery, costumes, lights, sound, etc. — into a unified whole. Directors must maintain high standards, seeking excellence rather than mediocrity in the selection of the play and in the technical and interpretative aspects. Finally, they must inspire and work harmoniously with their cast and crews, guiding and encouraging them to fully use their talents.

To achieve these aims the director needs an extensive knowledge of the theatre, a vivid imagination for visualizing scenes and movement, and an enthusiasm for the work. He or she must be competent not only as an artist in creating the right touch for the play, but as an executive in organizing the rehearsal schedules and the many backstage crews.

Duties

Being responsible for the complete production, the director has much work to do before ever casting and rehearsing the show. Let us view these duties.

1. The director selects the play (See Chapter 27), sets the dates for performance, reserves the stage for rehearsal use, obtains production permission from the publishers, and orders acting copies.

2. The director thoroughly studies the play by investigating the play's background: its previous productions and what the critics have said about it. (*The Reader's Guide* and the *New York Times Index* list drama reviews.) The director studies the period of the play, learning through books, magazines, and picture albums about the people, their lives, dress, and habits. In order to decide how best to achieve the author's purpose, the director analyzes the play for theme, style, mood, form, and language. Recognizing the structure and the climaxes allows the show to be divided into rehearsal scenes or units. Generally a new scene occurs either when a new idea is approached in the dialogue, when a new character enters, when there is a change of dominance between characters, or after a climax.

    The director should understand the lines, their rhythm, meaning, and importance. Key speeches should be marked to insure their communication to the audience. The relationship of each character and the motivating desire of each must be known in order to plan purposeful movement.

    Such thorough knowledge of the script will allow the director to make the necessary changes and cuts in the play, such as: shortening long scenes; deleting distasteful words; clarifying certain lines; and combining two or three bit parts into one role. All changes should be minor and avoid obscuring the author's intent.

3. The director determines the use of each technical tool (makeup, costumes, scenery, lights, properties, publicity, sound, music) in order to achieve unification. We have already discussed the backstage elements of makeup and costumes. Following this chapter, we shall study the other production aspects.

4. The director prepares the prompt book, a three-holed loose-leaf binder. In the prompt book, the director "produces the play on paper," with complete plans of the show. The contents contain detailed descriptions and charts of all backstage elements, a ground or floor plan (a flat skeleton diagram that indicates walls, doors, windows, and furniture, and that is drawn to scale), a copy of the play, and notations of all basic movement and business. Generally each page of the script is glued onto notebook paper that has a square hole cut in the center which allows both sides of the script to be visible. Provide wide margins for writing in movement, light warnings, and entrances.

5. The director plans the blocking, or the basic movement of the actors, notating it at the proper place in the prompt book's script. Advance blocking is important because of the rehearsal time saved in having the movement organized and unified. However, the director must be versatile in allowing blocking changes if the actors evolve better ideas during rehearsal.

6. The director conducts tryouts, casting, and rehearsals. We will discuss these aspects in Chapter 27, "Producing A Play."

Blocking

Now that you have a composite view of the director's job, let us concentrate on the specific duty of blocking. This involves the movement and arrangement of the actors from one stage picture to the next. Directors generally avoid using movement suggestions printed in acting copies. These directions are usually not complete and are often intended for large stages.

A director should always block a show to fit production interpretation and stage facilities. As a novice director, you may wonder how to provide proper movement. Keep in mind that stage composition must be meaningful, functional, and artistic. These three aspects are closely related and work together, but for study purposes let us analyze each separately.

Meaningful Movement

To be meaningful to the audience, the actor's movements must carry out the plot. Juliet must swallow the sleeping potion, and Hamlet must stab Polonius, if the stories are to follow the author's intent. Meaningful movement also communicates character, showing desires, giving vent to emotions, and indicating relationships with the other characters. What a character does is often more important than what he or she says!

Movement may suggest normal, daily living such as primping in the mirror, thumbing through a magazine, or buttoning a coat. Furthermore, the character may make contact with the furniture such as leaning against a bookcase or sitting on the arm of a chair. Movement should also picture relationships by physically associating the characters. People who like each other or who have strong emotions about each other move close together, whether it be for an embrace, a fight, or a struggle. Characters who feel indifference avoid close contact. Even the way characters are grouped around furniture tells their relationship. For example, two people sitting on a sofa will establish different groupings according to whether they are lovers, people gossiping, people quarreling, or children playing.

Functional Movement — Director's Tools For Emphasis

Besides being meaningful, movement should also be functional. The audience must be allowed to see and hear the important items. Therefore, it is the director's duty to emphasize the important aspects by creating a center of interest that catches and holds audience attention. Usually the director emphasizes the actor who is speaking important lines. Or, focus is put on lines and movement that explain later actions or that show secret feelings or a change of attitude. Sometimes audience attention is focused on an inanimate object. The director achieves a center of interest in subtle ways so that the audience gives their attention effortlessly. The following are the director's tools for emphasis. (You may find it fun to study famous paintings to see how the artist uses these same methods.)

Body Position —

The more open the character's position (the more one faces the audience), the more attention received. Usually full front is the most emphatic, followed by one-quarter, profile, three-quarter, and full back. (See Chapter 8 on body positions.) A standing position is usually more dominant than a sitting position; sitting is more emphatic than lying. An erect posture generally commands more attention than a slouched posture.

Stage Areas —

The following diagram shows the relative strength of stage areas, with number one being the strongest and six the weakest. The exception to area strength occurs when a downstage character assumes a three-quarter position in order to face an upstage character who is then emphasized.

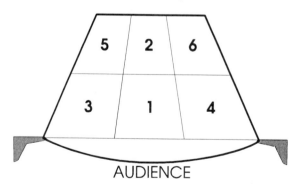

The director must choose the playing area according to the scene's importance. If it is a climactic scene, a strong area may be chosen. Or to weaken a strong action such as a gory stabbing, the director can soften the scene by playing it in a weak stage area. During the course of the play, the director should use all of the stage — the depth (up and down stage) as well as the width (right and left). Sometimes a scene is played in one area and the next scene in another area.

Some authorities point out that each stage area has an emotional value that is conducive to certain types of scenes. They relate DC to climactic scenes, where emotions explode; UC to scenes of dignity, royalty, or formality; DR to love scenes and other intimate, warm units; DL to routine business, soliloquies, or to scenes that build tension; UR to eavesdropping or foreshadowing events; and UL to horror scenes, ghosts, and unreality. *Note: The emotional value of these areas is not dogmatic and should be used with discretion.*

Levels —

The higher the level, the more attention a character receives. Not only is this because the audience can readily see raised figures, but there is also a psychological aspect of height dominating. For example, the tall person dominates the short person. Elevation can be varied by using platforms and stairs, as well as by having some figures stand, sit, and kneel.

Eye Focus —

People look where others look, so if characters A and B are looking directly at C, the audience will look at C also. This is called direct focus. To add variety, a director sometimes employs counter-focus, where A focuses on B who looks at C who looks at the speaking figure D. The audience will follow the pattern from A to B to C and finally to D.

Graphic Lines —

Graphic lines lead audience attention to the emphatic figure at either end, depending on the actor's eye focus. Straight lines are seldom used on stage because they are unnatural, except in cases of soldiers marching or people queuing for a specific reason. The director should also avoid semicircles, for they fail to allow emphasis. Unfortunately, many amateur productions are plagued with semicircle positions.

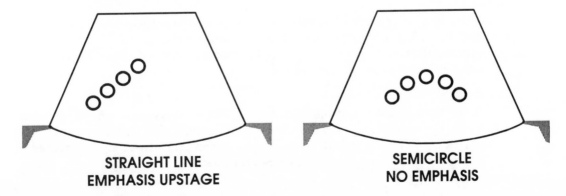

STRAIGHT LINE EMPHASIS UPSTAGE   **SEMICIRCLE NO EMPHASIS**

The most effective stage arrangement is the triangle, for the eyes of the audience travel along either side and focus on the figure at the apex. Generally the apex is upstage with the downstage characters turned in three quarter positions, as in the next diagram.

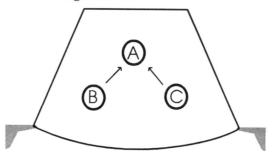

TRAINGLE — Emphasis on "A"

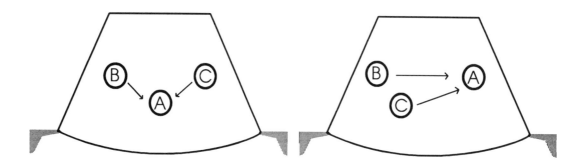

However, you may place the apex almost anywhere on stage and vary the size and angle of the triangles. Also, you may vary the heights of the characters within the triangle (standing, lying, etc.). Effective as the triangle is, avoid being obvious with it, and avoid overusing it.

Space —

A character surrounded by space draws attention because of being easily seen, and the audience wonders about the isolation from the group. The more space between the character and the group, the more emphasis. In the diagram at the top of the next page, "A" receives emphasis.

Contrast —

If one actor is different from all the rest, dominance is achieved through contrast. A person who sits and the others stand, or is in a full back position and the others are full front, or is dressed in one color and the others are all dressed in another color, will be accented through contrast.

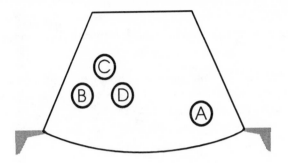

Reinforcement —

Any major figure who is reinforced or backed up by minor figures achieves attention. A business executive with three secretaries hovering behind is more emphatic than one without any secretaries. The king with his retinue, or the gang leader with thugs behind are impressive because of the reinforcement. Also, a character can be emphasized with scenery, such as being framed by an arch, a column, or a tree; or a person can be emphasized with furniture such as a high-backed chair, as illustrated in the next diagrams.

Light —

A character in a strong pool of light dominates those in a dim light.

Color —

The more brilliant the costume color, the more emphasis. Only principal characters should wear red or white, and these colors should be used with care, since they easily attract audience attention.

Speech —

The speaker dominates unless there is movement on stage.

Movement —

The moving figure achieves emphasis. Remember that forward movement is strong; retreating movement is weak. "Talky" scenes can be made more interesting if you add movement. To accent certain words in the dialogue, move before the line or phrase. Movement after the line, stresses the action, not the words. Movement during the line weakens the words, and so is often used when the lines are to be subordinated or "thrown away."

Artistic Movement

For stage movement to be artistic, it must satisfy the aesthetic desires of the spectators. The director achieves this artistry through variety, unity, and balance.

Variety —

Imaginative powers must be used to provide variety in emphasis, in the atmosphere of the scenes, in the speeches, and in the movement. The play should never be monotonous; nor should it be so constantly varied that the audience tires from the effort of watching everything.

Unity —

There must be unity in the variety of movements that the play requires. There must be a single purpose or a continuing line that links all the elements or all the scenes from start to finish. It is this unification that prevents the audience from being taken completely by surprise. The audience must always have a hunch that "something like that would happen." Unity requires careful handling; it must be neither too evident nor too complex.

Balance —

Balance is another aspect of the artistry of movement. It implies "dressing the stage" so that the elements on either side of the playing area seem to be equal. Of course it is impossible to keep the stage balanced constantly, but the director should aim at moving from one balanced picture to another.

    a. *Symmetrical balance* is achieved when there is an equal number of figures on each side of the stage, placed equidistant from the center. This composition is usually artificial and extremely formal. It is used sparingly to indicate state occasions, or church and courtroom scenes requiring formality. It is also used in certain comedies demanding stylized acting, such as *The Importance of Being Earnest.*

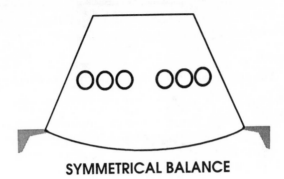

SYMMETRICAL BALANCE

b. *Asymmetrical balance* is informal, with both sides balancing in a more subtle way. The teeter-totter principle is employed here. A lighter figure on one side balances a heavier figure on the other side, if the lighter figure is farther from the center. In asymmetrical balance, the distance of the lighter figure from the side should approximately equal the distance of the opposite person from the center.

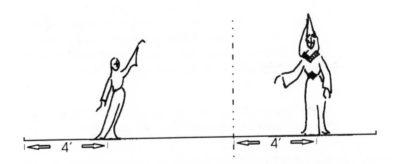

Using asymmetrical balance, a character on one side can balance a group on the other side. For example, if X balances two characters on the other side, he or she must take one step more toward the wall than would be needed for balancing just one character. For X to balance three figures, two steps closer to the side are needed. For more than three figures, X will not have to move any closer to the wall. There is a point on stage where one character can balance a large group no matter how many are in it. See the diagram at the top of page 212.

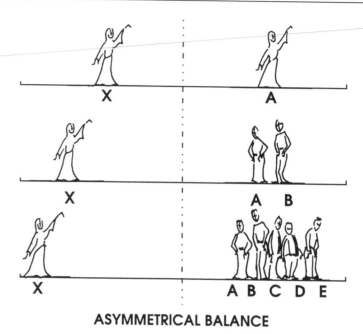

ASYMMETRICAL BALANCE

c. *Aesthetic Balance* is sometimes called psychological balance, which gives the impression of equal weight on both sides of the center, even though the actual weight is not equal. For instance, one major character in the play gives the impression of outweighing several less important characters. A standing figure gives the impression of balancing several seated people. The speaker has more weight than the listener, and a character reinforced by scenery can balance a large group on the opposite side. Strong movement and bright colors also balance large masses.

A word about scene balance: if only one stage area is used for a scene and that area is balanced, the audience will be oblivious to the rest of the empty stage.

Plotting the Blocking

Now that we have discussed the ways to make stage movement meaningful, functional, and artistic, let us see how the director plots the blocking. Before beginning blocking, he or she must draw the ground or floor plan of the set and place the furniture. Furniture grouping must provide a variety of playing areas. Keep important entrances and exits free. While there should be ample space on stage for movement, there should be enough furniture to prevent the stage from looking bare, unless that is the desired effect.

The director then goes through each scene, recording the basic crosses of each character in the margins of the prompt book. It is usually advisable to block the climactic scenes first to prevent repetition of the climax pictures in earlier, less important scenes. To work out the blocking, the director sometimes uses chessmen, buttons, or inverted golf tees for characters, moving them in various positions on a large floor plan. When a movement is effective, it is notated in the prompt book by drawing in the margin a small rough draft of the stage floor with its furniture placement. Using a different colored pencil for each character, the character's position is labeled and an arrow drawn to indicate new movement. Each move is numbered using a corresponding number notated in the script at the exact place in the dialogue where the movement is to be made.

Each director has an individual method of notation. Some use dots or crosses to indicate characters. Other use stick figures to visualize the picture. Stick figures are sometimes preferred, for the director can show characters standing or sitting, and in which direction they are facing.

Example: Blocking Notation

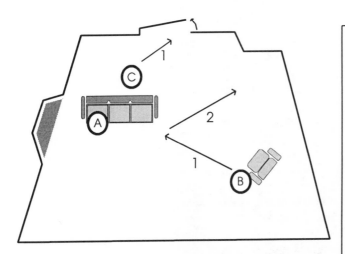

(script)

Орш кф ①хие хкое жру бнн зррд о
жру бнн зррд оеп хр грое хр хие бкд рж
хр грое хр хие бкд рж хиеку гршпхуъ. О
бкд рж хиеку грцпхуъ. Орш кф хие хкое
грцпхуъ. Орш кф хие хкое жру бнн зр
кф хие хкое жру бнн зррд оеп Фие тцкг

Орш кф хие хкое жру бнн зррд оеп хр
грое хр хие бкд рж хиеку грцпхуъ.
Орш кф хие хкое жру бнн зррд оеп хр
грое хр хие бкд рж хиеку грцпхуъ.
Орш кф хие хкое жру бнн зррд оеп
грое хр хие бкд рж хиеку
Оие тцкгм вуршп жрщ ②лц
Орш кф хие хкое жру бнн зррд
грое хр хие бкд рж хиеку
Орш кф хие хкое жру бнн
хр грое хр хие бкд рж
Оие тцкгм вуршп

(A is sitting on the sofa; B is standing by the chair; C is UR. For move #1, C exits UC and B crosses to sofa. In the dialogue where #2 is marked, B crosses UL.)

ASSIGNMENT AND ITS PURPOSE

You are to assume the director's duties by choosing and analyzing a scene and by blocking it on paper. Then following your planned blocking, you will direct classmates in the scene until the movement is believable and smoothly executed.

You will be graded on your ability to achieve meaningful, functional, and artistic movement. Your instructor will give special attention to how well your blocking creates proper emphasis, achieves variety, establishes balance, and communicates character relationships.

Tartuffe by Molière
Utah Shakespearean Festival,
Photo by John Running

Tartuffe attempts to seduce Elmire. Notice the period costume and the modified realism in the setting.

HOW TO PREPARE

1. Select a one-act play that has literary value and one that you like.

2. Quickly read and analyze the play in order to determine its theme, style, mood, form, and structure. (See Chapter 18.) Analyze the characters for motivation and relationships. Decide how these elements will affect movement.

3. Select a 4 – 6 minute scene from the play, preferably one with only two or three characters in it. Copy the scene on 8½ x 11 paper, leaving wide margins for your blocking notations. Make as many copies as there are characters, so that each of your actors will have a script from which to read.

4. On the activity sheet for this chapter, found in the teacher's manual, complete your master ground plan, using your classroom playing area for stage size. Draw the necessary furniture, doors, and windows as near to scale as you can approximate. Fill out the rest of the activity sheet.

5. Visualize the scene action; and, as you do so, block the complete scene on the margins of your script. (Do not write on the actors' scripts.) Use a small, rough floor plan, label the characters, and indicate with arrows and lines each cross you want them to make.

   Remember, the actor's movement must be motivated, simplified, and heightened. (See Chapter 9.) In addition, use your imagination and the suggestions in this chapter to provide emphasis, variety, balance, and group relationships within the stage composition.

   Include ample movement! Nothing bores an audience more than to witness a scene where the actors look like marble statues. If the scene you have chosen is "talky," break up the speeches with motivated movement.

6. Review your planned movements until you feel that you can direct your cast with confidence and poise.

HOW TO PRESENT

This assignment will take several class periods, in order to give you and each of your classmates a chance to direct your respective scenes. Each day several scenes will be rehearsed and presented. One day you will direct your planned scene; the other days you will act in a classmate's scene. Your instructor will appoint each cast. If possible, take your actors to the stage, or to an empty room where there is space to work. If there are no additional rooms available, do the best you can in a corner of the drama room. Set up makeshift furniture and provide your group with scene copies. As they read the scene aloud, direct them according to your planned blocking which you have plotted on your script.

As you direct, call each actor by the character's name. Ask the actors to write down their crosses on their script. This will enable them to reproduce the blocking accurately. If necessary, explain your reasons for wanting certain movement. While your directions should be concrete, your aim is to guide, not dictate, so be pleasant and patient.

Rehearse several times, until the actors feel sure of the movement. (Other scenes will simultaneously be in rehearsal.) When your instructor calls time, all rehearsal should stop. Then each scene will be presented individually to the class. When the instructor calls for your scene, turn in your activity sheet, set up the furniture in the playing area, briefly introduce your cast, and announce the play's title. Then join the audience, watching your scene objectively.

Your instructor may ask for constructive criticism and if necessary may provide demonstrations to show more effective movement. Accept the criticism cheerfully, for your purpose is to learn. Your instructor may also wish to check your master blocking script.

ADDITIONAL PROJECTS ON THE DIRECTOR'S DUTIES

1. Using one, big, overstuffed armchair, see how many varied groupings you can achieve with two characters. Do the same thing with a sofa or with two chairs grouped around a window.

2. Block scene "pictures" which reveal the following situations:
   a. Three people whispering
   b. Two people quarreling
   c. Four people looking for something
   d. A messenger bringing good news to a group of people
   e. Five people showing surprise
   f. Three people telling a story to four other people

3. Study famous paintings and identify the artist's use of balance and emphasis. Relate this technique to the theatre. Suggested paintings for study:

   Cezanne, *Card Players*

   De Hooch, *A Dutch Courtyard*

   Giorgione, *Adoration of the Shepherds*

   Degas, *Classe de Danse*

   da Vinci, *The Last Supper*

4. Report on the "Golden Section" and relate its principle to stage composition. (See Sievers, *Directing for the Theatre.*)

5. Create a living room setting that has a variety of usable levels.

Chapter
25 SETTING THE STAGE

Time Limits: 4 – 5 minutes for extemporaneous oral report explaining choice, style, color, line, etc., of scenery.

Activity Sheet: Fill out the special form for this chapter, found in the teacher's manual. Hand it to your instructor before giving your talk.

PROMPTINGS

1. Identify basic stage equipment.
2. List and describe the five requirements of stage scenery.
3. Explain the concerns of the scenery designer.
4. Discuss equipment used in set construction.
5. Describe the correct procedure for constructing a flat.
6. Explain correct scenery painting procedures including texturing.
7. Discuss three-dimensional pieces.
8. Relate how to combine drapes and flats for scenery.
9. Discuss placement of entrances and furniture in the set.
10. Provide a rationale for each stage and shop safety precaution.

THEATRE LANGUAGE

Acoustics
Arena theatre
Construction
Cutouts
Drop
Dutchman
Flats

Formalized
Ground plan
Ground row
Header
Practical
Raked
Screens

Scrim
Set pieces
Simplified realism
Strike
Stylization
Symbolism
Texturing

(Plus designated list of stage equipment in this chapter)

BACKGROUND NOTES

Fortunate is the school that has adequate stage facilities, for too many theatres are poorly equipped, built for the lecturer rather than for the actor. In some schools, a stage is placed at the end of a gymnasium with the results that acoustics are often bad, audience sight lines poor, and bleachers uncomfortable and noisy.

To provide maximum satisfaction for both spectator and participant, a school stage should be housed in a theatre with raked seating (floor sloping up toward the back of the house so that audience members can see over those sitting in front). The stage should offer an acting area between 30 and 35 feet wide, at least 12 feet high, and at least 15 feet deep. The stage floor should be of soft wood; then the scenery can be secured by braces screwed into the floor. There should be ample backstage space for storing and handling scenery and properties, plus space above for rigging and flying scenery. Light units, plugs, and an adequate dimming system are needed. In addition, there should be suitable dressing and makeup rooms.

If your school theatre is antiquated or poorly planned, many problems arise in producing a play and providing scenery for it. Some schools, finding that their stage is too tiny and their facilities too limited, have turned to arena theatre and do their shows "in the round." (See Chapter 28.) Other schools, while lacking the best facilities, are able to do excellent staging through imaginative use of equipment at hand. Limitations often provide challenges that are exciting and stimulating to meet!

To acquaint you with your school stage, your instructor may wish to conduct a class tour of the auditorium. On the tour, study audience sight lines to see if the complete stage can be seen from all parts of the house. Measure the acting area. Using the list below as a guide, identify the following items so that you will know what is available on your school stage.

Stage Equipment

Act or Front Curtain: curtain that masks the acting area from the audience. The front curtain is opened at the beginning of the play and closed between acts or scenes. It is usually a draw curtain that parts in the middle.

Apron: narrow acting area between the front edge of the stage and the front curtain.

Back Wall: opposite the proscenium opening. If painted white and finely spattered with colors, when lighted it is a good background for exterior sets.

Backing: flats used behind scene windows and doors to mask backstage areas from audience view.

Battens: long pipes from which curtains, lights, or flats are hung.

Borders: short curtains hung at intervals above the acting area to mask lights and scenery from the audience.

Cyclorama or *Cyc:* background curtain covering stage back and sides.

Flies: area above stage where scenery is hung out of view.

Fly Gallery: narrow platform about halfway up the backstage side wall from which the lines for flying scenery are worked. Some schools do not have a fly gallery, but work their fly lines from the backstage floor.

Gridiron or *Grid:* framework of beams above the stage; supports riggings for flying scenery.

Ground Cloth: canvas to cover floor of acting area.

Legs: Drapes hung in pairs, stage right and left, behind the tormentors to mask the backstage.

Pin Rail: rail on fly gallery or on backstage wall to which lines are pulled and tied off.

Proscenium Arch: frame for the opening.

Proscenium Opening: opening through which the audience views the play.

Right-Hand Stage: curtain pulled at stage right. Left-hand stage is when curtain is pulled at the left side.

Teaser: heavy curtain or canvas-covered wooden frame hung above the proscenium opening to adjust the height of the opening.

Tormentors: curtain or flat at each side of the proscenium opening; used to regulate the width of the opening.

Trap: opening in stage floor.

Stage Scenery Requirements

The type of scenery you use for each play will depend upon the stage facilities, the available technicians and crews, the play's budget, and the time available for making scenery. Regardless of the setting you choose, it must meet the following requirements.

1. *The setting should provide a suitable background for the play's action.* There must be adequate space for movement, including several acting areas or levels to provide variety and interest and to motivate the actors into using the whole stage in the course of the play. There must be adequate doors, windows, and

levels. Furthermore, the color of the setting should contrast with the actor's faces so that the actors will be readily seen. Busy or violent wallpaper patterns should not be used.

2. *The setting must communicate adequate information about the play.* The locale, the time and period, the cultural, social, and economical status of the characters must all be revealed in the set.

3. *The setting must suggest the play's style and mood.* From observing the scenery with its particular color and line design, the audience should immediately be able to tell when the curtain rises whether the play is comic, tragic, fantastic, realistic, etc. There are numerous types of scene design to use for establishing atmosphere.

   a. *Realism* presents a set that appears lifelike in every detail but that has been designed with artistic selectivity to create the desired mood.

   b. *Simplified realism* suggests reality through the use of simplified scenery or drapes. In this style, some factors may appear unreal, but because they are not distracting, the audience accepts them.

   c. *Symbolism* exaggerates a sign to convey an idea or mood. For example, a barren tree silhouette may symbolize evil; a huge painted wishbone may symbolize a character's hope.

   d. *Stylization* exaggerates and repeats a period motif or a decorative style. For example, the fleur-de-lis may be emphasized and repeated in scenery, costumes, and props for a frivolous French play. Stripes, circles, a Greek key design, a lotus leaf pattern, etc., may be emphasized for effect. Stylization lends itself particularly to fantasies, to musicals, and to period plays by such authors as Molière, Sheridan, Goldsmith, and Wilde.

   e. *Formalized design* sometimes termed plastic or space, uses levels, platforms, ramps, stairs, and arches against a neutral, permanent background such as drapes. Greek and Shakespearean plays adapt themselves to this design.

   f. *Constructivism* incorporates an architectural framework that allows the audience to see the basic structure of the walls and platforms. Rafters, studding, etc., are exposed, enabling the audience to view the play's action through the building skeleton.

   (These are just a few of the many scenery types. For additional information, you should study a scene design text.)

4. *The setting must be technically practical or usable.* Doors and windows must open if they are to be used. Stairs, platforms, and ramps must be built firmly, if they are to bear the actor's weight. If there are set changes, scenery must be planned for quick shifts.

5. *The setting should be aesthetically pleasing to the eye, being:*

   a. *Unified* —

In tragedies the setting may be heavy and massive, lines may be vertical, colors may be dark and somber. In comedies, the scenery may be lively and frivolous with curved lines and light colors.

   b. *Balanced* —

If there is a big fireplace on one side, there must be something on the other side to convey equal weight.

   c. *Varied* —

There should be variety provided by levels, jogs, and alcoves. Sets using flats may be situated parallel to the front stage edge, or they may be placed on a ten- to twenty-five degree slant either to the right or left. Parallel sets are basic but sometimes monotonous unless jogs or levels are added to promote interest. Slanted sets lend themselves to plays rich with action, since diagonal lines suggest movement and excitement.

   d. *Unobtrusive* —

Whatever the setting, it must be unobstrusive. Of course when the curtain opens, the audience will be aware of the set, but as the action begins, the audience should be able to forget the scenery and concentrate on the play. Any setting or mechanical device that calls attention to itself and distracts from the play is poor theatre.

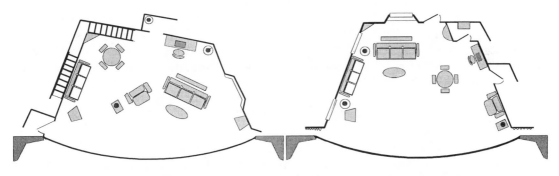

SLANTED SET   **PARALLEL SET**

While elaborate scenery is often identified with the professional theatre and is sometimes considered to be the ultimate in staging, there is a growing trend both on and off Broadway toward simplified scenery. Certainly school groups should work within the limitations of their stage and technical facilities. Most schools should aim at simplicity in their setting, whether they use flats, drapes, or a combination of both. Simplified scenery that employs suggestion can be used to great advantage, for it not only solves technical deficiencies, but it allows the audience to exercise its imagination, which is in itself a satisfying activity.

Ground Plan & Elevation Sketch

When designing scenery, the technician studies the play and consults with the director to determine the style, line, and color desired. When these elements are decided, he or she draws a ground plan if the director has not already done so. The ground or floor plan is a flat drawing of the set drawn to scale, which shows the doors, windows, walls, stairs, platforms, ramps, and furniture placement. (You draw the ground plan so that it looks like what you would see if you were suspended high above the stage and were looking down onto the floor.) The ground plan should be so specific that the stage crew can build the necessary scenery from it.

Next, the designer paints an elevation sketch that shows in color and perspective how the stage will look from the audience. This sketch and the ground plan will go into the prompt book. Many scene designers also construct a model that is an accurate miniature reproduction of the set, showing each flat, how each is joined together, the backing pieces, furniture, etc. When the ground plan, sketch, and model are complete, the scene construction and painting crews begin their work. Sets should be finished at least one week before production, allowing technicians and actors to rehearse with them several times.

Constructing Flats

With adequate equipment and knowledge and with assistance from the school's shop director, most groups work effectively with flats. These wooden frames are made from 1' x 3' white pine (grade C or better), which is a strong, straight, and lightweight wood. Most flats are twelve feet high and no wider than five feet, nine inches. Wider flats cannot be transported through doors and are hard to handle. Flats are covered with eight ounce flameproof canvas or six ounce muslin. While muslin is cheaper, it is not as durable as canvas. If you use muslin, be sure to flameproof it by using a recipe available in any stagecraft book or by obtaining a formula from your local fire department. The canvas is then glued to the flat and its surface is sized.

Basic construction techniques for a flat are as follows.

1. Cut the frame.

    a. To use a butt joint, which is the most common one used, cut the two rails the width you want the finished flat to be. Measure carefully: realize that lumber sizes are not exact to their label. For example, lumber marked 1" x 3" usually measures 3/4" x 2 5/8".

    b. Cut the two stiles the required height less the width of the two rails.

    c. Cut the toggle rails the width of the flat minus the width of the two stiles. Use one toggle rail about every five feet to be sure the frame stays the same width.

    d. Cut the keystones and corner blocks out of 1/4" plywood. Keystones are six inches long; corner blocks have eight inch legs.

2. Assemble the frame.
   a. Place the ends of the stiles against the edges of the rails.
   b. Using a squaring frame to assure square corners, over the butt joints nail the corner blocks, setting them 3/4" inside all outer edges. (This border allows two flats to be tightly placed together at right angles.)
   c. Set in the toggle rails and secure them between the stiles with keystone blocks and clout nails.
   d. Attach the two corner braces (cut approximately the length of the rail) on the same side to prevent the flat from twisting.
   e. Use mending plates and corrugated fasteners to secure every joint.
3. Fasten on the hardware.
   a. Screw in lashline cleats for connecting flats as a wall.
   b. Screw in a tie off cleat about two feet from the floor.

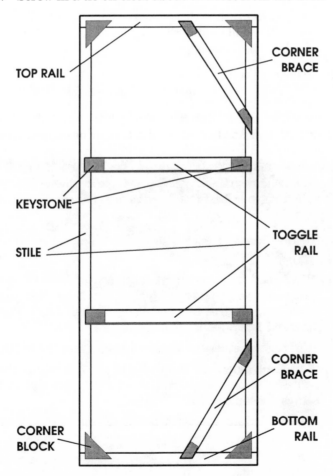

4. Cover with flame-proofed canvas or muslin.
   a. Turn the flat over so that the braces are underneath.
   b. Cut the fabric to overlap the frame size.
   c. Tack or staple every four or five inches along the stiles to hold the fabric free of wrinkles while it is being glued.
   d. Lift the fabric and glue along the sides. Then bring the muslin over the glued surface, smoothing it with a wooden block. The muslin should sag a bit because it will tighten with a coat of sizing.
   e. Repeat stapling and gluing the rails. Do not glue braces or toggle rail.
   f. Tack the outer edges, spacing tacks to fall between the staples already placed.

5. Paint the flat with sizing — a glue-water mixture that seals and stretches the muslin taut, and provides a good painting surface.

6. Trim the fabric after it dries. Use a razor knife to cut off extra fabric 1/4" from the outer edge. To avoid pulling the muslin loose when shifting flats, do not trim the cloth flush to the outer edge.

7. Attach the lashline cord.
   a. Drill a hole in the upper right corner block.
   b. Thread a 1/4" cotton sash cord through the hole and knot it.
   c. Pull the cord tight and cut it off six inches longer than the flat.

Construction of stairs for a set. Utah Shakespearean Festival:
Master Carpenter, Mike Mattheus

Uprighting Flats

If your stage floor is wooden, use an adjustable stage brace and a cleat for erecting scenery. The cleat is attached a little over half way up the flat. A stage brace is hooked through the cleat; the brace is lengthened to the floor and anchored with a stage screw. If you are not allowed to use screws on the floor, substitute a wooden three-cornered frame brace jack, weighted across the base with a sandbag or stage weight.

Stage hands will erect the flats by "walking them up." One person will secure the bottom rail with the foot. Two others will lift the top and, placing hand over hand along the stiles, will raise the flat. To lower a flat, place a foot at the bottom and let the flat "float" to the floor face down.

Applying Dutchman

After the set is put together and if it is not to be shifted, cover the joining cracks with dutchman, a four-inch wide strip of muslin. Dip the dutchman in sizing or in the scene paint and lay it over the cracks, brushing out the wrinkles. When dry, it should have a smooth stretch and blend into the painted set.

Painting Flats

Most schools now use latex paint, as it comes in many colors and covers well. If you are using old flats, begin with a priming coat that gives a uniform color to all of the flats. Next comes the base coat which will be the foundation color of your scenery.

Texturing

Finally, texture the set to add depth, shading, and interest. Texturing methods include the following:

1. *Spattering —*
   Using at least one light and one dark color, dip a four-inch brush into the paint; wipe it almost dry, then standing about four feet from the set, hit the brush handle against the heel of your free hand and let the drops of paint spatter the flats.

2. *Stippling —*
   Gently touch the flat with a crumpled rag or sponge to leave clusters of paint.

3. *Dry brushing* (used for shading and also for simulating wood)
   Lightly stroke an almost dry brush in one direction with a light and then a dark color.

4. *Rag Rolling —*
   Dip a rag in paint and roll it over the flats for a rough appearance.

5. *Stenciling* —

Out of stiffened commercial stencil paper or plywood, cut a wall paper pattern. Lay the stencil on the surface, and to prevent running and destroying the pattern, pat the paint across the holes. Lift the stencil carefully to avoid smearing.

Remember, stage scenery construction and rigging requires a special technique that combines portability with durability. To learn more detailed ways of building, painting, bracing, and moving flats, consult several stagecraft books.

Additional Scenery Choices

In addition to flats, there are set pieces that are *three-dimensional*, such as practical rocks, stairs, and ramps. *Cutouts* are small flat sections of scenery cut out in a certain shape and supported at the back by a brace. Bushes are often made from cutouts. A *ground row* is a cutout placed on the floor at the back of the stage to suggest mountains, buildings, trees, etc., seen at a distance. A *drop* is a large painted cloth fastened to battens at both top and bottom and used to represent sky or scenery. Drops are often flown to provide quick scene changes such as are needed in musical comedies and restoration plays. A *scrim* is a drop of loose weave material (such as cheese cloth or shark's tooth scrim) that is often hung mid-stage. It may be painted with dye. When lighted from the front it is opaque; the audience sees the painted design. When lighted from the back, it becomes transparent, thus allowing the audience to see dream scenes, flash backs, and supernatural elements that occur upstage of the scrim.

Draperies and Screens

Since most school stages are equipped with cyc *drapes*, many groups effectively use them instead of flats for their setting. Drapes made of dull, heavy material such a velour, lined repp, monk's cloth, or burlap hang well and do not reflect light. Black is probably the best color, although blue and grey are used. These drapes should be hung in six-foot wide strips from a traverse track that allows the curtains to be moved to various positions. The curtains should have a wide hem to provide for cleaning shrinkage and should be weighted at the bottom. Two or three borders in matching fabric should be hung from battens above the stage. There should also be additional short sections that can be hung above door and window frames.

Draperies can be combined with flats to provide an unusual and often distinctive background. Of course, you must take great care so that the two elements will fuse together well. To use door and window pieces with drapes, construct the flats as suggested and support them with stage braces or with wooden rightangle brace jacks weighted with sand bags. Since the drapes will be pulled to each side of the scenery units, hang a header (a short curtain that matches the drapes) above the window frame and a skirt of the same material below it. Doors will need only a header. Place both door and window frames over the bottom edge of the headers for a smooth line.

WINDOW WITH HEADER & SKIRT   **DOOR WITH HEADER**

Drapes can also be used with flats that are placed on the floor horizontally to connect with door, window, fireplace, bookcase, or furniture units. This arrangement gives a more concrete suggestion of a room.

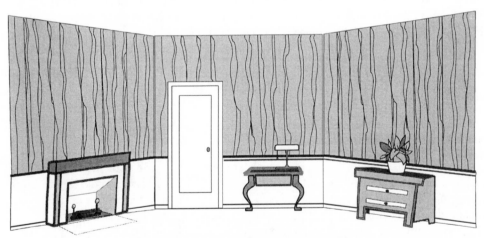

HORIZONTAL FLATS WITH DRAPES

Screens used with a drapery background are excellent simplified settings for stage and classroom use. Screens are double-faced flats having reversible hinges. Each of the two sides is painted differently. The screens can then be reversed for quick changes in plays having more than one set.

To obtain a variety of placements, you will need two twofold screens and one threefold screen. Screens should be about nine feet high, with each flat of the twofold screens being four to five feet wide. Threefold screens should be three and one half to four and one half feet wide. Some schools use only threefold screens, with the center fold measuring four feet wide and the two side folds each two feet wide, thus allowing the side pieces to meet when they are folded against the center.

Use your ingenuity to design a set of screens that will work well on your school stage and that will suggest the scenery needed. Construct the framework as you would for a flat, but use a two-inch corner brace at each corner instead of the usual corner block for flats. Cover both sides with canvas and use 7/8 inch reversible hinges on the panel edges at the top, middle, and bottom. With screens, you can also use cutouts, and door and window flats. A curtained pole placed between screens will provide curtained entrances and alcoves.

SCREEN AND DRAPE SET

Door & Window Placement

A door upstage center provides the best entrance; a side door provides the best exit. So decide which is the most important in the play and plan accordingly. Try to have more than one door. If you have two doors, avoid placing them side by side or on the same level. Staggered door placement will offer a more interesting movement pattern. Stage doors usually swing out and are hinged on the upstage side. Standard door openings are six feet eight inches high and two feet eight inches wide. Double doors are four feet wide.

If the actor must describe something he sees out of the window, place the window on a side wall so that the actor can face the audience as he looks out. Place the window on the back wall if the audience must see something through it. Windows and doors need proper backing flats to create the right illusion and to mask the backstage area.

Fireplace Placement

If a fireplace is to be used as a grouping center, place it on a downstage side wall. A fireplace on a back wall forces the actors to turn their backs to the audience.

Furniture Placement

Arrange furniture to provide acting areas both upstage and downstage. Avoid using too much furniture because actors need space to move.

Large or tall pieces of furniture should not be placed downstage of important entrances or exits. Also avoid any high pieces that will mask action occurring behind them. Large furniture is usually not placed in stage center since this is a strong acting area. Some furniture such as chairs should be situated at the downstage corners. This helps to finish the set while providing two more acting areas.

In choosing furniture, select pieces that will motivate or encourage actors to use them. Stools afford numerous groupings. Half-arm chairs, over-stuffed chairs, and straight back chairs all provide different types of movement for the imaginative actor. Sometimes actors may move chairs during the play to provide new groupings. Be sure that the furniture used reinforces the design line: columns and tall furniture provide height and a feeling of dignity; long low tables and railings add width and calmness. Small set props such as pillows, pictures, and knickknacks give the room a "lived-in" feeling.

ASSIGNMENT AND ITS PURPOSE

This project involves designing and drawing a ground plan to scale for a play. You must determine the style, color, and line needed for the play. Then, using the dimensions of your school stage and taking into account the facilities and technicians available, design a workable ground plan using either drapes, flats, or screens. Be prepared to substantiate your choice of design, set, and furniture placement in a short talk to the class.

You will be graded on the appropriate and imaginative choice of color, line, and style and on the effectiveness of the scenery and furniture placement.

HOW TO PREPARE

1. Read and analyze a play. (Your instructor may wish to assign you a play.) Determine the style, line, and color needed in the set to communicate the play's mood and locale. Decide the type of scenery (flats, drapes, screens) that lends itself to the play and to your school stage.

2. Determine the ground plan arrangement with all necessary doors, windows, furniture, platforms, and stairs. Provide unity, balance, and variety within your plan.

3. Fill in this chapter's activity sheet, found in the teacher's manual. This includes doing a drawing of the ground plan to scale (1/4 inch to equal 1 foot).

4. Prepare a 4-5 minute extemporaneous talk explaining your choice of color, line, style, and type of scenery. Tell how the set meets the five scenery requirements as listed in this chapter. If possible, prepare a large copy of the ground plan to show to the class during your talk.

5. Rehearse and time your report until you can give it in a smooth and interesting manner.

HOW TO PRESENT

When your name is called, hand both the activity and critique sheets to your instructor and walk to the front of the class. Pause and look at your audience before beginning to speak. Then present your talk as rehearsed. Remember, if you show interest and enthusiasm in what you are saying, your listeners will be interested and alert.

ADDITIONAL PROJECTS ON SETTING THE STAGE

1. Draw a colored, elevated sketch of the ground plan you drew for the previous assignment in this chapter.

2. Construct a model of a set you have designed.

3. From research, give class reports on the following:
   a. Constructing flats
   b. Covering flats
   c. Painting flats
   d. Assembling scenery
   e. Shifting scenery
   f. Constructing a practical rock, tree and/or column

4. Give a demonstration on —
   a. Making masks and properties with plastics.
   b. Using vacuum-formed plastic items for set and costume ornaments, armor, spear heads, stage jewelry, etc.

5. Using only drapes and screens, design a set that has two scene changes.

6. Choose a Shakespearean play and design a permanent set for it by using platforms, ramps, and stairs with a draped background.

7. Choose a musical, such as *Oklahoma!, West Side Story, Phantom of the Opera, Oliver,* or *Cats,* and design a backdrop for the set.

SAFETY HINTS FOR THE THEATRE

Everyone working in the theatre should be concerned about safety, for scene shops and stages abound with potential hazards. In the theatre, people work simultaneously at different jobs — sawing, nailing, painting, and moving sets. Ropes and cables are hung overhead to suspend heavy instruments, which if accidentally dropped, could cause severe injury. Often actors need to walk backstage in the dark amidst furniture, properties, and lighting cable. To prevent people from getting hurt, safety procedures must be followed.

General Safety Tips —

1. Be alert to safety — yours and others. As in defensive driving, awareness of what both you and the others are doing is crucial.

2. Know the location of fire extinguishers on stage, in the shop, and the control booth. Know how to use the extinguishers.

3. Know the location of a well equipped first-aid kit.

4. Report all injuries or potential hazards to your instructor.

5. Do not allow anyone to smoke backstage, in the shop, or in the control booth.

Shop Safety Tips —

1. Wear appropriate clothing for protection. Wear long pants, shirts, and hard-toed, hard-soled shoes. Avoid loose clothing that could get caught in power tools.

2. Tie back long hair to prevent its being caught in power tools.

3. Wear protective gear when necessary.

   a. Use dust masks when working with dust-producing materials.

   b. Wear masks that filter out fumes when working with vapor-producing materials.

   c. Wear earplugs when working around noisy equipment.

continued ...

Safety Hints ... continued

4. Always get instructions before using any tool. Each tool has its own safety regulations. Understand the warnings and obey the rules. If you don't know what you are doing, don't do it!

5. When operating tools, pay attention. Don't talk and become distracted.

6. Look for and correct any potential hazard, such as nails sticking out of boards.

7. Unplug all power tools immediately after using them.

8. Look where you are going. Keep your head up if people are working above. Also, don't work on the floor when someone is overhead on a ladder, as tools can fall.

9. Don't move a ladder with someone on it.

10. Keep the shop clean and organized with all items in their proper place.

11. Keep the shop well ventilated when dust and fumes are around.

12. Use Common Sense!

Time Limits: Your instructor will set the preparation time limit.

Activity Sheet: Fill out the light chart for this chapter, found in the teacher's manual, and hand it to your instructor when he or she calls for it.

PROMPTINGS

1. List and explain four basic requirements of stage lighting.
2. Compare Fresnels to Lekos.
3. Discuss the purpose of strip lights.
4. Explain the purpose of a light plot.
5. Explain the formula for determining wattage.
6. Describe several special lighting effects.
7. Discuss types of dimmers.
8. Compare the three types of colored light media.

THEATRE LANGUAGE

Borderlights
Color frame
Cross lighting
Dimmer
Ellipsoidal
Floodlight
Footlights

Fresnel
Gelatin
Lamp
Leko
Olivette
PAR-38; R-40
Pin connector

Roundels
Scoop
Spill
Spotlight
Stage cable
Strip lights
Swivel socket

BACKGROUND NOTES

It is a thrilling moment in the theatre. The house lights slowly dim. The audience becomes hushed. All eyes focus on the front curtain. To anxious spectators, seemingly endless seconds pass before the curtain parts and the play begins.

Interestingly, audience enjoyment of the production depends to a great extent on the show's lighting. It is important, therefore, that stage lighting meets four basic requirements:

1. Provide visibility

2. Establish emphasis

3. Create mood

4. Suggest light source

Lighting Requirements — Visibility & Emphasis

Comfortable visibility in the theatre is the prime requisite for stage lighting. Since too much light glares and too much darkness strains, light intensity must be carefully balanced to allow the audience to see what they are supposed to see without being unduly aware of the lights. Lighting, like all other technical aspects, must reinforce the play by being a unified part of the whole production. Lighting must not call attention to itself.

Closely allied to visibility is emphasis. Bright lights dominate and dim lights subordinate, so stage areas that carry the most important action need somewhat brighter and more dramatic lighting than the less important areas.

To provide visibility and to establish emphasis, we use spotlights, for they produce the necessary concentrated illumination. Spotlights contain a lamp (incandescent or the new, more efficient, longer-lasting tungsten-halogen bulb), a lens that focuses the light rays, a reflector, and a housing unit. Today, there are two basic types of spotlights. The Fresnel, a highly efficient light, has a step-like Fresnel lens, a T-type (tubular) lamp, and a spherical mirror. Beams from the Fresnel cast a diffused or soft-edged light pool that makes blending easy.

FRESNEL   *Photo Courtesy of Strand Lighting*

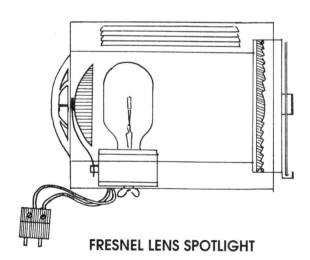

FRESNEL LENS SPOTLIGHT

The second type spotlight is called the Ellipsoidal Reflector or Leko light. It contains a plano-convex lens, a T-type lamp that burns base up, and an ellipsoidal reflector. These spots are excellent for long throws since their beam is strong and can be focused with such precision that there is no "spill" or unwanted light leakage. Their beam can also be made narrow or wide and will provide either a harsh or soft edge.

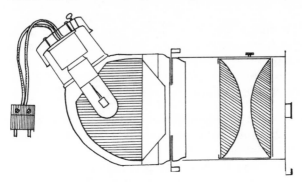

ELLIPSOIDAL REFLECTOR SPOTLIGHT

ELLIPSOIDAL REFLECTOR
Photo Courtesy of Strand Lighting

Spotlights must be properly positioned if they are to provide adequate visibility and emphasis. Because of their capacity for long throws of light, place Lekos out front either on beams in the auditorium ceiling or on stands in the balcony. Large stages need 1,000-watt Lekos, but smaller stages use 500-watt lights. Carefully focus Lekos to light the downstage areas and to prevent spill onto the audience or the proscenium arch. Light upstage areas with 500-watt Fresnels secured to the teaser batten with pipe clamps. If your school does not have a teaser batten, you can provide one by mounting vertical pipes on each side of the inner proscenium opening and attaching a horizontal pipe to them, positioning it directly behind the teaser curtain.

To prevent the actor's face from being in shadow, cross light each stage area with two spots, each placed on opposite sides of the stage or theatre at a 45-degree angle to the acting area and beamed down onto the area at a 45-degree angle. In focusing spots, stand an actor in each area and aim the center of the light pool on the face. Do not aim at the floor or the scenery. The set gets ample light from spill.

To enhance the natural shadows and highlights achieved by this 45-degree lighting, the spots on one side should have a warmer color than those on the opposite side. For example, if the spots on stage right are warm light pink, those on stage left may be a cool pale lavender. The actor's face will then have a three-dimensional appearance, as this color arrangement subtly provides highlights on the warm side and shadows on the cool side.

In the diagram labeled "Partial Light Plot," found on page 245, notice the basic light placement for downstage and upstage areas. Also notice that the beams of all the lights overlap. This prevents having "dead" places on stage where there is no light on the actor's face.

Lighting Requirement — Mood

To achieve the third lighting requirement, proper mood, you must blend together the spot pools by using border or strip lights and floodlights. These units provide general illumination: they tone the spotted areas without changing the contrast or emphasis provided by the specific spotlighting.

Border or strip lights are placed parallel to the front curtain and are hung from chains attached to overhead battens. Strips have either six or eight compartments with individual reflectors for each light, or they have compartments that take twelve PAR-38 or R-40 reflector floods. While some school stages have numerous border strips, only two are

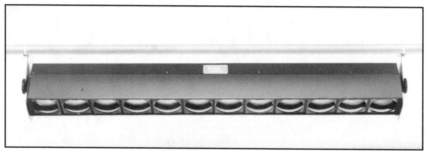

STRIP LIGHT FOR USE WITH R-40 OR PAR-38 LAMPS
Photo Courtesy of Strand Lighting

necessary. There should be a teaser unit of six or more compartments hung immediately upstage of the teaser curtain. It is generally placed in the center of the teaser batten with spots filling out the rest of the batten on both sides. The second border strip should be placed upstage to light and tone the top of the backdrop. These borders should be wired to three alternating circuits for red, blue, and green or amber coloring. A third and portable border is often used as a horizon strip to light the bottom of the sky drop. The horizon strip, placed on the floor about three and one-half feet downstage of the drop, is mounted on a wagon for easy movement off and on stage.

Floodlights are large lamps — 500 to 1,000 watts — that are mounted in an open-faced housing. Floodlights differ from spots in that they have no lens. They give a soft, widely diffused light that is good for lighting door and window backings and back drops. Called a scoop flood, this light has an ellipsoidal reflector and is equipped with a yoke for hanging the unit from battens with a pipe clamp.

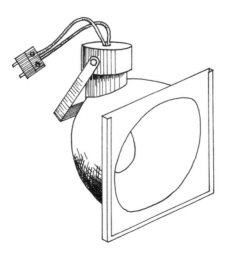

SCOOP FLOODLIGHT

Remember, the way you blend borders and floods depends upon the play's mood. For example, the more intense the conflict or emotion, the greater the contrast between specific and general illumination. If the play is a comedy, mix bright lights in predominantly warm colors. If the play is a tragedy or serious drama, blending should create a medium to low tone, throwing shadows and casting cool colors. Of course, lights should never be so dim as to prevent visibility. If a scene is to be played in relative darkness, start with dim lights to set the mood and then gradually sneak them up until the audience can see the action.

Lighting Requirement — "Logical" Light Sources

The last lighting principle applies only to realistic plays. It requires that you suggest to the audience the obvious source of the light such as the sun, moon, table lamps, candles, and fireplaces. By suggesting the source, you often can imply the time of day and the weather conditions. A cool daylight blue of low intensity apparently coming in through a window may suggest early morning. A bright warm amber light streaming in through French doors may indicate late afternoon on a warm, sunny day. (In nonrealistic plays it is not necessary for lighting to come from a logical source, so the lighting effects may be highly theatrical and imaginative.)

By using special effect lighting, you are able to suggest light source on stage. Special effects, of course, require much experimentation if they are to appear convincing. Try the following techniques; then consult a lighting text for additional hints.

Burning logs. The suggestion of burning logs can be made by placing an amber or orange light at the back of the logs. Attach a small, tin windmill in front of the light. The hot air rising from the lamp will turn the windmill and provide the necessary fire flicker. Or, you may achieve the burning log effect by screwing different colored lamps into flicker sockets (often used for Christmas tree lights) that are attached to a board and placed on the floor behind the logs. A small orange or amber flood will provide a warm glow while the lights give off a flicker.

Burning coals. To simulate burning coals, place small pieces of broken, amber colored glass or crumpled orange and red gelatin over an amber lamp placed in the bottom of the grate.

Lighted floor lamps & table lamps. On stage, all floor and table lamps should only use small wattage globes. The actual light should come from stage spots focused on the area.

Flash pot. A flash pot can be easily made by scraping out the plastic window in an ordinary low amperage household fuse, being careful not to damage the fuse wire. Fill the resulting hole with approximately 1/4 teaspoon of fine flash power. *Note: Do not tamp it down, as this could cause an explosion that could harm the technician.*

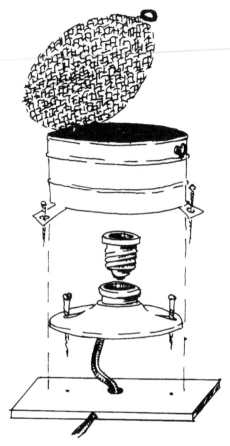

FLASH POT WITH SCREEN

Then screw the fuse into an outlet, such as a porcelain ceiling outlet mounted on a board. Place a 1/8-inch mesh metal window screen cover over the unit. When the outlet is turned on (or plugged in) the electric current will ignite the gunpowder and provide a loud flash and explosion so necessary in many plays dealing with magical or supernatural elements. Be sure you handle flash devices carefully, as they can be dangerous. *Note: Never place them where they may set fire to fabric or scenery. Always unplug the outlet before loading the fuse.*

Smoke. The effect of smoke can be achieved by placing dry ice in water — the hotter the water, the faster the smoke effect. Since this heavy gas falls quickly to the floor, you can help it rise by using a large container that has a small opening. With hot water, the gas will be quickly pushed through the narrow neck, escaping upward with force.

Lighting Connectors & Control Board

Now that we have seen how to satisfy the four stage lighting requirements, let us discuss how to connect stage lights properly. Lights are connected to the electric current by special stage connectors and cable. Some schools use twist lock connectors that provide a safe connection without having to worry about their being accidently pulled apart. Other groups prefer the more expensive pin connectors. While pin connectors must be tied with an overhand knot to insure their staying together, they are more durable than twist locks. In many states, new electrical codes require that schools use a grounded plug for all connections whether it be twist lock, pin connectors, or regular household two-blade plugs.

Always use heavy three-conductor grade cable for theatrical lighting, as it is equipped to carry a larger load than is ordinary household cord. Schools should use either #14-gauge cable that carries 15 amperes or #12 gauge that carries 20 amperes. Never use household cable on stage, as it is a fire hazard. In connecting lights be sure you do not overload the circuit. Wires will take only a certain amount of wattage. To determine how many watts your stage cable will carry, apply the formula $W=VA$, or # of watts equals # of volts multiplied by # of amperes. For example, if you are using #14 stage cable that carries 15 amperes, and if your current is 110 volts (with which most stages and homes are equipped) multiply the figures together, and you will find that cable #14 will safely carry 1,650 watts. Number 12 cable will safely carry 2,200 watts under the same conditions. Stage cable either plugs into electrical outlets on the walls or floors, or it plugs directly into the control board.

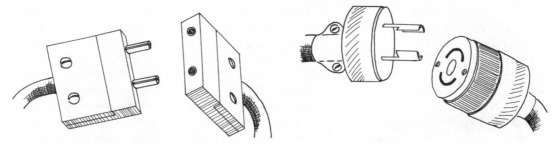

PIN CONNECTORS   **TWIST LOCK CONNECTORS**

The control board, if properly wired, contains individual switches for the various lights and circuit borders, and a master switch that turns off all of the lights for a blackout or for making repairs. The control board also contains the dimmers by which light intensity can be varied. If possible, all lights should be connected to dimmers so that their brightness can be changed. There are two basic types of dimmers: mechanical control (such as auto transformers), and the electronic control, where the load is regulated by low-voltage current. Electronic systems have remote control with preset scene devices and solid state components. The more sophisticated electronic dimmer is one with a computer-assisted memory. Portable units can be operated from any part of the theatre.

Basic Equipment

When you are to light a play, what equipment will you need? Ideally, you should have at least ten Fresnels for the lights on the teaser, six Ellipsoidal reflectors for auditorium spots, two floods, two strip lights (one teaser strip and one strip for lighting the back drop), and an adequate dimming system. Realistically, few schools have adequate lighting equipment. If some money is available each year for purchasing supplies, instead of buying small spotlights, save the money and eventually purchase Leko lights and Fresnels. When your drama department has a limited budget, you can make adequate spotlights or floods for mounting on the teaser. Purchase either the 150-watt PAR-38 (PAR stands for parabolic reflector) or R-40 (R stands for reflector) spots or floods.

LIGHTING CONTROL BOARD
Photo Courtesy of Strand Lighting

While PAR-38 spots are somewhat more expensive than R-40s, they provide more vivid illumination because of their parabolic reflector. PARs can also be safely used outside. However, the 150-watt R-40 is a popular choice for indoor use. (These are the lamps used in department store display windows). Both the PAR and R spots contain a built-in lens, reflector, and diffusing element. Of course, the light beam cannot be adjusted, but this limitation can be overlooked since these spots are most efficient and very inexpensive.

Whether you use PARs or Rs, screw them into clamp-on swivel sockets that you can mount on a batten. (You can obtain swivel sockets that screw into standard light sockets, if you need this type.) Swivel sockets make it possible to adjust the lamps to any angle.

Reflector spots and floods are now available in several colors, or you can use a clear lamp and attach spring tension holders that house special glass color filters. For greater color versatility, buy clear lamps and make frames for holding gelatin or plastic (special color media in transparent sheets).

LIGHTBOARD REMOTE
*Photo Courtesy of
Strand Lighting*

Cut each frame from large tin cans or from sheet aluminum available at the lumber yard or at a sheet metal shop. Fold the frame double, place the gelatin between the frames, and attach them together with brads at the top. Then wire the frame to the socket with coat hanger wire, allowing adequate ventilation between lamp and gelatin. Without proper ventilation, the heat generated by the lamps will burn out the color media.

If you do not wish to buy, make, and assemble these separate parts, you can purchase a complete unit for use with PARs and Rs that consists of a clamp-on swivel socket, an attached color holder for glass color filters, and a six-foot cord with plug. This is called an "air-cooled hanging swivel clamp unit" and is obtainable through theatre supply houses. If desired, spill-proof louvers can be purchased to fit over the color holder. While this "air cooled" unit is more expensive than a "do it yourself" unit, it is time saving, handy, and complete. Another choice is to purchase PAR-Cans from a lighting supply house. These cans have an attached yoke for hanging and will house a PAR 64 (a 1,000-watt lamp about eight inches wide). The beam is powerful, yet it has a soft edge.

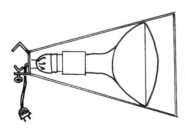

**DO-IT-YOURSELF
SPOT**

**SCREW-IN
SWIVEL SOCKET**

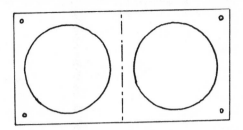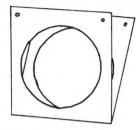

CUT-OUT COLOR FRAME

Colored Light — gelatins, plastics, & glass

To provide colored light on stage, three media are used: gelatins, plastics, and glass. Glass, called roundels, are colored discs used in some strip lights. With the exception of the glass color filters designated for PARs and Rs, roundels are not used for specific stage lighting because their intense color lowers illumination and makes blending difficult. Moreover, roundels come in a somewhat limited color range. For specific stage lighting, use gelatins or plastics — transparent sheets of color placed in a color frame that mounts in front of spotlights and floods. Gelatin is widely used because it comes in a variety of colors and is relatively inexpensive. It must be replaced frequently, however, since it becomes brittle and fades with use. Plastic costs more than gelatin, but it is much more durable and does not fade as quickly. In the long run, plastic is probably cheaper to use than gelatin. Both gelatin and plastic can be purchased in a wide range of colors from most theatrical or lighting supply houses. *Note: Never use cellophane over lights as it is highly flammable.*

Lighting Colors

Your choice of lighting colors will depend on the mood of the play, the time of day, the season, and the apparent light source. However, strip lights usually have a standard color combination with red, blue, and amber or green lights. When amber and blue are mixed, an almost white light is produced. It is generally best to use pale tints on the area spotlights. Pale tints won't drastically change costume and makeup colors, and they allow the most efficient showing of the light produced.

You will want to experiment with colors until you obtain the desired effect. As you experiment, you may wish to try the following combinations to see how they look with the scenery and costumes. (Write to theatre supply houses for sample color choices.)

General daylight:
        warm side — light scarlet
        cool side — frost

Morning light:
        warm side — light straw
        cool side — light blue

Late afternoon light:
        warm side — light amber
        cool side — daylight blue

Artificial light:
        warm side — light scarlet
        cool side — special lavender or light sky blue

Moonlight:
        warm side — steel blue
        cool side — frost

Lighting Plots, Charts, & Cue Sheets

If you are a member of the light crew, you should be familiar with the script in order to know the play's mood, the setting, the time of day, the season, weather, and any special effects needed. Then consult with the director and view the floor plan to ascertain the number and location of doors and windows, the light sources, such as a fireplace or table lamps, and the color of scenery and costumes. Next, determine the light plot by tracing over the ground plan of the setting and imposing on your copy the position of each light you are going to use for each scene. Number each light and indicate its color. Show all the light units, including foots, strips, spots, backing lights, and special lighting effects. Also, indicate the throw of the spot beams.

You should then make a light chart or instrument schedule, listing each light, its number, type, watt, color, and dimmer connection. Next, prepare a light cue sheet that tells the light reading and the changes needed at exact places in the script. On the next page are examples of a light chart and cue sheet that would be used by the light crews and that would appear in the prompt book.

Mount and connect lights for the play at least ten days before performance. Work when the stage is not in use. At least a week before production, your director will call a special light session for the purpose of focusing and setting lights and running through light changes. Be sure that all connections are securely fastened, that circuits are not overloaded, and that lights do not shine in the eyes of the audience. If you get unwanted shadows on the back wall, lower the brightness of the border strips.

During the week of dress rehearsal, use complete stage lighting and carefully rehearse all cues so that action and lights are synchronized. Nothing is more ludicrous than to have an actor supposedly turn off all the lights, only to have them remain on several seconds after the hand leaves the switch. To prevent such slips, a member of the light crew should be situated backstage where the action can be seen. Rehearse such light cues many times. Remember, when using dimmers, slowly provide the light changes; the audience should not be aware of the different intensity. *Note: Only designated light crew members should handle the lights and the control board. Never touch the board unless you are supposed to! Lighting equipment is expensive and should be handled only by experienced light people.*

INSTRUMENT SCHEDULE

Example: Instrument Schedule

Number	Instrument Type	Wattage	Color	Dimmer
T1	FRESNEL	500	#4 PINK	A4
T2	"	"	"	A7
T3	"	"	"	A5
T4	"	"	#17 LAU	A3
T5	"	"	"	A2
T6	"	"	"	A1
C1	ELLIPSOIDAL SPOT	1000	FROST	B1
C2	"	"	"	B2
C3	"	"	"	
C4				

CUE SHEET   Act 1 Scene I

Example: Cue Sheet

CUE 1   House Lights Full

CUE 2   Stage Lights — Or
         C1 & C4 — full
         C2 & C5 — full
         C3 & C6 — up 2/3
         Teaser Spots — full
         Border — up 2/3

CUE 3   Slowly dim house

CUE 4   Foots — up 2/3

CUE 5   HARRY " I'M TIRED "
         teasers on dimmers 4 & 7 — dim ½

CUE 6

ASSIGNMENT AND ITS PURPOSE

In this project you are to assume the initial duties of a lighting chairperson, by planning a light plot for a designated play. Employ your school's light equipment and any additional homemade spots that you wish to indicate. You will be graded on your ingenuity in making the best use of the available equipment, on the proper placement of lights for their maximum use, and on the extent that your light plot meets the four requirements of stage lighting as discussed in this chapter.

HOW TO PREPARE

1. Choose a play and make a ground plan of the set, or use the play and ground plan you employed in the previous chapter's assignment.

2. Using your school's lighting equipment and any additional homemade spots, plan your light plot. Decide the position of each light, its identifying number, its color, and its beam throw. Indicate footlights, strip lights, spots, floods, backing lights, and special lighting effects. Provide cross beams at approximately 45-degree angles. Be sure the important acting areas are well lighted. Choose colors that will establish the proper mood, light source, weather, time of day, and visibility. Provide highlighting and shadows with warm colors on one side and cool colors on the other.

3. Fill out the activity sheet for this chapter, found in the teacher's manual, and draw a ground plan as skeleton for your light plot. Draw in all the units you planned in Step #2. Be sure you show each light, its number, and color.

   For example, you may number your lights by the abbreviation C1 — standing for ceiling spot number one; T1 — signifying teaser spot number one, etc. Indicate the spot beams and be sure they overlap. Provide lighting for the complete play, including special effect lighting.

HOW TO PRESENT

In this assignment there will be no oral activity. When your instructor calls for your completed activity sheet, hand it in. It will be checked and returned to you at a later date.

PARTIAL LIGHT PLOT

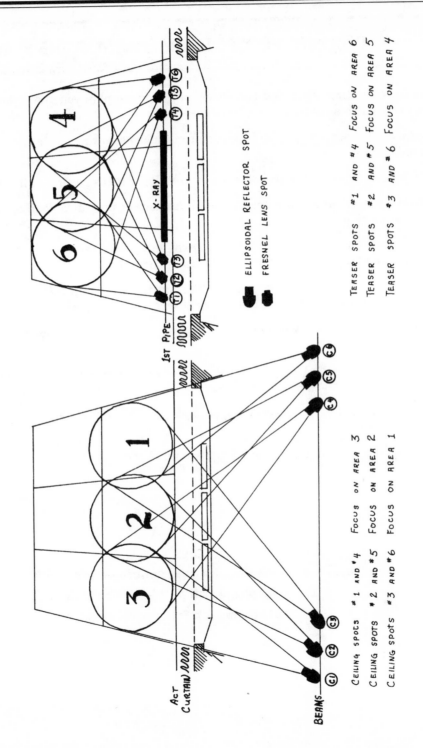

ELLIPSOIDAL REFLECTOR SPOT

FRESNEL LENS SPOT

X-RAY

1ST PIPE

ACT CURTAIN

BEAMS

TEASER SPOTS #1 AND #4 FOCUS ON AREA 6
TEASER SPOTS #2 AND #5 FOCUS ON AREA 5
TEASER SPOTS #3 AND #6 FOCUS ON AREA 4

CEILING SPOTS #1 AND #4 FOCUS ON AREA 3
CEILING SPOTS #2 AND #5 FOCUS ON AREA 2
CEILING SPOTS #3 AND #6 FOCUS ON AREA 1

ADDITIONAL PROJECTS ON LIGHTING THE STAGE

1. Make a lighting chart and cue sheet for the same play you chose for the assigned activity for this chapter.

2. Give class reports on special lighting effects such as how to obtain lightning, flames, a rainbow.

3. Make spotlights for the school stage from PARs or Rs as suggested in this chapter.

4. Wire a special sound board with push buttons that provide a doorbell, a door chime, and a telephone bell.

5. Report on the principles of electricity, explaining such terms as watt, ampere, volts, fuse, circuit, direct current, and alternating current.

6. Report on and show sketches of the different types of lamps: G, T, PS, etc.; and the different styles of lamp bases: screw, prefocus, mogul, bi-post, etc.

7. Discuss the different types of reflectors: parabolic, ellipsoidal, spherical. Show sketches of each type.

8. Report on tungsten-halogen (quartz) stage lamps, comparing their features and advantages to incandescent stage lamps.

9. Discuss use of lighting accessories, such as barn doors, funnels, and gobos. (See *Glossary*)

10. Demonstrate the effect of colored lights on different colored costumes and fabric textures.

"Photos used in this Chapter are courtesy of Strand Lighting
A company within the Film and Television Division of
The Rank Organisation PLC, United Kingdom"

LIGHTING SAFETY TIPS

1. Know the number and wattage of lighting instruments plugged into a circuit before turning it on.

2. Disconnect a plug by pulling the connector body — not the cord.

3. Check cables periodically and replace any that are worn.

4. Store cables by hanging them in a neat coil in the storage room.

5. When replacing tungsten-halogen lamps, use gloves and handle carefully. Grease or fingerprints on the lamp could cause it to explode when it reaches a high temperature.

Chapter
27 PRODUCING A PLAY

Time Limits: 4 weeks rehearsal in class

Activity Sheet: Fill out the top of the activity sheet at the end of this chapter, found in the teacher's manual. Hand it to your instructor when he or she calls for it.

PROMPTINGS

1. Describe the criteria a director should use in script selection.
2. Explain the director's pre-audition duties.
3. Discuss qualities a director considers when casting.
4. List and describe the types and duties of backstage crews.
5. List in order the six kinds of rehearsal units and discuss the object of each.
6. Defend the list of theatre courtesies for cast and crew.

THEATRE LANGUAGE

Audition	Double casting	Prompter
Blocking rehearsal	Dress rehearsals	Royalties
Business manager	House manager	Stage manager
Callbacks	Pages	Tryouts
Developing rehearsals	Polishing rehearsals	Understudies

BACKGROUND NOTES

"The play's the thing..." and its production is a culmination of the talent and technique of both actors and backstage staff. When doing a play, you should apply all of the aspects discussed in previous chapters. Furthermore, whether you act, student direct, or participate as a crew member, you should understand play choice criteria, tryout and casting procedures, rehearsal schedules, and theatre etiquette.

Considering the importance of play selection, it is lamentable that numerous schools devote their energies to inferior scripts. In production, countless individuals work hours over a period of several weeks. Certainly their efforts should be applied to a worthwhile play, enabling them to absorb the best. To spend talent and time on drivel is foolish! No amount of superior work will elevate inferior material. Remember, choice of play will either ruin or establish your drama department's reputation, so select judiciously.

Script Selection

What standards should you and your director meet in choosing a play?

1. The script should be one of high artistic quality, well written with a clear sequence of events that lead to a strong climax. There should be a worthwhile theme that truthfully shows life's problems. There should be lucid characterizations, expressive dialogue, and clean humor. Certainly the play should stimulate the emotions and intellect of all participants, challenging their artistic endeavors.

2. The play should be suitable to the audience. Never offend the community's religious beliefs or sense of good taste. Avoid vulgarity, profanity, and ultra-sophistication! Leave worldly Broadway scripts to the professional. Schools should lead the community in developing high standards for entertainment. Audience taste can be cultivated, and you can be assured that if you do a good play well, the majority will like it.

3. The play must be suitable to the available talent, equipment, and budget. While directors avoid pre-casting, if they are unable to think of anyone who can do the main roles, they are wise to select a different show. Likewise, the stage must be able to handle scenery demands, and the budget and box office returns should help to cover the cost of the production. Show expenses vary according to the demands of scenery, costumes, makeup, lights, ticket printing, publicity, and royalty. Royalty is payment to the author for the use of the play. Charges are from fifty dollars up. Unless you select a classic, choose a royalty play, for non-royalty shows are seldom worth doing. It should go without saying that your school must always pay the necessary royalties. Failure to do so is a punishable crime. As soon as the play is selected, and before tryouts, your director writes the publisher and asks permission to present the show; royalty payments are due one to two weeks before opening night.

4. The play should help provide a varied season. Actually, the wise director plans plays for a two or three year period, aiming at producing numerous types: classics (including Shakespeare), fantasies, romantic comedies, social problem plays, farces, folk plays, youth plays, mysteries, and perhaps a Broadway show. A well-rounded season begins with a popular play in the fall (one that the audience will readily like so that they will keep coming to the other offerings); a serious play in the winter months; and a light novelty, fantasy, or experimental show in the spring. Occasionally the school may wish to present a season of shows built

around one theme. Besides variety of type, play choice should offer variety in period, setting, gender, and cast size.

5. The director should like the play in order to do good work. After making the final choice of the play, the director writes the publisher for paperback acting copies.

Pre-Production Planning

Now, the most important creative directing work begins — providing the foundation upon which the success of the whole show depends. The director completely plans the production, studying the play for theme, mood, structure, style, etc. The prompt book is made by including ground plans, preliminary blocking, and basic crew plans. (For the director's preliminary work, see Chapter 24.) To the prompt book, the director later adds the rehearsal schedule, and the names, addresses, and phone numbers of cast and crew. Eventually the crews add their drawings, lists, and charts until there is a complete working record of the show. During preliminary planning, the director sets performance dates and obtains rehearsal use of the auditorium. When these jobs are completed, the director prepares for casting by choosing tryout scenes from the play.

Casting

Casting is usually accomplished through a series of tryouts or auditions. Time, date, place, and tryout procedures are published in the school paper. Some directors place scripts in the library, where those interested in auditioning may read them and prepare scenes. Other directors prefer sight reading tryouts. When possible, the director holds tryouts where the play is to be given. If you audition, you must fill out a casting sheet. (See sample on page 251.) At the beginning of tryouts, the director briefly describes the scenery, tells the plot, and discusses the characters. You are asked not to try out for or accept a part unless you are willing to also accept the responsibility of attending each rehearsal to which you are called. Then the director announces the first tryout scene and chooses those who wish to read. Scenes should be characteristic of the roles, about three minutes long, and contain two or three characters. When you audition, go to the stage and read the best you can. Try not to be nervous. Your director is eager to listen and give you serious consideration. When you are not auditioning, listen carefully to the others, for you may learn from them and be able to read better a second time

After preliminary tryouts, the director selects those actors who seem best suited for the parts. There may be three or four students chosen as possibilities for each character. These people attend callbacks. At callback, the director makes suggestions to see how you and the others take direction. You may be asked to memorize a speech, to move on stage, or to do improvisations.

In choosing the cast, the director looks at your appearance. Are you physically suited for the role? Does your ability as an actor fit the style of the play? For classroom work the director casts accordingly to each member's need for development. For public presentation, actors are selected who will give the best possible performance, possessing a flexible, expressive voice that is suitable for the part and that projects well; good diction; and effective movement and body rhythm or tempo. In addition, the director looks to see if you have vitality, imagination, and an emotional intensity that can be developed for the part. You must be an actor who arouses interest within the audience. Furthermore, actors who are dependable will be chosen, for they must attend rehearsals, study their parts, and cooperate with cast and crews. The director must be able to depend on actors maintaining good health and good study habits. A sick or worried actor can ruin a show!

During callbacks, the director selects a tentative cast who will work convincingly together. The actors chosen should be varied in their voice, body tempo, and appearance, yet they should provide enough unity to carry the main mood. Casting remains tentative for at least two weeks. Like members of an athletic team, if actors do not develop within a

SAMPLE CASTING SHEET

NAME _____ HEIGHT _____ YEAR IN SCHOOL _____

ADDRESS _____ WEIGHT _____ FEMALE _____ MALE _____

PHONE _____ HAIR COLOR _____

SPECIAL TALENTS (SING, DANCE, PLAY MUSICAL INSTRUMENT, ETC.) _____

_____

CHECK WHAT YOU WOULD LIKE TO WORK ON: (✔)

_____ COSTUMES   _____ MAKEUP   _____ PUBLICITY

_____ DIRECTOR'S ASSISTANT _____ PROMPTER   _____ STAGE MANAGER

_____ LIGHTING & SOUND   _____ PROPS

ON BACK OF PAGE, PLEASE LIST:

1. PREVIOUS ACTING EXPERIENCE (INCLUDE PLAY, ROLE, PLACE)

2. HOURS WHEN YOU CAN REHEARSE

3. OTHER COMMITMENTS (ORCHESTRA, FOOTBALL, ETC.)

DIRECTOR'S COMMENTS

APPEARANCE _____ ABILITY TO TAKE DIRECTION _____

VOICE _____ PERSONALITY _____

SPEECH _____ POSSIBLE FOR ROLE OF _____

INTERPRETATION _____ _____

MOVEMENT _____ _____

certain time limit, they may be replaced. Some schools double cast to provide opportunitya for more students. With a double cast, each group gives the same number of performances. However, double casting takes much extra rehearsal time, sometimes at the expense of a polished performance. Often it is better to select a single cast with understudies for the main roles. Certainly everyone who accepts a part must be available and must understand and prepare to meet his or her obligations!

While casting, and often before, the director selects backstage crews and their chairpersons. Not everyone can act in each play, so if you are not cast, cheerfully volunteer for a crew. Backstage work is vitally important to the show. With competent people it is fun, besides being good theatre experience. Many students prefer backstage work to acting and become proficient at lights, scene construction, costumes, and box office management. The director meets with all the technical crews to explain and assign duties and to give each crew a deadline for completing its work. Crew members are responsible to their chairperson, who in turn is responsible to the stage manager and/or director.

Backstage Personnel and Duties

Type and number of crews depend on the play and the way it is staged. The following is a list of backstage personnel and their duties.

Assistant to the director is a competent student who helps the director in conducting rehearsals, typing out notices, making phone calls, doing research, etc.

Stage manager is responsible to the director and the faculty technician (faculty member who designs sets and costumes and who supervises scenery construction). The stage manager has charge of all stage crews, seeing that they keep to schedule. He or she also assists the director. During dress rehearsal and performance, the stage manager has complete supervision of the stage, giving warning calls for lights, effects, and curtains. Before opening the curtain for each scene and act, "O. K." reports are received from each crew chairperson. After the final performance, he or she supervises and assists with strike and collects all crew reports, adding them to the prompt book.

Prompter is a dependable student who accepts the responsibility of attending every rehearsal to become familiar with the script, the cues, and the pauses. He or she sees that the practice room is ready and during rehearsal holds the prompt book, notating all movement and business that the director sets. All intentional pauses in the dialogue are marked to avoid prompting during them. All crew and entrance warnings are marked. At rehearsal, those actors who forget their lines are cued, using a medium voice, not a whisper. At dress, the prompter times the show and the scene shifts with a stop watch. If a prompter is used during performance, he or she should be able to immediately assist the actors with lines if they need help.

Stage crew constructs, paints, and sets up scenery. The crew also shifts scenery during the show. After each performance the crew sets up Act I for the next night's running. The stage crew helps strike after final performance.

Light crew prepares the light plots, charts, and cue sheets; hangs and focuses the lights and runs them during the show. The crew assists with strike.

Sound effects crew prepares a cue sheet and provides the necessary sound effects. The crew also selects necessary music for the overture, mood, and transitions.

Costume or *wardrobe* plans costumes, prepares costume charts, secures or makes costumes, and assigns dressing rooms. Members should hang each actor's costume in act sequence with accessories gathered in a marked box. The crew keeps all costumes mended and pressed, and assists actors in dressing and making quick changes. The crew also helps actors to keep dressing rooms clean. After the show, crew members store school costumes and return all borrowed or rented ones.

Makeup crew plans makeup for each actor, obtains necessary supplies, and arranges for a separate makeup room if possible. During dress rehearsal and performance, the crew assists actors in applying makeup. For large casts, the crew often provides a makeup "production line," where each crew member is responsible for doing one step in makeup application. For example, one crew member applies all the base; another does all the eyes. The crew also keeps the makeup room clean and puts away the supplies each night.

Property crew prepares detailed property lists for each scene and locates all props and furniture, including dummy props for rehearsal. The chairperson assigns each member specific props to set up and strike for each act. The crew organizes the props, keeping those for each scene in a separate basket or on a separate table. After the final performance the crew returns all borrowed properties and stores those belonging to the school.

Pages are used when the cast is large. They stand in the wings during dress and performance to receive warning entrance calls from the prompter or stage manager. They then call the actors from their dressing rooms. With a small cast, actors are responsible for their own entrances without being called.

Business manager is often a faculty member who has charge of the funds, serves as public relations officer, and supervises the chairperson of the following crews: publicity, ticket, and program.

Publicity crew advertises the show by giving the school and local newspapers various news stories concerning dates of performances, people involved, information about the play, author, costumes, unusual properties, etc. The crew should also be on the alert for feature stories, such as an amusing incident at rehearsal. The crew makes arrangements for newspaper pictures of the cast and crews. Besides newspaper publicity, the crew may place posters in store windows; with special permission, mail fliers with bank statements; mail post cards to patrons announcing the play; with permission, hang banners across a main street; display cast pictures in the school halls; or present short "teaser" scenes in an assembly and on television. Imaginative members may devise other publicity ideas. Be sure you advertise well so that you'll get a large audience.

Ticket crew designs the tickets and orders them early (specifying a different color for each night). When the tickets are printed, crew members number them for reserved seats. (If possible, have reserved tickets. They provide a "theatre" feeling as opposed to the movie house atmosphere.) The ticket crew sells tickets in advance. If possible, they hold a selling contest among cast and crew members. The person selling the most tickets may be given a prize.

```
ROW                    Name of School  presents            SEAT
    SECTION                 PLAY  TITLE            SECTION
        SEAT                — author —                  ROW
                    Place                   Time
                    Date                    Price
```

SAMPLE TICKET

Program crew is responsible for designing, planning, and printing of programs. Programs should include a title page or a cover that names the play, author, producing group, date, time, and place. The cover should also have some design, sketch, or picture that fits the play and its mood. The inside of the program should list the cast in order of appearance and tell the time and place of each scene and act. The opposite page should list all backstage members (production staff) and acknowledge the publishing house and any local business firms that have helped. The back of the program should contain information that creates interest and informs the audience about the play and your drama department. Include a short summary of the plot (unless such knowledge will destroy audience enjoyment), a brief sketch of the author, and a statement concerning the production.

For advance publicity, announce your next production and drama activities. You may also mention the aims of your group. For good public relations, some schools print the names of their drama patrons and patronesses (school board members, officials, and citizens who support the school plays). Whether you hire the printing done or do it yourself, make the programs look smart and professional. Be sure all names are spelled correctly.

House manager is responsible for the seating and comfort of the audience. The house manager sees that the auditorium is cool (crowds and stage lights warm it up), that the doors are open early at each performance, and that ample programs are available for distribution. He or she also supervises the ushers by helping them to become familiar with the seating arrangement.

Ushers hand out programs and escort the audience to their seats. Since plays are festive occasions, ushers and the house manager should dress in good clothes or in appropriate costumes, planned and approved by the director. Manager and ushers should be pleasant and courteous to the audience. If possible, the house manager should rehearse the ushers in meeting audience members courteously and seating them quickly. Ushers should seat no one after the curtain goes up. Latecomers should wait to be seated until a scene break. As soon as the theatre empties after each performance, the house manager and ushers should check all rows for lost articles and should pick up programs and rubbish.

Rehearsals

While backstage crews are planning and executing their specific duties, the director and cast are occupied with rehearsals. It is important that the director organizes rehearsals carefully in order to make the best use of available time. A director should efficiently utilize the actor's time and energy by grouping scenes together that have the same characters. With proper rehearsal arrangement only needed actors are called. Therefore, actors can avoid long waits. At the beginning of rehearsals, the director hands out copies of the rehearsal schedule to the cast and crews. One copy is also tacked to the stage call board. Usually this schedule cannot be altered, so plan to meet it.

How you behave at rehearsal greatly determines your success in the production. You must expect to maintain standard theatre policies by attending all rehearsals when you are called. Even if your part is a walk on, you must appear when called! Some schools require students and their parents to sign a contract stating that the students will attend all rehearsals. Certainly, you should always be prompt and should be on your best behavior. Practicing a show is serious work, but if everyone cooperates as a team, rehearsal provides adventuresome fun in working toward an artistic goal.

Rehearsal schedules vary according to the difficulty of the play, the experience of the actors, and the time available. For three-act plays, schools need at least five to six weeks of rehearsal after casting. Rehearsals should be five or six days a week, from two to three hours long. Classic or costume shows take more practice time. For one-act plays, provide three to four weeks of rehearsal, three or four times a week. Always have as many rehearsals as you can possibly squeeze in, so that you can maintain excellent performance standards. Some casts practice after school and some in the evenings. Plan on at least two, long, Saturday rehearsals. Usually your director provides specific goals for each session. The following indicates standard rehearsal sequence.

Reading rehearsals immediately follow casting. All cast and crews attend, with the cast sitting around a large table. The purpose of this rehearsal is to help the group gain an understanding of the play. The director's interpretation of the play and concept of the characters is discussed, as well as the theme and climaxes. The ground plans are shown, and possibly a watercolor sketch of the set. The actors read their parts, with the director correcting any mispronunciation or misinterpretation. The director may ask questions about each character. For example, "Why does your character say that? What does he mean? What does this speech reveal about the character?" Actors should also ask questions that lead to stimulating discussions about motivation and character relationships, and how these relate to the theme. The director may require a written analysis of each character. Reading rehearsals may take several sessions, depending on the show's difficulty.

Blocking rehearsals are conducted on stage or in a large room where the floor plan is drawn to scale on the floor and marked with masking tape. Blocking rehearsals coordinate lines with basic movement, groupings, entrances, exits, and crosses. As the director indicates your moves, write them in your script with pencil. Don't use ink. If movement is changed, you will have to erase. Always take a pencil to rehearsal while you have books in hand and notate all directions. (At home underline your cues and your character's name in red or highlight the speeches.) Your director blocks one act at a time, scene by scene, repeating each segment to set the movement in your mind. Be sure you justify or motivate all movement given you, and that you read all lines with interpretation. After one act is set, memorize your lines for that act. You should memorize Act I as you begin blocking II; memorize II as you block III. All lines should be learned at least two weeks before opening night.

Developing rehearsals begin on each act when blocking is set. During the first rehearsal without scripts, the director details business. (As you redo business, you are repeating lines, which is helpful to memory.) Other developing rehearsals are devoted to characterization, motivation, and belief in your part. Also, attention is given to projecting emotion and reacting or relating to others. During developing rehearsals you should start using dummy props. If you are doing a costume play, begin rehearsing in practice costumes. At these sessions your director may work on stage with you part of the time, going out front for an occasional overall view. He also calls private rehearsals for developing love scenes, fights, and crowd scenes.

Polishing rehearsals find the director out front, testing stage pictures from all angles and giving attention to the countless details that make good theatre. Some rehearsals concentrate on only one act, some on difficult scenes, and some are complete uninterrupted run-throughs of the entire show. Polishing rehearsals are critical; they are what make a sparkling performance. Unfortunately, many schools through poor rehearsal planning never have time to polish their show.

In polishing, the director works on audibility, on the pointing of important lines, and on developing vocal nuances. Business and movement are made more concise, with any unnecessary action deleted. All group scenes are coordinated to provide for troupe ensemble playing. The director makes sure both major and minor roles are effectively characterized, tempo and rhythm create vigorous climaxes that alternate with less intense scenes, and that you pick up your cues to prevent the play from exhibiting the "amateur drag." He or she checks to see that the acting is fresh with the illusion of the first time. Every detail is addressed, for little escapes audience attention.

Technical rehearsals must be conducted on stage. Their purpose is to synchronize technical and acting aspects. The first technical rehearsal is long and arduous. It is held without the actors. Crews set up scenery, place furniture, hang curtains, mount lights, etc. They also practice scenery shifts, working for a quick and quiet change. (Crew members should wear crepe soled shoes to help mask foot noise.) The second technical rehearsal is with the cast. The director asks only for those scenes requiring scene shifts, light changes, effects, and prop changes. Crews now mark furniture positions on the floor with masking tape. The stage manager practices opening and closing the act curtain. If possible, the cast members put on their costumes and parade across the stage under the proper lights. Crews can then make necessary color alterations.

Dress rehearsals should be held at least three times. Prior to the first dress, the director gives written instructions to cast and crews informing them about time, procedure, and requirements of each dress and performance. Every dress rehearsal should begin promptly, whether or not all cast and crews are ready. Dress starts early, at six or seven p.m. (Rehearsal will then finish early.) Contrary to belief, nightmare dress rehearsals generally mean poor performances. Certainly a bad final dress rehearsal indicates an inefficient director or uncooperative cast and crews. Dress should go relatively smoothly if previous work has been efficient. Never leave details to the last minute. Everyone involved deserves a good final dress rehearsal that will give them confidence in a strong performance.

   a. The *first dress rehearsal* is the most hectic since it coordinates all sound, lights, scenery shifts, and properties. The cast wears full costume. The director sits out front; and in order to watch the stage constantly, can dictate notes to an assistant. The prompter times the show and the scene shifts. Shifts should be a matter of seconds. Act intermissions should be no longer than ten minutes. There should be few, if any, interruptions during this rehearsal, since the director gives a critique at the end.

   b. The *second dress rehearsal* adds makeup to the other technical aspects. Also, the cast rehearses planned curtain calls. When the curtain opens for the first call, all supporting roles should be on stage in specified places. Then the major roles enter in pairs. Actors should smile and bow in character, maintaining poise and suppressing giggles. The stage manager quickly closes and then opens the curtain again as the whole company bows. The curtain is closed each time after the applause reaches a climax; there should be no additional curtain calls when applause wanes or when houselights come on.

After this dress rehearsal, take necessary photographs, starting with Act III and working backwards. This reverse sequence facilitates scenery shifts and costume changes. The director plans pictures in advance, handing out copies of the sequence. The director may give a critique at the end of this dress, or may hand out individual notes. Some directors prefer to withhold critique until the beginning of the final dress.

c. *Third* or *final dress rehearsal* should be run exactly like performance. There should be absolutely no interruptions and every detail should be complete. Some directors make this an invitational dress where guests are invited. This is often done when the play is a comedy and the cast needs practice in holding for laughs. Before this rehearsal begins, the cast should give the crews appreciative applause backstage.

Fiddler on the Roof by Stein, Brock, & Harnick
Topeka West High School: Director, Doug Goheen

Action celebrating the wedding.

Performance

After weeks of concerted rehearsal, it seems wasteful to have but one performance. Try to schedule at least three shows. Before and during performance, only those with specific jobs should be allowed backstage. Crews should arrive early enough to have the stage completely set up one hour before curtain. The cast should arrive at least one hour before curtain in order to warm-up, dress, apply makeup, and check their hand props. When makeup is finished, each cast member should stay quietly in the dressing room getting into character. The stage manager calls roll in the greenroom about fifteen minutes before curtain. There the director talks to the assembled cast and crew, reminding everyone not to change anything, regardless of what friends say. Do each show as rehearsed! If you have rehearsed well, you can be confident that you'll have a good show. Give your best each night. If you make a small error, such as calling a character by the wrong name, don't correct yourself. The audience probably won't notice the error. Rectify only those mistakes that are vital to the action. If a character fails to enter on time, fill in with inconsequential talk or business. Don't say, "I wonder where ____ is."

As in dress rehearsal, the stage manager has charge of performance. The director sits out front in an inconspicuous place, where he or she takes necessary notes and observes audience reaction. Always start the show on time! If you do so consistently, your audience will learn to be prompt. Many schools refuse to seat latecomers until after the first scene or act. Do not allow announcements or skits between acts. It is also a poor policy to give flowers and gifts on stage. Send such items to the dressing rooms where they can be enjoyed privately after the show. The applause from the audience and the thrill from knowing you have done a good job should be "flowers" enough for all.

After each performance, remove makeup and costumes and tidy the dressing rooms. Actors should never leave a mess for the crews. After the final show, while enthusiasm is still keen, crews should immediately strike the set and properties. (Take them down and put them away.) Return borrowed items the next workday. Assemble all completed charts in the prompt book. It is fun to have a cast party for actors, crews, and faculty directors. This is often held on stage after strike, or if it is too late, the party is given on another evening.

Sample Rehearsal Schedule for Three-Act Plays

(Adjust to fit play and circumstances. This schedule calls for five rehearsals a week, three Saturday rehearsals, and three performances.)

Preparation week:
Tryouts, callbacks, final readings with tentative cast, meetings with crews.

1st week:
Monday	Read complete play with cast and crews.
Tuesday	Read first half; discussion and analysis.
Wednesday	Read second half; discussion and analysis.
Thursday	Act I; block first half; repeat to set.
Friday	Act I; block remainder; repeat to set.

2nd week:

Monday	Act I; characterization and motivation.
Tuesday	Act II; block first half; repeat to set.
Wednesday	Act II; block remainder; repeat to set.
Thursday	Run through Acts I and II; adjust groupings if necessary.
Friday	Act II; characterization and motivation.
Saturday	Special private rehearsals for love scenes, fight scenes, etc.

3rd week:

Monday	Act I memorized; no books; work on detailed business.
Tuesday	Run through Act I (no books) and Act II; work on belief and response; actors should look at each other and listen to each other.
Wednesday	Act III; block first half; repeat to set.
Thursday	Act III; block remainder; repeat to set.
Friday	Act II memorized; no books; work on business detail.
Saturday	Run through Acts I and II memorized; clarify business detail; use hand props.

4th week:

Monday	Act III; characterization and motivation.
Tuesday	Run through Acts I–II–III; work on audibility, groupings, characterization. Concentrate on minor roles.
Wednesday	Polish Act I; business, lines, tempo, climax, props.
Thursday	Polish Act II; business, lines, tempo, climax, props.
Friday	Act III memorized; no books; work on business detail.
Saturday	Polish Act III. Give it extra time. Work on business, lines, tempo, climax, and props. (After this rehearsal, crews may start to set up the stage if it is clear for the next two weeks.)

5th week:

Monday	Run through Acts I–II–III; work on audibility, unity, tempo, climax, line pickup, transitions, ensemble playing. Check for spontaneity. Actors must not anticipate lines or mouth the lines of others.
Tuesday	Polish difficult scenes, climaxes, etc. Concentrate especially on Act III.
Wednesday	Technical rehearsal without actors. Set up scenery, furniture, lights, etc. Practice shifts. Actors may run a line rehearsal with the prompter. No movement; just say lines and pick up cues readily.
Thursday	Technical rehearsal with actors. Repeat scenes needed for technical changes. Do costume review.
Friday	Run through complete show with set, lights, props.

6th week:

Monday	First dress; full costume, lights, sound, props, scenery, and shifts.
Tuesday	Second dress; as Monday,+ makeup. Plan curtain calls; take pictures.
Wednesday	Invitational dress; performance level.

Thursday   Opening night performance.
Friday   Performance.
Saturday   Performance, strike, and cast party.

ASSIGNMENT AND ITS PURPOSE

For this assignment the class will work together producing a one-act play for an assembly, an invitational performance, or a festival entry. If the class is small, the instructor will direct the play and each class member will have either a role, a backstage job, or both. If the class is large, produce two or three one-acts, using a student director for each while the instructor supervises. If possible, do the play in proscenium, using screens and drapes. If you have a classroom stage, use it for an "intimate" theatre proscenium presentation. This assignment will consume about four weeks of class time: one week for casting and other preparations; three weeks for rehearsals.

You will be graded according to the check list on the activity sheet for this chapter, found in the teacher's manual. Review it now to see what is expected of you.

HOW TO PREPARE

1. Your instructor will select the student directors if more than one play is to be given.

2. You will be given several acceptable scripts from which the class will choose those they wish to do. If you produce more than one play, plan a varied program of both comedy and serious drama.

3. Each student director should study the script and do all preliminary work including drawing a ground plan, blocking the action, and scheduling rehearsals. Plan approximately fifteen class rehearsals and five outside of class (noon, after school, evenings, or Saturdays). Modify the three-act rehearsal schedule in this chapter to fit scenes in the one-act.

4. With the help of the instructor, student directors will cast their show to include both experienced and inexperienced people in each cast. After deciding tentative cast lists, hold a reading rehearsal, making any necessary adjustments in the cast from insight gained from the readings.

5. Decide crew heads and members. Your instructor will appoint crew jobs to those not cast, so that each class member has a responsibility. A student serving in both cast and crew should work on the same play.

6. Crews are responsible for all work connected with their job, including charts and plans. Crew chairpeople should detail work to members while accepting

their share of duties. (See Chapters 21 through 26.) Crews should meet deadlines assigned by the director.

7. In class, work according to the planned rehearsal schedule, concentrating on different aspects each time. Use separate rooms for each cast, if possible. Otherwise, work quietly in separate corners of your drama room.

8. Each actor is responsible for knowing lines by the deadline and for seriously studying the part outside of class.

(*Note: If some students are not going to be occupied throughout the rehearsal weeks, the instructor may assign one or more of the additional projects.*)

HOW TO PRESENT

Follow the basic performance procedure as discussed in this chapter. Work toward giving a good show. If you present the play for a very small invitational audience of parents and friends, your class may wish to serve refreshments at the intermission. If possible, have programs to distribute at the door. All ushers should dress up. Make the occasion festive!

ADDITIONAL PROJECTS ON PRODUCING A PLAY

1. Write a report on a famous actor or actress from information gained from such books as Katharine Cornell's *Curtain Going Up*, Funke and Booth's *Actors Talk About Acting*, Cornelia Otis Skinner's *Family Circle*, Ellen Terry and G. B. Shaw's *A Correspondence*, Gertrude Lawrence's *A Star Danced*, Kenneth Tynan's *Alec Guinness*, Marinacci's *Leading Ladies*.

2. Write a report on a famous scene designer or stage director such as Adolphe Appia, Gordon Craig, Robert Edmond Jones, David Belasco, Jo Mielzinger, Constantine Stanislavski, Max Reinhardt, Lee Strasberg, Tyronne Guthrie, Peter Brook, or Jerzy Growtowski.

3. Write a report on a summer festival theatre in the United States or Canada. Suggestions for Shakespearean Festival Theatres: Ashland, Oregon; San Diego, California; Cedar City, Utah; Central Park, New York City; Stratford, Connecticut; Washington, D.C.; or Stratford, Ontario. Other suggestions: the Passion Play at Spearfish, South Dakota; summer repertories at Virginia City, Montana; Buck County Playhouse, Penn-

sylvania; Mineola Playhouse, Long Island; Canal Fulton Summer Arena, Ohio; Boothbay Playhouse, Maine.

4. See a video of a great play and evaluate it:

> *Importance of Being Earnest* (Gielgud and Evans)
>
> *J. B.* (Plummer and Massey)
>
> *The Lady's Not for Burning*
>
> *Medea* (Anderson)
>
> *The Rivals* (Evans and Brown)
>
> *St. Joan* (McKenna)
>
> *Death of a Salesman*
>
> Any reputable Shakespeare production

5. Collect and arrange material for an interesting bulletin board display in your drama class.

6. Do a complete prompt or production notebook for a three-act play in which you present all phases of production. Include the following:

    a. Short summary of the plot

    b. Theme in one sentence

    c. Floor plan drawn to scale

    d. Description of set, its color, line, and mood

    e. Water color sketch of set, in perspective

    f. Light cue sheet, plot, chart

    g. Sound cue sheet

    h. Costume plot for each character

    i. Makeup chart for each character

    j. Property list for each scene, telling where each property should be placed

    k. Publicity schedule; poster and ticket design

    Make the notebook as inclusive as possible. Your instructor may want to delete or enlarge certain sections, depending on the play. For example, if the cast is large, you may be asked to plan costumes and makeup for only two main characters.

7. Write a dramatic criticism of each one-act play performed in class. Evaluate the play, the acting, the staging, and the audience response. (See Chapter 30.)

8. Write a dramatic criticism of the one-act play in which you participated. Tell the benefits you derived from your experience.

9. See a professional or amateur full length play presentation, and write a critique on it as though you were a professional critic. In your paper, discuss the play, the acting, the production, and the audience response.

10. Prepare and present to the class a 30 – minute oral review of a three-act play. In your solo presentation, cut and arrange the script so that as you narrate the story, you read the scenes that disclose character, theme, and climax. Edit the script carefully and rehearse painstakingly. Stay within your time limits. Be sure that your delivery seems spontaneous and is believable and that your speech is distinct, with proper interpretation and characterization. If properly presented, your review should delight and/or inspire your audience.

 "Great art does not call attention to itself."

Books on Careers in Theatre

Babcock, Dennis, and Preston Boyd. *Careers in the Theatre*. Minneapolis, MN: Lerner, 1975.

Blum, Richard. *Working Actors*. Stoneham, MA: Focal Press, 1989

Cohen, Robert. *Acting Professionally: Raw Facts About Careers*. 3rd ed. Mountain View, CA: Mayfield, 1982.

Fridell, Squire. *Acting in Television Commercials for Fun and Profit*. New York: Crown, 1980.

Greenberg, Jan. *Theatre Careers*. New York: Holt, Rinehart and Winston, 1983.

Hines, Terence, and Suzanne Vaughn. *An Actor Succeeds: Career Management*. New York: Samuel French, 1989.

Logan, Tom. *How to Act and Eat at the Same Time*. 2nd ed. Washington, D.C.: Communication Press, 1988.

Moore, Dick. *Opportunities in Acting Careers*. Skokie, IL: National Textbook Company, 1985.

Padol, Brian, and Alan Simon. *The Young Performer's Guide: How to Break into Show Business*. Crozet, VA: Better Way, 1990.

THEATRE COURTESIES

1. Always be prompt for rehearsals.
2. Come to rehearsals prepared to work.
3. Study your part when you are not on stage; also study it at home.
4. When not studying your part, actively watch the others on stage. You will learn from their errors and achievements.
5. Don't leave rehearsals until you are dismissed by the director.
6. Cooperate with all cast and crew members. There are no "stars" in a show; each person is needed to create a good production.
7. Accept criticism cheerfully.
8. Allow the director to direct. When you are given directions, listen. If you are asked to write down criticism, do so and then incorporate the suggestions in the next rehearsal.
9. Avoid a display of temperament. Be patient and pleasant. Don't criticize others.
10. Be quiet in the wings and auditorium.
11. Be ready for entrances without having to be called. Never be late for an entrance.
12. Remain in character whenever on stage. Never break and laugh.
13. Don't look at the prompter if you forget a line. Remain in character and wait for the prompt. Listen to it carefully.
14. Do not "mouth" other actors' lines.
15. When the director interrupts rehearsal for another actor, stand quietly in character, ready to start again when the interruption is finished.
16. If anything accidentally falls on the stage floor, pick it up.
17. Never appear in makeup or costume except backstage and on stage.
18. Don't touch items such as lights or props that are under the jurisdiction of another crew.
19. When entering the theatre, leave personal problems behind.
20. Give your best performance for every audience.
21. Don't confuse acting with living.
22. Never peek through the main curtain at the audience!
23. When the stage manager gives warning calls or instructions, always say, "Thank you," in reply.
24. Keep up your grades. If you can't participate in drama and simultaneously maintain good grades, don't accept a role.

Chapter 28 ACTING IN THE ROUND AND THRUST

Time Limits: 4-10 minute Shakespearean scene

Activity Sheet: Fill out the top part of the activity for this chapter, found in the teacher's manual, and hand the sheet to your instructor when you are asked.

PROMPTINGS

1. Relate the historical background to arena and thrust staging.
2. Discuss advantages to arena and/or thrust theatre.
3. Describe various arena arrangements for placing audience.
4. Compare acting in arena to that in proscenium.
5. Compare directing in arena or thrust to that in proscenium.
6. Describe how lighting should be placed and used in arena.
7. Explain the importance of detail in arena's furniture, properties, and costumes.

THEATRE LANGUAGE

Arena theatre
Dionysian festival
Flexible theatre
Funnels

Horseshoe staging
Light trees
Louvers

Pageant wagon
Recorders
Thrust theatre

BACKGROUND NOTES

"A rose by any other name would smell as sweet." And so it is with acting in the round. Whether you call it arena theatre, circle, central, circus, penthouse, horseshoe, flexible, thrust, or theatre-in-the-round, it is a boon to both dilettante and professional thespians.

The essence of arena theatre and thrust is the intimacy. The audience encircles the actors, except in horseshoe or thrust staging where the audience sits on three sides. In either situation, actors and spectators are usually three to five feet apart. Because of this closeness and because scenic effects are slight, arena has been called the actors' theatre. Acting dominates and is carried to satisfying heights through the imagination of both actor and audience.

Arena staging is not new. It is a revival of the ancient practice of primitives who danced and told stories around a campfire; of the ancient Greek Dionysian festivals conducted in a semicircle; of the Medieval pageant wagons around which guild members and townspeople flocked; of the Elizabethan performances with their platforms extending into the groundling area. Today's non-proscenium theatre was revived by such men as Reinhardt and Appia in their experimental work. Interest grew until, in the late 1930s, the first permanent arena theatre, "The Penthouse," was constructed under the guidance of Glenn Hughes at the University of Washington. In the 1940s, Margo Jones created her "Theatre-in-the-Round" in Dallas, Texas. Since then numerous university, community, and professional groups have established flexible theatres in rooms where seats and playing areas can be positioned for any style of intimate presentation.

Advantages & Disadvantages

There are several advantages to arena or flexible staging. It allows you to present good theatre without proscenium facilities. If you lack an auditorium, if your school stage is outdated, or if the stage is constantly being used by other groups, turn to arena. Your theatre can then be almost any large room. A second advantage is that arena is inexpensive. There is no costly building and painting of scenery. Expense lies mainly in costumes and lights. Third, arena is intimate. The audience likes this immediate contact, for it is easy to establish empathy (see Chapter 3). Arena parallels the "close ups" of movies and television.

Like all art forms, arena presents some problems that need special handling. Difficulties arise because of the lack of aesthetic distance. (See Chapter 7.) Sometimes the audience generates excess empathy that in turn destroys the theatrical illusion. Embarrassment may occur during intense love scenes, quarrels, or fights. To counter this problem, plays must be carefully chosen, and acting must be subtle. Lack of distance also makes it difficult to achieve certain illusions. Shootings, stabbings, etc., must be carefully planned and precisely executed if they are to carry belief. In fact, arena theatre demands that every item be accurate in detail. Costumes, furniture, and properties must bear close inspection. In addition, the actor must constantly and completely be in character, using a perfected technique that appears natural.

Characteristics of Arena Productions

Let us view the characteristics of arena production. Arena can be housed in any room that is large enough for an audience and a playing area and that allows a view unobstructed by columns. Room size may vary, although you should avoid one that is long and narrow. A room 40 x 60 feet will easily seat 150 people and give you a suitable acting area of about 18 x 20 feet. Ceilings should be between 12 and 20 feet high for proper lighting. In selecting a room, consider the availability of rest rooms, dressing rooms, and audience lobby. You can perform in a classroom, a library, on a large stage, in a band room (particularly good if it has its own risers), or a gymnasium. If you choose the gym, provide an intimate feeling by using one end, and by curtaining or screening off the rest of the area. Whatever room you select, attempt to give it a theatre feeling that is cozy.

FORMS OF ARENA THEATRE

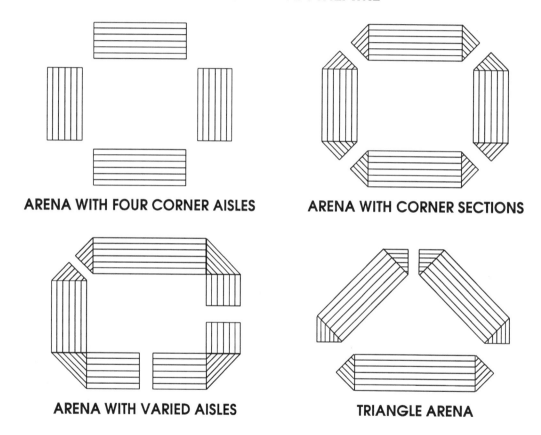

ARENA WITH FOUR CORNER AISLES

ARENA WITH CORNER SECTIONS

ARENA WITH VARIED AISLES

TRIANGLE ARENA

Whether you place the audience on three or four sides, ideally you should elevate their seats for unobstructed vision. Three levels are usual with the first row raised one foot (to prevent light spill on the audience), the second row raised two feet, and the third and last row raised three feet and placed against the wall of the room. If band risers are available, use them. Otherwise construct sturdy platforms. Eight-foot long sections are easy to handle. Make them three feet deep to accommodate chairs and to provide a small front aisle. If possible, build triangular corner sections so that the corners turn toward the playing area. If you cannot raise the first row, put the chairs three or four feet away from the acting area to prevent stage light from spilling on the audience. If you cannot raise any of the seats, stagger them and limit seating to three rows.

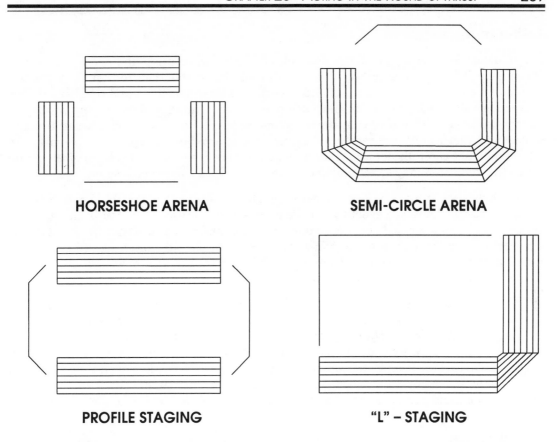

HORSESHOE ARENA   **SEMI-CIRCLE ARENA**

PROFILE STAGING   **"L" – STAGING**

When a large room is available, you can vary the theatre floor plan according to the demands of the play. Sometimes you may want to arrange the area as pure arena, sometimes as a horseshoe, perhaps even as a triangle. Use your imagination to gain flexibility. In your arrangement allow two or more aisles. The audience can then easily reach their seats, and the actors have entrance and exit ways.

Scripts for Arena

While most scripts can be adapted to arena theatre with a little imagination and ingenuity, it is best to be selective in your play choice. Generally you should avoid plays that depend heavily on spectacle. Peter Pan can believably fly all over the proscenium stage, but with arena it is a different matter. It is possible, of course, to include spectacle. One professional group succeeded in staging a visible oil well eruption in arena. But for amateurs, at least, it is wise to forego such technical problems. If possible, avoid large crowd scenes, since a small cast works easier in central staging. Unless you can simplify changes, it is best to avoid multiple sets and complex properties. Plays that require intense emotional scenes may prove an unwise choice unless handled with restraint.

Acting in Arena

There is no basic difference between acting for proscenium and acting for arena. The same principles are used but with modification. In flexible theatre there is a greater demand for concentration because of audience proximity. Latecomers and coughers can be distracting unless you, the actor, have complete concentration. Certainly you must constantly stay in character. If you slip for one moment, the audience will notice because insincerity and superficiality are readily perceived in arena. When not speaking, be sure you listen and react carefully, for your face may be the only one seen by a section of the audience. How you listen may affect audience response to the speaking character.

Arena acting requires less exaggeration. The audience will notice the slightest movement and gesture. A raised eyebrow may go undetected in proscenium, but in the round it can convey deep emotions. Economize your movement and make sure that what you use is significant and natural appearing. (You will even want to act with your back!) Also, acquire more subtlety in communicating emotions. Keep in control and utilize suggestion. The audience will imaginatively supply the rest.

Standard proscenium body positions are ineffective when playing to an audience on all sides. In arena, your main concern is to avoid covering other actors and to avoid being covered yourself. Instead of standing close to an actor while sharing a scene, step to one side and "open up" by providing space between the two of you. This position will prevent both you and your partner from being covered. Standing apart means, however, that you must look directly at the person to whom you are speaking so that proper focus can be established. Never stand parallel to another actor unless both of you have your backs to an aisle.

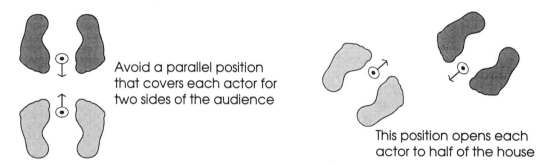

Avoid a parallel position that covers each actor for two sides of the audience

This position opens each actor to half of the house

Also note that during the course of the show you should play to all sides. Never favor one section. If you have no lines, but for certain reasons must stand for a long period (such as a servant may do), place yourself with your back to an aisle to keep from obstructing audience view.

Execute all business as precisely and naturally as possible. Whatever you do should bear close scrutiny. Little can be faked, for the audience is quick to catch mistakes. If you dial a phone, for example, be sure you dial the proper number of digits. If you drink coffee, be sure you swallow.

There is never a prompter in flexible theatre, so you must overlearn your lines. Also, do not be tricked by the smallness of the theatre. While you need not speak as loudly as for proscenium, you must be precise with your diction. Since you always have your back to part of the audience, speak to be heard not only in front, but all around you. Maintain good resonance, articulate clearly, and point your lines. A small theatre is no excuse for slovenly speech!

Directing for Arena

Directing practices are slightly modified for arena. In planning the stage setting the director uses fewer furniture pieces than in proscenium, while allowing enough chairs to seat all minor characters when necessary. Balance important furniture pieces as evenly as possible around the acting area, placing one major piece near the center to allow motivation for central action. Furniture placed on the periphery should motivate actors to the edges. Set pieces may also be placed in front of an unused aisle, though be sure to allow enough aisles for entrances and exits.

Since standard proscenium terms of stage right, left, etc., are not applicable to arena, directors use either compass positions or clock numbers for designating areas and giving directions. Entrances are usually marked 1-2-3 or A-B-C. When notating movement, both director and actors should indicate the direction to be faced.

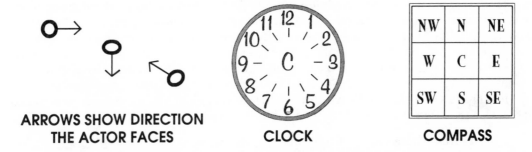

ARROWS SHOW DIRECTION
THE ACTOR FACES

CLOCK

COMPASS

In blocking for arena, never use the printed script directions intended for proscenium. Start anew. In arena, the director directs from all sides. There is no preferred seating since there are no strong or weak areas, unless the center can be considered strong.

One of the director's main problems in arena is to achieve emphasis. Body position and stage area cannot provide emphasis, since an actor facing one direction will have his or her back to part of the audience; and an area close to one audience section is distant to another. The director, therefore, achieves emphasis through level: the dominant characters stand while the minor characters sit; and through direct visual focus: the actors look at the important characters. Speaking and moving characters also receive emphasis.

The director plans open composition, maintaining space between characters so that they won't cover each other. Each section of the audience should see at least one actor's face all of the time. If there are only two characters on stage, never face them the same direction. If there are three characters on stage, use a triangular placement. Then each audience section will see a face. Do not allow actors to face each other in parallel position unless standing with their backs to an aisle, thus being covered completely only on the aisle line.

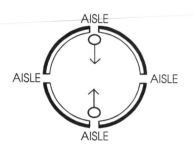

Accept the fact that stage composition cannot be ideal for all of the audience all of the time. Compensate by planning movement so that each quarter of the circle, square, or rectangular acting area has about one-fourth of the stage composition arranged especially for it. Avoid overusing one area and avoid crowding characters into the middle. Change focus by rotating the action frequently, for rotation allows the audience to see different backs and faces. Each basic move should bring new faces to each audience section. During a long speech, the speaker should plan motivation which shifts positions to various parts of the house. Of course the director must not create a merry-go-round effect that comes from over movement. Use only well-motivated, necessary action.

The director should time entrances and exits carefully. Some groups light their aisles and treat them as an acting area; the character is on stage upon entering the aisle. Other groups keep their aisles darkened and the character is onstage only when reaching the playing area. In horseshoe arrangement, doors are often placed in the open wall. Whatever you choose, all act and scene beginnings should be taken in full blackout since arena has no curtain. Warn the audience three minutes before curtain. Then at curtain time, blackout all lights to prevent the audience from seeing the actors approach the playing area. Luminous tape on the floor and on other crucial objects allows the actors to see their way to position. The last actor in place gives a sound cue for lights to come up. Try to work the sound into the opening scene. For example, a clicking of a tea cup may cue the lights, and when lights are on, the audience may see the characters grouped around a table drinking tea. Use the reverse procedure for exits: blackout to allow the actors to leave unseen.

Apart from these few modifications, the arena director carries through the same preparation and rehearsal schedule as necessary for proscenium shows.

Lighting for Arena

Of the backstage elements, lighting is crucial. Lights must be provided that will illuminate the actor from all four sides without lighting the audience. Brightness must be consistent unless otherwise desired. Fresnels (500-watt) provide the best light, but PAR-38 and R-40 reflectors with swivel sockets can also be used. (See Chapter 26.) All lights need louvers or funnels to prevent light spill from shining into the eyes of the au-

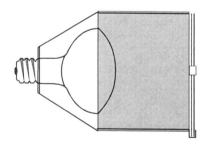

FUNNEL MADE FROM STOVE PIPE OR COFFEE CAN WITH A COLOR FRAME

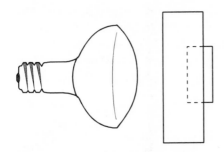

dience. You can purchase special "barndoor" louvers for Fresnels and spring clip louvers for reflector spots. Or you can make funnels for reflectors by using six-inch stove pipe or a two-pound coffee can with the bottom cut out. Attach to the pipe or can a wire flange and ring that will fit over the lamp. If you do not use colored lamps, you will also need to attach a color frame to the funnel.

PURCHASED LOUVER THAT CLIPS ONTO REFLECTOR LAMP

While proscenium lighting requires two spots per acting area, arena needs three to four spots for each area in order to light the actor on all sides. For example, if you have six playing areas in an approximate 18 x 20-foot rectangular stage and if you light with four spots to an area, you need twenty-four spots. If you light with three spots, you need eighteen units. A smaller playing area requires fewer spots. So does horseshoe staging.

If possible, mount lights on the ceiling, as this position facilitates achieving a 45-degree angle of light throw. If there are ceiling beams, attach porcelain receptacles to them

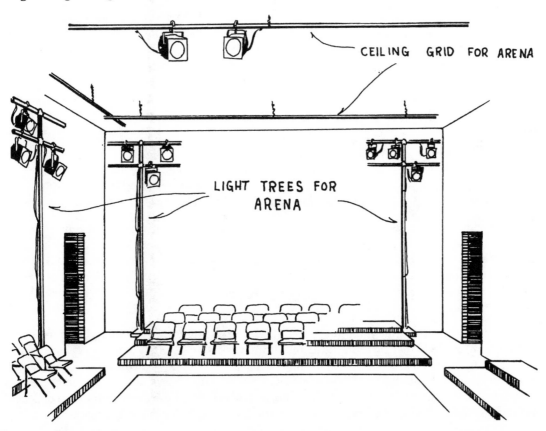

CEILING GRID FOR ARENA

LIGHT TREES FOR ARENA

and run lines to each receptacle. For greater flexibility construct a framework or grid 15 — 18 feet above the acting area. Use 1¼-inch pipe at right angles to the ceiling beams and hang units from the pipe. If there are no ceiling beams and you have a flat ceiling, hang pipe battens in a square or rectangular grid above the playing area. Be sure that all pipe battens extend a distance beyond the acting area to permit you to light the extreme edges and to focus all lights at a 45-degree angle onto the area.

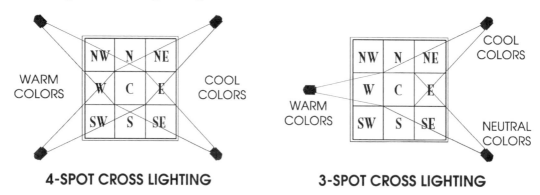

4-SPOT CROSS LIGHTING　　**3-SPOT CROSS LIGHTING**

When you use four spots per stage area, place them at 90-degree angles to each other. When you use three spots, set them about 120 degrees from each other. In focusing the light, direct each 45-degree angle beam about five feet from the floor onto the center of every acting area. To blend and tone all the areas and to give more prominence to the center, hang a 300-watt reflector flood directly over the center. Be sure the flood is equipped with a masking hood. If you desire, you can mask ceiling lights by hanging short drapes around the grid. This is not necessary, however, as the audience apparently does not mind seeing the units.

If you cannot mount lights on the ceiling, use six or eight light trees: tall pipe stands (on a heavy base) with cross bars to which light units are attached. Make the trees as high as the ceiling will allow, or at least high enough to obtain a 45-degree light throw. Place the trees behind the audience and focus the lights onto the acting area.

Color placement of lights differs in arena. If you use four cross spots, place warm colors opposite cool colors. If you use three cross spots, you must have three colors — warm, neutral, and cool — used in the same sequence, clockwise around each playing area. (Warm colors are usually thrown the longest distance.) For neutral colors, use either light flesh pink, special lavender, or frost. Be sure all colors used in arena are relatively pale and mix well.

It is important that you have full control of arena lights, since the lights must serve as a curtain. Place all acting area lights on dimmers. If you situate your arena theatre on a large stage, you can use the existing stage dimmers. Otherwise, you will need several small individual portable dimmers or one portable console. Auto transformers are good for this purpose and are not too expensive. If possible, have the house lights on dimmers, too. Blackouts will be smoother, and then you can dim the houselights for curtain warning.

The "open" stage or thrust of the Stratford Shakespearean Festival Theatre.

Ontario, Canada
Photographer,
Peter Smith

Properties and Set Pieces for Arena

In arena, properties must establish what scenery does in proscenium. Consequently, they must be chosen carefully if they are to create the proper illusion of mood, locale, and economic status. All furniture must be low. Sofa, tables, and chairs must not obscure audience sight lines. If possible, choose backless chairs and sofas. Keep all lamps, flower arrangements, etc., low. Try to get variety in furniture by utilizing chairs, loveseats, benches, stools, sofas. All props must bear close scrutiny, being as authentic as possible. You cannot fake arena properties. A papier-mâché sword may pass in proscenium, but in the round you need a real sword. Cold mashed potatoes may look like vanilla ice cream in proscenium, but to the arena audience, they look just like cold mashed potatoes!

In arena, eliminate stairs and fireplaces if possible. Eliminate windows or use low benches to denote window seats. Keep bookcases to a three-foot height. Eliminate pianos or use a small spinet. Food should be that which is actually designated. Newspapers must be actual. If the *New York Times* is needed, get a *New York Times*. You can fake headlines by gluing proper ones on but handle the paper so that the fake is not obvious. It is best not to use firearms in flexible theatre.

Cover the acting area with a carpet to outline the playing area and to set the play's mood. For example, a well-worn rug may denote a poor family. If you cannot vary the rug, choose a neutral color that you can use for any play. Light grey softens facial shadows; rose beige reflects a flattering color. Avoid extremely light and dark carpets since they either reflect or absorb too much light. If possible, carpet the aisles to mask entrance and exit sounds.

Sometimes scenery is used in the form of cutaway walls or fences. If you use cutaway scenery, be sure it is low and complete on all sides. In horseshoe staging, scenery is sometimes used at the open end.

Conduct all property and scene changes in full view of the audience. The audience enjoys this procedure immensely, and the crews can make an exact and quick change because they can see what they are doing. Shift crews should be cleanly dressed in uniform work clothes or in stylized costumes. If there are servants in the play, allow them to change the props. Sometimes the servants can do amusing pantomimes as they take their shift. In one whimsical arena show, all scene shifts were done to ballet steps by two servant girls in black dresses and lace aprons. Whatever the shift, rehearse it carefully. Shifts should be quickly executed and performed in keeping with the play. During shifts, use houselights rather than acting area lights. It is also pleasant to have background music.

Sound for Arena

In fact, sound is very important in flexible theatre. A tape deck and amplifier should be available for music to set the mood and cover curtain blackouts. Place the speakers near the acting area to bring the sound from there. In arena, sound effects such as wind and rain are usually on recordings. However, telephone rings should come from a bell that rings in the phone. Doorbells should come offstage near the entrance.

Costumes and Makeup for Arena

Like properties, costumes must be perfect in every detail. Little can be faked. Fabrics cannot be substituted and sewing must be well finished. Unless you want the opposite effect, costumes must fit exceedingly well. They should also be clean and pressed. Before entering the playing area, check for powder, hair, and lint on your costumes. If you rent costumes for a period play, tell the company you are using them for arena. You may receive better-looking and fitting garments.

Accessories must also be authentic and believable. Be careful of wearing your own jewelry. Class rings and fraternity pins immediately stand out as local and break the illusion of the play.

Makeup must appear real at close range. The audience should never be aware of theatrical makeup! Consequently, use makeup sparingly and apply it subtly. Pancake is often a good choice for foundation. Blend all highlights and shadows. Never leave harsh lines. Old-age makeup on young people is difficult in arena. Age should be conveyed primarily through body movement. Subtle modeling plus the graying of hair will suggest age. If you use beards and mustaches, work with them until they look natural. Be sure you skillfully dress all hair.

ASSIGNMENT AND ITS PURPOSE

Arena acting is an enjoyable experience for both actor and audience. For this assignment your class will present group Shakespearean scenes in arena style to an invited audience. Scenes will vary in length from about four to ten minutes long. All scenes will be student directed, acted, and produced. When the scenes are at performance level, you will present them in your classroom as an hour program.

You will be graded on acting, blocking, and staging as specified on the critique sheet for this chapter, found in the teacher's manual.

HOW TO PREPARE

1. Your instructor will divide the class into groups. He or she will assign each group a Shakespearean scene and designate the cast, the student director, and the student technician who will handle all necessary backstage elements for the specific group.

2. Your instructor will also select one student to serve as class stage manager. This student will arrange the order of scene presentation, provide publicity, programs, and lights. The stage manager will also conduct dress rehearsals and performance as well as prepare the room for the invited arena audience.

3. The following are scene suggestions:

   As You Like It
   > Act I, Scene III; serious. Celia, Rosalind, Duke Frederick
   > Act III, Scene II; comic. Orlando and Rosalind
   >> Begin: Rosalind, "I pray you, what is't a'clock?"

   Hamlet
   > Act I, Scene III; serious-comic. Laertes, Ophelia, Polonius
   >> End: Laertes, "Farewell"
   > Act III, Scene I; serious. Hamlet and Ophelia
   >> Begin: Hamlet, "To be, or not to be. . ."
   >> End: Hamlet, "The rest shall keep as they are. To a nunnery go."
   > Act V, Scene I; serious. Hamlet, Horatio, First Clown
   >> Begin: First Clown, "In youth, when I did love."
   >> End: Hamlet, "Here comes the King."

   Henry The Fifth
   > Act III, Scene IV; comic. Katharine and Alice (This short scene is in French)
   > Act V, Scene II; comic-serious. King Henry, Katharine, Alice
   >> Begin: King Henry, "Fair Katharine, and most fair, Will you vouchsafe to teach a soldier . . ."
   >> End: King Henry, "Here comes your father."

Julius Caesar
   Act II, Scene I; serious. Portia and Brutus
      Begin: Enter Portia, "Brutus, my lord."
      End: Brutus, "Leave me with haste."
   Act IV, Scene III; serious. Cassius and Brutus
      End: Brutus, "He'll think your mother chides, and leave you so."

Macbeth
   Act I, Scene V; serious. Lady Macbeth, Messenger, Macbeth
   Act II, Scene II; serious. Lady Macbeth, Macbeth
   Act V, Scene I; serious. Lady Macbeth, Doctor, Gentlewoman

Merchant of Venice
   Act I, Scene II; serious-comic. Portia, Nerissa, Servant
   Act III, Scene I; serious. Solanio, Salerio, Shylock, Tubal, Servant
      Begin: Solanio, "How now, Shylock. What news among the merchants?"

Midsummer Night's Dream
   Act III, Scene II; serious-comic. Lysander, Helen, Demetrius, Hermia
      Begin: Lysander, "Why should you think that I should woo in scorn?"
      End: Hermia, "I am amazed and know not what to say."

Much Ado About Nothing
   Act IV, Scene I; serious. Benedict and Beatrice
      Begin: Benedict, "Lady Beatrice, have you wept all this while?"
   Act V, Scene II; comic. Benedict, Margaret, Beatrice, Ursala

Romeo and Juliet
   Act II, Scene V; comic. Juliet and Nurse

Twelfth Night
   Act I, Scene III; comic. Sir Toby, Maria, Sir Andrew
   Act II, Scene V; comic. Sir Toby, Sir Andrew, Fabian, Maria, Malvolio

Additional Shakespearean scenes with excellent suggestions appear in Samuel Selden's *Shakespeare: A Player's Handbook of Short Scenes*, Holiday House, 1960, and Marchette Chute and Ernestine Perrie's *The Worlds of Shakespeare*, Dutton Co., 1963.

4. Outside of class you should read the complete play and make preliminary preparations. Your instructor will help you on interpretation problems. Each student director should block the scene for arena; each cast member should secure a script; the technical person should decide on costumes, props, and sound effects, and provide necessary charts and cue sheets. (If your school has a wardrobe collection that can be converted to believable Shakespearean costumes, use it. Or if time warrants, make the necessary costumes. Otherwise, do the scenes in appropriate modern dress.) The stage manager should attend to the duties as listed in step two.

5. When preliminary planning is complete, each group should simultaneously block and rehearse its scene in class. As soon as movement is set, begin memorizing lines. It will take many class periods of concentrated work to achieve performance level for the scenes.

6. The stage manager will conduct at least two dress rehearsals (three if done in Shakespearean costume). Go straight through the program as it is to be presented. Your instructor may offer a critique to tie each scene into a unified program. Double-check to be sure costumes, props, and makeup will stand close audience scrutiny. Carefully rehearse scene shifts that take but seconds each. Scene shifters should be dressed in appropriate and consistent attire.

HOW TO PRESENT

Make this as much of an actual theatre experience as possible. Drape your classroom windows to darken the room and provide adequate spotlights for lighting the playing area. Set rows of chairs in arena placement.

Use background music to establish the mood. You can obtain tapes or CD's of harpsichord and recorder music that suggest Shakespearean work. Or invite your school's choir leader to provide three or four madrigal singers for the occasion.

If you do not hand out programs, a designated student should announce each scene and give a brief, well-worded play synopsis of the circumstances leading up to each scene.

Present the program as rehearsed, striving for a polished, enjoyable performance.

ADDITIONAL PROJECTS ON ACTING IN THE ROUND AND THRUST

1. Do a one-act play in arena or thrust style. Follow the same basic procedure for preliminary planning, blocking, rehearsal, etc., as suggested in Chapter 27, but adapt it for intimate staging.

2. Prepare a short (30 to 40 minutes) children's play in arena style. Troupe the play to local elementary schools, playing in classrooms.

College of Southern Idaho

Actors rehearse on a thrust stage with the orchestra to be positioned audience right. This theatre's thrust can be hydraulically lowered, if desired, to create an orchestra pit.

UNIT VI

THEATRE APPRECIATION

Chapter
29   ATTENDING A PLAY

Time limit: Turn in your report no longer than three days after attending the theatre.

Activity sheet: Complete the activity sheet for the chapter, found in the teacher's manual, and attach it to your two-page report.

PROMPTINGS

1. Discuss the purpose and value of all types of theatre.
2. Compare movies and television to live theatre.
3. Compare other art forms to live theatre.
4. Discuss the differences in acceptable audience behavior for TV, movies, and live theatre.
5. Describe appropriate attire and behavior for attendance at live theatre plays.

THEATRE LANGUAGE

Edit   Metaphor
Empathy   Transitory
Etiquette

BACKGROUND NOTES

"All of the world's a stage," said Jacques in Shakespeare's *As You Like It*. Today that seems particularly true as we are inundated with theatre in the form of movies, videos, and television. While you undoubtedly feel comfortable with these media, perhaps your experience in seeing live theatre may be limited.

Certainly, the aim of all types of theatre should be to help us understand ourselves better as we learn about other people and the world. Types of theatre differ, however, in their offerings.

Movies and videos, at first glance, seems similar to live theatre in that there is a script, there are actors, directors, and backstage elements. The same plot is there too, as it is in a live stage version of the story. However, the experiences of seeing movies and attending plays are very different. When we see a film, we are witnessing pictures that have been arranged into a series of scenes, usually shot out of sequence and shot many times before the final "take." Every bit is edited to control permanently what we see. Countless viewings give us the same production. The show is frozen in time.

In contrast, live theatre is transitory. It is always in the "now." Each moment as it passes is gone forever, as is true in life. Even if the play is given night after night, each performance is a unique experience, because every night there is a different audience, and varying degrees of energy flow from the actors. Also, as an audience member watching a play, we can look at anything on stage we want to see. Our focus is not completely controlled by the editing room as it is in film and television.

Television, too, differs from live theatre. It has invaded our homes with everything from sit-coms to national disasters, sporting events, and wars. What we see in our living room often seems distorted as the events are presented with quick cuts and blatant commentary to accommodate the medium. Even though real events spill from TV into our homes, we sometimes feel estranged from life around us, because there is no sense of community, no feeling of the empathic response that we experience in live theatre.

Unlike other art forms such as paintings that forever remain constant, or novels which present the past reported in the present, theatre lets us experience that which is happening right now. Actors speak as if for the first time. There is immediacy as theatre gives us a metaphoric statement of life. When we attend theatre, we have a sense of occasion, of sharing with others the essence of the human condition.

Hopefully this class has encouraged you to see live theatre. When you attend, it is important for you to observe appropriate audience behavior. Society mandates what modes of conduct are acceptable for various situations. When you watch TV in your home, it is usually considered all right to talk out loud during a program, to leave and return to the room whenever you want, and to eat in front of the set. At rock concerts, as an audience member you sometimes shout, stomp your feet, stand up and move around. But in live theatre that behavior is inappropriate. The audience is expected to observe certain manners that will ensure an enjoyable evening for all in attendance.

ASSIGNMENT AND ITS PURPOSE

With a group of friends, attend a live play and observe audience response and behavior. Also analyze your own reactions. Write a two-page report on your impression and observations, noting differences between live theatre and the movies and television that you regularly see.

HOW TO PREPARE

1. With friends choose a play performance you wish to see and buy tickets in advance.

2. Dress up to attend this occasion.

3. Arrive early at the theatre.

4. Accept your responsibilities of a thoughtful and responsive audience member.

5. Be aware of your own response as well as that of other audience members.

HOW TO PRESENT

The next day write your comments and polish them. Include your receptiveness to the live show, noticing the differences between your experiences there and that which you have when attending movies or watching TV. Also report on audience behavior and attitude. Be sure you give specific examples to explain your statements.

Fill out the activity sheet for the chapter, found in the teacher's manual, and use it as a cover sheet for your report. Turn it in when your instructor calls for it.

ADDITIONAL PROJECT ON ATTENDING A PLAY

Research your library for articles by playwrights, painters, and other artists that discuss how their art form differs from the other fine arts.

THEATRE ETIQUETTE

1. Since theatre is a type of celebration with most people securing advance tickets and making special plans to attend, you should dress up for this festive occasion.

2. Arrive early to be seated and to read your printed program. After the curtain is up most theatres will not seat people until a scene break, so latecomers miss part of the show.

3. When you enter a row to get to your seat, face the people already seated. Do not turn your back to them as you cross to your seat.

4. Turn off the beeper on your watch or pager. An unexpected beep or alarm not only disturbs those around you but annoys the actors as well.

5. Remove hats and caps so that those seated behind you can see.

6. Don't put your feet on the seatback in front of you, whether or not someone is sitting there.

7. Avoid talking during the performance. It is discourteous to talk or whisper. Save comments until the intermission.

8. Do not take food or drink into the theatre. Also avoid unwrapping noisy candy and gum papers.

9. Respond to the play. Give it a chance to work its magic.

10. Don't leave during the play except for an emergency.

11. At the end, don't leave until the house lights are turned on. It is bad manners to slip out early.

12. To show that you enjoyed the performance, applaud at the end during the curtain call.

13. Do not give a standing ovation for every play. Reserve such a tribute for the truly outstanding performance.

14. Do not send flowers or gifts to the cast on stage. Instead, have such items delivered backstage.

15. If you sincerely enjoyed the performance, write a congratulatory note to the director and group. You will "make their day."

Chapter
30   EVALUATING A PLAY

Time Limits: 13 – 15 minutes or as your instructor designates

Activity Sheet: Write a critique of a play on the activity sheet for this chapter, found in the teacher's manual. Before you participate in the group discussion, hand the sheet to your instructor

PROMPTINGS

1. Define dramatic criticism.
2. Discuss ways you can learn about a production's quality.
3. Explain the three basic requirements of a critic.
4. Discuss the theatre's obligations to the audience.
5. List and explain Goethe's three general principles of criticism.
6. Discuss specific criteria for measuring a theatre production.
7. Explain the playgoer's obligations when serving as critic.

THEATRE LANGUAGE

Criteria   Dramatic criticism
Critique   Goethe's principles (gû´te)

BACKGROUND NOTES

Dramatic criticism is a field that everyone invades. Viewers of plays, movies, and television are quick to evaluate, to criticize, or to judge. In so doing, they are stating their opinion, for dramatic criticism is mainly that — personal opinion.

But opinions vary and often there are conflicting views concerning the same subject. One critic may praise a play; another may discredit it. How, then, are you to know whose opinion to respect? There are two ways. You may confront the critic with the question, "Why?" "Why was the play good?" "Why was it weak?" The viewer who shrugs and says, "I don't know. . . It just was," is not worth your consideration. But the critic who can intelligently answer the challenging why, who can back up opinions with valid reasons based on understanding and keen insight, is one whom you can respect. That opinion merits attention.

Another way to decide whether or not a play is good is to see it yourself and make your own judgment. But again, the worthiness of your opinion rests solely on what you bring to the play. If you have a background in theatre and a training in its various aspects, you can develop into an intelligent, discerning critic because you will know why something is good or why it is inadequate. In addition, your drama training and your subsequent appreciation of that art will lead to your increased enjoyment of good theatre.

Unfortunately, the word criticism has a derogatory connotation, and in practice, many critics only find fault. The purpose of criticism is, however, to evaluate, to show both the good and bad points. Such evaluation should in turn help to guide listeners, readers, or participants.

In the classroom, criticism is an important learning tool when it is properly handled. From a critique, students discover their strong points as well as those aspects that need improvement. With effort, such awareness enables them to raise their performance level.

In the professional field, dramatic criticism works in an absolute way. Professional critics attend first night performances and cast written judgment on the quality of the show. Thumbs up and the show lives; thumbs down and it closes, for New York audiences seem to prefer following the advice of their favorite critic, rather than seeing the play and forming their own opinions.

While you may never become a professional critic, as a student of drama you can learn how to give worthwhile judgment that will be respected by your listener. Of utmost importance is your background. It is imperative that you have:

1. A sound knowledge of all phases of the theatre, for the critic considers every aspect before making an appraisal.

2. A sense of good taste, which is the ability to discriminate with wisdom. It is nurtured from study, from being exposed to numerous productions, and from analyzing professional reviews.

3. An acceptable standard of criteria upon which to base your evaluation.

From your study in this course you are undoubtedly cognizant of the obligations of the theatre. Theatre must emotionally move the audience. It can challenge, thrill, or inspire us. But if it bores us, it has failed. Furthermore, the theatre must create a concentrated or intensified illusion of reality. We must be able to see more of life on stage than we could possibly live in the same amount of time; and what we see must appear real, truthful, or believable for the moment. Characters, events, and dialogue must remain consistent with the established style, whether the play be fantasy or realism. We must momentarily accept what we see and hear.

Keeping the theatre's obligations in mind, let us establish a general foundation for evaluation. Critics in numerous fields agree that the principles of Goethe (1749–1832), a great German philosopher, critic, and playwright, are sound and usable as a basis for criticism. Goethe always asked three things:

1. *What was the artist (author, actor, director, technician) trying to do?* Did the author aim at writing a tragedy? A fantasy? A farce? What was the author trying to say? Was the actor showing off his or her own personality or attempting to create the character? What was the director's purpose? The scene designers, etc.?

2. *How well did the artist do it?* Was the artist successful? Does the author's farce contain the necessary requirements to be a farce? Does the tragedy contain the elements indicative of that art form? Were the actor's technique and the director's method effective? In order to decide these questions, you will need to apply specific criteria pertaining to dramatic art. We will discuss this criteria in a moment.

3. *Was it worth doing?* Here you must form your opinion as to whether or not the time and effort was worthwhile for both artist and audience. Even if the artist succeeds in achieving his or her aim, the efforts may not be of value. After considering the whole production, you must decide its worth.

As general criteria, the above three questions are valuable, for they allow you to judge the work of an artist only after you have considered purpose, use of technique, and the value of the efforts. You will be wise to learn these three questions and apply them to many fields.

Criteria for Evaluating the Artist

Under item two of Goethe's principles, we stated that you must have a specific yardstick for measurement. The following may serve as criteria for evaluating the artist's success in the theatre.

I. Play Writing

Did the play have:

A. The necessary elements of its genre?

B. Universal appeal?

C. Individuality and freshness of style?

D. Subtle suggestion?

E. Clear organization with events rising to a strong climax?

F. Lucid, believable characterizations that arouse audience empathy?

G. Expressive dialogue?

H. Unified effect that provides interest through variety and contrast?

I. Balance of emotional climax and release?

II. Acting

A. *Belief.* Was each character convincing and believable? Was each true to the play, the production, and the theatrical conditions? Was the acting spontaneous (illusion of the first time)?

B. *Voice.* Were the quality, interpretation, and projection suitable for the character? Were proper tempo and rhythm achieved in line delivery and cue pickup?

C. *Body.* Were gestures, movement, and business motivated, clear, varied, and appropriate? Was proper stage technique incorporated with ease?

D. *Emotions.* Was there proper balance between emotion and control? Were reactions true? Was mood sustained? Were climaxes achieved?

E. *Relationships.* Were the proper relationships established among characters? Was there team work? Ensemble playing?

F. *Projection.* Did the characters project orally and visually to the audience? Did they communicate with economy, clarity, control, and conviction?

III. Directing

A. Were all aspects unified and faithful to the author's purpose?

B. Was stage composition handled effectively and smoothly with proper emphasis, balance, variety, and contrast?

C. Did rhythm and tempo provide the correct mood, with appropriate climax and release in each scene and act?

D. Was there correct balance of aesthetic distance and empathy?

IV. Staging

A. *Set.* Did it unobtrusively provide appropriate background and mood for the play?

B. *Lights.* Did they establish proper visibility, emphasis, and mood?

C. *Costumes and Makeup.* Was each in harmony with the character, period, mood, and style?

D. *Mechanics.* Were lights, sound effects, curtains, etc., handled effectively and on cue? Were scene shifts provided quickly and quietly?

V. Audience Response

A. Was the audience attentive? Interested?

B. Did it respond consistently to the play's aims — laugh at the proper moments; cry at the proper times?

C. Did it appreciate the dramatic situation? The witty repartee? The beautiful phrases?

D. Was the applause heartily spontaneous or dutifully polite?

E. During intermission and after the show, did audience members enthusiastically discuss the play?

Before you use the above questions for evaluation, you should be aware of the critic's obligation — the ethics of the field. Always respect the following do's and don'ts.

DO —

1. Back up all your opinions with valid reasons based on appropriate standards. It is your right to agree or disagree with others only if you soundly substantiate your opinion.

2. Be objective and fair. Realize your own prejudices and make the necessary allowances for them. Always keep an open mind. Be guided not only by your reactions but by those of the audience.

3. Evaluate the whole production. Take into consideration the five major areas for evaluating the artist's success described previously.

4. Be constructive. Indicate good points along with those that need improvement. This is particularly important in class and in rehearsal where performers often profit more from praise than from adverse comments. Whatever the criticism, be diplomatic. Rather than saying something is awful or bad, label it as "needing improvement."

5. Be sincere. Believe what you say. The opinion must be yours and not that of someone else. Certainly, in many cases you can be guided by professional critics, but you must learn to develop your own beliefs that are grounded in knowledge and understanding.

DON'T —

1. Don't be constantly negative.

2. Don't be clever at the expense of the artist. Your purpose is to evaluate, not ridicule.

3. Don't be overly critical. Always approach a performance with an attitude of enjoying it. If you constantly look for something wrong, you can't possibly give a fair review. Don't dwell on minute mishaps such as the fluffing of a line, unless their abundance obscures the total picture.

4. Don't be arrogant. Any judge needs humility, understanding, and kindness.

ASSIGNMENT AND ITS PURPOSE

The fun and enjoyment of a theatre party is yours in this assignment. As a group, you are to attend a local play performance and afterwards prepare a critique. Then, in class you will air your views in a group discussion.

You will be graded on your conduct at the theatre, how well you substantiate your opinions with sound reasoning, your objectivity, your sincerity, and your constructive appraisal of the whole performance based on an evaluation of its parts.

HOW TO PREPARE

1. As a class, choose a play performance you would like to attend. If possible, the class should go together as a group. Otherwise, divide into sections, with each group attending a different night's performance.

2. Appoint co-chairpersons to make all necessary arrangements such as obtaining reserved seats, collecting ticket money, and deciding on a place for the group to assemble before the performance.

3. Dress up to attend the theatre.

4. Be on your best behavior at the theatre. Loud talking, shouting, and scuffling only announce your poor taste and your inexperience as an audience member. Act with poise; be gracious and polite so that you and everyone else will enjoy the occasion. (See Chapter 29, Theatre Etiquette.)

5. Accept the responsibility of an audience member. Be in a receptive mood, ready to enjoy, to laugh, to cry. Allow your imagination to function. Suspend disbelief and enter the realm of theatre.

6. Enjoy the show, making notations only during the intermission and after the final curtain. When you arrive home, you may wish to list a few more items while they are fresh in your mind.

7. The next day, write your critique. First, judge each area — play, acting, directing, staging, and audience response — according to Goethe's three principles. Under principle number two, include the specific drama criteria described previously in this chapter. Then, on the activity sheet write a critique in which you evaluate the whole production, as dependent upon the parts. Substantiate your opinions with specific examples and sound reasons.

HOW TO PRESENT

Your instructor will divide the class into five discussion groups. In each, a leader will be appointed and each group will be assigned one critical aspect (play, acting, directing, staging, or audience response). It is important that the topic be assigned after you have seen the play, so that you won't be concentrating on just one phase as you watch the show.

Each group will have 15 minutes to prepare. The leader should devise pertinent questions to stimulate discussion. Questions should be phrased to prevent a "yes or no" answer. If your group is to discuss acting, the leader may include such questions as "How would you evaluate the believability of the acting?" "What aspects were particularly effective?" "How could that problem be solved?" "Why do you believe that this was weak?" etc. Discussion members should use the 15 minutes to quietly assemble their thoughts and to make necessary notes.

When your group is called upon, hand your activity sheet to your instructor and then sit at the table placed in front of the room. The leader will introduce the discussion by stating the topic and asking an initial question. Each group member should volunteer his or her opinions and reasons, stating them clearly, sincerely, and courteously. Don't wait for the leader to call on you. Do your part to help the leader by keeping the talk active. There is no time to be bashful in a group discussion. Get in and participate, so that at the end of the time limit, you will have adequately viewed the topic.

Each group will be allowed 13–15 minutes. The timekeeper will signal after thirteen minutes. The leader should then summarize the major opinions of the group and offer a suitable conclusion. When the group is through, return with poise to your desk.

ADDITIONAL PROJECTS ON EVALUATING A PLAY

1. Compare the criticisms of two different professional critics concerning the same Broadway play. Suggested sources: *The New York Times, The Washington Post, The New Yorker, Time, Saturday Review.* Notice any differences between reviews hurriedly written for a daily newspaper and those written for a weekly magazine.

2. View a play, movie, or television show and write a critique of it. Read your evaluation to the class.

3. Divide the class into five or six groups and assign each group a different television program. Within each group, members will individually view the same show and write a critique. In class, group members will read aloud and compare each of their evaluations. If possible, compare class criticism with that of a professional television critic.

Chapter 31 EXPLORING THEATRE HISTORY

Time limits: To be arranged with your instructor

Activity Sheet: The scope of this assignment allows numerous projects which are suggested at the end of each segment. Discuss your choice with your instructor and describe it on this chapter's activity sheet, found in the teacher's manual.

PROMPTINGS

1. Discuss the beginnings of theatre including the Primitive and Egyptian contributions.

2. Show the importance of ancient Greek theatre by relating it to civic and religious implications.

3. List the three great Greek tragedians and their contributions.

4. Compare Roman theatre to Greek theatre.

5. Discuss Eastern and Oriental theatre.

6. Plot the development of Medieval theatre in Europe.

7. Describe the social climate in Elizabethan England.

8. Relate details about Shakespeare's life, his plays, and characteristics.

9. Discuss Jonson and Marlowe's theatre contributions and plays.

10. Explain the structure of outdoor theatres in Elizabethan times, relating conjecture about the Globe theatre.

11. Describe major theatre contributions that came from the Italian and French Renaissance.

12. Discuss Restoration and 18th century drama.

13. Compare Romanticism to Realism in the 19th century drama.

14. Describe early American drama and theatre activities.

15. Discuss highlights of 20th century drama including trends and playwrights.

16. Describe the U.S. theatre today, including influences of regional theatre and the emerging voices.

THEATRE LANGUAGE

Avant-garde	Kyogen	Soliloquy
Blank verse	Miracle play	Thespian
City Dionysia	Morality Play	Trilogy
Closet drama	Mystery play	Trope
Comedy of manners	Noh drama	Passion play
Commedia dell'arte	Realism	Vaudeville
Hubris	Regional theatre	Wooden-O
Kabuki	Ritual	

BACKGROUND NOTES

A knowledge of theatre history is a rich possession. To know the development of theatre is to know the development of the human race. As the theatre grows, civilization grows; when it flourishes, humans flourish; and when it is suppressed, people walk in darkness.

Theatre and the human race are as related as mirror and reflection, as self and shadow. Study theatre of a particular era, and you learn the religious, social, political, and economic influences of that time. You learn the people's desires, ideals, and needs. And perhaps more important, you gain insight into the present from what has gone before. A comparison of past eras not only emphasizes the evolution of drama, but it elucidates the theatre of today and prognosticates that of tomorrow.

Our study here will give you only the major aspects of theatre history. For greater depth and details, you may want to read some of the books on theatre background. You may also wish to take a special college course in theatre history.

PRIMITIVE TRIBES

Drama, a Greek word, means to do or to act. But drama itself is much older than the Greek civilization. It was born out of the dance of primitive people, when instinctive rhythmic movements and desire to imitate evolved into pantomimes that told or showed or mimicked something.

There were initiation dances to teach the tribe's customs to boys reaching manhood; war dances to kindle bravery in the warriors; story dances to imitate events of the hunt or battle; and religious dances to appease the numerous unseen spirits that the savage felt controlled the world.

From these religious dances evolved a ritual. The chief representative of the gods — the medicine man, shaman, witch doctor, or priest — would don a mask believed to have powerful magic and would pray, exorcise spirits, and chant while the tribe assisted or watched.

Out of this religious ritual, performed in a circle in front of the temple, drama emerged with its speaking actor.

Today we can still see some primitive dramatic forms in the dances of South African and Australian tribes. Remnants of ancient ritual are equally evident in the Hawaiian hula and in the American Indian dances, such as the snake dance, the corn dance, and the sun dance.

Suggested Projects —

1. From current articles, such as those in the *National Geographic*, report on the drama of today's primitives. Show pictures if possible.

2. Write a paper on the importance of imitation in the development of primitive drama.

   Suggested sources:

   > Macgowan, Kenneth, and Herman Ross. *Masks and Demons*.
   > Macgowan, Kenneth, and William Melnitz. *The Living Stage*.
   > Fraser, James. *The Golden Bough*.
   > Roberts, Vera. *On Stage*.

EGYPTIAN THEATRE

As far as we know, the Egyptians were the first people to establish a type of drama, performing plays as early as 3000 B.C. The Egyptian people were primarily concerned with life after death, and those who could afford it had huge pyramids built and splendidly furnished, for they intended to live in them in the afterworld. Their philosophy of life and death is exemplified in their drama.

There were five types of Egyptian plays, all of them serving more as religious ritual than as pure theatre, performed either in special tombs or in the temples.

1. The *Pyramid* plays were written on the tomb walls and included not only the plot and characters but basic stage directions. These religious dramas, enacted by the priests, show the ascent of the soul to become a star and symbolize the resurrection of the body.

2. The *Coronation Festival* play was performed at the crowning of a new pharaoh.

3. The *Heb Sed* or *Coronation Jubilee* play celebrated the pharaoh's thirtieth year on the throne, enacting the events of his reign.

4. The *Medicinal* play evolved around magical healing. The plot concerned the goddess Isis, whose child is bitten by a scorpion. Isis heals her son by using artificial respiration and a magic cure.

5. The *Abydos Passion* play again developed the resurrection theme. Set, the god of evil, becomes jealous of his brother, Osiris. Tricking Osiris into a coffin, Set nails it shut and throws it into the Nile. Isis, the wife of Osiris, finds the coffin and buries her husband; but Set digs him up, dismembers the body, and throws it over the earth. Isis collects the pieces and buries them again. Osiris is then resurrected and becomes King of the Dead, ruling over those mortals who ascend to heaven.

The annual production of this play, given as part of a religious festival, would last several days. It included a mock water battle on the Nile and a funeral procession in which the audience participated.

Suggested Projects —

1. Show pictures and report on the ancient Egyptian civilization. If possible, as a class, visit a museum showing Egyptian artifacts.

2. Write a paper showing the relationship between the Abydos Passion play performed by the ancient Egyptians, and the Oberammergau passion play performed today in Germany.

HEBREW THEATRE

Although there is mention of dance and ritual in the Old Testament, there is no reference to a definite theatre in Judea. However, two books of the Bible read as dramatic literature. The *Song of Solomon*, which was probably chanted at wedding festivals, contains beautiful poetic dialogue spoken by a bride and groom.

The *Book of Job* is almost like a five-act drama with a prologue and epilogue. There is no record, though, of its having ever been performed in ancient times. Today it is usually classified as dramatic poetry rather than drama. However, there have been several modern adaptations of the story which have been successful on stage.

Suggested Projects —

1. Read the *Book of Job* in the Bible, and the modern version, *J. B.* by Archibald MacLeish. Compare the two for dramatic structure and tell how each reflects the time in which it was written.

2. Enact a scene from *J. B.* by Archibald MacLeish. Present it to the class.

GREEK THEATRE

With ancient Greek theatre, we have a drama so outstanding that it has never been surpassed. Only the Elizabethans came close to achieving such an apogee. The Golden Age of Greece (500–400 B.C.) brought us the greatest tragedies of all time, as well as outstanding creativity in such fields as architecture and government.

Greek theatre had its beginnings in the Dionysian rites that paid homage to Dionysus, the god of wine and fertility. These public celebrations were held around stone altars at the

foot of hilly vineyards. There was much dancing and singing of hymns or dithyrambs to honor Dionysus, and as these religious celebrations gained impetus, choral groups were organized with vocal contests among them.

Ruins of ancient Greek Theatre of Dionysus at Athens
Courtesy of Alienari-Art Reference Bureau

A statue, possibly of an actor with a mask, apparently was one of many that decorated the front of the paraskene at the Theatre of Dionysus.

Out of these dithyrambic rituals developed tragedy, which literally means goat song *(tragos)*. There is disagreement among scholars as to why it was thus called. There are several possibilities. Perhaps the chorus wore goat skins, or they draped the altar with one, or a goat was sacrificed at the end of the festival as an offering to the gods.

Of the four Dionysian festivals, the one held in March, the City Dionysia, developed into a festival of tragedies, where a coveted prize was awarded the best series of plays. The festival, which took place in Athens, was both a national and religious ceremony. Since business was suspended for a week, everyone participated. Crowds came from the surrounding villages, and if someone could not afford the nominal ticket price, the state would pay their entrance fee. Both sexes attended, although theatre production and acting were restricted to males (as was true worldwide for many centuries).

The annual festival lasted five or six days. The first day included a procession that carried the image of Dionysus to the city limits where a day of religious rites, wine drinking, merrymaking, and singing was spent. At night the image was returned to the theatre (*theatron* or seeing place) by candlelight.

The next day or two were given to dithyrambic contests performed by various choral groups. The final three days were reserved for the play contests. In festive mood the audience assembled at dawn to see the long performances. Each day a different dramatist was featured. He would offer four plays: a trilogy, or three tragedies centered around one theme; and a satire, or farce, that burlesqued the same tragic figures and provided the comic relief necessary after the heavy trilogy. At the end of the festival the winning author and his financial backer *(choregus)* were allowed to wear the coveted ivy garland.

It should be pointed out that comedies (from *komos*, meaning a band of revellers) were sometimes given in the afternoon during the City Dionysia. However, most comedies were performed at the Lenaea festival (in early February) where prizes were awarded for the best comic writer.

Plays were performed out-of-doors. At first, the theatre consisted of crude benches placed on a sloping hill and looking down on a circle of hard-packed ground, where the chorus performed around an altar. Later, the side of the mountain was scooped out into a bowl shape, something like our amphitheaters today, and tiers of stone seats in concentric semicircles were built on the hill. These theatres often seated as many as 20,000 spectators, with a special first row being reserved for dignitaries. The acting area, called the orchestra, was the circular space marked out on the ground at the foot of the hill. It varied from sixty-five feet to eighty-five feet in diameter.

The actors changed costumes in the *skene,* a small building first situated at the side of the orchestra and later permanently placed behind it. The *skene,* from which we derive the word scene, had three doors in its facade through which actors would enter. To the right and left between the *skene* and the orchestra was a wide passageway, called the *parodos,* which was used for the chorus to enter and exit. Eventually, a platform called a *Proskenion* (from which we get the term proscenium) was placed in front of the *skene* for the actors. On each side, two wings called the *Paraskenia* were introduced.

The structure of this theatre, as is true of any playhouse, influenced acting and presentation. Since the theatre was large and the distance between audience and playing area was great, the drama was rhetorical, containing more speech than action. The actors, all men, of necessity used broad gestures and declamatory speaking. To project to the audience, the actor made himself taller by wearing thick soled shoes, called *cothornus,* and a high headpiece, called an *onkus.* In addition, he wore wooden, cork, or linen masks that fitted over the entire head. These masks not only denoted the character, station in life, and emotion, but they projected the actor's voice through a type of inside megaphone.

Costumes of both the actor and the chorus consisted of standard Greek attire: the sleeveless *chiton,* or tunic, belted below the breast; the *himation,* or long mantle, draped around the right shoulder; and the *chlamys,* or short cloak. These costumes were very color-ful and often had elaborately embroidered patterns on them.

Staging was accomplished simply with the use of *pinakes,* or scenery painted on boards and placed against the *skene,* and *periaktois,* or triangular prisms that could be revolved for scenery changes. A few properties were also used. Drums were sounded for thunder, and the *eccyclema,* a small wagon platform, was wheeled in to show a corpse to the audience (all killing had to occur off stage and be reported to the audience by the chorus or a messenger). The *deus-ex-machina* was a unique mechanical crane used for lowering and raising gods. Its name is still employed today for labeling any device, such as the death of a rich uncle, that unexpectedly occurs to assist the main character in solving problems conve-niently.

Sketch of Theatre at Epidaurus

The Theatre of Dionysus in Athens by Arthur Wallace Pickard-Cambridge.
Reprinted by permission of Oxford University Press.

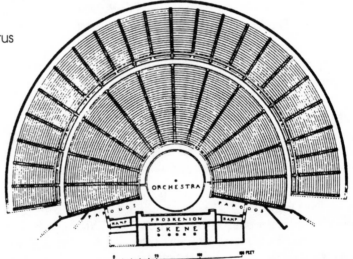

The Greek tragedies were based on ancient myths which were well known and en-joyed by the audience. Most of the plays encompassed certain elements that Aristotle (384–322 B.C.) later identified in his *Poetics.*

Aristotelian Elements for Tragedy

1. The tragedy must provide catharsis, or a spiritual purge, that is attained when the audience feels pity and terror from what they see on stage. The plays inspire the audience to live better lives.

2. The hero, who must be in a high social position (kings, gods), must possess a tragic flaw: something in his character or a failure in his judgment that brings disaster.

3. There must be a change of fortune involving reversal (the character's efforts boomerang) or discovery (the character moves from ignorance to knowledge).

4. The plays must be written in the highest form of poetry.

5. The plots must conform to the three unities of:
    a. Action: a series of closely related events.
    b. Time: action takes place within twenty-four hours.
    c. Place: action takes place in only one locale.

(It should be pointed out that many of the Greek plays did not observe the unity of place and time, but Aristotle still included this element in his treatise.)

Besides containing the previous qualities, most of the tragedies followed a set form.

➤ The *Prologue* introduced the play.

➤ The *Parados* was a song that brought on the chorus.

➤ The *Epeisodion* (of which there were usually five) was a passage of dialogue that alternated with...

➤ The *Stasimon* or song by the chorus.
    As the chorus chanted or sang, often to the accompaniment of music, they moved with slow dance-like grace so that the songs were broken into two passages:
    • The *strophe* as the chorus moved left; and
    • The *antistrophe* as they moved back to the right.

➤ The *Exodus* took the chorus offstage and ended the play.

The first tragedian to win the City Dionysia playwriting prize was Thespis. In his plays that year (534 B.C.), he introduced a leader for the chorus. The leader would speak, and the chorus would respond in chants. Thus, the leader became the first Greek actor. Thespis also instigated another first in his theatre: the use of masks. It is from his name that actors today are called thespians.

Three great writers of tragedy developed during the Golden Age. Their few extant plays are still performed today throughout the world. Aeschylus (525–456 B.C.), who has been termed the Father of Tragedy, is considered by many scholars to be the greatest tragic poet of all time. He was a rugged individual and a warrior at the Battle of the Marathon. Aeschylus frequently participated in the City Dionysia, winning first prize thirteen times. He is attributed with inventing the trilogy and adding a second actor to the plays. He reduced the chorus from fifty to twelve, but that august group still handled most of the play, relating the events and setting the mood. Aeschylus loved spectacle and his plays abounded with it. He had Prometheus, the god, fall off a cliff, and he dressed the Furies in such frightful masks that it is said women and children fainted upon seeing them.

As was current for his day, Aeschylus accepted the gods and the fate they decreed for man. While all of his plays reflect with dignity and simplicity this "predestination" philosophy, they also show the worth of man and man's sense of responsibility. Of Aeschylus' ninety plays, only seven are extant. You should at least be familiar with his Oresteia trilogy or the story of the house of Atreus, since the other two great Greek dramatists also wrote about this legend.

The Oresteia trilogy encompasses two religious beliefs of the ancient Greeks. The *Sin of Hubris* decreed that one must suffer for too much pride or arrogance; the *Vengeance Theme* made it a religious obligation to avenge a wrong done to one's family. In *Agamemnon*, the first play of the Oresteia trilogy, Agamemnon returns home from ten years of war, commits the Sin of Hubris, and is killed by his wife Clytemnestra, who has never forgiven him for sacrificing their eldest daughter to the gods. In *Libation Bearers*, Electra, the remaining daughter of Agamemnon, talks her brother Orestes into killing their mother in revenge. The third play, *The Furies*, finds Orestes being chased throughout the world because of the murder. Finally, he is pardoned by the gods.

The second great writer of tragedies was Sophocles (497–406 B.C.). He was a handsome, well educated man of many talents: musician, singer, and athlete. He was also interested in civic affairs, becoming the treasurer of Athens. Sophocles, like Aeschylus, had a brilliant career in theatre. He wrote over 100 scripts and won eighteen Dionysia Festivals. In his plays he introduced a third actor and changed the chorus to fifteen. Sophocles was a polished literary craftsman who had keen theatrical sense. His plays abound with beautiful language, a well-balanced plot, and excellent character portrayal. Today his work is considered the essence of great Greek drama. The best known of his seven extant plays are *Electra*, in which he handles the Oresteia theme; *Oedipus Rex*, in which Oedipus unknowingly kills his father and marries his own mother in an effort to resist fate; and *Antigone*, a "sequel" to Oedipus.

Euripides (485–406 B.C.), although apparently good at boxing and painting, confined himself to a literary life. He would often retire to a cave overlooking the sea and there he would meditate and write. Sometimes considered the "First Modern," Euripides was an unorthodox thinker who questioned the traditional religious ideas and gods. His plays emphasize psychological motivations and social consciousness, particularly accentuating the plight of women and the problem of the outsider. He was the first to "humanize" drama with little household details and events that appeal to the emotions. His *Medea* is a potent tragedy that shows the mental anguish of Medea who is driven mad by jealousy. In *Alcestis*, Euripides wrote a tragicomedy that combined both the serious and the humorous.

Besides these three great tragedians, two writers of comedy gained note. Aristophanes (circa 450–380 B.C.) is considered the finest comic writer of ancient Greece. His biting, bawdy satire on Athenian life produced vigorous plays that abound with humorous ideas and bold attacks. His comic fantasy *The Birds* appeals most to today's taste since its humor is less dated. His other plays include: *The Frogs*, a satire on Euripides; and *The Clouds*, a satire on Socrates.

Menander (circa 342–291 B.C.) was also a celebrated writer of comedy. Unlike Aristophanes who wrote on social aspects, Meander burlesqued domestic or private life. His plays teem with cunning servants, parasitic relatives, protective fathers, and young lovers. Until the 20th century, only fragments of Menander's plays were extant; our knowledge of his work was gleaned mainly from ancient Roman writers who copied him extensively. But in 1957, *The Curmudgeon*, a complete farce by Menander, was discovered. This lively spoof shows us his comic genius.

Finally, the great Grecian drama began to deteriorate as Caesar's armies marched over the land. From Greek drama, the victorious Romans established their theatre, but their imitation greatly deviated from the Attic original.

Suggested Projects —

1. Report on the ancient Greek physical theatre, showing pictures of its gradual development. See *On Stage* by Vera Roberts, and *Development of the Theatre* by Allardyce Nicoll.

2. Read one of the following plays and give a class report on it:

   Agamemnon, Aeschylus   *Oedipus Rex*, Sophocles
   Libation Bearers, Aeschylus   *Antigone*, Sophocles
   The Furries, Aeschylus   *Medea*, Euripides
   Prometheus Bound, Aeschylus   *Alcestis*, Euripides
   Electra, Sophocles   *The Curmudgeon*, Menander
                                        (printed in *Horizon*, July, 1959, pp. 79–89)

3. Read O'Neill's *Mourning Becomes Electra* and compare its theme and style with the Oresteia trilogy.

4. Read Robert Turney's *Daughters of Atreus* and report on it to the class, showing its handling of the Oresteia. Draw a sketch of the Atreus' family tree so that relationships are made clear.

5. See a video of one of the Greek tragedies and report on it.

6. Rehearse and present a scene from one of the Greek plays.

7. Construct a mask similar to one used in ancient Greek Theatre. Explain the character's personality, social position, and age as symbolized in the mask.

8. Diagram an approximate "time chart" showing the life span of Aeschylus through Menander, so that you can more readily see the period relationship of these dramatists.

9. Report on the training of actors in ancient Greece. Compare your information with what you know of today's actors. See *On Stage* by Vera Roberts.

10. Provide a bulletin board display with a set of pictures of Greek and Roman theatres obtained from University Prints, 15 Brattle Street, Harvard Square, Cambridge, Massachusetts 02138.

ROMAN THEATRE

As the Romans invaded Grecian territory, they began to take special interest in Greek literature and art. Soon, Rome's crude native drama was replaced by translations and adaptations of the Greek plays.

Since theatre was frowned upon by the aristocratic Romans, audiences consisted mainly of the lower classes. Their desire was for entertainment. Scoffing at the aesthetic and intellectual, they demanded spectacle and vulgarity. Thus, the imitated Greek theatre became decadent and hollow. Tragedies gradually degenerated and comedies slipped into vulgar slapstick.

Because the Senate was hostile to theatre, at first Roman playhouses were merely portable wooden platforms around which the audience stood. But in 61 B.C., Pompey had a huge outdoor auditorium built. In order to make it legal, he erected a small statue of Venus at the top and called it a temple of worship. The "steps" of this temple, of course, served as seats for the theatre.

Not to be outdone, Caesar ordered a playhouse built that was in the shape of two wooden theatres, back to back, each of which could be revolved to face the other. After a play presentation, the seats could be swung around into an amphitheatre for chariot races and gladiatorial contests.

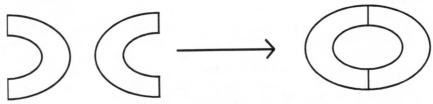

Other permanent theatres gradually were built. Usually the stage was a raised narrow platform called the *pulpitum* (from which we derive the word pulpit). This was backed by a three-storied wall filled with ornate carvings and statues. The semicircular seating area was connected to the stage, creating a single unit. Awnings were sometimes placed over the audience area, and later, permanent wooden roofs were erected.

The Romans were the first to use a front curtain. It rolled up and down from a trough in the downstage floor. Roman theatre also instigated the claque, a person paid to arouse the audience into clapping and shouting.

Of Rome's comic writers, we need mention only two. Plautus (254–184 B.C.) copied Greek plots, added stock characters, and lavishly sprinkled the action with slapstick. His plays are important mainly because they served as a pattern for later writers. For example, his *Menaechmi* influenced Shakespeare's *Comedy of Errors*, and his *Pot of Gold* served as Molière's pattern for *The Miser*. The second noted writer of comedy, Terence (185–159 B.C.), continued to borrow plots from the Greeks, styling his plays after Menander.

Only one tragedian, Seneca (circa 4 B.C.–65 A.D.), was a major playwright. He too borrowed plots from the Greeks, but his plays are so bombastic and abound with such gory details that they make better "closet" drama (plays to be read) than actual performances. However, Seneca had a great influence on later drama, since his works were rediscovered during the early Renaissance and served as models for numerous playwrights throughout Europe and England.

Soon Roman theatrical activity gained impetus, with plays and other entertainment being presented for every holiday. And there were many Roman holidays, numbering 175 at one time, which, would have occupied about six months' time.

The production of plays was eventually overshadowed by sensational spectaculars. In the colosseums, gladiatorial contests were interspersed with Christians being fed to the lions. Special arenas called *naumachiaes* were filled with water, and slaves on ships fought until all hands were killed.

Finally, theatre entertainment became so base that when Rome fell in 475 A.D. and the Christian church took over, all theatrical activity was banned. For hundreds of years afterward, theatre lay dormant throughout the Continent. The East, however, did not suffer the darkness of Europe. Instead, theatrical forms that had been nurtured from years past, gained impetus throughout India and the Orient.

Suggested Projects —

1. Show pictures and report on the various Roman playhouses, including the arenas.

2. Compare the social position of actors in Rome with those in Greece. Include a report on Roscius, the noted Roman actor. (See *On Stage* by Vera Roberts)

HINDU THEATRE

Dramatic form in India is ancient, dating back to 1500 B.C. when dialogue was used in the Vedic or religious hymns. According to Hindu mythology, Brahma invented theatre and commanded the first playhouse built; but real theatre did not emerge until the fifth century B.C. Then plays were written concerning the subject matter of the two great epics, the *Mahabharata* and the *Ramayama*.

The great flourishing of Indian drama came between the 4th and 10th century A.D. Then such plays as *The Little Clay Cart* by King Shudraka, and the masterpiece of Indian drama, *The Fatal Ring* by Kalidasa, were written. Both of these plays were composed in Sanskrit, the literary language used and understood only by the aristocrats. In fact, most Hindu drama was for the upper classes, being performed in either the gardens or court-yards of the palaces, or in specially built palace playhouses. The stage was situated at one end of the room with the audience sitting around. The only scenery was a decorated wall with doors leading to a green room where the actors changed.

Theatre patrons had a great love of beauty, and so we find Hindu theatre intimate, delicate, and restrained, performed strictly for pleasant entertainment with the plays always ending happily. As far as we know, Hindu theatre was the first to permit women to act on stage.

Suggested Projects —

1. Read aloud to the class the lovely poem "Salutation to the Dawn" by Kalidasa. Compare its style and mood to early Hindu theatre.

2. Read and report on *Shakuntala (The Fatal Ring)* by Kalidasa.

CHINESE THEATRE

Chinese drama dates back to 2000 B.C., when interpretative dancing took on a dramatic form, as ritualistic ancestor worship and military celebrations were staged. These early performances, however, were not presented as entertainment. The Chinese revered their ancestors; dramatic ritual was solely religious with only the emperor, the priests, and the court as participants and audience.

Later, the religious ritual developed into definite plays, but it was not until the 8th and 9th century A.D. that Chinese drama blossomed, led by Emperor Ming Huang (713–756), who founded a school for actors in his pear tree garden. The school was so successful that Chinese actors are traditionally called "Children of the Pear Tree Garden." Ming Huang continues as the patron saint of theatre, with actors burning incense to his statue before they go on stage.

The drama of Ming Huang's time was highly formal. It dealt primarily with three themes: ancestor worship, military glory, and faithfulness to husband. It was written in classical Chinese that only the exceptionally well educated could understand. This classical tradition changed, however, when the Mongols invaded in 1280 A.D. Lacking in cultural background, the Mongols demanded action, acrobatic stunts, songs, and dances, instead of the established long literary passages. It was in this flourishing period that such plays as *Lady Precious Stream*, *The Chalk Circle*, and *The Lute Song* were written, and it is interesting to note that these three pieces are sometimes performed today in the English-speaking world.

The dramas associated with the Mongolian influence became traditional theatre, and throughout the centuries they were enacted in their original form until the Communists took over China after World War II. After 1949, the Communist government rewrote many of the classical plays to preach government policy.

The Chinese stage dates back to Ming Huang's time and is still used today with slight modifications. At first it had a platform that extended into the audience, with the audience sitting on three sides. Today, however, the platform has been pushed behind a proscenium arch, and instead of patrons sitting at tea tables, there are rows of seats in front of the stage.

The traditional Chinese stage has no curtain and no scenery. Scene changes are suggested by the chorus and the dramatic action. On the backstage wall there are two doors through which the actors enter. The musicians sit on stage left; the chorus on stage right. These groups accompany the play much like the musicians of our silent movie days. Performances are very long, since several plays are given. Often the audience spends the whole day at the theatre, where they used to be served both dinner and supper but now are offered only light refreshment and tea.

Most of the acting is done by men who also take women's parts. Acting is regarded as a life study. It is highly artificial and symbolic. While movements are graceful, they are always traditional, with every gesture meaning something specific. For example, a sleeve passed over the eye denotes weeping; a shaking of the shoulders signifies grief.

Properties also have symbolic meaning. White paper falling from a red umbrella means snow; a man with a whip indicates that he is on horseback; an actor carrying a flag indicates an army; a flag with wavy lines symbolizes a river. Properties are handed to the actor by a prop man, supposedly "invisible" because he is dressed in black. The actors wear elaborate, dazzling costumes and thick makeup in which color signifies character: red means faithfulness; blue, cruelty; white, evil; etc.

Because Chinese drama has much chanting, singing, and musical accompaniment, in the last century Westerners began calling it Peking Opera. The style of Peking Opera can still be seen today, along with new trends that have been influenced by the West. Although Chinese drama seems strange to the Western world, the basic symbolic quality has influenced such playwrights as Thornton Wilder in his *Our Town*. The greatest influence of Chinese drama, of course, has been in Japan.

Suggested Projects —

1. As a class, read aloud Benrimo and Hazelton's *Yellow Jacket*, a 20th century play in the Chinese tradition.

2. Report on today's "Peking Opera," which has toured the United States and other western countries.

JAPANESE THEATRE

Early drama in Japan was probably based on the ritualistic dance of the Shinto religion, but in the fourteenth century the Japanese evolved the Noh plays. Similar in form and content to Chinese drama, these pieces were written in a formal, classical language meant only for the aristocrats. These plays, which have remained unchanged since the 14th century, are still performed today in Japan. They are short, serious, philosophical studies that combine poetry with dance and music. However, the dance is unlike Western dance with its vigorous movements. Instead, it is a series of sedate posturings in which an attitude is expressed.

Noh stages are always built to specific measurements. They are wooden eighteen-foot squares, with the audience sitting on three sides. The stage's pointed roof, a carry over from the early times when Noh was performed outside, is similar to that of a Shinto shrine and is supported by four pillars. The floor is of highly polished Japanese cypress, specially constructed with large empty jars underneath to provide a unique resonant sound when the actor thumps his feet at a climactic moment.

The characters enter from the green room off right by means of the bridge, a narrow corridor upstage. As each character enters, he bows to the audience, announces his name, where he has come from, and what he will do. The chorus, consisting of six to eight men, sits on stage left and provides chanting background music.

Scenery consists of a pine tree tapestry hung on the back wall. Only essential properties are used, and they are often a suggestion rather than an actual representation of the object. For example, a folding fan which the actor uses for his various acting poses may at times suggest a dagger, a tray, or a letter, depending on what is needed.

Costumes are ornate silks, worn by all characters whether they are rich or poor. The cut of the costume and the makeup differentiates social class. Major actors wear carved wooden masks that have stereotyped expressions from one of the fifteen standard masks allowed in Noh plays.

To offset the often depressing, foreboding quality of the Noh plot, the Kyogen was developed as comic interlude. Kyogens are farce comedies played without music and without the actors being masked. Usually five Nohs are presented at one performance, interspersed with three Kyogens.

In the seventeenth century another form of Japanese theatre became popular. It is called Bunraku or doll theatre, which features four-foot tall, complete figured, wooden marionettes, carved in such realistic detail that eyelids, eyebrows, mouth, and fingers can be moved. Each doll is elaborately costumed. While narrators read the dialogue and a musician plays the *samisen* (a three-string, flutelike instrument), three attendants dressed in black and wearing gauze masks (to symbolize that they are to seem invisible) manipulate the dolls.

The common man's drama is called the Kabuki. It began around 1600 when O-Kuni, a woman, began singing and dancing to crowds in the street. This popular entertainment developed into a theatrical form that was promoted by men when women were banned from the stage in 1629.

Kabuki, which incorporates song and dance, is more melodramatic and sensational than the Noh plays. Kabukis have a wide range of subject matter. There are heavy, tension-filled historical tragedies that realistically portray scenes of suicide, murder, and torture; there are domestic love triangles; and there are unspoken dance dramas that often feature grotesque demons.

The Kabuki playhouse uses a wide extended platform, but it dispenses with the roof, pillars, and bridge of the Noh theatre. Actors enter from a "flowerway," a ramp that extends through the audience from the back of the auditorium up to the stage. The stage floor contains trap doors where actors may also make spectacular entrances and exits. Since 1793, most Kabuki theatres have been equipped with a revolving stage which allows quick and impressive scene shifting. Such theatrical devices as the ramp, trap door, and revolving stage have been borrowed from Japan by the Western world in recent years.

Kabuki is noted for its lavish use of color in elaborate silk costumes. Although masks are not used, thick stylized mask-like makeup is applied. Wigs are worn that denote a character's station, personality, and age, and that often weigh as much as twenty-five pounds. Kabuki also utilizes colorful, extravagant scenery.

In Kabuki and Noh, acting skill is all important. Actors are traditionally men who are versatile at impersonating women. Today, women may act in Kabuki, although few do. For centuries the acting profession in Japan has been inherited, with children as young as five sometimes appearing momentarily on stage as they begin their lifelong profession. Not until actors are middle-aged do they gain fame.

Acting follows the Chinese tradition. It is highly symbolic, artificial, and rhythmical, moving slowly from one studied pose to another. A tilt of the finger, a flutter of an eyelash has meaning. Actors often take as long as thirty minutes to make an entrance up the flowerway in their art of striking an attitude that will evoke a certain mood in the audience. Today, these ancient theatre types are still performed along with more modern, westernized drama.

Suggested Projects —

1. Read several Japanese *haikus* (special, short poems) and discuss how this literary form relates to Japanese acting.

2. Report on modern theatre trends in Japan, including the "westernization" of Japanese drama.

3. Report on the use of puppets in the Far East, including the Japanese doll the-

atre, Bunraku. (See Haar's *Japanese Theatre*, pp. 43-87 for excellent pictures and information on Bunraku.)

MEDIEVAL THEATRE

Now let us return to the Middle Ages in Europe, often called the Dark Ages because there was little or no cultural activity. The Middle Ages began with the fall of Rome and continued until sometime in the 12th or 13th centuries. During this period of the despotic feudal system, illiteracy predominated, and travel and an exchange of ideas all but vanished. For approximately 400 years there was no theatre, except for sparse folk festivals and a few wandering jugglers and minstrels, who managed to stir the theatrical coals that were constantly being extinguished by the Church.

Yet strange as it may seem, the Church that buried drama in the fifth century resurrected that same art sometime during the ninth century as it introduced the trope, short dramatized scenes, into the mass. The trope began in France, but the idea soon spread throughout the Continent. At first, brief Easter and Nativity tableaux were given to help the illiterate congregation understand the service. Pantomimes soon gave way to dialogue, first in Latin and then in the vernacular, as priests and choir boys enacted this liturgical drama.

Scenes became so popular that whole stories began to be enacted. Small platforms called mansions or stations were placed within the cathedral. Separate scenes were performed on these with the crowd moving from one mansion to another until they had seen the whole story. In the tenth century, a nun, Hrosvitha, wrote religious comedy that was performed on the cathedral mansions.

Three types of plays, often called the "Three M's," were presented. The Mystery plays had as their subject matter the Bible stories; the Miracle plays enacted the lives of the saints; and the Morality plays taught right from wrong, with the characters personifying abstract qualities. An excellent example of a morality play is *Everyman*, which is still occasionally performed today. As Everyman journeys to Death, his Friends, Worldly Goods, etc., all leave him. Only Good Deeds accompanies him to the grave.

Finally, drama in the church became boisterous when comedy was added, and the crowds became so great that in the thirteenth or fourteenth century, productions were moved outside to the market place, and the drama again became secularized. The comedy vein persisted. Herod became a devil and the audience laughed at his antics; Noah's wife stubbornly refused to enter the ark and had to be carried protestingly inside; devils with pitchforks prodded the wicked.

Spectacular staging devices were contrived. One, called Hell's Mouth to represent the Inferno, contained a dragon's jaw that would open and close amid smoke and flames. A rack showing tortured souls was sometimes added, with realistic screams.

Eventually the trade guilds sponsored the plays, with each guild presenting an applicable episode: the Cooks would handle Hell's Mouth, as they were used to smoke and flames; the Shipbuilders would stage Noah's Ark; etc. Each scene was prepared in great detail and was carefully rehearsed. The productions were often spectacular, being presented to throngs of people on festival days in an atmosphere of gaiety and fun.

In some towns the mansions were arranged in a single line with heaven at one end, hell at the other, and the rest of the settings placed in-between. In other villages, the stations were located around a market place, so that the audience would move from one station to the next as the episodes were enacted. In England, France, and the Netherlands, pageant wagons were often utilized. These were double-decked wagons. The lower story was curtained off and served for costume changing. The play's action was staged on the upper section and sometimes on the street around the wagon. Audience members would find vantage points and remain there as the wagons were brought to them, episode by episode — something like our parade floats today.

Model of Late Medieval Pageant Wagon
The Cleveland Museum of Art

In England the plays performed on pageant wagons were termed cycles, and they were given in the spring on Corpus Christi day. Four of these cycles are extant: those of York, Chester, Wakefield, and Coventry. These old plays are periodically performed today in England during special summer festivals.

One other type of drama, the Passion play, evolved during the late Middle Ages. It depicted scenes from Christ's life, showing particularly his last days of suffering and his resurrection. Of these, the passion play at Oberammergau is still performed. Over three hundred years ago, residents of that small Bavarian village prayed that if they would be spared the Black Plague that was ravishing the Continent, they would periodically drama- tize a passion play. When their village was saved, they kept their vow and in 1633, they presented their first play. Since then, the Oberammergau Passion Play has been performed every ten years, at the turn of the decade. Only in 1940, during the war, were they unable to give a show. Today thousands of people throng to see this intriguing play from the past.

A similar passion play, though on a smaller scale, is enacted in the United States each summer at Spearfish, South Dakota, and during the winter at Lake Wales, Florida. There is also a passion play at Eureka Springs, Arkansas.

In addition to these Medieval religious plays, a few secular comedies were written and performed. In 1470, *Master Pierre Patelin* appeared, delighting audiences then as it does today, as it pokes fun of an unscrupulous lawyer who tricks a client and then finds himself tricked.

The effects of Medieval staging were to be felt in later drama. Because audience members were brought close to the performers, and because the playing area provided increased freedom, acting became more important than dialogue. Medieval drama also brought in a mixture of the comic and the serious, a combination that was soon to be carried out by both the Commedia players in Italy, and the Elizabethan writers in England.

Suggested Projects —

1. Read one of the following plays and discuss the elements in it that depict life and philosophy in the Middle Ages:
   The Second Shepherd's Play   *Master Pierre Patelin*
   Everyman   *Gammer Gurton's Needle*

2. As a class, select scenes from one of the extant mystery cycles and prepare them for presentation. Play sources: Hussey, Maurine, ed. *The Chester Mystery Plays*. (London: Heinemann, 1957); and Purnis, J. O., ed. *The York Cycle of Mystery Plays*. (Macmillan, 1950).

3. Report to the class on the Oberammergau Passion play, telling production prepa- ration, playing procedures, etc. Or, if someone in the community has attended this play, have them tell the class about it.

4. Read Simonson's description of Medieval staging in his book *The Stage is Set* and report on the information, supplementing your report with any other perti- nent material of the period.

5. Write a plot outline for a morality play. List sequence of events, and name and describe each character.

6. Enact a scene from *Everyman* or *The Second Shepherd's Play*.

ITALIAN & SPANISH RENAISSANCE THEATRE

The Renaissance (about 1400–1600) was an exciting time in which to live. The travels of the Crusaders and such men as Marco Polo (circa 1254–1324) did much to stimulate curiosity. Then as the ancient classic writers were rediscovered, a "rebirth" of learning occurred throughout Europe, with vigorous activity in all of the arts and sciences. The Renaissance started in Italy, and such men as Petrarch, Leonardo da Vinci, Michelangelo, and Machiavelli contributed to a great flowering of knowledge and ideas.

An important form of theatre to originate in Italy at this time was the Commedia dell'Arte. Developed years before from mimes and pantomimes that may have been remnants of ancient Roman comedy, this art was flourishing by 1550. Commedia dell'Arte was professional, improvised comedy performed in the streets for the masses. A company, consisting usually of seven men and three women, would ad-lib action, dialogue, song, and dance around a scenario (plot skeleton) that usually involved love and intrigue. In order to improvise, actors had to be inventive, clever, and witty, with agile bodies for the many acrobatic stunts, fights, and dances.

Stock characters evolved: Harlequin, who wore patches that became his stylized diamond costume of today, was the clever, witty one; Pierrot was lovelorn and moody; Columbine, flirtatious and pretty; Pantalone, who wore baggy trousers and from whom we get the term pantaloons, was the gullible father. Actors, which included the first women on the stage since Indian drama, wore half masks. The popularity of this art form spread throughout Europe and was particularly well received in France, where it later influenced the writings of Molière.

In juxtaposition to the Commedia for the common man was the drama for the Italian nobility. It is termed "pseudo-classicism" because it attempted to copy ancient Roman forms. For this drama noblemen such as the Medici family built ornate private indoor theatres where the acting area was framed by a proscenium arch. The first permanent proscenium theatre was the Theatre Farnese built in Parma in 1618.

The newly created opera, however, supplanted the popularity of plays. For opera, huge theatres were constructed with the audience being seated in tiers of narrow horseshoe-shaped galleries. The auditorium was splendidly furnished as a social gathering place for the aristocracy. Spectacular scenery evolved, which included the use of perspective drawings on ornately painted backdrops. It was at this time that stage floors were built on a rake (upstage sloping toward the audience) to further the perspective illusion.

While Italy was developing its Commedia and opera, Spain became interested in drama. From about 1550 to 1680, Spanish theatre flourished, being influenced by both Commedia dell'Arte and Italian court staging.

Three major playwrights evolved: Cervantes (1574–1616), who is better known today for *Don Quixote* than for his thirty plays; Lope de Vega (1562–1635), who wrote a phenomenal two thousand plays, many of them full of beautiful poetry, vigorous action, and dashing romance; and Calderon (1600–1681), who created two hundred plays, distinguished by their spiritual emphasis and elevated poetry.

These dramatists were all successful in establishing an original art form, free from the classical rules that fettered so many Italian and French writers. Spanish dramatists ignored the unities of time and place, wrote beautiful flowing dialogue, and evolved their action around "cape and sword" adventure, romance, and chivalry.

Spanish playhouses were somewhat like those of Elizabethan England. At first, stages were erected at one end of an open courtyard. Later, permanent enclosed buildings were constructed, with the audience standing or sitting in front of the raised stage, and a balcony with side boxes reserved for the nobility.

Public theatre used simplified settings, but the occasional court performances demanded elaborate scenery. Costumes were rich, no matter where the play was staged. Owing to the popularity of Italian Commedia in Spain, women were allowed to act on stage with the men. That plays were immensely popular is apparent by the fact that forty theatres existed in Madrid when the "Golden Age" of Spain's theatre came to an end with Calderon's death.

Although the theatrical activity in both Italy and Spain advanced Renaissance drama, it was not in these countries where drama realized its greatest potential. Instead, we look to England for a unique form that reached unbelievable heights.

Suggested Projects —

1. Report on each of the Commedia dell'Arte characters, describing their stock personalities and their costumes.

2. Enact a puppet "Punch and Judy" show along the lines of the Commedia.

3. Pretend that you are an Italian manager of Commedia and write an original scenario from which your actors will improvise.

4. Compare the writing style of Spanish playwrights with those dramatists of Elizabethan England.

ELIZABETHAN THEATRE

There was great vitality, zest, and intellectual curiosity throughout England during Queen Elizabeth I's reign (1558–1603). Her country burgeoned with national pride over its voyages of discovery, its defeat of the Spanish armada, its expanding trade markets, and its increased literary vistas that resulted from Caxton's introduction of printed books in 1475.

Dramatic activity had continued from the Medieval cycles. Before Elizabeth mounted the throne, English university students were performing old plays by Seneca, and contemporary English writers were creating their own drama. Nicholas Udall wrote England's first comedy, *Ralph Roister Doister*, in 1550. *Gammer Gurton's Needle* was produced in 1552, and a tragedy, *Gorboduc* by Sackville and Norton followed in 1561.

When Elizabeth I mounted the throne, the theatre gained a friend, for even though the Lord Mayor and other civil authorities were hostile to drama (because the crowds spread disease and often caused fights), Elizabeth loved the theatre. She commanded many court performances, protected groups of players through court sponsorship, and looked upon London's feverish dramatic activity with approval.

The first public playhouse to be erected during this time was The Theatre, constructed by James Burbage in 1576, accommodating about 1500 people. It was placed outside of London to escape the city's jurisdiction. Other theatres, including The Rose, The Fortune, The Swan, Blackfriars, and Shakespeare's Globe, were soon built.

Although we do not know the exact nature of Elizabethan theatre structure, we know that the playhouses were modeled upon the inn-yards where earlier plays had been presented. Called "Wooden O's," the theatres were usually round or octagonal, with two or three tiers of thatched roof galleries surrounding an open court on three sides. One end served as a multiple acting area, with a large platform (equipped with trap doors) that was raised four to six feet and that extended into the open court. Each theatre also had a "discovery" space located between two doors at the back of the stage and used for small interior settings, such as Juliet's burial vault. There is much controversy about the particulars of this space. J. C. Adams calls it the "inner below" or "study," which was a small curtained inner stage receding between the two doors at the back. C. Walter Hodges maintains the rear stage jutted forward onto the platform, a position which would make sightlines better. From recent excavations of Elizabethan theatres, researchers are modifying their ideas to

Stage in an Inn-Yard, c. 1565

This reconstruction sketch is based upon one of the 16th century by Pieter Breughel the Younger, and on an almost identical one from Callot of the 17th century. Portable platforms upon which actors performed were set up in the inn-yards.

add continually to the disagreement on location, use, and size of the discovery space.
We do know that the two doors at the back
of the stage led to the "tiring house," or backstage area, where the actors would retire to
change costumes.

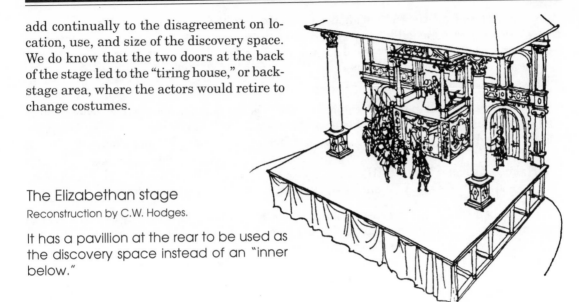

The Elizabethan stage
Reconstruction by C.W. Hodges.

It has a pavillion at the rear to be used as
the discovery space instead of an "inner
below."

On the second level of the stage facade, there was another acting space (an "inner
above"), as well as balcony windows and a terrace. A third level could also provide a playing
area but was used mainly for the musicians as they accompanied songs and dances, and
played musical interludes. A fourth level was a structure called the "hut" which housed
stage machinery for the special effects.

This style of playhouse did much to stimulate dramatic writing. A rapid succession
of scenes in different localities was possible because of the several stage areas. Furthermore, much action could be provided since there was ample space in which the actor could
move. With the audience so close to the stage, dramatists were also able to use expressive,
rich language to its fullest extent.

Plays were held in the afternoon (with the daylight serving as illumination), and to
announce performances, a flag — white for comedy, black for tragedy — was raised at the
top of the theatre. All classes of people attended, for the theatre was to Elizabethans not
only their drama, but their movies, novels, radio, television, and newspapers rolled into
one. The groundlings, consisting of tradesmen, soldiers, apprentices, and servants, paid a
penny and stood in the "pit" around the platform, guffawing at the comedy. Lords and ladies
paid more and had seats in the gallery. Their taste included a love of the poetry. A few rich,
young gallants would even occupy a portion of the stage. The whole atmosphere was joyful,
and at times boisterous. Peddlers sold oranges and nuts that were noisily eaten by the
audience.

There was no scenery. The spectators used their imagination as they assimilated
the playwright's descriptions and moods. Some properties were available and so were sound
effects. In fact, the burning of the Globe theatre in 1613 was the result of the thatch roof

catching a spark from the cannon shots that announced the King's entrance in *Henry VIII*. Since costumes were usually handsome styles of the day donated by patrons, there was little attempt made toward historical accuracy. Julius Caesar, along with Dr. Faustus, wore Renaissance clothes on the Elizabethan stage. Only a few stylized costumes for fairies, witches, lawyers, and churchmen were in use.

Actors were all men, with the ladies' parts being taken by young boys whose voices had not yet changed to masculine lowness. Acting paid well, but it was a strenuous life, for parts required singing, dancing, fighting, and fencing. Three great actors emerged: Richard Burbage (son of James Burbage), who played many Shakespearean tragic figures, including Hamlet, Othello, Richard III, and King Lear; Edward Alleyn, who acted tragedies by Marlowe and others; and William Kemp, who portrayed Shakespeare's great comic parts.

Unbelievable as it may seem, the Elizabethan period would still have been an age of dramatic giants if Shakespeare had never lived and written. There were many brilliant playwrights, and most of them wrote with great freedom, disregarding the classic unities of time and place, and the rule that violence should not be seen on stage. Moreover, they mixed poetry with prose and interspersed comedy with tragedy. Competent though they were, Thomas Kyd, John Lyly, Robert Greene, George Peele, John Webster, Thomas Dekker, Thomas Heywood, and Beaumont and Fletcher were shadowed because of the three giants: Christopher Marlowe, Ben Jonson, and William Shakespeare.

Christopher Marlowe (1564–1593) graduated from Cambridge University with is B.A. degree. Later, when he attempted to obtain his Masters, he was refused because he had been absent from Cambridge. However, Queen Elizabeth I intervened and allowed him his degree, since she said that he had given her valuable service (probably in helping to discover a plot against the throne). Next to Shakespeare, Marlowe was the greatest dramatist of tragedy in England, even though he lived only to the age of twenty-nine, being killed in a tavern brawl.

Marlowe's perfected blank verse, that reminds us of the Greek grandeur, is often termed "Marlowe's Mighty Line." In his short life he wrote seven plays, with *Tamburlaine*, *Edward II*, *The Jew of Malta*, and *Dr. Faustus* being his best known. The latter is a rendition of the popular story of a man who sells his soul to the devil. From it we get the famous line:

> "Was this the face that launched a thousand ships
> And burnt the topless towers of Ilium.
> Sweet Helen, make me immortal with a kiss."

Ben Jonson (1573–1637) was also a college graduate and proud of his background in the classics. In fact, he scorned Shakespeare at first because Shakespeare knew "small Latin and less Greek." Jonson was a classic writer, always correct, always abiding by the Aristotelian unities. Much of his work is biting, humorous satire. *Everyman in His Humour*, *Volpone*, and *The Alchemist* are but a few of his plays. When James I inherited the throne, Jonson entertained the court with masques, great extravaganzas of song, dance, and recitation. It is said that on one Jonson production alone, James spent the equivalent of $500,000 in lavish costumes and sets designed by Inigo Jones, who had studied perspective scenery in Italy.

William Shakespeare (1564–1616) is considered to be the greatest of all English dramatists. On Shakespeare's death, his critic, Jonson, conceded that Shakespeare was "not of an age, but for all time."

Unfortunately, we know little about Shakespeare's life. Born in Stratford-upon-Avon where his father was a glover and for a time a respected town official, Shakespeare attended grammar school, his only formal education. At eighteen, he married Ann Hathaway, eight years his senior. Although the exact reason is not known, he left his wife and three children and went to London, where he began working in the theatre world as an actor, manager, and writer. By 1596, he was well established and in royal favor, for Queen Elizabeth granted him a coat of arms.

In the thirty-eight plays attributed to him, Shakespeare wrote histories, comedies, tragedies, and fantasies. His greatness lies in many areas—

1. In his skill as a dramatist, where he balanced
    a. Plot and character,
    b. The serious and the comic,
    c. The climax and the release;
2. In the universality of his ideas;
3. In his majestic use of language; and
4. In his masterly portrayal of characters that live in our memories:
    the melancholy Dane; the fat, braggart Falstaff; the impish Puck; the boyish Rosalind; the impetuous Hotspur; the youthfully passionate Romeo; the jealous Othello.

His majestic soliloquies (speeches where actors talk alone to reveal their thoughts aloud) encompass great breadth of vision and are beloved by learned people the world over. But, his less grand phrases are a part of us, too. We quote Shakespeare without even knowing it. "That blinking idiot," "grim necessity," "as luck would have it," "Greek to me," "the short and long of it," "a rose by any other name," "haven't slept a wink," "eating out of house and home," "all the world's a stage," "the unkindest cut of all," "salad days" — all are from his inventiveness.

When you read or see Shakespeare's plays: *Hamlet, Macbeth, Othello, Romeo and Juliet, King Lear, Henry V, Richard III, Taming of the Shrew, The Tempest, Twelfth Night, Midsummer Night's Dream* — plus many more — you are exposed to the most noble dramatist and the greatest poet in the English language.

The political unrest that had been brewing during the reign of James I (1603–25) continued after Charles I was crowned in 1625. Actual civil war broke out and finally Oliver Cromwell, the Puritan leader, gained control. Charles was beheaded and the rest of the Stuart line fled to France. The Puritans, always against the theatre, closed those "dens of iniquity" in 1642. Public theatre died in England until the Stuarts regained control in 1660. However, plays were performed surreptitiously, as the many arrests of actors and audience members attest.

Suggested Projects —

1. Rehearse and present a Shakespearean scene to the class. Read the complete play from which the scene is taken, so you will better understand the character's motivation.

2. Give class reports on Shakespeare and his London. Show pictures obtained from the Folger Shakespeare Library, Washington, D.C. Good background sources are: *Shakespeare in London* by Marchette Chute; *Shakespeare Without Tears* by Margaret Webster; *Shakespeare's Life and Times* by Roland Frye; and "Shakespeare," *Time*, July 4, 1960.

3. Read one of the following plays and report on it in class: *Dr. Faustus*, Marlowe; *Volpone*, Jonson; *Edward II*, Marlowe; any of Shakespeare's.

A modern adaptation of the Globe Theatre.
The Adams' Theatre, Utah Shakespearean Festival

4. Compare Elizabethan theatres with those of Renaissance Spain. (See *The Living Stage*, Macgowan and Melnitz.)

5. Compare Leslie Hotson's ideas of Shakespeare's theatre (*Shakespeare's Wooden O*. Macmillan, 1960) with those of John C. Adams (*The Globe Playhouse*. Cambridge University Press, 1942).

6. See and study the Shakespeare video series by the Royal Shakespeare Company. Many public libraries have these to loan.

FRENCH RENAISSANCE THEATRE

Because of France's many wars, and because one theatre group had exclusive rights to the public playhouse, the Renaissance came late to French theatre, taking place during the 17th century. At that time the increased theatre activity gave rise to what is termed "neoclassicism," where dramatists were supposed to observe the classic unities and write in a restricted verse form.

This French drama developed into entertainment mainly for the royalty. Playhouses were ornate, following the Italian plan of sumptuous surroundings for the nobles. Guilded carvings, velvet-covered seats, and lavish drapes were abundantly displayed.

Three French playwrights gained importance. Pierre Corneille (1606–1684), whose work is highly moralistic and eloquent, ignored the classic form only once to write his best-known work, the tragedy *Le Cid*. Jean Racine (1639–1699) followed the rigid classic rules in writing what is termed "polite tragedy." *Phaedra* is his most well-known play.

Molière (1622–1673) is the high point of French theatre. He wrote such effulgent, scintillating satire that his plays still entertain audiences around the world today. Molière's real name was Jean Baptiste Poqueline, but when he chose the theatre as a life-work, he also chose another name so that his parents would not be disgraced by having an actor in the family.

Molière acted "on the road" for twelve years, participating in Commedia dell'Arte. As he began to write comedies, he drew from the Commedia's farcical style. His many plays, performed both for the public and for the court of Louis XIV, are masterpieces of brilliant satire, a perfect blend of the humorous and the caustic. In *The Doctor in Spite of Himself*, he burlesques the field of medicine; in *Tartuffe*, he lampoons hypocrisy; in *The Imaginary Invalid* he spoofs hypochondria.

Throughout his writing career, Molière continued to act. In his last years he was ill from tuberculosis, and he ironically died on stage after completing a performance of *The Imaginary Invalid*. After his death, Molière's great dream came true. In 1680, a state-supported theatre was inaugurated under the name Comédie Française. This company, still functioning under that title, is the most important theatre group in France today.

Suggested Projects —

1. Read and act out scenes from one of Molière's comedies such as: *The Doctor in Spite of Himself; The Would-Be Gentleman; The Miser; The Affected Young Ladies; The Imaginary Invalid; Tartuffe.*

2. Present to the class an oral reading of Chapter 2, "Death of the Man Who Laughed at Death," on Molière in John Allen's *Great Moments in The Theatre.*

RESTORATION & 18th CENTURY ENGLISH THEATRE

When Charles II returned from France and was restored to the English throne in 1660, he started a new era of drama that was fashioned after the theatre he had seen in Paris.

Since the Elizabethan playhouses had been torn down by the Puritans, new indoor theatres were built with a deep apron on which to act and with a proscenium arch, behind which a series of flats were painted in perspective and were set parallel to the curtain. These flats were spaced upstage of each other to give the illusion of distance. Candles and oil lamps provided lighting in these indoor theatres, and women were allowed to perform on stage.

18th CENTURY THEATRE

The audience was the sophisticated aristocracy: witty, insincere, immoral, and dissipated. The plays staged at this time were comedies of manners that satirized the artificiality of the day, and so they, too, were witty and often immoral.

Plays of the Restoration include John Dryden's *All for Love*, George Etherage's *Love in a Tub*, William Wycherly's *The Country Wife*, George Farquhar's *The Beaux' Stratagem*, and William Congreve's *The Way of the World*.

The Restoration ended in 1737, when Parliament passed the Licensing Act which limited the public playhouses to two: Covent Garden and Drury Lane. All others were illegal. Thus, we get the term "legitimate" theatre, which today refers to all live play performances. With the enforcement of the Licensing Act, plays and their performances had to pass a censoring board.

Later in the century and roughly corresponding to the period of the American Revolution, two other English writers carried on the comedy of manners tradition with a brilliancy and with a cleanliness that must have pleased the licensing board. Oliver Goldsmith (1728–1774) brought forth his happy *She Stoops to Conquer,* and Richard Brinsley Sheridan (1751–1816) fashioned such delightful comedies as *The Rivals* and *School for Scandal*. The latter is considered the best English comedy since those of Shakespeare.

Sheridan was a most unusual man. Handsome and a witty conversationalist, he was the life of the party. Not only was he a success at writing comedy, but he also gained fame for writing operas. He was elected to Parliament where his orations were so brilliant that it is said people would pay large sums of money to hear him speak. Unfortunately, Sheridan was a spendthrift and he died a poor man.

During this period, some great actors crossed the English stage. David Garrick (1717–1779), both actor and director, is credited with establishing a less bombastic style of acting. He did many Shakespearean revivals, often rewriting, deleting, or adding to the scenes. The tragic actress Sarah Kemble Siddons (1755–1831) and her brother John Phillip Kemble (1757–1823) were also famous stage personalities. Later, Edmund Kean (1787–1833) achieved great acclaim, particularly in his role of Shylock.

Suggested Projects —

1. Present an oral biographical sketch of one of the following: Oliver Goldsmith, Richard Brinsley Sheridan, David Garrick, Sarah Kemble Siddons, John Phillip Kemble, or Edmund Kean.

2. Enact scenes from *The Rivals, School for Scandal,* or *She Stoops to Conquer.*

3. Present to the class an oral reading of Chapter 5, "Shakespeare by Lightning," on Edmund Kean in John Allen's *Great Moments in The Theatre*.

19th CENTURY CONTINENTAL THEATRE

The dramatic style that firmly established itself in the early 19th century was Romanticism, an emotional escape into adventure, beauty, and sentimental idealism. Started by Goethe (1749–1832) and Schiller (1759–1805) in Germany, the movement blossomed in France under Victor Hugo (1802–1886) and the elder Alexander Dumas (1802–1870), who adapted for the stage his well-read adventures such as *The Three Musketeers*. In England, romantic plays that can only be labeled "closet drama" were written by the poets Byron, Tennyson, Shelley, Arnold, and Browning.

In mid-nineteenth century, however, drama took a decided turn in the opposite direction. Realism, that depicts a selected view of real life, gained impetus. The major dominating figure was Henrik Ibsen (1828–1906), a Norwegian who is often called the "Father of Realism." His work was well written and constructed, with keen insight into characterization. Although his plays seem mild to today's audiences, his themes completely revolutionized the theatre of his time, shocking the spectators and bringing on a storm of criticism about the way he exposed current social problems. In *The Doll's House*, Nora slammed the door on her husband and children and presented to the world a new position of women in society. Ibsen's other plays, among them *The Master Builder*, *An Enemy of the People*, and *Ghosts*, have equally provocative themes that realistically showed the problems of that era. His work influenced that of many other dramatists such as Strindberg of Sweden, who wrote expressionistic drama that became the forerunner of today's avant-garde theatre. Chekhov's *The Cherry Orchard*, and Gorki's *Lower Depths* continued the revolt against Romanticism. Stanislavski (1863–1938), the great Russian director, also contributed to the movement with his experimental theatre for actors where a technique of realistic acting evolved.

In England, George Bernard Shaw (1856–1950) introduced Ibsen to the theatre world by producing *Ghosts*. Shaw then continued his own realistic bent by writing comic satire in which he attacked all cherished beliefs, leaving little untouched by his biting, yet delightful wit. Considered the finest English playwright since Shakespeare, Shaw left a long list of plays. *Androcles and the Lion*, *Pygmalion*, *Major Barbara*, *The Devil's Disciple*, *Arms and the Man*, *The Doctor's Dilemma*, and *Candida* are but a few of his successes. Shaw hoped that his comic writings would reform the world. That they failed, he felt, was not his fault.

Although realism grew to great heights, many authors around the world continued to write noteworthy romantic, symbolic, or mystic plays. In England Oscar Wilde (1856–1900) produced witty farces. His *Importance of Being Earnest* is in the best 18th century comedy of manners style. Sir William Gilbert (1836–1911) and Sir Arthur Sullivan (1842–1900) wrote the finest of satiric operettas with their *Mikado*, *HMS Pinafore*, and many others. In France, Rostand wrote *Cyrano de Bergerac* (1897); in Russia, Gogol wrote *The Inspector General* (1836); in Belgium, Maeterlinck wrote *The Bluebird* (1908); and in Italy, Pirandello created *Six Characters in Search of an Author* (1921).

Among the famous continental actors of the 19th century were France's Sarah Bernhardt and Coquelin; Italy's Eleanora Duse; and England's Sir Henry Irving and his leading lady, Ellen Terry — both largely responsible for bringing respectability again to the acting profession.

Suggested Projects —

1. With a partner, choose a scene from this period to rehearse and present.

2. Read and report on one of the following plays, briefly giving its plot and telling how it realistically shows life at the time it was written.
    The Doll's House, Ibsen
    An Enemy of the People, Ibsen
    The Cherry Orchard, Chekhov
    Arms and the Man, Shaw
    The Devil's Disciple, Shaw

3. Read and report on one of the following plays, showing its contribution to the dramatic world:
    The Importance of Being Earnest, Wilde
    Cyrano de Bergerac, Rostand
    The Inspector General, Gogol
    Six Characters in Search of an Author, Pirandello

4. Discuss the influence of the Duke of Saxe-Meininger's (1826–1914) company on staging and acting.

5. With two other readers, present an oral reading program to the class, using Chapter 6, "Revolutions in the Air," on Hugo and Romanticism; Chapter 8, "Antoine and the Theatre Libre," on Naturalism; and Chapter 7, "A Masterpiece of Horror," on Henry Irving in John Allen's *Great Moments in the Theatre*.

19th CENTURY AMERICAN THEATRE

It was in the 19th century that American drama grew and developed its own national flavor. Up to that time the few theatre activities that prevailed had been mainly borrowed from the English theatre.

Early drama in the colonies was sparse, since most people regarded theatre as sinful. In fact, in the New York colony the Governor's council passed an act in 1709 forbidding "playacting and prizefighting." Theatre fared better in the Virginia colony where students of the College of William and Mary performed a play in 1702, and where the first playhouse in America was built in Williamsburg in 1716. On the whole, though, drama had a difficult time. In 1778, the Continental Congress denounced stage shows during the Revolution because they "diverted the minds of the people from . . . the defense of their country."

The first American play worthy of consideration was written by Royal Tyler in 1787. Called *The Contrast,* it was a pleasing comedy dealing with American problems. Apparently the play was most successful, for when it was published, President George Washington's name was first on the subscription list. In fact, Washington was a theatre lover and periodically attended plays where he saw Shakespeare and other classic revivals that dominated the boards.

In the 19th century, theatre blossomed as most of the moralist opposition disappeared. Numerous showboats entertained up and down the Mississippi. Playhouses were built in major American cities. These buildings followed the new trend of smaller auditoriums, narrow aprons, box settings (instead of wings and backdrops), and after 1880, incandescent lighting. Actors began using greasepaint that was developed in 1865 by Leichner, a German opera singer. The use of historically accurate costumes was also initiated in the 19th century to accompany the realistic settings that came into vogue.

Powerful theatre managers formed stock companies where groups of actors received excellent training in repertory theatre. This was the age of the actor, and many outstanding stars were immortalized in their work. Edwin Booth (1833–1893) was considered to be America's greatest actor; appearing as Hamlet, he played one hundred nights, a record broken by few other Hamlets. Joseph Jefferson (1829–1905) made a name for himself with his *Rip Van Winkle*; Richard Mansfield (1857–1907) brilliantly starred in many productions; Maude Adams delighted audiences in such plays as *Peter Pan*; and Mrs. John Drew, whose daughter married a Barrymore and started that famous acting family, found success in *The Rivals*.

Many of these actors toured America with their shows, playing frequently in one-night stands. During this time "the road," as it was called, was lucrative business. For over fifty years road companies toured until the competition of radio and the movies and the increased railroad rates brought the decline of trouping, with only a few name stars touring in the 20th century. With the disappearance of road shows and repertory companies, the "long-run" performances on Broadway were established, and New York City became the theatrical center of the United States. There, the theatre burgeoned into big business.

Three major types of native theatrical activity developed in 19th century America. The Minstrel shows, done in black face and featuring Negro songs and jokes, were exceptionally popular throughout America and England. Vaudeville was liked perhaps even better. It was a variety show, featuring everything: trained seals, singers, acrobats, jugglers, dancers, comedians, dog and pony acts. Shows were kept free of off-colored jokes so that the entertainment was for the whole family. Vaudeville was "big time" for years until movie and radio competition closed it. Now it is almost a lost art, except for a few night club variety shows. Melodrama that reeked with over sentimentalism thrived during this time, as audiences throughout the country wept at the plight of the poor heroine in the clutches of the villain. *East Lynn* was one such melodrama played by every stock troupe in the country.

Suggested Projects —

1. Give biographical sketches on a great American actor or actress of the 19th century.

2. Create and stage a class version of an "authentic" vaudeville show.

3. Provide a bulletin board display with an excellent set of inexpensive pictures on "Actors and Actresses" obtained from University Prints, 21 East Street, P.O. Box 271, Winchester, Massachusetts 01890.

20th CENTURY THEATRE

At the turn of the 20th century, new scenecraft methods revolutionized staging. Through the creativity of such men as Switzerland's Adolphe Appia and England's Gordon Craig, the theatre was introduced to impressionistic settings, revolving stages, projected scenery, and fluid lighting.

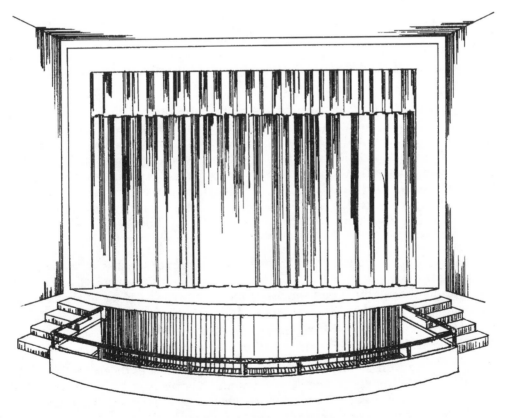

20th CENTURY THEATRE

Continental playwrights made numerous contributions. In Germany, Bertholt Brecht (1898–1956) developed his Epic theatre, where he hoped to encourage audience members to think critically in order to promote social reform through political action. To do so, Brecht purposely created an "alienation" where he broke the realistic illusion and stressed theatricalism. He deliberately inserted narration and songs between episodic scenes; he made stage light units visible to the audience; he used placards, projections, and any other effect to get the spectator to think and ask questions that would encourage societal changes. His most popular plays include *Mother Courage*, *The Caucasian Chalk Circle*, *The Good Woman of Setzuan*, and *The Three Penny Opera*.

In France, Jean Giraudoux (1882–1944) wrote the popular *Tiger At the Gates*, *Ondine*, and *Madwoman of Chaillot*. Jean Anouilh (1910–1987) wrote a modern version of *Antigone* and a play about Joan of Arc called *The Lark*. In each he showed an uncompromising protagonist maintaining integrity by choosing death.

In Spain, Federico Lorca (1898–1936) achieved acclaim with themes of love and honor in *Blood Wedding* and *The House of Bernarda Alba*. In Italy, Luigi Pirandello (1867–1936) wrote about appearance versus reality in *Six Characters in Search of An Author*.

Ireland's John M. Synge (1871–1909) wrote in poetic prose about the Irish people and a conflict between a desire for freedom and a life that was oppressive. *The Playboy of the Western World* and *In The Shadow of the Glenn* promoted these themes. Sean O'Casey (1884–1964) dealt with the effects of the Irish Rebellion on ordinary people in *The Shadow of a Gunman*, *Juno and The Paycock*, and *The Plough and the Stars*.

Popular English dramatists in the first half of the century include: T. S. Eliot (1888–1965), who wrote poetic drama in the *Cocktail Party* and *Murder in a Cathedral*; Christopher Fry (1907–), who created intellectual comic verse plays with *The Lady's Not For Burning* and *Venus Observed*; J. B. Priestly (1894–1984), who wrote mysteries such as *An Inspector Calls*; James M. Barrie (1860–1937), who wrote *Peter Pan*; and Noel Coward (1899–1973), who developed witty, sophisticated comedies that include *Blithe Spirit* and *Private Lives*. Opening up a new post-World War II era were John Osborne's *Look Back in Anger*, David Storey's *Home*, Peter Shaffer's *Equus*, and Tom Stoppard's *Rosencrantz and Guildenstern Are Dead*.

One set of playwrights we will combine together, not because of nationality, but because they are exponents of the avant-garde theatre called absurdism. In their plays the absurdists argue that all life is meaningless. Characters speak and act at random with no societal rules. Theatre of the absurd includes Samuel Beckett's *Waiting for Godot*, Eugene Ionesco's *The Bald Soprano*, Jean Genet's *The Balcony*, Harold Pinter's *The Dumb Waiter*, and Edward Albee's *The Sandbox*.

In the early 20th century, America became stage struck as theatre activities multiplied. The country began developing its own unique theatre, largely through the efforts of Professor George Pierce Baker and his playwriting course at Harvard. There he nurtured new notable American dramatists. Phillip Barry, Robert Sherwood, Sidney Howard, S .H.

Behrman, and Eugene O'Neill were aided by Baker and two theatre companies —The Washington Square Players and the Provinceton Players — that produced their work.

Of these new playwrights, Eugene O'Neill (1888–1953) became the leading American dramatist in the first part of the 20th century. His plays were both realistic and expressionistic dealing often with psychological truths. After becoming a master of the one-act, O'Neill turned to writing longer scripts. *The Emperor Jones, The Hairy Ape, Strange Interlude, Ah Wilderness, Mourning Becomes Electra,* and many other plays made him and American theatre famous throughout the world.

Other United States playwrights who became prominent are: George S. Kaufman and his comedies *You Can't Take It With You* and *The Man Who Came to Dinner*; Lillian Hellman with *The Little Foxes* and *The Children's Hour*; Robert Sherwood with *Idiot's Delight* and *Abe Lincoln in Illinois*; Maxwell Anderson, who wrote poetic drama in *Winterset* and *Elizabeth the Queen*; and Clifford Odets with *Waiting for Lefty* and *The Golden Boy*.

Special attention should be given to four American dramatists. Thornton Wilder (1897–1975) contributed one of the best loved and frequently produced American plays, *Our Town*. It depicts small town life in the early 1900s and shows the eternal patterns of human existence. In *The Skin of Our Teeth* he shows the human ability to overcome disasters. Tennessee Williams (1911–1983) featured unique, often neurotic, Southern characters that he clothed in a poetic quality in *Glass Menagerie, A Streetcar Named Desire*, and *Cat On A Hot Tin Roof.*

Arthur Miller (1915–) writes of the dilemma of American families and the tragedy of common citizens in *The Death of a Salesman* and *All My Sons*. Neil Simon (1927–) continues to be one of the most popular and prolific writers of comedy. He combines wisecracks and barbed wit with family realism and serious overtones. Some of his plays are *Barefoot in the Park, Star Spangled Girl, The Odd Couple, Prisoner of Second Avenue, Brighton Beach Memoirs*, and *Biloxie Blues.*

New American playwrights include Sam Shepard (*Buried Child*), David Mamet (*American Buffalo*), Lanford Wilson (*Tally's Folly*), Arthur Kopit (*Wings*), A. R. Gurney (*The Dining Room*), and Christopher Durang (*Sister Mary Ignatus Explains It All For You*).

American theatre is also seeing female playwrights with scripts that often explore basic feminist issues. Among these dramatists are Marsha Norman (*'Night, Mother*), Beth Henley (*Crimes of the Heart*), María Irene Fornés (*Fefu and Her Friends*), Wendy Wasserman (*The Heidi Chronicles*), and Tine Howe (*Painting Churches*).

African American theatre has been enriched with Lorraine Hansberry (1930–1965) who wrote *A Raisin in the Sun*, and with August Wilson (1945–) who is writing a history of Black America with plays set in different decades of the 20th century. His shows include *Ma Rainey's Black Bottom, Fences*, and *Piano Lesson*. Charles Fuller (1939–) won success with *A Soldier's Play*. He is writing a series of plays about African Americans since the freeing of the slaves.

Besides playwrights, this century has also brought forth notable stage actors. The list includes: Sarah Bernhardt, Eleanora Duse, John and Ethel Barrymore, John Gielgud, Laurence Olivier, Ralph Richardson, Judith Anderson, Katharine Cornell, Helen Hayes, Edith Evans, Peggy Ashcroft, Alfred Lunt, and Lynn Fontanne.

Directors such as Elia Kazan, Peter Hall, Joshua Logan, Zelda Fichandler, Tony Richardson, Peter Brock, and Alan Scheider contribute exceptionally fine professional productions.

One other American contribution to the theatre world needs mention: the musical comedy. Under the inspiration of Richard Rodgers and Oscar Hammerstein, there was born in 1943 the delightful musical, *Oklahoma!*, to be followed later with *The King and I, Carousel*, and *South Pacific*. Alan Lerner and Frederick Lowe created *Brigadoon* and *My Fair Lady*. Other long running hits include *West Side Story, Fiddler on the Roof, Man of La Mancha,* and *Music Man*. Lately, the American musical comedy has had a difficult time. The expense of large casts and elaborate staging has made new shows risky business. Consequently, the focus has turned to London and the work of Andrew Lloyd Webber. His musicals, *Evita, Cats, Les Misérables*, and *Phantom of the Opera,* have bridged the Atlantic and proven extremely popular in the United States.

Today, the theatre is alive with abundant activity. Broadway is still considered the hub of professional theatre, but rising costs have kept producers away from many new ventures. Most shows are comedies or musicals with mass appeal to insure a hit. Consequently, new playwrights, shows, and actors have had to look elsewhere for experience. Off-Broadway theatre (theatres seating less than 299 people) welcomes new names and plays because shows can be done less expensively. Not being tied so tightly to the box-office allows experimental productions to be staged. Some of these shows become hits and occasionally move to Broadway.

Professional live productions are also available outside of New York City. In the 1960s, Regional theatres (sometimes called Resident theatres) were established in major cities. The first began in 1963 in Minneapolis, and was under the direction of Tyrone Guthrie. Later, other companies opened in San Francisco, Louisville, Seattle, Dallas, Los Angeles, and Denver, to mention a few. These nonprofit, professional theatres offer a season of several months to an audience usually consisting of subscribers. Many groups also have touring companies or outreach programs for school and community organizations. The major problem for these Regional theatres is lack of permanent funding because they rely mainly on state and federal money, as well as on private and corporate help. Yet despite financial hazards, the Regional theatre movement manages to maintain strength and provide high quality theatre to the nation.

These resident companies encourage new talent and playwrights, including those who represent various ethnic groups and social minorities. For example, David Hwang writes about the Chinese culture, as does Frank Chin and James Yoshimura. Luis Valdez and José Rivera feature the Hispanic. Other writers focus on senior citizens, handicapped people, and children.

Nonprofessional community theatre is productive almost everywhere. Community theatres usually perform "New York successes" and sometimes classical plays. They attempt to involve many townspeople and their enthusiasm and imagination help them to overcome the barriers of often having inadequate facilities.

Throughout the nation, most secondary schools, colleges, and universities provide a variety of drama classes and school productions. These shows allow training for young actors and technicians, and provide students with a knowledge and an appreciation of the theatre.

Many groups are also doing Readers Theatre, with its presentational style that allows great imagination and staging flexibility within the limited budgets that schools often face.

Summer festivals ranging from Shakespeare to old-time melodrama draw huge crowds. Look and you shall undoubtedly find a summer theatre near your town.

In recent years, voices have sporadically cried that our theatre is becoming decadent, with plays of questionable merit. Theatre, of course, depends to a great extent upon the audience. If an audience demands good theatre — that which not only entertains but stimulates worthwhile thinking and feeling — and insists that its wishes be satisfied, then the theatre must accordingly respond if it is to live. You who are today's dedicated student of drama will be tomorrow's talent and audience member. Your expectations will be the boundaries of future theatre horizons.

Suggested Projects —

1. Report on one of the following in the U.S. Discuss growth and contribution:

Community Theatre	Regional Theatre	Motion Pictures
Children's Theatre	Musical Comedy	Television
Readers Theatre		

2. Present a report on the history of the American musical comedy. Include famous song excerpts from recordings of the musicals.

3. Hold a panel discussion on "Television and Its Contribution to the Theatre World."

4. Read one of the plays by 20th century authors as listed in the above material. Report on how the play mirrors our society today.

5. As a class, attend a community or university theatre production. Visit backstage, if possible. In class, discuss the qualities of the play, of the acting, and of the production.

6. Report on how the Elizabethan stages have influenced the style of our modern thrust stages, such as the one at the Minneapolis Repertory Theatre or the one at Stratford, Ontario, Canada.

7. Report on the Abbey Theatre movement in Ireland. Include information on dramatists Synge, Yeats, Gregory, and O'Casey.

8. Report on the style and success of famous actors in the 20th century.

9. Rent and see video cassette tapes on modern theatre.

BOOKS FOR LEISURE READING & THEATRE HUMOR

Allen, John. *Great Moments in the Theatre*. London: Phoenix House, 1958.

Barranger, Milly and Jessica Tandy. *A BIO Biography*. New York: Performing Arts, 1991.

Brook, Peter. *The Empty Space*. New York: Atheneum, 1968.

Cottrel, John. *Laurence Olivier*. Englewood Cliffs, NJ: Prentice Hall, 1975.

DeMille, Agnes. *And Promenade Home*. New York: Little, Brown, 1958.

Dolbier, Maurice. *All Wrong on the Night*. New York: Walker, 1966. Vignettes of humorous theatrical errors.

Funke, Lewis and John Booth. *Actors Talk About Acting*. New York: Random House, 1961. Very good for the serious drama student.

Gielgud, John. *Stage Directions*. New York: Random House, 1963.

Gillmore, Margalo. *Four Flights Up*. New York: Houghton Mifflin, 1964. Most entertaining.

Grotowski, Jerzy. *Towards a Poor Theatre*. New York: Simon and Schuster, 1968.

Guthrie, Tyrone. *Life in the Theatre*. New York: McGraw-Hill, 1959.

Hart, Moss. *Act One*. New York: Random House, 1959. Excellent.

Hay, Peter. *Broadway Anecdotes*. New York: Oxford University Press, 1989.

Hay, Peter. *Theatrical Anecdotes*. New York: Oxford University Press, 1987.

Hayes, Helen. *My Life in Three Acts*. New York: Touchstone, 1991.

Holbrook, Hal. *Mark Twain Tonight*. New York: McKay, 1959.

Houseman, John. *Final Dress*. New York: Touchstone, 1984.

Lewes, George. *On Actors and the Art of Acting*. New York: Grove Press. 1957.

Martin, Mary. *My Heart Belongs*. New York: William Morrow, 1976.

Mosel, Tad, and Gertrude Macy. *Leading Lady: Katharine Cornell*. Boston, MA: Little, Brown, 1978.

Redgrave Michael. *The Actor's Ways and Means*. London: Heinemann Ltd., 1953.

Stanislavski, Constantin. *My life in Art*. New York: Theatre Arts Books, 1948.

UNIT VII

MONOLOGUES & SCENES

MONOLOGUES

MONOLOGUES FOR WOMEN

1. *Romeo and Juliet* by William Shakespeare.
2. *Saint Joan* by George Bernard Shaw.
3. *The Madwoman of Challiot* by Jean Giraudoux.
4. *Fences* by August Wilson.
5. *The Prisoner of Second Avenue* by Neil Simon.

Romeo and Juliet by William Shakespeare

Attending a dance, Juliet meets Romeo and they fall in love. Later, Romeo hides in her garden. When she walks onto her balcony and romantically speaks aloud to herself about Romeo, he discloses his presence. Embarrassed, Juliet addresses him.

JULIET. Thou know'st the mask of night is on my face,
Else would a maiden blush bepaint my cheek
For that which thou hast heard me speak tonight.
Fain would I dwell on form, fain, fain deny
What I have spoke; but farewell compliment!
Dost thou love me? I know thou wilt say "Ay,"
And I will take thy word; yet, if thou swear'st,
Thou mayst prove false: at lovers' perjuries
They say, Jove laughs. O gentle Romeo,
If thou dost love, pronounce it faithfully;
Or if thou think'st I am too quickly won,
I'll frown and be perverse and say thee nay,
So thou wilt woo; but else, not for the world.
In truth, fair Montague, I am too fond,
And therefore thou mayst think my 'haviour light;
But trust me, gentleman, I'll prove more true
Than those that have more cunning to be strange.
I should have been more strange, I must confess,

But that thou overheard'st, ere I was ware,
My true love's passion; therefore pardon me,
And not impute this yielding to light love,
Which the dark night hath so discovered.

Saint Joan by George Bernard Shaw

Joan of Arc has been sentenced to life in prison, instead of burning at the stake, for leading soldiers into battle based on voices she has heard from Heaven. When she realizes that she is to be continually confined, she recants her confession and boldly addresses her inquisitors.

JOAN. Yes: they told me you were fools [*the word gives great offence*], and that I was not to listen to your fine words nor trust to your charity. You promised me my life; but you lied [*indignant exclamations*]. You think that life is nothing but not being stone dead. It is not the bread and water I fear: I can live on bread; when have I asked for more? It is no hardship to drink water if the water be clean. Bread has no sorrow for me, and water no affliction. But to shut me from the light of the sky and the sight of the fields and flowers; to chain my feet so that I can never again ride with the soldiers nor climb the hills; to make me breathe foul damp darkness, and keep from me everything that brings me back to the love of God when your wickedness and foolishness tempt me to hate Him: all this is worse than the furnace in the Bible that was heated seven times. I could do without my warhorse; I could drag about in a skirt; I could let the banners and the trumpets and the knights and soldiers pass me and leave me behind as they leave the other women, if only I could still hear the wind in the trees, the larks in the sunshine, the young lambs crying through the healthy frost, and the blessed, blessed church bells that send my angel voices floating to me on the wind. But without these things I cannot live; and by your wanting to take them away from me, or from any human creature, I know that your counsel is of the devil, and that mine is of God.

The Madwoman of Chaillot by Jean Giraudoux

Although ostensibly not mentally normal, the Countess shows worldly common sense and goodness. In trying to coax a young man from committing suicide, she delves into her world of the past to spur him to enthusiasm for life.

COUNTESS. To be alive is to be fortunate, Roderick. Of course, in the morning, when you first awake, it does not always seem so very gay. When you take your hair out of the drawer, and your teeth out of the glass, you are apt to feel a little out of place in this world. Especially if you've just been dreaming that you're a little girl on a pony looking for strawberries in the woods. But all you need to feel the call of life once more is a letter in your mail giving you your schedule for the day — your mending, your shopping, that letter to your grandmother that you never seem to get around to. And so, when you've washed your face in rosewater, and powdered it — not with this awful rice-powder they sell nowadays, which does nothing for the skin, but with a cake of pure white starch — and put on your pins, your rings, your brooches, bracelets, earrings and pearls — in short, when you are dressed for your morning coffee — and have had a good look at yourself — not in the glass, naturally — it lies — but in the side of the brass gong that once belonged to Admiral Courbet — then, Roderick, then you're armed, you're strong, you're ready — you can begin again.

Fences by August Wilson

In the early 1960s, when Cory returns home from the military for his estranged father's funeral, his mother, Rose, tries to explain the father's behavior and her relationship in the marriage.

ROSE. You can't be nobody but who are you, Cory. That shadow wasn't nothing but you growing into yourself. You either got to grow into it or cut it down to fit you. But that's all you got to make life with. That's all you got to measure yourself against that world out there. Your daddy wanted you to be everything he wasn't...and at the same time he tried to make you into everything he was. I don't know if he was right or wrong...but I do know he meant to do more good than he meant to do harm. He wasn't always right. Sometimes, when he touched he bruised. And sometimes when he took me in his arms he cut.

When I first met your daddy, I thought..Here is a man I can lay down with and make a baby. That's the first thing I thought when I seen him. I was thirty years old and had done seen my share of men. But when he walked up to me and said, "I can dance a waltz that'll make you dizzy," I thought, Rose Lee, here is a man that you can open yourself up to and be filled to bursting. Here is a man that can fill all them empty spaces you been tipping around the edges of. One of them empty spaces was being somebody's mother.

I married your daddy and settled down to cooking his supper and keeping clean sheets on the bed. When your daddy walked through the house he was so big he filled it up. That was my first mistake. Not to make him leave some room for me. For my part in the matter. But at that time I wanted that. I wanted a house that I could sing in. And that's what your daddy gave me. I didn't know to keep up his strength I had to give up little pieces of mine. I did that. I took on his life as mine and mixed up the pieces so that you couldn't hardly tell which was which anymore. It was my choice. It was my life and I didn't have to live it like that. But that's what life offered me in the way of being a woman and I took it. I grabbed hold of it with both hands.

The Prisoner of Second Avenue by Neil Simon

When Edna's husband Mel, an executive of a New York company, is laid off work, she takes a job to tide them over. Although the playwright deals with a serious subject, he adds humor with numerous funny lines. Here, Edna has rushed home to eat with Mel during her lunch break.

EDNA. Mel?...Mel, I'm home. (*She closes door and crosses to living room, turns off radio, then into kitchen.*) You must be starved. I'll have your lunch in a second...(*Takes things out of package.*)...I couldn't get out of the office until a quarter to one and then I had to wait fifteen minutes for a bus...God, the traffic on Third Avenue during lunch hour....I got a cheese souffle in Schrafft's, is that alright? I just don't have time to fix anything today, Mr. Cooperman wants me back before two o'clock, we're suddenly swamped with work this week...He asked if I would come in on Saturdays from now until Christmas but I told him I didn't think I could...(*She is crossing into kitchen and getting out pots.*)...I mean we could use the extra money but I don't think I want to spend Saturdays in that office too. We see each other little enough now as it is...Come in and talk to me while I'm cooking, Mel, I've only got about thirty-five minutes today...(*Edna has put the casserole on the stove and is now crossing into kitchen, setting up two places with dishes and silverware.*)...My feet are absolutely killing me. I don't know why they gave me a desk because I haven't had a chance to sit at it in a month...Hi, love. I bought you Sports Illustrated...Mr. Cooperman told me there's a terrific story in there about the Knicks, he thought you might be interested in it...(*Mel tosses the magazine aside with some contempt...*)...You just can't move up Third Avenue because there's one of those protest parades up Fifth Avenue, or down Fifth Avenue, whichever way they protest...Fifteen thousand women screaming "Save the Environment" and they're all wearing leopard coats...God, the hypocrisy...Come on, sit down, I've got some tomato juice first...(*She pours tomato juice into two glasses. Mel listlessly moves to table and sits.*)...Isn't that terrible about the Commissioner of Police?...I mean *kidnapping* the New York Commissioner of Police?...Isn't that insane? I mean if the cops can't find him, they can't find anybody...(*She sits, picks up her glass of juice and sips.*)...

MONOLOGUES FOR MEN

1. *Julius Caesar* by William Shakespeare.
2. *As You Like It* by William Shakespeare.
3. *Hamlet* by William Shakespeare.
4. *Cyrano De Bergerac* by Edmond Rostand.
5. *The Devil and Daniel Webster* by Stephen Vincent Benét.
6. *Death of a Salesman* by Arthur Miller.

Julius Caesar by William Shakespeare

Caesar has been assassinated on the steps of the Roman forum by Brutus and other trusted friends. At the funeral, Anthony cleverly begins to turn the crowd from praising Brutus to avenging Caesar's death.

> Friends, Romans, countrymen, lend me your ears!
> I come to bury Caesar, not to praise him.
> The evil that men do lives after them,
> The good is oft interred with their bones;
> So let it be with Caesar. The noble Brutus
> Hath told you Caesar was ambitious,
> If it were so, it was a grievous fault.
> And grievously hath Caesar answer'd it.
> Here, under leave of Brutus and the rest—
> For Brutus is an honourable man;
> So are they all, all honourable men—
> Come I to speak in Caesar's funeral.
> He was my friend, faithful and just to me;
> But Brutus says he was ambitious,
> And Brutus is an honourable man.
> He hath brought many captives home to Rome,
> Whose ransoms did the general coffers fill;
> Did this in Caesar seem ambitious?
> When that the poor have cried, Caesar hath wept;
> Ambition should be made of sterner stuff;
> Yet Brutus says he was ambitious,
> And Brutus is an honourable man.
> You all did see that on the Lupercal
> I thrice presented him a kingly crown,

Which he did thrice refuse. Was this ambition?
Yet Brutus says he was ambitious,
And, sure he is an honourable man.
I speak not of disprove what Brutus spoke,
But here I am to speak what I do know.
You all did love him once, not without cause;
What cause withholds you then to mourn for him?
O judgement! thou art fled to brutish beasts,
And men have lost their reason. Bear with me;
My heart is in the coffin there with Caesar,
And I must pause till it come back to me.

As You Like It by William Shakespeare

When the Duke banishes Lady Rosalind, for protection she disguises herself as a man and travels into the woods with her girl friend Celia. Frolicking romance ensues with mistaken identities. In this famous speech Jacques, a courtier who attends the Duke, philosophizes on the passages within a person's life.

JACQUES.   All the world's a stage,
And all the men and women merely players.
They have their exits and their entrances,
And one man in his time plays many parts,
His acts being seven ages. At first the infant,
Mewling and puking in the nurse's arms.
Then the whining schoolboy with his satchel
And shining morning face, creeping like snail
Unwillingly to school. And then the lover,
Sighing like furnace, with a woeful ballad
Made to his mistress' eyebrow. Then a soldier,
Full of strange oaths and bearded like the pard,
Jealous in honor, sudden and quick in quarrel,
Seeking the bubble Reputation
E'en in the cannon's mouth. And then the justice,
In fair round belly with good capon lin'd,
With eyes severe and beard of formal cut,
Full of wise saws and modern instances;
And so he plays his part. The sixth age shifts
Into the lean and slipper'd pantaloon,
With spectacles on nose and pouch on side;

His youthful hose, well sav'd, a world too wide
For his shrunk shank, and his big manly voice,
Turning again toward childish treble, pipes
And whistles in his sound. Last scene of all,
That ends this strange eventful history,
Is second childishness and mere oblivion,
Sans teeth, sans eyes, sans taste, sans everything.

Hamlet by William Shakespeare

Polonius, who is the Danish court's Lord Chamberlain, bids good-bye to his son Laertes who is returning to a French university. Polonius gives some fatherly advise.

POLONIUS. Yet here, Laertes? Aboard, aboard, for shame!
The wind sits in the shoulder of your sail,
And you are stayed for. There--my blessing with thee,
And these few precepts in thy memory
Look thou character. Give thy thoughts no tongue,
Nor any unproportioned thought his act.
Be thou familiar, but by no means vulgar.
Those friends thou hast, and their adoption tried,
Grapple them unto thy soul with hoops of steel;
But do not dull thy palm with entertainment
Of each new-hatched, unfledged courage. Beware
Of entrance to a quarrel, but being in,
Bear't that th' opposed may beware of thee.
Give every man thy ear, but few thy voice;
Take each man's censure, but reserve thy judgment.
Costly thy habit as thy purse can buy,
But not expressed in fancy; rich not gaudy,
For the apparel oft proclaims the man,
And they in France of the best rank and station
Are of a most select and generous chief in that.
Neither a borrower nor a lender be,
For loan oft loses both itself and friend,
And borrowing dulls th' edge of husbandry.
This above all, to thine own self be true,
And it must follow as the night the day
Thou canst not then be false to any man.
Farewell. My blessing season this in thee!

Cyrano de Bergerac by Edmond Rostand

Although charming and witty, the 17th Century poet Cyrano has an exceptionally large nose that brings him excessive ridicule. Tiring of mundane comments about his nose, he imaginatively describes what could be said about it by a clever person.

CYRANO.   I'm afraid your speech was a little short, young man. You could have said...oh, all sorts of things, varying your tone to fit your words. Let me give you a few examples.

In an aggressive tone."If I had a nose like that, I'd have it amputated!"

Friendly. "The end of it must get wet when you drink from a cup. Why don't you use a tankard?"

Descriptive. "It's a rock, a peak, a cape! No, more than a cape: a peninsula!"

Curious. "What do you use that long container for? Do you keep your pens and scissors in it?"

Gracious. "What a kind man you are! You love birds so much that you've given them a perch to roost on."

Truculent. "When you light your pipe and the smoke comes out your nose, the neighbors must think a chimney has caught fire!"

Solicitous. "Be careful when you walk; with all that weight on your head, you could easily lose your balance and fall."

Thoughtful. "You ought to put an awning over it, to keep its color from fading in the sun."

Pedantic."Sir, only the animal that Aristophanes calls the hippocam-pelephantocamelos could have had so much flesh and bone below its forehead."

Flippant."That tusk must be convenient to hang your hat on."

Grandiloquent."No wind but the mighty Arctic blast, majestic nose, could ever give you a cold from one end to the other!"

Dramatic."When it bleeds, it must be like the Red Sea!"

Admiring."What a sign for a perfume shop!"

Lyrical."Is that a conch, and are you Triton risen from the sea?"

Naive."Is that monument open to the public?"

Respectful."One look at your face, sir, is enough to tell me that you are indeed a man of substance."

Rustic."That don't look like no nose to me. It's either a big cucumber or a little watermelon."

Military."The enemy is charging! Aim your cannon!"

Practical."A nose like that has one advantage: it keeps your feet dry in the   rain." . . .

There, now you have an inkling of what you might have said to me   if you were witty and a man of letters.

The Devil and Daniel Webster by Stephen Vincent Benét

Jabez Stone has sold his soul to the Devil. When the Devil comes to collect, Jabez asks his friend, the great statesman Daniel Webster, to defend him. The jury is comprised of the ghosts of men from America's past. In order to win his case, Webster appeals to the love of country that the jury feels.

WEBSTER.   Be still!
I was going to thunder and roar. I shall not do that.
I was going to denounce and defy. I shall not do that.
You have judged this man already with your abominable
        justice. See that you defend it. For I shall not speak of this
        man.
You are demons now, but once you were men. I shall speak to
        every one of you.
Of common things I speak, of small things and common.
The freshness of morning to the young, the taste of food to the
        hungry, the day's toil, the rest by the fire, the quiet sleep.
These are good things.
But without freedom they sicken, without freedom they are
        nothing.
Freedom is the bread and the morning and the risen sun.
It was for freedom we came in the boats and the ships. It was
for freedom we came.
It has been a long journey, a hard one, a bitter one.
But, out of the wrong and the right, the sufferings and the
        starvations, there is a new thing, a free thing.
The traitors in their treachery, the wise in their wisdom, the
valiant in their courage — all, all have played a part.
It may not be denied in hell nor shall hell prevail against it.
Have you forgotten this?

Death of a Salesman by Arthur Miller

Biff has returned home for a short time. With his brother, Happy, as a sounding board, Biff confesses that he has wasted his life and still does not know what to do. He is torn between the demands of his father Willy and his own self-desires.

BIFF. Well, I spent six or seven years after high school trying to work myself up. Shipping clerk, salesman, business of one kind or another. And it's a measly manner of existence. To get on that subway on the hot mornings in summer. To devote your whole life to keeping stock, or making phone calls, or selling or buying. To suffer fifty weeks of the year for the sake of a two-week vacation, when all you really desire is to be outdoors, with your shirt off. And always to have to get ahead of the next fella. And still — that's how you build a future....

Hap, I've had twenty or thirty different kinds of jobs since I left home before the war, and it always turns out the same. I just realized it lately. In Nebraska when I herded cattle, and the Dakotas, and Arizona, and now in Texas. It's why I came home now, I guess, because I realized it. This farm I work on, it's spring there now, see? And they've got about fifteen new colts. There's nothing more inspiring or — beautiful than the sight of a mare and a new colt. Add it's cool there now, see? Texas is cool now, and it's spring. And whenever springs comes to where I am, I suddenly get the feeling, my God, I'm not gettin' any-where! What the hell am I doing, playing around with horses, twenty-eight dollars a week! I'm thirty-four years old, I ought to be makin' my future. That's when I come running home. And now, I get here, and I don't know what to do with myself. *(After a pause)* I've always made a point of not wasting my life, and every time I come back here I know that all I've done is to waste my life.

SCENES

The Imaginary Invalid by Molière, adapted by Fran Tanner

In this 17th Century French satire, the young girl Louison is teasing her father, Argan, by refusing at first to disclose that her older sister, Angelique, is seeing a gentleman. When forced to speak, she enjoys embellishing her story.

(Louison, a girl of twelve or thirteen, enters.)

LOUISON. Did you call me, papa?

ARGAN. Yes, little one. Come here. *(She advances part way.)*

ARGAN. *(Beckoning slyly.)* A little closer.

(Louison comes closer.)

ARGAN. Now then. Look at me.

LOUISON. *(With seeming innocence.)* Yes, papa?

ARGAN. Don't you have something to tell me?

LOUISON. *(Sweetly.)* Well, I can tell you a story. Would you like to hear the Donkey's Skin or the fable of the Raven and the Fox?

ARGAN. *(Angrily.)* That's not what I had in mind.

LOUISON. My apologies, papa.

ARGAN. Don't you obey your father?

LOUISON. Of course, papa.

ARGAN.   And didn't I ask you to report all that you see?

LOUISON.   Yes, papa.

ARGAN.   Have you told me everything?

LOUISON.   *(With some doubt.)* Yes, papa.

ARGAN.   Haven't you seen something today?

LOUISON   No, papa.

ARGAN.   No?

LOUISON.   *(Quite doubtful.)* No...

ARGAN.   Aha. Then I shall have to renew your memory. *(Picks up his cane and starts toward Louison.)*

LOUISON.   *(Frightened.)* Oh, papa.

ARGAN.   Is it not true that you saw a man with your sister Angelique?

LOUISON.   *(Crying.)* Oh, dear.

ARGAN.   *(Raising his cane to hit her.)* I shall teach you to lie.

LOUISON.   Oh, forgive me, papa. Angelique made me promise not to tell. But I'll tell you now.

ARGAN.   Very well. You shall tell me, but only after I have punished you for telling a lie.

LOUISON.   Don't whip me, dear papa. Please don't whip me.

ARGAN.   I shall! *(Raises his cane and strikes once.)*

LOUISON.   *(Louison backs against the couch, crying loudly, pretending to be hurt.)* Oh, I'm hurt. Papa, stop. I'm hurt. Oh I'm dying, I'm dead. *(She falls on couch, pretending to be dead, but keeping one eye open to see what her father will do.)*

ARGAN.   What's this? Louison, my little one. Louison, what have I done to you? Oh, dear. My poor Louison. Oh, my poor child.

LOUISON.   *(No longer able to hide her laughter, sits up suddenly.)* Come, come, papa. It's all right. I'm not quite dead.

ARGAN.   *(Surprised, but relieved.)* Oh, you imp, you. What a rascal I have. Well, I'll overlook it this once, but you must tell me everything.

LOUISON.   Yes, papa. But don't tell Angelique I told.

ARGAN.   Of course not.

LOUISON.   *(Looks to be sure no one is listening.)* Well, while I was in Angelique's sitting room, a handsome man came, looking for her.

ARGAN.   *(Eagerly.)* Yes?

LOUISON. When I asked what he wanted, he said he was her new music teacher.

ARGAN. Aha. So that is their little plan. Continue.

LOUISON. Then Angelique came and when she saw him she said *(over dramatically.)* "Oh, go away, for my sake, leave."

ARGAN. *(Disappointed.)* Oh.

LOUISON. But he didn't leave. He stayed and talked to her.

ARGAN. *(Eagerly.)* What did he say?

LOUISON. He told her . . . *(Teasing her father.)* many things.

ARGAN. Yes?

LOUISON. That he loved her passionately, and that she was the most glorious creature in the world.

ARGAN. And then?

LOUISON. And then he fell on his knees before her —

ARGAN. *(Excitedly.)* Yes, yes

LOUISON. *(Dramatically.)* And kissed her hand — *(Giggles.)*

ARGAN. *(Eagerly.)* And then?

LOUISON. And then — *(Pause full of suspense, followed by a matter of fact.)* Mama came and he ran away.

ARGAN. *(Disappointed)* That's all? Nothing more?

LOUISON. No, papa. There was nothing more. *(She giggles and runs out. Argan groans and sinks into a chair.)*

The School for Scandal by Richard Brinsley Sheridan

Sir Peter is chastising his young wife for her extravagance. She humorously confronts him with her determination to do as she pleases, in this 18th Century comedy of manners.

SIR PETER. Lady Teazle, Lady Teazle, I'll not bear it!

LADY TEAZLE. Sir Peter, Sir Peter, you may bear it or not, as you please; but I ought to have my own way in everything, and what's more, I will, too. What! Though I was educated in the country, I know very well that women of fashion in London are accountable to nobody after they are married.

SIR PETER.   Very well, ma'am, very well; so a husband is to have no influence, no authority?

LADY TEAZLE.   Authority! No, to be sure, if you wanted authority over me, you should have adopted me, and not married me. I am sure you were old enough.

SIR PETER.   Old enough! Ay, there it is. Well, well, Lady Teazle, though my life may be made unhappy by your temper, I'll not be ruined by your extravagance.

LADY TEAZLE.   My extravagance! I'm sure I'm not more extravagant than a woman of fashion ought to be.

SIR PETER.   No, no, madam, you shall throw away no more sums on such unmeaning luxury. 'Slife! To spend as much to furnish your dressing-room with flowers in winter as would suffice to turn the Pantheon into a greenhouse and give a *fête champêtre* at Christmas.

LADY TEAZLE.   And am I to blame, Sir Peter, because flowers are dear in cold weather? You should find fault with the climate, and not with me. For my part, I'm sure, I wish it was spring all year round, and that roses grew under our feet.

SIR PETER.   Oons! Madam, if you had been born to this, I shouldn't wonder at your talking thus; but you forget what your situation was when I married you.

LADY TEAZLE.   No, no, I don't; 'twas a very disagreeable one, or I should never have married you.

SIR PETER.   Yes, yes, madam; you were then in somewhat a humbler style, the daughter of a plain country squire. Recollect, Lady Teazle, when I saw you first sitting at your tambor, in a pretty figured linen gown, with a bunch of keys at your side; your hair combed smooth over a roll, and your apartment hung round with fruits in worsted, of your own working.

LADY TEAZLE.   Oh, yes! I remember it well, and a curious life I led — my daily occupation to inspect the dairy, superintend the poultry, make extracts from the family receipt book, and comb my aunt Deborah's lap-dog.

SIR PETER.   Yes, yes, ma'am, 'twas so indeed.

LADY TEAZLE.   And then, you know, my evening amusements! To draw patterns for ruffles, which I had not materials to make up; to play Pope Joan with the curate; to read a sermon to my aunt; or to be stuck down to an old spinet to strum my father to sleep after a fox-chase.

SIR PETER. I am glad you have so good a memory. Yes, madam, these were the recreations I took you from; but now you must have your coach — *viz–à–viz* — and three powdered footmen before your chair; and in the summer, a pair of white cats to draw you to Kensington Gardens. No recollection, I suppose, when you were content to ride double, behind the butler, on a docked coach-horse?

LADY TEAZLE. No; I swear I never did that. I deny the butler and the coach-horse.

SIR PETER. This, madam, was your situation; and what have I done for you? I have made you a woman of fashion, of fortune, of rank; in short, I have made you my wife.

LADY TEAZLE. Well, then, and there is but one thing more you can make me to add to the obligation, and that is —

SIR PETER. My widow, I suppose?

LADY TEAZLE. Hem! Hem!

SIR PETER. I thank you, madam; but don't flatter yourself for though your ill conduct may disturb my peace, it shall never break my heart, I promise you; however, I am equally obliged to you for the hint.

LADY TEAZLE. Then why will you endeavor to make yourself so disagreeable to me, and thwart me in every little elegant expense?

SIR PETER. 'Slife, madam, I say, had you any of these little elegant expenses when you married me?

LADY TEAZLE. Lud, Sir Peter! Would you have me be out of the fashion?

SIR PETER. The fashion, indeed. What had you to do with the fashion before you married me?

LADY TEAZLE. For my part, I should think you would like to have your wife thought a woman of taste.

SIR PETER. Ay, there again: taste! Zounds! Madam, you had no taste when you married me!

LADY TEAZLE. That's very true indeed, Sir Peter; and after having married you, I should never pretend to taste again, I allow. But now, Sir Peter, if we have finished our daily jangle, I presume I may go to my engagement at Lady Sneerwell's.

SIR PETER. Ah, there's another precious circumstance; a charming set of acquaintances you have made there!

LADY TEAZLE. Nay, Sir Peter, they are all people of rank and fortune, and remarkable tenacious of reputation.

SIR PETER.	Yes, egad, they are tenacious of reputation with a vengeance; for they don't choose anybody should have a character but themselves! Such a crew! Ah! Many a wretch has rid on a hurdle who has done less mischief than these utterers of forged tales, coiners of scandal, and clippers of reputation.
LADY TEAZLE.	What! Would you restrain the freedom of speech?
SIR PETER.	Ah! They have made you just as bad as any one of the society.
LADY TEAZLE.	Why, I believe I do bear a part with a tolerable grace. But I vow I bear no malice against the people I abuse. When I say an ill-natured thing, 'tis out of pure good humor; and I take it for granted, they deal exactly in the same manner with me. But, Sir Peter, you know you promised to come to Lady Sneerwell's too.
SIR PETER.	Well, well, I'll call in just to look after my own character.
LADY TEAZLE.	Then indeed you must make haste after me, or you'll be too late. So, good-bye to ye. *(Exit)*
SIR PETER.	So, I have gained much by my intended expostulation; yet, with what a charming air she contradicts everything I say, and how pleasingly she shows her contempt for my authority! Well, though I can't make her love me, there is great satisfaction in quarreling with her; and I think she never appears to such advantage as when she is doing everything in her power to plague me. *(Exit)*

A Marriage Proposal by Anton Chekhov, adapted by Fran Tanner

In this delightful Russian comedy, Ivan Vassiliyitch Lomov's proposal of marriage to his neighbor's daughter, Natalia, is thwarted as they quarrel about ownership of the meadows separating their land.

NATALIA.	Oh, hello. Father said there was someone here to see me with an important question. How are you Ivan Vassiliyitch?
LOMOV.	I am fine my dear Natalia Stepanovna.
NATALIA.	You must excuse me for wearing my apron and looking like this, but I've been working. Do sit down. Goodness, you haven't visited us for ages. You should come more frequently. *(They sit.)* May I offer you something to eat?

LOMOV.   No, thank you. I've just had lunch.

NATALIA. Well, do smoke if you wish. There are some matches. It's hard to believe that the weather is so wonderful today, when yesterday it rained so much we couldn't work outside. How many bricks have you made? Wouldn't you know it. I had the workmen mow all of the hay, and now I'm worried for fear it will rot. I suppose I should have waited longer. *(Notices his suit.)* Oh, but what have we here. Why, you are all dressed up. Are you going to a party? You certainly look nice. What is the occasion?

LOMOV.   *(Excitedly)* It's — well — my dear Natalia Stepanovna — I have something to ask you—something that will be a surprise, I know, but you must not be angry — for — I — well — *(Aside.)* How cold it is in here!

NATALIA. What are you talking about? *(Pause.)* Well?

LOMOV.   Briefly — we have been friends for a long time — since childhood. My aunt and uncle, who gave me their estate — as you know — greatly admired your parents. Indeed your family and my family have been on good terms with each other for generations. In fact, as you know, my property is adjacent to yours. My meadows touch your woods.

NATALIA. Excuse me, Ivan Vassiliyitch, but those meadows. Did you call them yours?

LOMOV.   Yes, they are mine.

NATALIA. Well, I'm sorry to differ with you, but the meadows belong to us, not to you.

LOMOV.   Not mine? Now my dear —

NATALIA. Why, I've never heard the like of this. What makes you think they belong to you?

LOMOV.   Because I'm speaking of the meadows that run between your woods and my brick ground.

NATALIA. Precisely. They belong to us.

LOMOV.   No, they belong to me. You are quite mistaken. As far back as I can remember they have belonged to my family.

NATALIA. Not so.

LOMOV.   But it is on record, my dear. True, at one time the ownership was disputed, but now it is common knowledge that the meadows are mine, without argument. In fact, my aunt's grandmother permitted your great grandfather's servants to use the land rent-free while they made bricks for my grandmother.

They used the meadows for over forty years, with my family's permission. However, when —

NATALIA. But you are mistaken. My great grandfather's land touched the swamp, so the meadows of course are ours. There is nothing more to say. I can't understand your reasoning.

LOMOV. I'll be glad to show you the records, Natalia Stepanovna.

NATALIA. That is not necessary. Either you are joking or you are trying to make me angry. Whichever the case, you ought to be ashamed of yourself. It is most unpleasant to hear all of a sudden that the property we have owned for almost 300 years is not ours. I will be the first to admit that the meadows are not worth much. They cover less than five acres and would probably sell for only a few hundred rubles, but the principle of the thing is what interests me. I cannot stand peacefully by while you take my land.

LOMOV. Please, let me finish speaking. Your great grandfather's peasants, as I have already stated, made bricks for my aunt's grandmother. She wanted to be nice to them, so she —

NATALIA. Grandmother! Grandfather! Aunt! I don't know a thing about your ancestors but I do know the meadows are mine. And that's that!

LOMOV. No, the meadows belong to me!

NATALIA. You can talk until you're blue in the face, and put on full evening dress for all I care, but the meadows are, and always will be, mine — mine — mine. I have no intention of taking your land, but neither will I relinquish that which rightfully belongs to my family!

LOMOV. Well, the meadows mean nothing to me. I don't need them. Please, let us stop this. I present the meadows to you as a gift.

NATALIA. How can you give them to me when they belong to me? Ridiculous. Here we have always considered you to be our good friend. Why only last year we loaned you our threshing machine when we needed it ourselves—and now you are stealing our property. How dare you give me my own land. I call that a very dirty trick. In fact, to give you a piece of my mind, I'd say —

LOMOV. You are calling me a thief? My dear lady, I'll have you know that I have never taken anyone's land and I will not be accused of doing so now. The meadows belong to me!

NATALIA. Liar. They are mine!

LOMOV. Mine!

NATALIA.	So. We'll see who they belong to. This afternoon I'll order my reapers into my meadows.
LOMOV.	You'll what?
NATALIA.	My reapers will go into my meadows — today.
LOMOV.	Then I'll have the pleasure of kicking them out.
NATALIA.	How dare you.
LOMOV.	The meadows belong to me. Can't you understand. They are mine!
NATALIA.	It's not necessary to shout. If you want to rant and rave, please leave. In my house you must conduct yourself like a gentleman.
LOMOV.	Oh. If my head wasn't throbbing and my heart beating wildly, I would handle you the way you should be handled. *(Loudly.)* The meadows are mine!
NATALIA.	Mine!
LOMOV.	Mine!

A Doll's House by Henrik Ibsen, translated by Michael Meyer

In this Norwegian play written in 1879, the question of Women's Rights is addressed. Nora is a wife who is treated as a child by her husband Torvald Helmer. In this scene, Nora realizes what she must do to achieve her own identity.

NORA.	*(Looks at her watch.)* It isn't that late. Sit down here, Torvald. You and I have a lot to talk about. *(She sits down on one side of the table.)*
HELMER.	Nora, what does this mean? You look quite drawn —
NORA.	Sit down. It's going to take a long time. I've a lot to say to you.
HELMER.	*(Sits down on the other side of the table.)* You alarm me, Nora. I don't understand you.
NORA.	No, that's just it. You don't understand me. And I've never understood you — until this evening. No, don't interrupt me. Just listen to what I have to say. You and I have got to face facts, Torvald.
HELMER.	What do you mean by that?
NORA.	*(After a short silence.)* Doesn't anything strike you about the way we're sitting here?

HELMER. What?

NORA. We've been married for eight years. Does it occur to you that this is the first time that we two, you and I, man and wife, have ever had a serious talk together?

HELMER. Serious? What do you mean, serious?

NORA. In eight whole years — no, longer — ever since we first met — we have never exchanged a serious word on a serious subject.

HELMER. Did you expect me to drag you into all my worries — worries you couldn't possibly have helped me with?

NORA. I'm not talking about worries. I'm simply saying that we have never sat down seriously to try to get to the bottom of anything.

HELMER. But, my dear Nora, what on earth has that got to do with you?

NORA. That's just the point. You have never understood me. A great wrong has been down to me, Torvald. First by Papa, and than by you.

HELMER. What? But we two have loved you more than anyone in the world!

NORA. (Shakes her head.) You have never loved me. You just thought it was fun to be in love with me.

HELMER. Nora, what kind of a way is this to talk?

NORA. It's the truth, Torvald. When I lived with Papa, he used to tell me what he thought about everything, so that I never had any opinions but his. And if I did have any of my own, I kept them quiet, because he wouldn't have liked them. He called me his little doll, and he played with me just the way I played with my dolls. Then I came here to live in your house —

HELMER. What kind of a way is that to describe our marriage?

NORA. (Undisturbed.) I mean, then I passed from Papa's hands into yours. You arranged everything the way you wanted it, so that I simply took over your taste in everything — or pretended I did — I don't really know — I think it was a little of both — first one and then the other. Now I look back on it, it's as if I've been living here like a pauper, from hand to mouth. I performed tricks for you, and you gave me food and drink. But that was how you wanted it. You and Papa have done me a great wrong. It's your fault that I have done nothing with my life.

HELMER. Nora, how can you be so unreasonable and ungrateful? Haven't you been happy here?

NORA. No; never. I used to think I was; but I haven't ever been happy.

HELMER.   Not — not happy?

NORA.   No. I've just had fun. You've always been very kind to me. But our home has never been anything but a playroom. I've been your doll-wife, just as I used to be Papa's doll-child. And the children have been my dolls. I used to think it was fun when you came in and played with me, just as they think it's fun when I go in and play games with them. That's all our marriage has been, Torvald.

HELMER.   There may be a little truth in what you say, though you exaggerate and romanticize. But from now on it'll be different. Playtime is over. Now the time has come for education.

NORA.   Whose education? Mine or the children's?

HELMER.   Both yours and the children's, my dearest Nora.

NORA.   Oh, Torvald, you're not the man to educate me into being the right wife for you.

HELMER.   How can you say that?

NORA.   And what about me? Am I fit to educate the children?

HELMER.   Nora!

NORA.   Didn't you say yourself a few minutes ago that you dare not leave them in my charge?

HELMER.   In a moment of excitement. Surely you don't think I meant it seriously?

NORA.   Yes. You were perfectly right. I'm not fitted to educate them. There's something else I must do first. I must educate myself. And you can't help me with that. It's something I must do by myself. That's why I'm leaving you.

HELMER.   *(Jumps up.)* What did you say?

NORA.   I must stand on my own feet if I am to find out the truth about myself and about life. So I can't go on living here with you any longer.

HELMER.   Nora, Nora!

NORA.   I'm leaving you now, at once. Christine will put me up for tonight —

HELMER.   You're out of your mind! You can't do this! I forbid you!

NORA.   It's no use your trying to forbid me any more. I shall take with me nothing but what is mine. I don't want anything from you, now or ever.

HELMER.   What kind of madness is this?

NORA.   Tomorrow I shall go home — I mean, to where I was born. It'll be easiest for me to find some kind of a job there.

HELMER.   But you're blind! You've no experience of the world —

NORA.   I must try to get some, Torvald.

HELMER.   But to leave your home, your husband, your children! Have you thought what people will say?

NORA.   I can't help that. I only know that I must do this.

HELMER.   But this is monstrous! Can you neglect your most sacred duties?

NORA.   What do you call my most sacred duties?

HELMER.   Do I have to tell you? Your duties towards your husband, and your children.

NORA.   I have another duty which is equally sacred.

HELMER.   You have not. What on earth could that be?

NORA.   My duty towards myself.

Pygmalion by George Bernard Shaw

Acting on a wager, the phonetician Henry Higgins transforms Eliza, a Cockney flower girl, into a socially acceptable lady. After winning the wager, he dismisses Eliza. With hurtful disappointment, she confronts Higgins about her future.

HIGGINS.   *(In despairing wrath outside.)* What the devil have I done with my slippers? *(He appears at the door.)*

LIZA.   *(Snatching up the slippers, and hurling them at him one after the other with all her force.)* There are your slippers. And there. Take your slippers; and may you never have a day's luck with them!

HIGGINS.   *(Astounded.)* What on earth — ! *(He comes to her.)* What's the matter? Get up. *(He pulls her up.)* Anything wrong?

LIZA.   *(Breathless.)* Nothing wrong — with you. I've won your bet for you, haven't I? That's enough for you. *I* don't matter, I suppose.

HIGGINS.   You won my bet! You! Presumptuous insect! *I* won it. What did you throw those slippers at me for?

LIZA.   Because I wanted to smash your face. I'd like to kill you, you selfish brute. Why didn't you leave me where you picked me out of — in the gutter? You thank God it's all over, and that now you can throw me back again there, do you? *(She crisps her fingers frantically.)*

HIGGINS. *(Looking at her in cool wonder.)* The creature is nervous, after all.

LIZA. *(Gives a suffocated scream of fury, and instinctively darts her nails at his face!!)*

HIGGINS. *(Catching her wrists.)* Ah! Would you? Claws in, you cat. How dare you show your temper to me? Sit down and be quiet. *(He throws her roughly into the easy-chair.)*

LIZA. *(Crushed by superior strength and weight.)* What's to become of me? What's to become of me?

HIGGINS. How the devil do I know what's to become of you? What does it matter what becomes of you?

LIZA. You don't care. I know you don't care. You wouldn't care if I was dead. I'm nothing to you — not so much as them slippers.

HIGGINS *(Thundering.)* Those slippers.

LIZA. *(With bitter submission.)* Those slippers. I didn't think it made any difference now. *(A pause. Eliza hopeless and crushed. Higgins a little uneasy.)*

HIGGINS. *(In his loftiest manner.)* Why have you begun going on like this? May I ask whether you complain of your treatment here?

LIZA. No.

HIGGENS. I presume you don't pretend that I have treated you badly?

LIZZA. No.

HIGGINS. Has anybody behaved badly to you? Colonel Pickering? Mrs. Pearce? Any of the servants?

LIZA. No.

HIGGINS. I am glad to hear it. *(He moderates his tone.)* Perhaps you're tired after the strain of the day. Will you have a glass of champagne? *(He moves towards the door.)*

LIZA. No. *(Recollecting her manners.)* Thank you.

HIGGINS. *(Good-humored again)* This has been coming on you for some days. I suppose it was natural for you to be anxious about the garden party. But that's all over now. *(He pats her kindly on the shoulder. She writhes.)* There's nothing more to worry about.

LIZA. No. Nothing more for you to worry about. *(She suddenly rises and gets away from him by going to the piano bench, where she sits and hides her face.)* Oh God! I wish I was dead.

HIGGINS. *(Staring after her in sincere surprise.)* Why? In heaven's name, why? *(Reasonably, going to her.)* Listen to me, Eliza. All this irritation is purely subjective.

LIZA. I don't understand. I'm too ignorant.

HIGGINS. It's only imagination. Low spirits and nothing else. Nobody's hurting you. Nothing's wrong. You go to bed like a good girl and sleep it off. Have a little cry and say your prayers: that will make you comfortable.

LIZA. I hear your prayers. "Thank God it's all over!"

HIGGINS. *(Impatiently.)* Well, don't you thank God it's all over? Now you are free and can do what you like.

LIZA. *(Pulling herself together in desperation.)* What am I fit for? What have you left me fit for? Where am I to go? What am I to do? What's to become of me?

HIGGINS. *(Enlightened, but not at all impressed.)* Oh, that's what's worrying you, is it? *(He thrusts his hands into his pockets, and walks about in his usual manner, rattling the contents of his pockets, as if condescending to a trivial subject out of pure kindness.)* I shouldn't bother about it if I were you. I should imagine you won't have much difficulty in settling yourself somewhere or other, though I hadn't quite realized that you were going away. *(She looks quickly at him: he does not look at her, but examines the dessert stand on the piano and decides that he will eat an apple.)* You might marry, you know. *(He bites a large piece out of the apple and munches it noisily.)* You see, Eliza, all men are not confirmed old bachelors like me and the Colonel. Most men are the marrying sort (Poor devils!); and you're not bad-looking: it's quite a pleasure to look at you sometimes — not now, of course, because you're crying and looking as ugly as the very devil; but when you're all right and quite yourself, you're what I should call attractive. That is, to the people in the marrying line, you understand. You go to bed and have a good nice rest; and then get up and look at yourself in the glass; and you won't feel so cheap.

(Eliza again looks at him, speechless, and does not stir. The look is quite lost on him: he eats his apple with a dreamy expression of happiness, as it is quite a good one.)

HIGGINS. *(A genial afterthought occurring to him.)* I daresay my mother could find some chap or other who would do very well.

LIZA. We were above that at the corner of Tottenham Court Road.

HIGGINS. *(Waking up.)* What do you mean?

LIZA.   I sold flowers. I didn't sell myself. Now you've made a lady of me I'm not fit to sell anything else. I wish you'd left me where you found me.

HIGGINS.   *(Slinging the core of the apple decisively into the grate.)* Tosh, Eliza. Don't you insult human relations by dragging all this cant about buying and selling into it. You needn't marry the fellow if you don't like him.

LIZA.   What else am I to do?

HIGGINS.   Oh, lots of thing. What about your old idea of a florist's shop? Pickering could set you up in one: he has lots of money. *(Chuckling.)* He'll have to pay for all those togs you have been wearing today; and that, with the hire of the jewelry, will make a big hole in two hundred pounds. Why, six months ago you would have thought it the millennium to have a flower shop of your own. Come! You'll be all right. I must clear off to bed; I'm devilish sleepy. By the way, I came down for something: I forget what it was.

LIZA.   Your slippers.

HIGGINS.   Oh yes, of course. You shied them at me.

SCENES FOR TWO MEN

1. *The Importance of Being Ernest* by Oscar Wilde.
2. *Box and Cox* by John Madison Morton.
3. *Everyman,* Anonymous.
4. *The Inspector General* by Nicolai Gogol.
5. *You Can't Take It With You* by Moss Hart and George Kaufman.
6. *Fences* by August Wilson.
7. *Brighton Beach Memoirs* by Neil Simon.

The Importance of Being Earnest by Oscar Wilde

In this 19th Century English comedy, Algernon is quizzing Jack about the latter's proposal of marriage to Gwendolen. The two men spar with adroit repartee, for which author Oscar Wilde is famous.

ALGERNON.   Didn't it go off all right, old boy? You don't mean to say Gwendolen refused you? I know it is a way she has. She is always refusing people. I think it is most ill-natured of her.

JACK.   Oh, Gwendolen is as right as a trivet. As far as she is concerned, we are engaged. Her mother is perfectly unbearable. Never met such a gorgon... I don't really know what a gorgon is like, but I am quite sure that Lady Bracknell is one. In any case, she is a monster, without being a myth, which is rather unfair... I beg your pardon, Algy, I suppose I shouldn't talk about your own aunt in that way before you.

ALGERNON.   My dear boy, I love hearing my relations abused. It is the only thing that makes me put up with them at all. Relations are simply a tedious pack of people who haven't got the remotest knowledge of how to live, nor the smallest instinct about when to die.

JACK.   Oh, that is nonsense!

ALGERNON.   It isn't.

JACK.   Well, I won't argue about the matter. You always want to argue about things.

ALGERNON.   That is exactly what things were originally made for.

JACK. Upon my word, if I thought that, I'd shoot myself. *(A pause.)* You don't think there is any chance of Gwendolen becoming like her mother in about a hundred and fifty years, do you Algy?

ALGERNON. All women become like their mothers. That is their tragedy. No man does. That's his.

JACK. Is that clever?

ALGERNON. It is perfectly phrased! And quite as true as any observation in civilized life should be.

JACK. I am sick to death of cleverness. Everybody is clever nowadays. You can't go anywhere without meeting clever people. The thing has become an absolute public nuisance. I wish to goodness we had a few fools left.

ALGERNON. We have.

JACK. I should extremely like to meet them. What do they talk about?

ALGERNON. The fools! Oh, about the clever people, of course.

JACK. What fools!

ALGERNON. By the way, did you tell Gwendolen the truth about your being Ernest in town, and Jack in the country?

JACK. *(In a very patronizing manner.)* My dear fellow, the truth isn't quite the sort of thing one tells to a nice sweet refined girl. What extraordinary ideas you have about the way to behave to a woman!

ALGERNON. The only way to behave to a woman is to make love to her, if she is pretty, and to someone else if she is plain.

JACK. Oh, that is nonsense.

ALGERNON. What about your brother? What about the profligate Ernest?

JACK. Oh, before the end of the week I shall have got rid of him. I'll say he died in Paris of apoplexy. Lots of people die of apoplexy, quite suddenly, don't they?

ALGERNON. Yes, but it's hereditary, my dear fellow. It's a sort of thing that runs in families. You had much better say a severe chill.

JACK. You are sure a severe chill isn't hereditary, or anything of that kind?

ALGERNON. Of course it isn't.

JACK. Very well, then. My poor brother Ernest is carried off suddenly in Paris, by a severe chill. That gets rid of him.

ALGERNON. But I thought you said that... Miss Cardew was a little too much interested in your poor brother Ernest? Won't she feel his loss a good deal.

JACK.	Oh, that is all right. Cecily is not a silly romantic girl, I am glad to say. She has got a capital appetite, goes for long walks, and pays no attention at all to her lessons.
ALGERNON.	I would rather like to see Cecily.
JACK.	I will take very good care you never do. She is excessively pretty, and she is only just eighteen.
ALGERNON.	Have you told Gwendolen yet that you have an excessively pretty ward who is only just eighteen?
JACK.	Oh! One doesn't blurt these things out to people. Cecily and Gwendolen are perfectly certain to be extremely great friends. I'll bet you anything you like that half an hour after they have met, they will be calling each other sister.
ALGERNON.	Women only do that when they have called each other a lot of other things first. Now, my dear boy, if we want to get a good table at Willis's, we really must go and dress. Do you know it is nearly seven?
JACK.	*(Irritably.)* Oh! It always is nearly seven.
ALGERNON.	Well, I'm hungry.
JACK.	I never knew you when you weren't...
ALGERNON.	What shall we do after dinner? Go to the theatre?
JACK.	Oh, no! I loathe listening.
ALGERNON.	Well, let us go to the Club.
JACK.	Oh, no! I hate talking.
ALGERNON.	Well, we might trot round to the Empire at ten?
JACK.	Oh, no! I can't bear looking at things. It is so silly.
ALGERNON.	Well, what shall we do?
JACK.	Nothing!
ALGERNON.	It is awfully hard work doing nothing. However, I don't mind hard work where there is no definite object of any kind.

Box and Cox by John Madison Morton.

In this farce that is set in 19th Century England, two men unknowingly rent and share the same room — one by day and one by night. In the following scene, they try to decide who gets to marry Penelope Ann. Humorously, neither wants the girl.

BOX.   I say, sir!

COX.   Well, sir?

BOX.   What's your opinion of duelling, sir?

COX.   I think it's a barbarous practice, sir.

BOX.   So do I, sir. To be sure, I don't so much object to it when the pistols are not loaded.

COX.   No, I dare say that does make some difference.

BOX.   And yet, sir — on the other hand — doesn't it strike you as rather a waste of time, for two people to keep firing pistols at one another, with nothing in 'em?

COX.   No, sir — not more than any other harmless recreation.

BOX.   Hark ye! Why do you object to marry Penelope Ann?

COX.   Because, as I've observed already, I can't abide her. You'll be quite happy with her.

BOX.   Happy? Me! With the consciousness that I have deprived you of such a treasure? No, no, Cox!

COX.   Don't think of me, Box — I shall be sufficiently rewarded by the knowledge of my Box's happiness.

BOX.   Don't be absurd, sir!

COX.   Then don't you be ridiculous, sir!

BOX.   I won't have her!

COX.   I won't have her!

BOX.   I have it! Suppose we draw lots for the lady — eh, Mr. Cox?

COX.   That's fair enough, Mr. Box.

BOX.   Or, what say you to dice?

COX.   With all my heart! Dice, by all means. *(Eagerly.)*

BOX.   *(Aside.)* That's lucky! Mrs. Bouncer's nephew left a pair here yesterday. He sometimes persuades me to have a throw for a trifle, and as he always throws sixes, I suspect they are good ones. *(Goes to the cupboard and brings out the dice.)*

COX.   *(Aside.)* I've no objection at all to dice. I lost one pound, seventeen and sixpence, at last Barnet Races, to a very gentlemanly looking man, who had a most peculiar knack of throwing sixes; I suspected they were loaded, so I gave him another half-crown, and he gave me the dice. *(Takes dice out of his pocket.)*

BOX   Now then, sir!

COX   I'm ready, sir. *(They seat themselves at opposite sides of the table.)* Will you lead off, sir?

BOX   As you please, sir. The lowest throw, of course wins, Penelope Ann?

COX   Of course, sir.

BOX   Very well, sir!

COX   Very well, sir!

BOX   *(Rattling dice and throwing.)* Sixes!

COX   That's not a bad throw of yours, sir. *(Rattles dice and throws.)* Sixes!

BOX   That a pretty good one of yours, sir. *(Throws.)* Sixes!

COX   *(Throws.)* Sixes!

BOX   Sixes!

COX   Sixes!

BOX   Sixes!

COX   Sixes!

BOX   Those are not bad dice of yours, sir.

COX   Yours seem pretty good ones, sir

BOX.   Suppose we change?

COX.   Very well, sir. *(They change dice.)*

BOX.   *(Throwing.)* Sixes!

COX.   Sixes!

BOX.   Sixes!

COX.   Sixes!

BOX.   *(Flings down the dice.)* Pooh! It's perfectly absurd, your going on throwing sixes in this sort of way, sir.

COX.   I shall go on till my luck changes, sir!

BOX.   Let's try something else. I have it! Suppose we toss for Penelope Ann?

COX.   The very thing I was going to propose! *(They each turn aside and take out a handful of money.)*

BOX.   *(Aside, examining money.)* Where's my tossing shilling? Here it is!

COX.   *(Aside.)* Where's my lucky sixpence? I've got it!

BOX.   Now then, sir — heads win?

COX.   Or tails lose — whichever you prefer.

BOX.   It's the same to me, sir.

COX.   Very well, sir. Heads, I win — tails, you lose.

BOX.   Yes. *(Suddenly.)* No. Heads win, sir.

COX.   Very well — go on.

BOX.   *(Tossing.)* Heads!

COX.   *(Tossing.)* Heads!

BOX.   Heads!

COX.   Heads!

BOX.   Ain't you rather tired of turning up heads, sir!

COX.   Couldn't you vary the monotony of our proceedings by an occasional tail, sir?

BOX.   Heads!

COX.   Heads!

BOX.   Heads? Stop, sir! Will you permit — *(Taking Cox's sixpence.)* Holloa! Your sixpence has got no tail, sir!

COX.   *(Seizing Box's shilling.)* And your shilling has got two heads, sir!

BOX.   Cheat!

COX.   Swindler!

Everyman, Anonymous, adapted by Fran Tanner

Morality plays were popular in late Medieval times. In them, a lesson was taught by personifying abstract qualities. Everyman, the main character, resists Death, who has come for him. When Everyman realizes he must die, he searches a companion to accompany him. His friends, such as Wealth, Wit, and Kin, abandon him. He finds that the only person who will go with him to the grave is Good Deeds.

DEATH.   I, Death, will in the world go run overall,

And cruelly outsearch both great and small;
Every man will I beset that liveth beastly
Out of God's laws, and dreadeth not folly.
He that loveth riches I will strike with my dart,
His sight to blind, and from heaven to depart...
In hell for to dwell, world without end.
Lo, yonder I see Everyman walking.
Full little he thinketh on my coming;
His mind is on fleshy lusts and his treasure,
And great pain it shall cause him to endure
Before the Lord, Heaven King.

(Enter Everyman.)

Everyman, stand still! Whither art thou going
Thus gaily? Has thou thy Maker forgot?

EVERYMAN. Why askest thou?
Wouldest thou know?

DEATH. Yea, sir; I will show you.
In great haste I am sent to thee
From God out of his majesty.

EVERYMAN. What, sent to me?

DEATH. Yea, certainly.
Though thou have forgot him here,
He thinketh on thee in the heavenly sphere,
As, ere we depart, thou shalt know.

EVERYMAN. What desireth God of me?

DEATH. That shall I show thee.
A reckoning he will needs have
Without any longer respite.

EVERYMAN. To give a reckoning longer leisure I crave;
This blind matter troubleth my wit.

DEATH. On thee thou must take a long journey;
Therefore thy book of count with thee thou bring,
For turn again thou cannot by no way.
And look thou be sure of thy reckoning,
For before God thou shalt answer, and show
Thy many bad deeds, and good but a few;
How thou hast spent thy life, and in what wise,
Before the chief Lord of Paradise...

EVERYMAN. Full unready I am such reckoning to give.
I know thee not. What messenger art thou?

DEATH.   I am Death, who dreadeth no man;
             For every man I arrest, and no man spareth;
             For it is God's commandment
             That all to me should be obedient.

EVERYMAN.   O Death, thou comest when I had thee least in mind;
             In thy power it lieth me to save;
             Yet of my goods will I give thee, if thou will be kind;
             Yea, a thousand pound shalt thou have,
             If defer this matter till another day.

DEATH.   Everyman, it may not be, by no way.
             I set not by gold, silver, nor riches,
             Nor by pope, emperor, king, duke, nor princes;
             For, if I would receive gifts great,
             All the world I might get;
             But my custom is clean contrary.
             I give thee no respite. Come hence, and not tarry.

EVERYMAN.   Alas...I may say Death giveth no warning!
             To think on thee, it maketh my heart sick,
             For all unready is my book of reckoning.
             But twelve year and I might have abiding,
             My counting-book I would make so clear
             That my reckoning I should not need to fear.
             Wherefore, Death, I pray thee, for God's mercy,
             Spare me till I be provided of remedy.

DEATH.   Thee availeth not to cry, weep, and pray;
             But haste thee lightly on that journey,
             And prove thy friends if thou can;
             For, know thou well, the tide abideth no man,
             And in the world each living creature
             For Adam's sin must die of nature.

EVERYMAN.   Death, if I should this pilgrimage take,
             And my reckoning surely make,
             Show me, for saint charity,
             Should I not come again shortly?

DEATH.   No, Everyman; and thou be once there,
             Thou mayst never more come here, Trust me verily.

EVERYMAN.   O gracious God in the high seat celestial,
             Have mercy on me in this most need!
             Shall I have no company of mine acquaintance,
             To lead me from this vale terrestrial?

DEATH.   Yea, if any be so hardy
             That would go with thee and bear thee company...

	What, suppose thou thy life is given thee,
	And thy worldly goods also?
EVERYMAN.	I had thought so, verily.
DEATH.	Nay, nay; it was but lent thee;
	For as soon as thou art gone,
	Another a while shall have it, and then go therefrom
	Even as thou has done.
	Everyman, thou art mad; thou has they wits five,
	And here on earth will not amend thy life;
	For suddenly I do come.
EVERYMAN.	O wretched caitiff, whither shall I flee,
	That I might scape this endless sorrow?
	Now, gentle Death, spare me till tomorrow,
	That I may amend me
	With good advisement.
DEATH.	Nay, thereto I will not consent...
	And now out of thy sight I will me hie;
	See thou make thee ready shortly,
	For thou mayst say this is the day
	That no man living may scape away.
	(Exit Death.)
EVERYMAN.	Alas, I may well weep with sighs deep!
	Now have I no manner of company
	To help me in my journey, and me to keep;
	And also my book of accounts is full unready.

The Inspector General by Nikolai Gogol, adapted by Fran Tanner

Arriving penniless in a Russian village, Khlestakov is treated shabbily. But when he poses later as a government official, the villagers pamper his every wish. Thus, the playwright pokes fun at the crookedness of politicians and the gullibility of people. In this early scene of the play, Khlestakov orders supper from a servant who has been told to refuse this beggar.

SERVANT.	The manager sent me to see what you want.
KHLESTAKOV.	Ah, good to see you, old man. How are things going?
SERVANT	All right, thank you.
KHLESTAKOV.	Is business booming here at the hotel?

SERVANT.   Yes, sir. Thank you, sir.

KHLESTAKOV.   Lots of guests?

SERVANT.   Adequate, sir.

KHLESTAKOV.   Well fine! You know, it's almost past dinner time and I haven't eaten yet. Do a good turn and bring me a tray immediately, or I shall be late for my appointment.

SERVANT.   Sorry, sir, but the manager will charge no more dinners to you. In fact, today he almost sent a complaint about you to the police.

KHLESTAKOV.   A complaint? That's ridiculous. After all, I've got to eat or I shall starve. The truth of the matter is, I'm quite famished!

SERVANT.   Be that as it may. He said he wasn't going to give you anything else until you had cleared up your bill.

KHLESTAKOV.   Well, can't you talk to him? Put in a good word for me!

SERVANT.   But what can I say?

KHLESTAKOV.   Talk to him seriously and tell him I've got to have something to eat. The money — well — tell him just because his kind can go all day without food, doesn't mean that other people can. Preposterous idea!

SERVANT.   Yes, sir, I'll tell him. *(Exit Servant.)*

KHLESTAKOV.   How disgusting if he refuses to send up dinner. I've never been so hungry. I wonder if I could pawn my clothes? My trousers? No, I'd rather not eat than go home without my Petersburg suit. Too bad that Yokhim wouldn't let me rent a carriage. It would have been great to drive up in style to a landlord's house with my carriage lanterns on and Osip behind in uniform. How impressed they would be. "Who is it? Who has come?" Then my footman would announce *(He imitates footman.)* "Ivan Alexandrovich Khlestakov of Petersburg. Will you receive him?" Those country dunces, though, wouldn't even know what that meant. If any farmer visits them, he stumbles right into the living room like a bear. Hmmm. I'd go up to a pretty young girl and say "Mademoiselle, I am so happy —" Huh! *(He spits.)* I'm so hungry I feel nauseated.

(Enter the Servant.)

KHLESTAKOV.   Yes, what do you want?

SERVANT.   I'm bringing dinner.

KHLESTAKOV.   *(Claps his hands and jumps into his chair.)* Ah, dinner. At last, dinner.

SERVANT.	The manager says this is the last dinner he will send you.
KHLESTAKOV.	Oh, the manager. Who cares about the manager. What's there to eat?
SERVANT.	Soup and roast beef.
KHLESTAKOV.	You mean that is all?
SERVANT.	That's all, sir.
KHLESTAKOV.	Nonsense. I won't hear of it. That's not enough.
SERVANT.	On the contrary, sir, the manager says it's far too much!
KHLESTAKOV.	But what about the gravy?
SERVANT.	There isn't any.
KHLESTAKOV.	Why not? When I passed the kitchen I saw them making a lot, and earlier in the dining room, I saw two short-looking men eating salmon and other good things.
SERVANT.	Well, there is some and then there isn't.
KHLESTAKOV.	What do you mean?
SERVANT.	I mean, there isn't any, sir.
KHLESTAKOV.	No salmon? No gravy? No chops?
SERVANT.	No, sir. Well, yes, sir. But only for those who pay, sir.
KHLESTAKOV.	Oh, you, knucklehead. Why should I go hungry while they eat. Aren't I as good as they?
SERVANT.	No, sir. Well, yes, sir, but the difference is, they have money.
KHLESTAKOV.	Oh, it's a waste of time to argue with you. *(Tastes soup.)* What awful soup. Why, it's only hot water you've poured into the bowl. There's no taste at all, only a dreadful smell. I'll not eat it! You must bring me some other.
SERVANT.	Sorry, sir. The manager said if you didn't like this, you could go without.
KHLESTAKOV.	*(Holding his bowl and plate.)* Well, then leave it. Only, don't talk like that to me. I'll not have it. (Tastes soup again.) Heavens, what soup. *(Continues to eat it.)* I'm probably the first to ever eat soup like this. Why, there's even a feather floating on top. *(Spoons a piece of chicken in the soup.)* Ah, even the fowl is foul. Pass me the roast beef. Here, Osip, there's some soup left for you. *(Cuts meat.)* You call this roast beef? It most certainly is not!
SERVANT.	Then what is it?
KHLESTAKOV.	Only the devil knows, but it is not beef. It tastes more like leather. Cheaters! What they won't give a person. Why, my jaw

aches from chewing just one bite. (Picks teeth with finger.) It's even worse than tree bark. I can't get it out. Such food is enough to ruin one's teeth *(Wipes mouth with napkin.)* Isn't there anything else?

SERVANT. No, sir.

KHLESTAKOV. What cheaters they are. Not even dessert. It's terrible the way they always take advantage of travelers!

You Can't Take It With You by Moss Hart and George Kaufman

In this American comedy, the Sycamore family is considered eccentric because of their unusual philosophy. Grandpa Sycamore explains to the stalwart Mr. Kirby that people should not work at jobs they dislike.

KIRBY. (*Outraged.*) I beg your pardon, Mr. Vanderhof. I am a very happy man.

GRANDPA. Are you?

KIRBY. Certainly I am.

GRANDPA. (*Sits.*) I don't think so. What do you think you get your indigestion from? Happiness? No, sir. You get it because most of your time is spent in doing things you don't want to do.

KIRBY. I don't do anything I don't want to do.

GRANDPA. Yes, you do. You said last night that at the end of a week in Wall Street you're pretty near crazy. Why do you keep on doing it?

KIRBY. Why do I keep on — why, that's my business. A man can't give up his business.

GRANDPA. Why not? You've got all the money you need. You can't take it with you.

KIRBY. That's a very easy thing to say, Mr. Vanderhof. But I have spent my entire life building up my business.

GRANDPA. And what's it got you? Same kind of mail every morning, same kind of deals, same kind of meetings, same dinners at night, same indigestion. Where does the fun come in? Don't you think there ought to be something *more*, Mr. Kirby? You must have wanted more than that when you started out. We haven't got too much time, you know — any of us.

KIRBY.   What do you expect me to do? Live the way *you* do? Do nothing?

GRANDPA.   Well, I have a lot of fun. Time enough for everything — read, talk, visit the zoo now and then, practice my darts, even have time to notice when spring comes around. Don't see anybody I don't want to, don't have six hours of things I *have* to do every day before I get one hour to do what I like in — and I haven't taken bicarbonate of soda in thirty-five years. What's the matter with that?

KIRBY.   The matter with that? Suppose we *all* did it? A fine world we'd have, everybody going to zoos. Don't be ridiculous, Mr. Vanderhof. Who would do the work?

GRANDPA.   There's always people that like to work — you can't *stop* them. Inventions, and they fly the ocean. There're always people to go down to Wall Street, too — because they *like* it. But from what I've seen of you I don't think you're one of them. I think you're missing something.

KIRBY.   I am not aware of missing anything.

GRANDPA.   I wasn't either, till I quit. I used to get down to that office nine o'clock sharp no matter how I felt. Lay awake nights for fear I wouldn't get that contract. Used to worry about the world, too. Got all worked up about whether Cleveland or Blaine was going to be elected President — seemed awful important at the time, but who cares now? What I'm trying to say, Mr. Kirby, is that I've had thirty-five years that nobody can take away from me, no matter what they do to the world. See?

KIRBY.   (*Crossing to table.*) Yes, I do see. And it's a very dangerous philosophy. Mr. Vanderhof. It's — it's un-American.

Fences by August Wilson

Now a garbage collector, Troy, a former star of the Negro baseball league, is bitter because he was excluded from major league baseball. When in 1957 his son Cory wants a chance at professional sports, which are now integrated, Troy refuses to let him try. Feeling fenced in by society, Troy does not realize that his own actions fence in his own family.

CORY.   The Pirates won today. That makes five in a row.

TROY.   I ain't thinking about the Pirates. Got an all-white team. Got that boy... that Puerto Rican boy... Clemente. Don't even half-play him. That boy could be something if they give him a chance. Play him one day and sit him on the bench the next.

CORY.   He gets a lot of chances to play.

TROY.   I'm talking about playing regular. Playing every day so you can get your timing. That's what I'm talking about.

CORY.   They got some white guys on the team that don't play every day. You can't play everybody at the same time.

TROY.   If they got a white fellow sitting on the bench... you can bet your last dollar he can't play! The colored guy got to be twice as good before he get on the team. That's why I don't want you to get all tied up in them spots. Man on the team and what it get him? They got colored on the team and don't use them. Same as not having them. All them teams the same.

CORY.   The Braves got Hank Aaron and Wes Covington. Hank Aaron hit two home runs today. That makes forty-three.

TROY.   Hank Aaron ain't nobody. That's what you supposed to do. That's how you supposed to play the game. Ain't nothing to it. It's just a matter of timing... getting the right follow-through. Hell, I can hit forty-three home runs right now!

CORY.   Not off no major-league pitching, you couldn't.

TROY.   We had better pitching in the Negro leagues. I hit seven home runs off of Satchel Paige. You can't get no better than that!

CORY.   Sandy Koufax. He's leading the league in strikeouts.

TROY.   I ain't thinking of no Sandy Koufax.

CORY.   You got Warren Spahn and Lew Burdette. I bet you couldn't hit no home runs off of Warren Spahn.

TROY.   I'm through with it now. You go on and cut them boards.

(Pause.)

Your mama tell me you done got recruited by a college football team? Is that right?

CORY.   Yeah. Coach Zellman say the recruiter gonna be coming by to talk to you. Get you to sign the permission papers.

TROY.   I thought you supposed to be working down there at the A & P. Ain't you suppose to be working down there after school?

CORY.   Mr. Stawicki say he gonna hold my job for me until after the football season. Say starting next week I can work weekends.

TROY.   I thought we had an understanding about this football stuff? You suppose to keep up with your chores and hold that job down at the A & P. Ain't been around here all day on a Saturday. Ain't none of your chores done... and now you telling me you done quit your job.

CORY. I'm gonna be working weekends.

TROY. You damn right you are! And ain't no need for nobody coming around here to talk to me about signing nothing.

CORY. Hey, Pop... you can't do that. He's coming all the way from North Carolina.

TROY. I don't care where he coming from. The white man ain't gonna let you get nowhere with that football noway. You go on and get your book-learning so you can work yourself up in that A & P or learn how to fix cars or build houses or something, get you a trade. That way you have something can't nobody take away from you. You go on and learn how to put your hands to some good use. Besides hauling people's garbage.

CORY. I get good grades, Pop. That's why the recruiter wants to talk with you. You got to keep up your grades to get recruited. This way I'll be going to college. I'll get a chance...

TROY. First you gonna get your butt down there to the A & P and get your job back.

CORY. Mr. Stawicki done already hired somebody else 'cause I told him I was playing football.

TROY. You a bigger fool than I thought... to let somebody take away your job so you can play some football. Where you gonna get your money to take out your girlfriend and whatnot? What kind of foolishness is that to let somebody take away your job?

CORY. I'm still gonna be working weekends.

TROY. Naw... naw. You getting your butt out of here and finding you another job.

CORY. Come one, Pop! I got to practice. I can't work after school and play football too. Coach Zellman say...

TROY. I don't care what nobody else say. I'm the boss... you understand? I'm the boss around here. I do the only saying what counts.

CORY. Come on, Pop!

TROY. I asked you... didn't you understand?

CORY. Yeah...

TROY. What?!

CORY. Yessir.

TROY. You go on down there to that A & P and see if you can get your job back. If you can't do both... then you quit the football team. You've got to take the crookeds with the straights.

CORY.   Yessir.

Brighton Beach Memoirs by Neil Simon

This humorous and sometimes poignant play depicts a struggling family in 1937 who live in crowded, modest circumstances. In this scene Stan, 18, reveals to his 14 year old brother, Eugene, that he is going to leave home, because he has lost in a poker game his week's pay of seventeen dollars.

Eugene.   Aunt Blanche is leaving.

Stan.   *(Sits up.)* For where?

Eugene.   *(Sits on his own bed.)* To stay with some woman in Manhattan Beach. She and Mom just had a big fight. She's going to send for Laurie and Nora when she gets a job.

Stan.   What did they fight about?

Eugene.   I couldn't hear it all. I think Mom sorta blames Aunt Blanche for Pop having to work so hard.

Stan.   *(Hits pillow with his fist.)* Oh, God!...Did Mom say anything about me? About how I lost my salary?

Eugene.   You told her? Why did you tell her? I came up with twelve terrific lies for you. *(Stanley opens his drawer, puts on a sweater.)*

Stan.   How much money do you have?

Eugene.   Me? I don't have any money.

Stan.   *(Puts another sweater over the first one.)* The hell you don't. You've got money in your cigar box. How much do you have?

Eugene.   I got a dollar twelve. It's my life's savings.

Stan.   Let me have it. I'll pay it back, don't worry. *(He puts a jacket over sweaters, then gets a fedora from closet and puts it on. Eugene takes cigar box from under his bed, opens it.)*

Eugene.   What are you putting on all those things for?

Stan.   When I'm gone, you tell Aunt Blanche what happened to my salary. Then she'll know why Mom was so angry. Tell her please not to leave because it was all my fault, not Mom's. Will you do that? *(He takes coins out of cigar box.)*

Eugene. I have eight cents worth of stamps, if you want that too.

Stan. From the Police Athletic League. I didn't know you still had this.

Eugene. You gave it to me. You can have it back if you want it.

Stan. It's not worth anything.

Eugene. It is to me.

Stan. Sure. You can keep it.

Eugene. Thanks... Where will you go?

Stan. I don't know. I've been thinking about joining the army. Pop says we'll be at war in a couple of years anyway. I could be a sergeant or something by the time it starts.

Eugene. If it lasts long enough, I could join too. Maybe we can get in the same outfit.

Stan. You don't go in the army unless they come and get you. You go to college. You hear me? Promise me you'll go to college.

Eugene. I'll probably have to stay home and work, if you leave. We'll need the money.

Stan. I'll send home my paycheck every month. A sergeant in the army makes real good dough... Well, I better get going.

Eugene. *(On the verge of tears.)* What do you have to leave for?

Stan. Don't start crying. They'll hear you.

Eugene. They'll get over it. They won't stay mad at you forever. I was mad at you and I got over it.

Stan. Because of me, the whole family is breaking up. Do you want Nora to end up like one of those cheap boardwalk girls?

Eugene. I don't care. I'm not in love with Nora anymore.

Stan. Well, you should care. She's your cousin. Don't turn out to be like me.

Eugene. I don't see what's so bad about you.

Stan. *(Looks at him.)*... Take care of yourself, Eug. *(They embrace. He opens the door, looks around, then back to Eugene.)* If you ever write a story about me, call me Hank. I always liked the name Hank.

SCENES FOR TWO WOMEN

1. *Romeo and Juliet* by William Shakespeare.
2. *Othello* by William Shakespeare.
3. *The Importance of Being Ernest* by Oscar Wilde.
4. *The Glass Menagerie* by Tennessee Williams.
5. *The Miracle Worker* by William Gibson.
6. *A Shayna Maidel* by Barbara Lebow.

Romeo and Juliet by William Shakespeare

Wanting to marry Romeo secretly, Juliet has sent her nurse to make the arrangements with him. When the nurse returns, she teasingly prolongs giving the news to an impatient Juliet.

JULIET. The clock struck nine when I did send the nurse;
In half an hour she promis'd to return.
Perchance she cannot meet him: that's not so;
O, she is lame! love's heralds should be thoughts,
Which ten times faster glide than the sun's beams,
Driving back shadows over louring hills;
Therefore do nimble-pinion'd doves draw love,
And therefore hath the wind-swift Cupid wings.
Now is the sun upon the highmost hill
Of this day's journey, and from nine till twelve
Is three long hours, yet she is not come.
Had she affections and warm youthful blood,
She would be as swift in motion as a ball;
My words would bandy her to my sweet love, And his to me;
But old folks, many feign as they were dead;
Unwieldy, slow, heavy and pale as lead.

(Enter Nurse and Peter.)

O God, she comes! O honey nurse, what news?
Hast thou met with him? Send thy man away.

NURSE. Peter, stay at the gate. *(Exit Peter.)*

JULIET. Now, good sweet nurse, —
O Lord, why look'st thou sad?
Though news be sad, yet tell them merrily;
If good, thou sham'st the music of sweet news

By playing it to me with so sour a face.

NURSE. I am a–weary, give me leave awhile.
Fie, how my bones ache! What a jaunt have I had!

JULIET. I would thou hadst my bones, and I thy news.
Nay, come, I pray thee, speak; good, good nurse, speak;

NURSE. Jesu, what haste? Can you not stay awhile?
Do you not see that I am out of breath?

JULIET. How art thou out of breath, when thou has breath
To say to me that thou art out of breath?
The excuse that thou dost make in this delay
Is longer than the tale thou dost excuse.
Is thy news good or bad? Answer to that;
Say either, and I'll stay the circumstance.
Let me be satisfied, is't good or bad?

NURSE. Well, you have made a simple choice; you know not how to
choose a man. Romeo! No, not he, though his face be better
than any man's, yet his leg excels all men's; and for a hand, and
a foot, and a body, though they be not to be talk'd on, yet they
are past compare: he is not the flower of courtesy, but I'll
warrant him, as gentle as a lamb. Go thy ways, wench; serve
God. What, have you din'd at home?

JULIET. No, no: but all this did I know before.
What says he of our marriage? What of that?

NURSE. Lord, how my head aches! What a head have I!
It beats as it would fall in twenty pieces.
My back o't other side, — O, my back! My back
Beshrew your heart for sending me about,
To catch my death with jaunting up and down!

JULIET. I' faith, I am sorry that thou art not well.
Sweet, sweet, sweet nurse, tell me, what says my love?

NURSE. Your love says, like an honest gentleman, and a courteous, and
a kind, and a handsome, and, I warrant, a virtuous — Where is
your mother?

JULIET. Where is my mother! Why, she is within;
Where should she be? How oddly thou repliest!
'Your love says, like an honest gentleman,
Where is your mother?'

NURSE. O God's lady dear!
Are you so hot? Marry, come up, I trow;
Is this the poultice for my aching bones?
Henceforward do your messages yourself.

JULIET.   Here's such a coil! Come, what says Romeo?

NURSE.   Have you got leave to go to shrift today?

JULIET.   I have.

NURSE.   Then hie you hence to Friar Laurence' cell;
There stays a husband to make you a wife.
Now comes the wanton blood up in your cheeks,
They'll be in scarlet straight at any news.
Hie you to church; I must another way,
To fetch a ladder, by the which your love
Must climb a bird's nest soon when it is dark.
I am the drudge and toil in your delight,
But you shall bear the burden soon at night.
Go, I'll to dinner, hie you to the cell.

JULIET.   Hie to high fortune! Honest nurse, farewell.

(Exeunt.)

Othello by William Shakespeare

Othello believes that his wife, Desdemona, has been unfaithful. Jealous with rage, he sends her to her room with the intent of later killing her. Desdemona is blameless and cannot understand Othello's anger. As she prepares for bed, she discusses the situation with her maid servant Emilia, defending Othello and singing a song to quiet her fears.

EMILIA.   How goes it now? He looks gentler than he did.

DESDEMONA.   He says he will return incontinent;
And hath commanded me to go to bed,
And bade me to dismiss you.

EMILIA.   Dismiss me?

DESDEMONA.   It was his bidding; therefore, good Emilia,
Give me my nightly wearing, and adieu.
We must not now displease him.

EMILIA.   I would you had never seen him!

DESDEMONA.   So would not I: my love doth so approve him,
That even his stubbornness, his checks, his frowns, —
Prithee, unpin me, — have grace and favor in them.

EMILIA.   I have laid those sheets you bade me on the bed.

DESDEMONA.   All's one.

Good faith, how foolish are our minds!
If I do die before thee, prithee, shroud me
In one of those same sheets.

EMILIA.   Come, come, you talk.

DESDEMONA.   My mother had a maid call'd Barbara:
She was in love, and he she lov'd prov'd mad
And did forsake her.
She had a song of "willow";
An old thing 't was but it express'd her fortune,
And she died singing it. That song tonight
Will not go from my mind; I have much to do
But to go hang my head all at one side
And sing it like poor Barbara.
Prithee, dispatch.

EMILIA.   Shall I go fetch your nightgown?

DESDEMONA.   No, unpin me here.
This Lodovico is a proper man.

EMILIA.   A very handsome man.

DESDEMONA.   He speaks well.

EMILIA.   I know a lady in Venice would have walked barefoot to Palestine for a touch of his nether lip.

DESDEMONA.   (Singing.)
"The poor soul sat sighing by a sycamore tree,
    Sing all a green willow;
Her hand on her bosom, her head on her knee
    Sing willow, willow, willow.
The fresh streams ran by her, and murmur'd her moans;
    Sing willow, willow, willow;
Her salt tears fell from her, and soften'd the stones;
    Sing willow, willow, willow."

Lay by these; —
(Singing.)
"Willow," —
Prithee, hie thee; he'll come anon; —

(Singing.)
"Sing all a green willow must be my garland.
Let nobody blame him, his scorn I approve, —"
Nay, that's not next. —
Hark! Who is 't that knocks?

EMILIA.   It's the wind.

DESDEMONA. (Singing.)
     "I call'd my love false love; but what said he then?
       Sing willow, willow, willow.
     If I court moe women, you'll couch with moe men.—"

     So, get thee gone; good-night.
     Mine eyes do itch;
     Doth that bode weeping?

EMILIA. 'T is neither here nor there.

DESDEMONA. I have heard it said so. O, these men, these men!
     Dost thou in conscience think, — tell me, Emilia, —
     That there be women do abuse their husbands
     Is such gross kind?

EMILIA. There be some such, no question.

DESDEMONA. Wouldst thou do such a deed for all the world?

EMILIA. Why, would not you?

DESDEMONA. No, by this heavenly light!

EMILIA. Nor I neither by this heavenly light; I might do't as well i' th'
     dark.

DESDEMONA. Wouldst thou do such a deed for all the world?

EMILIA. The world's a huge thing; it is a great price
     For a small vice.

DESDEMONA. In troth, I think thou wouldst not.

EMILIA. In troth, I think I should; and undo't when I had done.
     Marry, I would not do such a thing for a joint-ring, nor for
     measures of lawn, nor for gowns, petticoats, nor caps, nor any
     petty exhibition; but, for all the whole world,— 'ud's pity, who
     would not make her husband a cuckold to make him a mon-
     arch? I should venture purgatory for it.

DESDEMONA. Beshrew me, if I would do such a wrong
     For the whole world.

EMILIA. Why, the wrong is but a wrong i' th' world; and having the
     world for your labour, 't is a wrong in your own world, and you
     might quickly make it right.

DESDEMONA. I do not think there is any such woman.

EMILIA. Yes, a dozen; and as many to th' vantage as would store the
      world they play'd for.
     But I do think it is their husbands' faults
     If wives do fall. Say that they slack their duties
     And pour our treasures into foreign laps,

'Or else break out in peevish jealousies.
Throwing restraint upon us; or say they strike us.
Or scant our former having in despite;
Why, we have galls, and though we have some grace,
Yet have we some revenge. Let husbands know
Their wives have sense like them; they see and smell
And have their palates both for sweet and sour
As husbands have. What is it that they do
When they change us for others? Is it sport?
I think it is. And doth affection breed it?
I think it doth. Is 's frailty that thus errs?
It is so too. And have not we affections,
Desires for sport, and frailty, as men have?
Then let them use us well; else let them know,
That ills we do, their ills instruct us so.

DESDEMONA.   Good-night, good-night. Heaven me such uses send,
Not to pick bad from bad, but by bad amend.

The Importance of Being Earnest by Oscar Wilde

In this scene from the 19th Century comedy of manners that satirizes English mores, Cecily and Gwendolen meet for the first time. Both believe they are engaged to Ernest Worthing. But Cecily's fiance is really Algernon Moncrief and Gwendolen's intended is really Jack Worthing — both men deceitfully saying their name is Ernest. In this farcical situation, the two women must show arched politeness and artificiality.

(Enter Gwendolen.)

CECILY.   *(Advancing to meet her.)* Pray let me introduce myself to you. My name is Cecily Cardew.

GWENDOLEN.   Cecily Cardew? What a sweet name. Something tells me that we are going to be great friends. I like you already more than I can say. My first impressions of people are never wrong.

CECILY.   How nice of you to like me so much after we have known each other such a comparatively short time. Pray sit down.

GWENDOLEN.   *(Still standing up.)* I may call you Cecily, may I not?

CECILY.   With pleasure.

GWENDOLEN.   And you will always call me Gwendolen, won't you?

CECILY.   If you wish.

GWENDOLEN. Then that is all settled, is it not?

CECILY. I hope so. *(A pause. They both sit down together.)*

GWENDOLEN. Perhaps this might be a favorable opportunity for my mentioning who I am. My father is Lord Bracknell. You have never heard of Pappa, I suppose?

CECILY. I don't think so.

GWENDOLEN. Outside the family circle, pappa, I am glad to say, is entirely unknown. I think that is quite as it should be. The home seems to me to be the proper sphere for the man. And certainly once a man begins to neglect his domestic duties he becomes painfully effeminate, does he not? And I don't like that. It makes men so very attractive. Cecily, mamma, whose views on education are so remarkably strict, has brought me up to be extremely shortsighted; it is part of her system; so do you mind my looking at you through my glasses?

CECILY. Oh, not at all, Gwendolen. I am very fond of being looked at.

GWENDOLEN. *(After examining Cecily carefully through a lorgnette.)* You are here on a short visit I suppose.

CECILY. Oh no. I live here.

GWENDOLEN. *(Severely.)* Really? Your mother, no doubt, or some female relative of advanced years, resides here also?

CECILY. Oh no! I have no mother, nor, in fact, any relations.

GWENDOLEN. Indeed?

CECILY. My dear guardian, with the assistance of Miss Prism, has the arduous task of looking after me.

GWENDOLEN. Your guardian?

CECILY. Yes, I am Mr. Worthing's ward.

GWENDOLEN. Oh! It is strange he never mentioned to me that he had a ward. How secretive of him! He grows more interesting hourly. I am not sure, however, that the news inspires me with feelings of unmixed delight. I am very fond of you, Cecily, I have liked you ever since I met you! But I am bound to state now that I know you are Mr. Worthing's ward, I cannot help expressing a wish you were — just a little older than you seem to be — and not quite so very alluring in appearance. In fact, if I may speak candidly —

CECILY. Pray do! I think that whenever one has anything unpleasant to say, one should always be quite candid.

GWENDOLEN. Well, to speak with perfect candor, Cecily, I wish that you were fully forty-two, and more than usually plain for your age. Ernest has, a strong upright nature. He is the very soul of truth and honor. Disloyalty should be as impossible to him as deception. But even men of the noblest possible moral character are extremely susceptible to the influence of the physical charms of others. Modern, no less than ancient history, supplies us with many most painful examples of what I refer to. If it were not so, indeed, history would be quite unreadable.

CECILY.   I beg your pardon, Gwendolen, did you say Ernest?

GWENDOLEN.   Yes.

CECILY.   Oh, but it is not Mr. Ernest Worthing who is my guardian. It is his brother — his elder brother.

GWENDOLEN.   Ernest never mentioned to me that he had a brother.

CECILY.   I am sorry to say they have not been on good terms for a long time.

GWENDOLEN.   Ah! That accounts for it. And now that I think of it I have never heard any man mention his brother. The subject seems distasteful to most men. Cecily, you have lifted a load from my mind, as I was growing almost anxious. It would have been terrible if any cloud had come across a friendship like ours, would it not? Of course you are quite, quite sure that it is not Mr. Ernest Worthing who is your guardian?

CECILY.   Quite sure. (A pause.) In fact, I am going to be his.

GWENDOLEN.   I beg your pardon?

CECILY.   (Rather shy and confidently.) Dearest Gwendolen, there is no reason why I should make a secret of it to you. Our little county newspaper is sure to chronicle the fact next week. Mr. Ernest Worthing and I are engaged to be married.

GWENDOLEN.   (Quite politely.) My darling Cecily, I think there must be some slight error. Mr. Ernest Worthing is engaged to me. The announcement will be in the 'Morning Post' on Saturday at the latest.

CECILY.   (Very politely.) I am afraid you must be under some misconception. Ernest proposed to me exactly ten minutes ago. (Shows her diary.)

GWENDOLEN.   (Examines diary through her lorgnette carefully.) It is certainly very curious, for he asked me to be his wife yesterday afternoon at 5:30. If you would care to verify the incident, pray do so. (Produces her diary.) I never travel without my diary. One should always have something sensational to read in the train. I am so sorry, dear Cecily, if it is any disappointment to you, but

I am afraid I have the prior claim.

CICELY. It would distress me more than I can tell you, dear Gwendolen, if it caused you any mental or physical anguish, but I feel bound to point out that since Ernest proposed to you he clearly has changed his mind.

GWENDOLEN. If the poor fellow has been entrapped into anything foolish, I shall consider it my duty to rescue him at once, and with a firm hand.

CICELY. *(Thoughtfully and sadly.)* Whatever unfortunate entanglement my dear boy may have got into, I will never reproach him with it after we are married.

GWENDOLEN. Do you allude to me, Miss Cardew, as an entanglement? You are presumptuous. On an occasion of this kind it becomes more than a moral duty to speak one's mind. It becomes a pleasure.

CICELY. Do you suggest, Miss Fairfax, that I entrapped Ernest into an engagement? How dare you? This is no time for wearing the shallow mask of manners. When I see a spade, I call it a spade.

GWENDOLEN. *(Satirically.)* I am glad to say that I have never seen a spade. It is obviously evident that our social spheres have been widely different.

The Glass Menagerie by Tennessee Williams

In an attempt to help her daughter, Laura, gain skills for the job market, Amanda scrapes up the money to send Laura to typing school. But in her shyness and embarrassment from having a lame foot, Laura quits the school without telling her mother. In the following scene, Amanda has just discovered her daughter's deceit and confronts her.

LAURA. Mother, I was just...

AMANDA. I know. You were just practicing your typing, I suppose. *(Behind chair R.)*

LAURA. Yes.

AMANDA. Deception, deception, deception!

LAURA. *(Shakily.)* How was the D.A.R. meeting, Mother?

AMANDA. *(Crosses to Laura.)* D.A.R. meeting!

LAURA. Didn't you go to the D.A.R. meeting, Mother?

AMANDA. *(Faintly, almost inaudibly.)* No, I didn't go to any D.A.R. meeting. *(Then more forcibly.)* I didn't have the strength — I didn't have the courage. I just wanted to find a hole in the ground and crawl in it and stay there the rest of my entire life. *(Tears type charts, throws them on floor.)*

LAURA.   *(Faintly.)* Why did you do that, Mother?

AMANDA.   *(Sits on R. end of day-bed.)* Why? Why? How old are you, Laura?

LAURA.   Mother, you know my age.

AMANDA.   I was under the impression that you were an adult, but evidently I was very much mistaken. *(She stares at Laura.)*

LAURA.   Please don't stare at me, Mother! *(Amanda closes her eyes and lowers her head. Pause.)*

AMANDA.   What are we going to do? What is going to become of us? What is the future? *(Pause.)*

LAURA.   Has something happened, Mother? Mother, has something happened?

AMANDA.   I'll be all right in a minute. I'm just bewildered — by life...

LAURA.   Mother, I wish that you would tell me what's happened!

AMANDA.   I went to the D.A.R. this afternoon, as you know; I was to be inducted as an officer. I stopped off at Rubicam's Business College to tell them about your cold and to ask how you were progressing down there.

LAURA.   Oh...

AMANDA.   Yes, oh–oh–oh. I went straight to your typing instructor and introduced myself as your mother. She didn't even know who you were. Wingfield, she said? We don't have any such scholar enrolled in this school. I assured her she did. I said my daughter Laura's been coming to classes since early January. "Well, I don't know," she said, "unless you mean that terribly shy little girl who dropped out of school after a few days' attendance?" No, I said, I don't mean that one. I mean my daughter, Laura, who's been coming here every single day for the past six weeks! "Excuse me," she said. And she took down the attendance book and there was your name, unmistakable, printed, and all the dates you'd been absent. I still told her she was wrong. I still said, "No there must have been some mistake! There must have been some mix-up in the records!" "No," she said, "I remember her perfectly now. She was so shy and her hands trembled so that her fingers couldn't touch the right keys! When we gave a speed-test — she just broke down completely — was sick at the stomach and had to be carried to the washroom! After that she never came back. We telephoned the house every single day and never got any answer." *(Rises from day-bed, crosses R.C.)* That was while I was working all day long down at that department store, I suppose, demonstrating those — *(With hands indicates brassiere.)* Oh! I felt so weak I couldn't stand up! *(Sits in armchair.)* I had to sit down while they got me a glass of water! *(Laura crosses up to phonograph.)* Fifty dollars' tuition. I don't care about the money so much, but all my hopes for any kind of future for you — gone up the spout, just gone up the spout like that. *(Laura winds phonograph up.)* Oh, don't do that, Laura! — Don't play that victrola!

LAURA.   Oh! *(Stops phonograph, crosses to typing table, sits.)*

AMANDA.   What have you been doing every day when you've gone out of the house pretending that you were going to business college?

LAURA.   I've just been going out walking.

AMANDA.   That's not true!

LAURA.   Yes, it is, Mother, I just went walking.

AMANDA.   Walking? Walking? In winter? Deliberately courting pneumonia in that light coat? Where did you walk to, Laura?

LAURA.   All sorts of places — mostly in the park.

AMANDA.   Even after you'd started catching that cold?

LAURA.   It was the lesser of two evils, Mother. I couldn't go back. I threw up on the floor!

AMANDA.   From half-past seven till after five every day you mean to tell me you walked around in the park, because you wanted to make me think that you were still going to Rubicam's Business College?

LAURA.   Oh, Mother, it wasn't as bad as it sounds. I went inside places to get warmed up.

AMANDA.   Inside where?

LAURA.   I went in the art museum and at the birdhouses at the Zoo. I visited the penguins every day! Sometimes I did without lunch and went to the movies. Lately I've been spending most of my afternoons in the Jewel-box, that big glass house where they raise the tropical flowers.

AMANDA.   You did all that to deceive me, just for deception! Why? Why? Why? Why?

LAURA.   Mother, when you're disappointed, you get that awful suffering look on your face, like the picture of Jesus' mother in the Museum!

	(Rises.)
AMANDA.	Hush!
LAURA.	*(Crosses R. to menagerie.)* I couldn't face it. I couldn't.

AMANDA.   *(Rising from day-bed.)* So what are we going to do now, honey, the rest of our lives? Just sit down in this house and watch the parades go by? Amuse ourselves with the glass menagerie? Eternally play those worn-out records your father left us as a painful reminder of him? *(Slams phonograph lid.)* We can't have a business career. No, we can't do that — that just gives us indigestion. *(Around R. day-bed.)* What is there left for us now but dependency all our lives? I tell you, Laura, I know so well what happens to unmarried women who aren't prepared to occupy a position in life. *(Crosses L, sits on day-bed.)* I've seen such pitiful cases in the South — barely tolerated spinsters living on some brother's wife or a sister's husband — tucked away in some mousetrap of a room —encouraged by one in-law to go on and visit the next in-law — little birdlike women — without any nest — eating the crust of humility all their lives! Is that the future that we've mapped out for ourselves? I swear I don't see any other alternative. And I don't think that's a very pleasant alternative. Of course — some girls do marry. My goodness, Laura, haven't you ever liked some boy?

LAURA.	Yes, Mother, I liked one once.
AMANDA.	You did?
LAURA.	I came across his picture a while ago.
AMANDA.	He gave you his picture, too? *(Rises from day-bed, crosses to chair R.)*
LAURA.	No, it's in the yearbook.
AMANDA.	*(Sits in armchair.)* Oh — a high-school boy.
LAURA.	Yes. His name was Jim.

The Miracle Worker by William Gibson

Anne Sullivan has been hired by the Keller family to try to teach their young daughter Helen, who is deaf and blind, how to communicate. Arriving at this, her first job, Anne is met at the train station by Mrs. Kate Keller. It is the late 1800's in a small Alabama town.

KATE. *(Simply.)* We've met every train for two days.

> *(Annie looks at Kate's face, and her good humor comes back.)*

ANNIE. I changed trains every time they stopped, the man who sold me that ticket ought to be tied to the tracks — ....

> *(Kate is studying her face, and Annie returns the gaze; this is a mutual appraisal, southern gentlewoman and working-class Irish girl, and Annie is not quite comfortable under it.)*

> You didn't bring Helen, I was hoping you would.

KATE. No, she's home.

> *(A pause. Annie tries to make ladylike small talk, though her energy now and then erupts; she catches herself up whenever she hears it.)*

ANNIE. You — live far from town, Mrs. Keller?

KATE. Only a mile.

ANNIE. Well. I suppose I can wait one more mile. But don't be surprised if I get out to push the horse!

KATE. Helen's waiting for you, too. There's been such a bustle in the house, she expects something, heaven knows what. *(Now she voices part of her doubt, not as such, but Annie understands it.)* I expected — a desiccated spinster. You're very young.

ANNIE. *(Resolutely.)* Oh, you should have seen me when I left Boston. I got much older on this trip.

KATE. I mean to teach anyone as difficult as Helen.

ANNIE. I mean to try. They can't put you in jail for trying!

KATE. Is it possible, even? To teach a deaf-blind child half of what an ordinary child learns — has that ever been done?

ANNIE. Half?

KATE. A tenth.

ANNIE. *(Reluctantly.)* No.

> *(Kate's face loses its remaining hope, still appraising her youth.)*

> Dr. Howe did wonders, but — an ordinary child? No, never. But then I thought when I was going over his reports — *(She indicates the one in her hand.)* — he never treated them like

ordinary children. More like — eggs everyone was afraid would break.

KATE.   *(A pause.)* May I ask how old you are?

ANNIE.   Well, I'm not in my teens, you know! I'm twenty.

KATE.   All of twenty.

(Annie takes the bull by the horns, valiantly.)

ANNIE.   Mrs. Keller, don't lose heart just because I'm not on my last legs. I have three big advantages over Dr. Howe that money couldn't buy for you. One is his work behind me, I've read every word he wrote about it and he wasn't exactly what you'd call a man of few words. Another is to be young, why, I've got energy to do anything. The third is, I've been blind.

(But it costs her something to say this.)

KATE.   *(Quietly.)* Advantages.

ANNIE.   *(Wry.)* Well, some have the luck of the Irish, some do not.

(Kate smiles; she likes her.)

KATE.   What will you try to teach her first?

ANNIE.   First, last, and — in between, language.

KATE.   Language.

ANNIE.   Language is to the mind more than light is to the eye. Dr. Howe said that.

KATE.   Language. *(She shakes her head.)* We can't get through to teach her to sit still. You are young, despite your years, to have such — confidence. Do you, inside?

(Annie studies her face; she likes her, too.)

ANNIE.   No, to tell you the truth I'm as shaky inside as a baby's rattle!

(They smile at each other, and Kate pats her hand.)

KATE.   Don't be.
We'll do all we can to help, and to make you feel at home. Don't think of us as strangers, Miss Annie.

ANNIE.   *(Cheerily.)* Oh, strangers aren't so strange to me. I've known them all my life!

A Shayna Maidel by Barbara Lebow

Set in New York City in 1946, this play portrays a family separated by the Holocaust. Although born in Poland, Rose, now in her twenties, came with her father to the United States when she was four. Her mother and sister were unable to follow and were put in concentration camps. In this scene her sister Lusia, now grown, has just arrived in New York. Her old world ways are a sharp contrast to Rose's "Americanization." Lusia's intent is to find and be united with her husband Duvid. The two sisters discuss their early memories.

(Saturday, mid-morning. Rose is heard softly humming a popular song. The morning light slowly comes up on her. She is wearing a robe and slippers, but looks dressed up. She is setting the table, trying to be quiet so as not to wake Lusia, although Lusia is not in sight and her bed is made. Rose enjoys arranging the small feast. The doorbell rings, startling her. She goes to the front door.)

ROSE.   Lusia! *(Rose follows Lusia as she puts down her handbag. Lusia is wearing the same clothes as when she arrived.)* I thought you were still sleeping. I've been tiptoeing around. What were you doing? Where could you go?

LUSIA.   To place I come to first. Where you come to get me.

ROSE.   Whatever for? Did you forget something? I'm surprised they're even open today. You went all by yourself?

LUSIA.   *(Struggling with language.)* I go read list. In books they got. And new names every day. People they find yet from the camps. Some coming yet from out woods where they been hiding.

ROSE.   I know. I know, Lusia. But surely by now —

LUSIA.   New names every day. And so I make mine list. You see? And sometimes maybe I find a person some place alive, some family, some friend. And this how I find Duvid, or he finding me, too.

ROSE.   But that would take a miracle.

LUSIA.   Is no miracle. Duvid is a… a *mensch.* Is only knowing Duvid is alive.

ROSE.   *(Covering her discomfort.)* I see. Come, you'll tell me more. We'll eat. *(Rose proudly leads Lusia to the laden dinette table. Lusia shrinks back, overwhelmed.)*

LUSIA.   Too much food! *So* much. No, *too* much, I think.

ROSE.   You must eat, Lusia. You've got to eat enough. And there's plenty, really, *(Piling food on Lusia's plate.)* I know you're the big sister, but you've got to let me take care of you, for now. Then, when everything's normal again, you'll be the big sister. *(Rose pours a glass of milk. Lusia sips at it, picks at the food. As they continue talking, they remain contrasted in manner. Lusia is still, Rosa animated, using her hands a lot.)*

LUSIA.   Funny, big sister, baby sister. I have baby sister one time, long time...

ROSE.   Ago.

LUSIA.   Long time ago. So beautiful I think, and I take for walk in ...

ROSE.   Carriage?

LUSIA.   Carriage, yes, I take for walk and show to friends mine baby *shvester*. Make me feel good. Happy. Then gone. And many years no sister but picture from America and letter from Papa and lady who takes care of.

ROSE.   Mrs. Greenspan. *Tanta* Perla.

LUSIA.   Yes. And then no more letter. No more sister. *(Voice.)* And carriage stays empty for too much years... And baby *shvester* woman now who want take care *me*.

ROSE.   I don't remember at all. I wish I did.

LUSIA.   You don't remember even Mama? *(Rose shakes her head.)* Nothing?

ROSE.   I was only four when we left. It's so strange that you have memories of me, that I was part of your life. That I was born in another world. I don't remember any of it. Just a feeling, maybe. Sometimes there's a particular smell when something's cooking or a song comes on the radio and all of a sudden I feel different, like I'm in another place.

LUSIA.   How you feel then?

ROSE.   Warm. Safe. Sad.

LUSIA.   Mama, that is. The feeling from Mama. *(Rose and Lusia look at one another silently across the table, each mirror to the other for a moment.)*

ROSE.   Eat some more, Lusia. You're not eating enough. *(Pause while Lusia picks at food.)* Lusia, have you wondered about it, thought why you got sick and not me?

LUSIA.   Mama says was plan from God. But she keeps hold our passage, our tickets, till could not read no more. Till thin like old leaf. Till long time after no good, no one... they no loz no one... no one... *(She is frustrated, trying to find the English word.)*

ROSE.   Allowed.

LUSIA.   Allowed leave Poland no more.

ROSE.   And I was playing stickball and going to the movies and eating

Mello-Rolls!

LUSIA. What means this?

ROSE. Oh, it doesn't matter. *(She pushes away from the table, gets up.)* He should have gotten you out!

LUSIA. Mama told how whole America changes mind, wants no new Jewish, no new people no more. All fast like this *(Snaps her fingers.)* something happens no one got money. From streets with gold to nothing. And everyone, not just mine father.

ROSE. That was the Depression. It kept you away, but it didn't make any difference in my life. I remember having bad dreams when I was little, but I don't know what about. Everything else stayed the same; the food, the stories on the radio and *Tanta* Perla, like a bird chirping around me trying to give comfort after the bad dreams. But she never could.

LUSIA. *De varemsteh bet iz de mamas. Farshtaist?*

ROSE. Yeah, but how could I tell? Mama wasn't real to me. They'd never say her name, or yours. They called you "Them," talking in whispers or in certain looks so I could just pick up little bits of what was going on. And when I was older and could have understood, I knew it was forbidden, Papa wouldn't talk. Not about you, not about Mama. He would just say he was working it out or, later, that Roosevelt would take care of everyone over there. I tried to make myself a family out of the photographs and letters, but they were in Yiddish and I only learned to read English. Tanta Perla used to read them to me and translate. Papa never would. Then, when there were no more letters, I began to forget completely. By the time the war came, it was as if there had been no one there at all... until Papa found you. I still don't know exactly how to feel. I mean, I've had it pretty easy and you —

LUSIA. Mine father don't know I'm here yet?

ROSE. He'll be in *shul* all day. We can call him tonight or even go out there.

LUSIA. No. Tuesday I suppose to come on boat.

ROSE. Papa was going to come with me to meet you. He'll be mad if we don't let him know you're here.

LUSIA. This I remember good about Papa. He gets so mad. He makes a big voice, everybody is... *(She shakes.)*

ROSE. Nervous.

LUSIA. Nervous.

ROSE.   In that way, he hasn't changed.

LUSIA.   I remember him. Papa was a man very... pretty?

ROSE.   Handsome? Papa?

LUSIA.   Handsome. And I know from pictures, too. But everything must be certain way or he is so mad. And very... *(She gestures.)*

ROSE.   Strict.

LUSIA.   Strict. But very proud when we all dress up. You, too. And Mama. Family all go out together. I see his face and I'm thinking how happy he is, how proud. He don't say nothing, but I can see. You know this face?

ROSE.   I've never seen that look. *(Pause.)* We'll have to call him tomorrow.

A Shayna Maidel
by Barbara Lebow
College of Southern Idaho:
Director, Tony Mannen

The body position of the two women creates a triangle which focuses on the standing character.

SCENES FOR MIXED GROUPS

1. *Macbeth* by William Shakespeare.
2. *Blithe Spirit* by Noel Coward.
2. *The Dining Room* by A.R. Gurney, Jr.

Macbeth by William Shakespeare

After helping her husband kill King Duncan, Lady Macbeth is obsessed with her terrible deed. In this sleepwalking scene, her gentlewoman asks the doctor to observe and diagnose the problem.

GENTLEWOMAN.	Lo you, here she comes! This is her very guise, and upon my life, fast asleep. Observe her. Stand close.
DOCTOR.	How came she by that light?
GENTLEWOMAN.	Why, it stood by her. She has light by her continually, 'tis her command.
DOCTOR.	You see, her eyes are open.
GENTLEWOMAN.	Aye, but their sense is shut.
DOCTOR.	What is it she does now? Look how she rubs her hands.
GENTLEWOMAN.	It is an accustomed action with her to seem thus washing her hands. I have known her continue in this a quarter of an hour.
LADY MACBETH.	Yet, here's a spot.
DOCTOR.	Hark! She speaks. I will set down what comes from her, to satisfy my remembrance the more strongly.
LADY MACBETH.	Out, damned spot! Out I say! One, two — why, then 'tis time to do 't. Hell is murky. Fie, my lord, fie! A soldier, and afeard? What need we fear who knows it, when none can call our power to account? Yet who would have thought the old man to have had so much blood in him?
DOCTOR.	Do you mark that?
LADY MACBETH.	The Thane of Fife had a wife. Where is she now? What, will these hands ne'er be clean? No more o that, my lord, no more o' that. You mar all with this starting.
DOCTOR.	Go to, go to. You have known what you should not.

GENTLEWOMAN.	She has spoke what she should not, I am sure of that. Heaven knows what she has known.
LADY MACBETH.	Here's the smell of the blood still. All the perfumes of Arabia will not sweeten this little hand. Oh, oh, oh!
DOCTOR.	What a sigh is there! The heart is sorely charged.
GENTLEWOMAN.	I would not have such a heart in my bosom for the dignity of the whole body.
DOCTOR.	Well, well, well —
GENTLEWOMAN.	Pray God it be, sir.
DOCTOR.	This disease is beyond my practice. Yet I have known those which have walked in their sleep who have died holily in their beds.
LADY MACBETH.	Wash your hands, put on your nightgown, look not so pale. I tell you yet again, Banquo's buried, he cannot come out on's grave.
DOCTOR.	Even so?
LADY MACBETH.	To bed, to bed, there's knocking at the gate. Come, come, come, come, give me your hand. What's done cannot be undone. To bed, to bed, to bed. *(Exit.)*

Blithe Spirit by Noel Coward

After holding a seance for research on his book, Charles finds that the spirit of his dead wife, Elvira, has appeared. Since only Charles (and the audience) can see her, his present wife, Ruth, thinks he is crazy. In trying to convince Ruth that the spirit of Elvira is indeed present, the following humorous scene ensues.

(Elvira enters by the windows, carrying a bunch of grey roses. She crosses to the writing-table up stage R., and throws the zinnias into the wastepaper basket and puts her roses into the vase. The roses are as grey as the rest of her.)

ELVIRA.	You've absolutely ruined that border by the sundial. It looks like a mixed salad.
CHARLES.	Oh, my God!
RUTH.	What's the matter now?
CHARLES.	She's here again!
RUTH.	What do you mean? Who's here again?
CHARLES.	Elvira.

RUTH.   Pull yourself together and don't be absurd.

ELVIRA.   It's all those nasturtiums; they're so vulgar.

CHARLES.   I like nasturtiums.

RUTH.   You like what?

ELVIRA.   *(Putting her grey roses into the vase.)* They're all right in moderation, but in a mass like that they look beastly.

CHARLES.   *(Crosses over to R. of Ruth, C.)* What did you mean about nasturtiums?

CHARLES.   *(Takes Ruth's hands and comes round to the L. of her.)* Never mind about that now. I tell you she's here again.

ELVIRA.   *(Comes to above the sofa.)* You have been having a nice scene, haven't you? I could hear you right down the garden.

CHARLES.   Please mind your own business.

RUTH.   If you behaving like a lunatic isn't my business, nothing, is.

ELVIRA.   I expect it was about me, wasn't it? I know I ought to feel sorry, but I'm not. I'm delighted.

CHARLES.   Ruth — darling — please...

RUTH.   I've done everything I can to help. I've controlled myself admirably. And I should like to say here and now that I don't believe a word about your damned hallucination. You're up to something, Charles — there's been a certain furtiveness in your manner for weeks. Why don't you be honest and tell me what it is?

CHARLES.   You're wrong — you're dead wrong! I haven't been in the least furtive — I —

RUTH.   You're trying to upset me. *(She moves away from Charles.)* For some obscure reason you're trying to goad me into doing something that I might regret. *(She bursts into tears.)* I won't stand for it any more. You're making me utterly miserable! *(She crosses to the sofa and falls into the R. end of it.)*

CHARLES.   *(Crosses to Ruth.)* Ruth — please —

RUTH.   Don't come near me!

ELVIRA.   Let her have a nice cry. It'll do her good. *(She saunters round to down stage L.)*

CHARLES.   You're utterly heartless!

RUTH.   Heartless!

CHARLES.   *(Wildly.)* I was not talking to you! I was talking to Elvira.

RUTH.   Go on talking to her then, talk to her until you're blue in the face, but don't talk to me.

CHARLES.   *(Crosses to Elvira.)* Help me, Elvira —

ELVIRA.   How?

CHARLES.   Make her see you or something.

ELVIRA.   I'm afraid I couldn't manage that. It's technically the most difficult business — frightfully complicated, you know — it takes years of study —

CHARLES.   You are here, aren't you? You're not an illusion?

ELVIRA.   I may be an illusion, but I'm most definitely here.

CHARLES.   How did you get here?

ELVIRA.   I told you last night — I don't exactly know —

CHARLES.   Well, you must make me a promise that in future you only come and talk to me when I'm alone.

ELVIRA.   *(Pouting.)* How unkind you are, making me feel so unwanted. I've never been treated so rudely.

CHARLES.   I don't mean to be rude, but you must see —

ELVIRA.   It's all your own fault for having married a woman who is incapable of seeing beyond the nose on her face. If she had a grain of real sympathy or affection for you she'd believe what you tell her.

CHARLES.   How could you expect anybody to believe this?

ELVIRA.   You'd be surprised how gullible people are; we often laugh about it on the Other Side.

(Ruth, who has stopped crying and been staring at Charles in horror, suddenly rises.)

RUTH.   *(Gently.)* Charles!

CHARLES.   *(Surprised at her tone.)* Yes, dear — *(Charles crosses to her, R.)*

RUTH.   I'm awfully sorry I was cross.

CHARLES.   But, my dear —

RUTH.   I understand everything now. I do really.

CHARLES.   You do?

RUTH.   *(Patting his arm reassuringly.)* Of course I do.

ELVIRA.   Look out — she's up to something.

CHARLES.   Will you please be quiet?

RUTH.   Of course, darling. We'll all be quiet, won't we? We'll be as quiet as little mice.

CHARLES.   Ruth dear, listen —

RUTH.   I want you to come upstairs with me and go to bed.

ELVIRA.   The way that woman harps on bed is nothing short of erotic.

CHARLES.   I'll deal with you later.

RUTH.   Very well, darling — come along.

CHARLES.   What are you up to?

RUTH.   I'm not up to anything. I just want you to go quietly to bed and wait there until Doctor Bradman comes.

CHARLES.   No, Ruth, you're wrong —

RUTH.   *(Firmly.)* Come, dear —

ELVIRA.   She'll have you in a straitjacket before you know where you are.

CHARLES.   *(Comes to Elvira — frantically.)* Help me — you must help me —

ELVIRA.   *(Enjoying herself.)* My dear, I would with pleasure, but I can't think how.

CHARLES.   I can. (Back to Ruth.) Listen, Ruth —

RUTH.   Yes, dear?

CHARLES.   If I promise to go to bed, will you let me stay here for five minutes longer?

RUTH.   I really think it would be better —

CHARLES.   Bear with me, however mad it may seem, bear with me for just five minutes longer.

RUTH.   *(Leaving go of him.)* Very well. What is it?

CHARLES.   Sit down.

RUTH.   *(Sitting down.)* All right. There!

CHARLES.   Now listen, listen carefully —

ELVIRA.   Have a cigarette; it will soothe your nerves.

CHARLES.   I don't want a cigarette.

RUTH.   *(Indulgently.)* Then you shan't have one, darling.

CHARLES.   Ruth, I want to explain to you clearly and without emotion that beyond any shadow of doubt, the ghost or shade or whatever you like to call it of my first wife Elvira is in this room now.

RUTH.   Yes, dear.

CHARLES.   I know you don't believe it and are trying valiantly to humor me, but I intend to prove it to you.

RUTH. Why not lie down and have a nice rest and you can prove anything you want to later on?

CHARLES. She may not be here later on.

ELVIRA. Don't worry — she will!

CHARLES. Oh God!

RUTH. Hush, dear.

CHARLES. *(To Elvira.)* Promise you'll do what I ask?

ELVIRA. That all depends what it is.

CHARLES. *(Between them both, facing upstage.)* Ruth — you see that bowl of flowers on the piano?

RUTH. Yes, dear, I did it myself this morning.

ELVIRA. Very untidily, if I may say so.

CHARLES. You may not.

RUTH. Very well — I never will again. I promise.

CHARLES. Elvira will now carry that bowl of flowers to the mantelpiece and back again. You will, Elvira, won't you? Just to please me.

ELVIRA. I don't really see why I should. You've been quite insufferable to me ever since I materialized.

CHARLES. Please!

ELVIRA. *(Goes over to the piano.)* All right, I will just this once. Not that I approve of all these Maskelyne and Devant carryings–on.

CHARLES. *(Crosses to the mantelpiece.)* Now, Ruth — watch carefully!

RUTH. *(Patiently.)* Very well, dear.

CHARLES. Go on, Elvira — take it to the mantelpiece and back again.

(Elvira takes a bowl of pansies off the piano and brings it slowly down stage, below the armchair to the fire; then suddenly pushes towards Ruth's face, who jumps up and faces Charles, who is at the mantel piece.)

RUTH. *(Furiously.)* How dare you, Charles! You ought to be ashamed of yourself.

CHARLES. What on earth for?

RUTH. *(Hysterically.)* It's a trick. I know perfectly well it's a trick. You've been working up to this. It's all part of some horrible plan...

CHARLES. It isn't — I swear it isn't. Elvira — do something else, for God's sake!

ELVIRA. Certainly — anything to oblige.

RUTH.   *(Becoming really frightened.)* You want to get rid of me — you're trying to drive me out of my mind —

CHARLES.   Don't be so silly.

RUTH.   You're cruel and sadistic and I'll never forgive you.

(Elvira picks up the chair from down stage L., holds it in midair as if to hit Ruth, Ruth flinches, then Elvira puts it back, and stands above the windows. Ruth makes a dive for the door, moving between the armchair and sofa. Charles follows and catches her.) I'm not going to put up with this any more.

CHARLES.   *(Holding her.)* You must believe it — you must —

RUTH.   Let me go immediately.

CHARLES.   That was Elvira — I swear it was.

RUTH.   *(Struggling.)* Let me go.

CHARLES.   Ruth — please —

(Ruth breaks away to the windows. Elvira shuts them in her face and crosses quickly to the mantelpiece. Ruth turns at the windows to face Charles.)

RUTH.   *(Looking at Charles with eyes of horror.)* Charles — this is madness-sheer madness — it's some sort of autosuggestion, isn't it? — Some form of hypnotism, swear to me it's only that — *(She rushes to Charles, C.)* Swear to me it's only that.

ELVIRA.   *(Taking an expensive vase from the mantelpiece and crashing it into the grate.)* Hypnotism my foot!

The Dining Room by A.R. Gurney, Jr.

This poignant scene is of a family celebrating Thanksgiving at their homestead. They are confronted with their elderly mother who is living in the past.

NANCY.   I've got the plates, Mrs. Driscoll. You've got your hands full with that turkey. *(She sets the plates and carving utensils at the head of the table and calls toward the hall.)* We're ready, everybody! Come on in! *(The singing continues as a Family begins to come into the dining room, to celebrate Thanksgiving dinner. The oldest son Stuart has his Mother on his arm. She is a very vague, very old Old Lady.)*

STUART.   ...Now, Mother, I want you to sit next to me, and Fred, you sit on Mother's left, and Ben, you sit opposite her where she can see you, and Nancy and Beth hold up that end of the table, and there we are. *(Genial chatter as everyone sits down. The two Sons push in their Mother's chair. After a moment the Old Lady stands up again, looks around distractedly.)* What's the matter, Mother?

OLD LADY.   I'm not quite sure where I am.

STUART.   *(Expansively; arm around her; seating her again.)* You're here, Mother. In your own dining room. This is your table, and here are your chairs, and here is the china you got on your trip to England, and here's the silver-handled caving knife which Father used to use.

OLD LADY.   Oh yes... *(Genial laughter, ad-libbing: "She's a little tired... It's been a long day..." The Old Lady gets up again.)* But who are these people? I'm not quite sure who these people are. *(She begins to wander around the room.)*

STUART.   *(Following her around.)* It's me, Mother: Stuart. Your son. And here's Fred, and Ben, and Nancy, and Beth. We're all here, Mother.

NANCY.   *(Going into the kitchen.)* I'll get the turkey. That might help her focus.

STUART.   Yes. *(To Old Lady.)* Mrs. Driscoll is here, Mother. Right in the kitchen, where she's always been. And your grandchildren. All your grandchildren were here. Don't you remember? They ate first, at the children's table, and now they're out in back playing touch football. You watched them, Mother. *(He indicates the French doors.)*

OLD LADY.   Oh yes... *(She sits down again at the other end of the table. Nancy comes out from the kitchen carrying a large platter. Appropriate Oh's and Ah's from Group.)*

STUART.   And look, Mother. Here's Nancy with the turkey... Put it right over there, Nancy... See, Mother? Isn't it a beautiful bird? And I'm going to carve it just the way Father did, and give you a small piece of the breast and a dab of dressing, just as always, Mother. *(He sharpens the carving knife officiously.)*

OLD LADY.   *(Still staring out into the garden.)* Just as always...

STUART.   *(As he sharpens.)* And Fred will have the drumstick — am I right, Fred? — And Beth gets the wishbone, and Ben ends up with the Pope's nose, am I right, Ben? *(Genial in-group laughter.)*

NANCY.	Save some for Mrs. Driscoll.
STUART.	I always do, Nancy. Mrs. Driscoll likes the second joint.
OLD LADY.	This is all very nice, but I think I'd like to go home.
STUART.	*(Patiently, as he carves.)* You are home, Mother. You've lived here fifty-two years.
BEN.	Fifty-four.
BETH.	Forever.
STUART.	Ben, pass this plate down to Mother...
OLD LADY.	*(Getting up.)* Thank you very much, but I really do think it's time to go.
NANCY.	Uh–oh.
STUART.	*(Going to her.)* Mother...
BETH.	Oh dear.
OLD LADY.	Will someone drive me home, please? I live at eighteen Summer Street with my mother and sisters.
BETH.	What will we do?
STUART.	*(Going to Old Lady.)* It's not there now, Mother. Don't you remember? We drove down. There's a big building there now.
OLD LADY.	*(Holding out her hand.)* Thank you very much for asking me... Thank you for having me to your house. *(She begins to go around the table, thanking people.)*
FRED.	Mother! I'm Fred! Your son!
OLD LADY.	Isn't that nice? Thank you. I've had a perfectly lovely time... Thank you... Thank you so much. *(She shakes hands with Nancy.)* It's been absolutely lovely... Thank you, thank you.
STUART.	Quickly. Let's sing to her.
BETH.	Sing?
STUART.	She likes singing. We used to sing to her whenever she'd get upset... Fred, Ben. Quickly. Over here.
OLD LADY.	*(Wandering distracted around.)* Now I can't find my gloves. Where would my gloves be? I can't go out without my gloves.
BEN.	What song? I can't remember any of the songs.
STUART.	Sure you can. Come on. Hmmmmmmmmm. *(He sounds a note. The others try to find their parts.)*
BEN & FRED.	Hmmmmm.
OLD LADY.	I need my gloves, I need my hat...

STUART.   *(Singing.)*

"As the blackbird in the spring...

OTHERS.   (Joining in.)

'Neath the willow tree...
Sat and piped, I hear him sing,
Sing of Aura Lee...

(They sing in pleasant, amateurish, corny harmony. The Old Lady stops fussing, turns her head, and listens. The other women remain at the table.)

MEN.   *(Singing.)*

Aura Lee, Aura Lee, Maid of Golden Hair...
Sunshine came along with thee, and swallows in the air."

OLD LADY.   I love music. Every person in our family could play a different instrument. *(She sits in a chair along the wall, Down Right.)*

STUART.   *(To his brothers.)* She's coming around. Quickly. Second verse.

MEN.   *(Singing with more confidence now; more daring harmony.)*

"In thy blush the rose was born,
Music, when you spake,
Through thine azure eye the morn
Sparkling seemed to break.
Aura Lee, Aura Lee, Maid of Golden Hair,
Sunshine came along with thee, and swallows in the air."

(The hold a long note at the end. The Old Lady claps. Everyone claps.)

OLD LADY.   That was absolutely lovely.

STUART.   Thank you, Mother.

OLD LADY.   But now I've simply got to go home. Would you call my carriage, please? And someone find my hat and gloves. It's very late, and my mother gets very nervous if I'm not home in time for tea. *(She heads for the hall.)*

STUART.   *(To no one in particular.)* Look, Fred, Ben, we'll drive her down, and show her everything. The new office complex where her house was. The entrance to the Thruway. The new Howard Johnson's motel. Everything! And she'll see that nothing's there at all.

FRED.   I'll bring the car around.

STUART.   I'll get her coat.

BEN.   I'm coming, too.

STRUART.   We'll just have to go through the motions.

GLOSSARY OF BASIC STAGE TERMS

Above: upstage.

Ad-lib: extemporize dialogue or movement.

Antagonist: main character who opposes the protagonist.

Apron: the stage floor between the front edge of the stage and front curtain.

Arena theatre: staging in the center of a room with audience sitting around the playing area.

Aside: words spoken by a character to the audience rather than to the other characters who supposedly do not hear the speech.

Audition: a tryout for a part in a play

Backdrop or **Drop**: painted curtain without fullness, hung from battens.

Backing: flats used behind window and door openings to mask audience view of backstage.

Backstage: area behind scenery not visible to audience.

Barndoors: lighting accessory for Fresnels that house moveable flippers to control the light beam.

Base: foundation color used for stage makeup.

Batten: horizontal pipe suspended over the stage, from which scenery, lights, and curtains are hung.

Below: downstage.

Blackout: all stage lights go off simultaneously.

Blocking: director's planned movement for the characters.

Border lights: strips of stage lights used for blending and toning.

Borders: short curtains hung over the stage to mask lights.

Build: increase of vocal intensity toward a climactic point.

Business: detailed bits of action such as knitting, setting the table, etc., as distinguished from broad stage movement.

Cable: electric cord; a special heavy cable; gauge #12 or #14 should be used for stage lighting.

Call: posted announcement of rehearsals, etc., placed on the call-board near stage entrance.

Cheat: to play toward the audience while seemingly conversing with others on stage.

Clear stage: warning for everyone who is not in the next scene to leave the acting area.

Climax: high point of the action.

Conflict: dramatic opposition of the protagonist with society, with his fellowman, or with himself.

Control board: switchboard for stage lights.

Counter-cross: a small movement in the opposite direction to the cross made by another actor.

Cover: to hide an actor, property, or some business from the audience view whether intentionally or not.

Crepe hair: material used for making beards and mustaches.

Critique: evaluation and suggestions.

Cross: an actor's move from one part of the stage to another.

Cue: (1) last words or action of one actor that immediately precede another actor's speech; (2) signal for light changes, curtain, etc.

Cut: (1) delete; (2) a command to stop action and dialogue.

Cyc or **Cyclorama**: sky drop that surrounds the back of the stage.

Dimmers: unit to control intensity of lights.

Dim out: gradually decrease light.

Dim up: gradually increase light.

Dock: area for scenery storage, often under the stage.

Downstage: area closest to the audience.

Drapes: large curtains hung in folds from battens on sides and back of acting area. They provide a neutral background.

Dress the stage: keep the stage picture balanced.

Exit: direction for an actor to leave the stage. Opposite "enter."

Flat: canvas-covered wooden frame used for scenery.

Flexible theatre: seats can be arranged for proscenium, arena, or horseshoe staging.

Flies: area above stage where scenery is hung or stored by lines from the grid.

Floodlights: lights without lens; used for blending and toning.

Floor cloth: canvas used to cover acting area floor.

Floor or **Ground plan**: flat skeleton diagram of the acting area shape and its corresponding furniture placement.

Focus: (1) center attention on; (2) center light beam on.

Footlights: row of colored lights usually sunk in the stage floor at front edge of apron and wired for three colors.

Fourth wall: imaginary wall between stage and audience.

Fresnel: spotlight with a fresnel lens that throws an efficient and soft beam; hung from the teaser batten to light upstage areas.

Funnels: Fresnel spotlight accessory that limits the beam to a circular pattern; also called a tophat.

Gelatin: transparent-colored medium used in front of stage lights.

Gesture: movement of separate parts of the body such as waving an arm or shrugging a shoulder.

Give: throw focus on the important character in a certain scene.

Gobo: a template of thin metal inserted into a Leko to create a shadow light pattern.

Greasepaint: theatrical makeup.

Greenroom: actor's lounge backstage.

Grid or **Gridiron**: framework high over stage from which are supported curtain and scenery riggings.

Grip: stage crew member who shifts scenery.

Ground plan: see "floor plan."

Ground row: low horizontal scenery that stands alone and is placed upstage to look like scenery in the distance.

Hand props: properties carried on stage by the actors during the play.

Holding for laughs: waiting for audience laughter to diminish before continuing dialogue.

Horizon strip: border lights usually mounted on a wagon and placed on the floor downstage of the sky drop for the purpose of lighting it.

House: auditorium.

Houselights: auditorium lights used before and after the play and during intermission.

Ingenue: young female character.

Juvenile: young male character.

Kill: eliminate; for example, "kill the noise" means to be quiet.

Left: stage area to actor's left as he faces the audience.

Legs: drapes hung right and left in pairs behind the tormentors to mark the backstage area.

Leko: spotlight with an ellipsoidal reflector; hung from the auditorium ceiling to light downstage acting areas.

Levels: platforms of various heights.

Mask: to cover something from audience view.

Mood: emotional state.

Motivate: to have a specific reason for saying or doing something; to show character's desires through voice and movement.

Notices: reviews by critics; dramatic criticism.

Open up: to play toward the audience.

Out-front: audience area.

Pantomime: bodily movement and expression without dialogue.

Pick up cues: to quickly begin a speech without allowing a pause between the first words of the speech and the cue.

Pin rail: bar to which rigging ropes are tied.

Pit or **Orchestra pit**: area between stage and first row of seats.

Places: warning for actors to assume their position on stage for the beginning of the scene.

Plant: to call attention to an idea or item that will be important later in the play.

Plot: (1) sequence of events in a play; (2) production plan of backstage items such as a light plot.

Pointing: emphasizing or stressing action or words.

Practical: usable, such as a door that the actor can open.

Project: increase voice or actions so they will carry to the audience.

Prompt book: contains script, blocking notations, warnings, crew charts, and other information necessary for producing the play.

Properties: set furnishings including furniture, pictures, ornaments, drapes, etc.

Proscenium: permanent framed opening through which the audience sees the play.

Protagonist: main character with whom audience empathy lies.

Quick study: one who can memorize a part rapidly.

Raked house or **seating**: slanted floor, allowing each row of the audience to see over the heads of those in front.

Ramp: sloping platform.

Right: stage area to actor's right as he faces the audience.

Ring down: command to close curtain.

Ring up: command to open curtain.

Roundels: colored glass discs used in footlights and border strips.

Royalty: money paid to an author for permission to stage his or her play.

Run: length of stage engagement.

Run through: rehearse scene without interruption.

Scoop: a floodlight with an ellipsoidal reflector; can be hung from battens.

Scrim: loose-weave curtain on battens used for "visions," "flashbacks," etc. Opaque when lighted from the front; transparent when lighted from the back.

Script: printed copy of the play.

Set: (1) scenery; (2) establish definite movements and lines.

Set piece: three-dimensional scenery piece which stands by itself, such as a practical rock.

Share: to assume a position of equal dramatic importance with another actor.

Shift: change scenery.

Soliloquy: long speech given by a character when alone on stage to show thoughts or to explain the plot; used frequently by Shakespeare.

Spill: light leakage from stage lights.

Spotlight: lights with beams that can be focused and that are used for specific illumination.

Stealing the scene: taking audience attention away from the proper focal point.

Strike: take down set and props after the show's final performance.

Tag line: final line of a play.

Take stage: to capture audience attention legitimately, as opposed to "give" and "share."

Teaser: overhead curtain that masks the first border of lights and that regulates the height of the proscenium opening.

Theme: basic idea of the play that gives unity to all elements.

The Method: refers to the Stanislavski approach to acting.

Throw away: under emphasize a line or action.

Timing: to give lines and movement at the exact, effective moment.

Topping: to exceed the tempo and pitch of the previous speech.

Tormentors: side curtains or flats that adjust the proscenium width at the extreme down right and left.

Trap: opening in stage floor that permits actors to enter from beneath the floor or to exit beneath it.

Tryouts: auditions for parts in a play.

Understudy: actor who is able to play a given role in an emergency.

Upstage: area farthest away from audience, toward the backstage wall.

Wagon: rolling platform on which horizon scenery or lights are placed for quick changes.

Walk-on: a part where the actor walks on and off stage without having any lines to say.

Warn: to notify that a cue is approaching.

Wings: offstage to right or left of the acting area.

Work lights: white lights used solely for rehearsal. In some theatres the strip lights are used in place of work lights.

X-ray border: compartmental lamps that hang on the first border to help blend acting area spots; usually wired for three colors.

INDEX

X

Y